Metaphor and Material Culture

Social Archaeology

General Editor
Ian Hodder, University of Cambridge

Advisory Editors
Margaret Conkey, University of California at Berkeley
Mark Leone, University of Maryland
Alain Schnapp, U.E.R. d'Art et d'Archeologie, Paris
Stephen Shennan, University College London
Bruce Trigger, McGill University, Montreal

Titles in Print
ENGENDERING ARCHAEOLOGY
Edited by Joan M. Gero and Margaret W. Conkey

SOCIAL BEING AND TIME
Christopher Gosden

IRON-AGE SOCIETIES
Lotte Hedeager

THE ARCHAEOLOGY OF ISLAM
Timothy Insoll

CONTEMPORARY ARCHAEOLOGY IN THEORY
Robert W. Preucel and Ian Hodder

AN ARCHAEOLOGY OF CAPITALISM
Matthew Johnson

MATERIAL CULTURE AND MASS CONSUMPTION
Daniel Miller

METAPHOR AND MATERIAL CULTURE
Christopher Tilley

In preparation

THE RISE OF MESO-AMERICA
Elizabeth Brumfiel

ARCHAEOLOGY AS CULTURAL HISTORY
Ian Morris

ARCHAEOLOGICAL INTERPRETATIONS
Robert W. Preucel

THE ARCHAEOLOGY OF LANDSCAPE
Edited by Wendy Ashmore and A. Bernard Knapp

Metaphor and Material Culture

Christopher Tilley

Copyright © Christopher Tilley 1999

The right of Christopher Tilley to be identified as author of this work has been asserted in accordance with the Copyright, Designs and Patents Act 1988.
Every effort has been made to contact copyright holders. Any omissions will be corrected at the first opportunity.

First published 1999

2 4 6 8 10 9 7 5 3 1

Blackwell Publishers Ltd
108 Cowley Road, Oxford OX4 1JF, UK

Blackwell Publishers Inc.
350 Main Street, Malden, Massachusetts 02148, USA

All rights reserved. Except for the quotation of short passages for the purposes of criticism and review, no part of this publication may be reproduced, stored in a retrieval system, or transmitted, in any form or by any means, electronic, mechanical, photocopying, recording or otherwise, without the prior permission of the publisher.

Except in the United States of America, this book is sold subject to the condition that it shall not, by way of trade or otherwise, be lent, resold, hired out, or otherwise circulated without the publisher's prior consent in any form of binding or cover other than that in which it is published and without a similar condition including this condition being imposed on the subsequent purchaser.

British Library Cataloguing in Publication Data

A CIP catalogue record for this book is available from the British Library.

Library of Congress Cataloging-in-Publication Data
Tilley, Christopher Y.
Metaphor and material culture / Christopher Tilley.
p. cm. – (Social archaeology)
Includes bibliographical references and index.
ISBN 0-631-19202-6 (alk. paper). – ISBN 0-631-19203-4 (pbk.: alk. paper)
1. Social archaeology. 2. Material culture. 3. Metaphor–Social aspects.
4. Metaphor in literature. 5. Metaphor in art.
I. Title. II. Series
CC72.4.T55 1999 930.1 – dc21
98-21302 CIP

Typeset in 11 on 13 pt Garamond
by Best-set Typesetter Ltd, Hong Kong
Printed in Great Britain by MPG Books Limited, Bodmin, Cornwall

This book is printed on acid-free paper

For Alice and Benjamin:
The Herons of Hambledon Hill

Contents

List of Plates	viii
List of Figures	ix
List of Tables	xii
Preface	xiv
Part I Metaphor and the Constitution of the World	**1**
1 Metaphor in Language, Thought and Culture	3
2 Solid Metaphor: The Analysis of Material Forms	36
Part II Text, Artefact, Art	**77**
Introduction	79
3 Frozen Metaphor: Megaliths in Texts	82
4 The Metaphorical Transformations of Wala Canoes	102
5 Body Metaphors in Southern Scandinavian Rock Art	133
Part III Landscapes and a Sense of Place	**175**
Introduction	177
6 The Beach in the Sky	185
7 Performing Culture in the Global Village	239
8 Conclusions	260
References	274
Index	287

Plates

2.1 A wooden *malangan* sculpture   60
2.2 Two women with *bilums*   63
4.1 Wala canoe prow figure-head   114
5.1 Högsbyn: rock 32   156
5.2 Högsbyn: Ormvindlingshällen   159
5.3 View of the carved rocks at Högsbyn in zone C seen from
    the south   162
6.1 The eastern end of the south Dorset Ridgeway   188
6.2 The Chesil Beach seen from Abbotsbury   190
6.3 The Martin's Down bank barrow at the western end of the
    Ridgeway   207
6.4 Part of the barrow line looking east from below Bronkham
    Hill towards Ridge Hill   222
6.5 The summit area of Bronkham Hill showing barrows and
    dolines   226
7.1 The central part of the 'Small Nambas' dancing ground:
    male side   241
7.2 Ancestor house with tree-fern carving   241
7.3 The 'Small Nambas' male dance troupe   242
7.4 The coral platform with displays of pigs' jaws   243
7.5 Serving *laplap*   244

Figures

1.1	'Horizontal' (metonymic) and 'vertical' (metaphoric) components of linguistic messages according to Jakobson	22
1.2	The relationship between twins and birds according to Lévi-Strauss	24
2.1	Diagram of Batammaliba house façade parts	42
2.2	Diagram of the Batammaliba house with its human parts	46
2.3	The social distribution of parts of the sacrificial beast among the Dinka	52
2.4	The classification of living creatures among Baan Phraan Maun villagers in Thailand	55
2.5	Yekuana *waja* representing *Awadi* the poisonous coral snake	71
2.6	Sabarl ceremonial axe showing named parts	73
3.1	The relative frequencies of generic usage of the term 'megalith' in the texts analysed	85
3.2	The mean frequency of occurrence of the term 'megalith' per page of text analysed	87
3.3	The frequency of different words linked with the term 'megalith'	90
3.4	Nilsson's comparison of the ground plans of Swedish passage graves and Eskimo houses	93

x LIST OF FIGURES

3.5	Some 'megalithic' textual journeys around Europe	96
4.1	The location of Wala and the Small Islands of Malekula, Vanuatu	105
4.2	Named parts of Wala canoes	107
4.3	The canoe as a big man	115
4.4	Sketches of traditional Small Island bird prow figure-head forms	116
4.5	Sketch of a large sea-going canoe from Atchin island	119
4.6	Sketch plan of Lowo dancing ground on Wala island	125
4.7	Relationship between the form of the dancing ground and the position of sacrificial boars in *Maki* ceremonies	127
5.1	The location of the Högsbyn rock carving site	134
5.2	The spatial distribution and characteristics of the Högsbyn carving site	136
5.3	Major design classes at Högsbyn	137
5.4	Examples of infilled designs taken from different carving surfaces at Högsbyn	146
5.5	Examples of sequencing and a concern with temporality in relation to cupmarks and wavy lines	147
5.6	The circle cross as seasonal marker	147
5.7	Varieties of circle-cross designs taken from different carving surfaces at Högsbyn	148
5.8	The consecutive monthly maximum north and south declinations of the moon during a year	149
5.9	Högsbyn: the carved designs on rock 32, eastern face	156
5.10	Högsbyn: the carved designs on the four carving surfaces of Ormvindlingshällen	160
5.11	Högsbyn: rock 19	164
5.12	Högsbyn: rock 1	166
5.13	Högsbyn: the changing character of human depictions from south to north of the carving area	169
5.14	Annotated sketch plan of the Högsbyn carving site showing viewing angle of the carved rock panels and paths of movement through the site	172
6.1	The south Dorset Ridgeway study area	187
6.2	Longitudinal section along the south Dorset Ridgeway	189
6.3	The distribution of finds of Palaeolithic and Mesolithic Portland chert in southern England	194
6.4	The distribution of Neolithic monuments in the south Dorset Ridgeway area	195

LIST OF FIGURES

6.5	The distribution of Bronze Age round barrows in the south Dorset Ridgeway area	209
6.6	Barrows in the vicinity of the Broadmayne bank barrow	213
6.7	Barrow groups along the south Dorset Ridgeway from Broadmayne to Bincombe Down	217
6.8	Barrow groups along the south Dorset Ridgeway from Bincombe Down to Bronkham Hill	217
6.9	Barrow groups along the Ridgeway from Bronkham Hill to the Black Down summit	223
6.10	Bronkham Hill: the distribution of barrows and dolines	227
6.11	The distribution of dolines and barrows in the summit area of Bronkham Hill	227
6.12	Barrow groups along the south Dorset Ridgeway from Black Down to Martin's Down	231
6.13	Plan of barrow group R2 towards the western end of the south Dorset Ridgeway	232

Tables

2.1 The relationship between marriage and sex rules, eating rules and rules of etiquette concerning house categories among Baan Phraan Maun villagers in Thailand 56
3.1 The sample of texts used in the analysis of 'megaliths' 84
3.2 Words linked with the term 'megalith' 88
3.3 Some alternative words to associate with the term 'megalithic' 89
3.4 The three most common words used in combination with 'megalith' 91
5.1 Motif types at Högsbyn in terms of number and relative frequency 137
5.2 Carving surfaces with only one identifiable design at Högsbyn 138
5.3 The frequency of carving surfaces with two different designs at Högsbyn 139
5.4 The frequency of design combinations on carving surfaces with three to eleven different designs at Högsbyn 140
5.5 The frequency of carving surfaces with different combinations of identifiable representational designs at Högsbyn 141
5.6 The frequency of carving surfaces with different combinations of identifiable abstract designs at Högsbyn 142

5.7	Cases of design superimposition or merging between different identifiable design classes at Högsbyn	143
5.8	The absolute and relative frequency of different designs according to a four-fold zonation of the Högsbyn carving area	152
5.9	The occurrence of left and right shoe-sole designs at Högsbyn in relation to a four-fold zonation of the carving site	170
6.1	Long barrows in south Dorset: morphological characteristics and relationships to other monuments	199
6.2	The landscape settings of the Neolithic monuments in the study area	200

Preface

To write about metaphor is immediately to enter into a multidisciplinary field, for metaphors have been extensively discussed by literary critics, linguists, cognitive psychologists, philosophers, educationalists, anthropologists, sociologists, geographers and art historians. This in itself might make it seem a particularly appropriate topic within a field of research such as material culture studies lacking a 'natural' disciplinary home (Miller and Tilley 1996). While many hundreds of books have been written about metaphor (see, for example, Shibles 1971) it has not been foregrounded within a consideration and analysis of material culture. Put into a nutshell, the purpose of this book is to exemplify the significance and use of the concept of metaphor in the study and writing of material forms. In essence, the work of the construction of human culture is doubly metaphorical in character. Language is, in part, a metaphorical construction of the world, as is material culture. It follows, therefore, that in the academic writing of material culture we are building metaphors on metaphors, or converting material or solid metaphor into linguistic metaphor, a matter of material and linguistic transformation.

In Part I of the book I attempt to provide a broad overview of the use and value of the concept of metaphor in the social sciences. Part II consists of three archaeological and ethnographic studies of metaphors: in text, contemporary Melanesian canoes and Scandinavian Bronze Age rock art. Part

III considers metaphor in relation to the social construction of landscape and the constitution of the meaning of place in the prehistoric past and the present. The development of the metaphorical significance of landscape is discussed in relation to long-term change from the Mesolithic to the end of the Bronze Age in the South Dorset Ridgeway area in Chapter 6. The next chapter considers a contemporary sense of place in Vanuatu in relation to global and local processes, heritage and tourism. In the Conclusions (Chapter 8) I attempt to develop elements of a theory of material forms as solid metaphor on the basis of the previous discussions. Together, these studies attempt to exemplify in both theory and practice the significance of metaphor for the analysis and understanding of past and present material forms and life-worlds.

The process of writing this book, perhaps more than any other, has transformed my understanding of text, and of the world. Previously, partially deadened by a conventional literalism, I was blissfully unaware of the constant use of metaphor in virtually every statement I attempted to make. In the course of writing the book, I became amused by the fact that the only way I could really express what I wanted to say was to use tropes. Personally, this resulted in a complete collapse in my conventional understanding of language. Before this, although I could accept intellectually that language had a fundamental figurative component, I still naively thought that it provided a domain in which I might be able to express what I wanted to say in a fairly straightforward and unambiguous literal manner. In writing the book I have inevitably used, like others before me, metaphor to assert the value and significance of metaphor.

I want to thank my students at University College London who stoically accepted the presence of the 'M word' in lecture courses on so many occasions. Danny Miller, Mike Rowlands and Buck Schieffelin were kind enough to make useful comments on Chapter 4. Thanks to Wayne Bennett for comments on Chapter 7 and to Jarl Nordbladh for criticism of a draft of Chapter 5. An earlier version of part of Chapter 5, now completely superseded by the analysis published here, has previously been published in the *Bulletin of the Institute of Archaeology*, University College, London, 1994. I am most grateful to Tommy Andersson for supplying me with unpublished recent documentation of the Högsbyn rock carvings and for discussions at the site. Another version of Chapter 8 has appeared in *Critique of Anthropology* 1997 and I am grateful to Sage Publishers for permission to publish it here. I am most grateful to Ian Hodder for constructive criticisms of a previous version of the entire book and to Tessa Harvey at Blackwell Publishers for her support and assistance.

Christopher Tilley, University College London, February 1998

Part I

Metaphor and the Constitution of the World

1

Metaphor in Language, Thought and Culture

Introduction

Metaphor is one of the tropes (twists and turns of language) of classical rhetoric, the other main ones being metonymy, synecdoche and irony. Rhetoric, in linguistic theory, is one of the primeval ancestors of structuralism. It was an attempt to analyse and classify the forms of speech which make language possible and intelligible. Going back to the ancient Greeks and Aristotle onwards there was an entire theory of rhetoric. With the development of a formal discourse on linguistics, the study of rhetoric fell somewhat into disrepute. It was the development of structuralism and semiotics during the 1960s that has done so much to revive a theory and interest in the tropes of language, an interest that is now paradoxically superseding structuralism itself in the form of various post-structuralist discourse theories. Like so many other so-called 'developments' in the social sciences the process of going forwards has entailed moving backwards to revive elements of a theory of language preceding the advent of structuralism.

To many contemporary linguistic theorists metaphor has been taken as the key, or most important trope, and often the term has been used to subsume all the others. Books on metaphor invariably consider the other tropes, but metaphor is taken as being the most important of all. While there have been many books and conferences on the subject of metaphor, such attention to metonymy or synecdoche seems unlikely. One reason is that metaphor has been considered to be the most complex, and therefore, the most interesting of the tropes to analyse. But there is something more: metaphor has become a figure for figurality in general (Culler 1981: 189), and conforming to this unwritten convention, this is the manner in which the term will function in the present account, where distinctions between it and other tropes are not explicitly made.

A usual division is made between literal language, language that means what it says and says what it means, and rhetorical or tropic or figurative use of language. Traditionally, it has been assumed that the language we use is predominantly literal. Tropes are an embellishment, an abuse, a deviation from the norm, performed for purposes of persuasion and ideology. We should therefore be somewhat suspicious of metaphor or properly confine it within a particular and limited domain. Metaphor has above all been linked with the imaginative faculties. The heartland domains of metaphor are literature and especially poetry. Fiction, in this view, is fundamentally opposed to facts and metaphors should not therefore be the domain of the serious social scientist. They, to use a metaphor, muddy an understanding of the world. Metaphor is linked with emotion and subjectivity and opposed to a disinterested and objective understanding.

The argument made here is that this is a tradition of thought that is fundamentally in error. An alternative position is that (1) without metaphor human communication would be nigh impossible; (2) metaphors provide the basis for an interpretative understanding of the world, the goal of the historical and social sciences.

Metaphor, metonymy, synecdoche: some initial definitions

Metaphor involves a move from a whole to one of its parts to another whole which contains that part, or from a member to a general class and then back again to a member of that class. In the most general sense metaphor involves comprehending some entity from the point of view, or perspective, of another. In this sense all knowledge and all interpretation may be claimed to be metaphorical. It is an illustrative device in which a term from one level or frame of reference is used within a different level or referential frame. It involves a transfer of one term from one system or level of meaning to another (*metaphora*: carrying over). From Aristotle we get the definitions that metaphor involves: the transference of a word to a sense different from its proper signification and 'giving the thing a name that belongs to something else' (Aristotle 1924: 1457b6–9). In this conceptualization, metaphor involves a transfer of meaning from the word that properly possesses it to another word belonging to the same shared category of meaning, a form of compressed analogy in which, unlike simile, the reader is made to do the work of establishing the connections, constructing the particular logic involved. By contrast, similes have less potential for producing an excess of meaning since the basis for the comparison is more controlled, stating explicitly that the terms are comparable and frequently providing the basis for the comparison: 'he struck out at her like a viper, his words were as if full of venom'. In metaphor, like simile, there are two conceptual domains, one being understood in terms of the other. An entire schematic structure involving two or more entities becomes mapped onto another. Some examples:

She is in full bloom (= maturity)
He is withering away (= dying)
He attacked my argument (arguments are war)
He was a lion in battle (= fierce etc.)
The foot of the hill
Time is money
His mind decayed
It was music to his ears
Our marriage is on the rocks

Metonymy

Metonymy involves a move from a part to a whole. In the statement 'Jane has been chasing those trousers' the trousers and the man are related as part of a notional or visual whole and related together. By contrast with metaphor, metonymy only involves one conceptual domain, so metonymic mapping occurs within a single domain rather than across domains. Consequently it involves an 'internal' rather than an 'external' relationship. One can refer to one entity within a schema by referring to another. One entity is taken as standing for another entity in the schema or, alternatively, for the schema as a whole. Metonymy accomplishes a transfer of meaning on the basis of associations that develop out of specific *contexts* and cultural traditions. Referring to the Queen by the phrase 'the crown' is only possible because of the historical association of queens and crowns. So metonymy, unlike metaphor, relies for its production of meaning on connections that build up over time or associations of usage. Some examples:

She's a pretty face (face for person, part for whole)
I hate to read Foucault (producer for product)
He hired a gun (object for user)
Clinton attacked Kuwait (controller for controlled)
Sainsbury's have introduced a new loyalty card (institution for people responsible)
The White House hasn't responded (place for institution)
Watergate changed our politics (place for event)

Synecdoche

Synecdoche is often regarded as being the most basic (and therefore relatively uninteresting) rhetorical device. It involves any series of part/whole relationships allowing one to move from a part to a whole or a whole to a part. Imagine we wish to talk about beech trees. A consideration of part to whole relations means that we can conceptualize beech trees in terms, for example, of woods, gardens, beech mast, doors, tables, spoons (things containing or made from beech). Alternatively, if we consider whole to part relationships we might understand beech trees themselves in terms of leaves, roots, trees or branches. A synecdoche involving a movement from a member to a class might involve a consideration of beech trees in terms of strong things or tall things or non-animate things. Movement from a class to a member might involve consideration of different varieties or shapes of beech trees.

Some further examples:

We need new blood in the company (= new people)
I've got a new set of wheels (= car, motorbike)
We need some good heads in the department (= intelligent people)

In general, synecdoche can be taken to be a special case of metonymy.

The Role of Metaphor or Why it is Important

Many scholars agree that metaphors arise because of inherent problems in the precise relationship between a world of words and a world of things, events and actions (Ortony 1975; Fainsilber and Ortony 1987; Gibbs 1994: 124ff.). Given that there always exists a gap between words and things and the actions and events that those words attempt to describe, capture or interpret (however many words I may try and use it is impossible to exactly reproduce in text the simplest of objects such as a chair, or of actions, such as a handshake), metaphorical expressions become necessary rather than contingent features of language. According to the *inexpressibility* thesis, metaphors provide ways of giving form to ideas and descriptions of the world virtually impossible in a literal language. The statement 'the ship is taking a bath' can serve to express far better the nature of childhood experience and the creation of meaning than any literal expression (Game and Metcalfe 1996: 48). In particular, emotions, feelings and understandings for others become positively banal when stated literally. Love requires the metaphor of the red rose. This general position has often been used to account for the power of poetry in stretching our imagination and producing insights into the nature of human lived realities. It provides a crucial link between metaphor, creativity and the human faculty of the imagination. Such a view forms the basis of Coleridge's philosophy. He understood metaphor as the power enabling the imagination to be put into *action*:

> The poet, described in *ideal* perfection, brings the whole soul of man into activity . . . He diffuses a tone and spirit of unity, that blends, and (as it were) *fuses*, each into each, by that synthetic and magical power, to which we have exclusively appropriated the name of the imagination . . . [It] reveals itself in the balance or reconcilement of opposite or discordant qualities: of sameness, with difference; of the general with the concrete; the idea with the image; the individual with the representative; the sense of novelty and freshness with old and familiar objects; a more than usual state of emotion with more than usual order. (Coleridge 1971: 253)

This is not so far from Ricoeur's more general statement that to 'present men "as acting" and all things "as in act" – such could very well be the *ontological* function of metaphorical discourse, in which every dormant potentiality of existence appears *as* blossoming forth, every latent capacity for action *as* actualized' (Ricoeur 1978: 43).

The *compactness* thesis suggests that metaphor often provides the simplest or most parsimonious means of communication between socialized individuals in the same culture. To describe the actions of a person as those of a fox or a viper, through commonly held cultural conventions of the connotations of the fox or the viper, can be a very succinct way of conveying information about him or her. Through metaphorical means it becomes possible to convey complex configurations of ideas with a very few words. Many metaphors cannot be paraphrased in a literal language. Often either a metaphor is used or nothing can be said (Ortony 1976).

Invariably linked with the previous two arguments is the *vividness* thesis. Metaphors facilitate the capturing of our phenomenological experience of the world in a unique way. They are a means of linking subjective and objective experience, conjoining them and resulting in a fresh 'fusion of horizons' (Gadamer 1975); they reside, therefore, at the heart of a hermeneutic or interpretative practice in the social sciences. This is also why, of course, metaphors are so common in poetry and literature: to create vivid and memorable images of the world.

It follows from this that metaphor and memory are frequently closely connected, and that the use of metaphor may enrich both the encoding and recall of information. A vivid metaphorical image, such as saying 'they cooked the land', is likely to be remembered far longer than a statement such as 'they burnt down the forest'. In so far as metaphors can evoke vivid mental images they facilitate memory. In this respect it is perhaps no coincidence that many of the titles of books and articles in the social and historical sciences exploit metaphors to the full.

One of the most important functions of metaphors in the process of understanding and interpreting the world is that they actively facilitate the production of novel understandings and interpretations. Metaphors provide a means by which we can connect together objects, events and actions that appear to be empirically (factually) disparate and unconnected. For example, by conceiving of human bodies as containers (of fluids and substances, with orifices – entrances and exits) one can begin to examine symbolic linkages between the body as container and other types of containers such as baskets or pots (Tilley 1996). Metaphor, then, provides an interpretative thread by means of which we can weave together into a fresh constellation the brute 'literal' facts of the world. In an empiricist or objectivist account of the world a body is a body and a pot is a pot. Metaphor provides a powerful means of overcoming this fragmented view of the world and examining systematic linkages between different cultural and material domains. Metaphor provides a way of mediating between concrete and abstract thoughts. A metaphor 'points to the existence of a given set of abstract relationships hidden within some immediately graspable image' (Beck 1978: 84).

In the most general sense metaphors promote self-reflexivity. An awareness of metaphor and its ubiquity helps us to understand better how and why we do research, and the extent to which we are trapped in the prison house of language, that our thought and writing is fundamentally metaphoric in character. We begin to see the metaphoric in what we take to be literal 'factual' or conventional statements about the world, an act of unmasking. Thinking about the metaphors we typically employ in interpretation leads us to a position in which we can begin to understand the manner in which the employment and emplotment of different metaphors leads to alternative conceptualizations and knowledges. If working with social science invariably involves working with metaphors this may help us to read better and write better.

Metaphor may not only serve as a binding element in providing an interpretative account of the world, it can also be conceived as a quality which links together individuals and groups. The fact that metaphors are culturally relative implies that members of the same culture may share many distinct metaphorical understandings in common. Others may be confined to distinct sub-cultures. Working out a speaker's attitudes and beliefs may be a key aspect of metaphorical understanding. Corradi Fiumara (1995), Gibbs (1994: 135ff.) and others have noted that metaphorical talk often presupposes and reinforces an intimacy between speaker and listener. Many figurative uses of language may be all but inaccessible to outsiders who do not share specific information about specific knowledges, beliefs and attitudes. The metaphors employed may very well be difficult to decode or understand by those who do not share the same frame of reference. In this manner metaphors may be utilized as vehicles of power in the sense of social domination and control. Those who do not understand the metaphorical meanings at work in culture, invariably linked to knowledges deemed fundamental to social reproduction, are almost inevitably those who have little or no authority. Learning metaphor becomes part and parcel of the process of the acquisition of cultural knowledges and the authority residing in their acquisition.

Metaphor has, of course, long been noted as a primary persuasive element in political rhetoric. Aristotle's tripartite division of language into logic, rhetoric and poetic in the *Poetics* (for discussions see Hawkes 1989; Derrida 1982) opposed rhetoric to logic, defining the former as having persuasion as its central role, the latter clarity. Both rhetorical and poetic language represented for him distinctive and specialized departures from ordinary language use which aimed at expressing things as clearly and as unambiguously as possible within a community of speakers. Conceived positively figurative use of language added spice, or seasoning, to its basic non-metaphorical nature. A great politician is, of necessity, a master of metaphor, and ever since Aristotle, this persuasive art of language use has been regarded with suspicion. This suspicion of the motives lying behind the use of metaphor has historically done considerable intellectual damage to the concept. Metaphor may become easily conceived as an ideological discourse, be accused of promoting manipulative representations of the world, a propagation of falsity. While metaphors may indeed produce a deliberate misrepresentation of the world this hardly seems to be a reason for speaking literally, since literal speech as much as metaphorical speech can be used to convey falsehoods. Metaphor itself is a mode of representation which can be used, abused and contested. The manner in which metaphor is employed in relation to social strategies and social struggles depends very much on the context of the events and actions and places in which it is set to work. But this persuasive purpose of metaphor is hardly confined to overt political discourse. All social scientific texts are motivated by an art of persuasion in which authors employ the powers of metaphor in conjunction with a presentation of empirical materials, or evidence, to convince their readers of the veracity and significance of the statements they are making.

Metaphor is fundamental to all belief systems. Myth and ritual may be reasonably argued to have their entire basis in a networking of metaphors. Fernandez (1986) writes of a 'mission of metaphor in expressive culture'. Defining metaphor as 'a strategic predication upon an inchoate pronoun (an I, a you, a we, a they) which makes a movement and leads to a performance' (ibid.: 8), he argues that the essence of religious experiences is a desire to change the way people feel about themselves and the world in which they live. Metaphors accomplish this end (ibid.: 23). By persuasion and performance they revitalize and empower the individual, connect things together, establish and re-establish, in symbolic strategies such as revitalization movements, a sense of wholeness and the relatedness of things in a reconstructive play of tropes (ibid.: ch. 8). This play of tropes in ritual achieves a number of ends. Amongst other things, it provides a sense of identity for inchoate subjects; enables movement in these subjects between states, provides a plan for ritual performance and enables the 'subject to return to the whole' (ibid.: 62). In short, metaphors provide a basis by means of which communities create and understand their collective experience. One of the most important points in Fernandez's thesis is the stress that he places on the metaphorical process as a form of movement linking together different domains. Metaphors provide a form of mediation between partial or abstract principles expressed in a verbal plane and concrete sensual images working on a non-verbal plane of experience. Beck advances this argument to suggest that metaphors mediate between the verbal and the non-verbal. Metaphors work to 'introduce nonverbal material into logically structured, semantic contexts.... Metaphor and the metonym are two sides of a single device used to bridge the gap between rational and sensory thought processes' (Beck 1978: 87). Rather than to suggest that metaphor is a mode of mediation between the verbal and non-verbal, between sensual experience of objects etc. and abstract thought, it seems far more to be the case that metaphorical processes are constitutive of both. Metaphor is in the artefact, in language, in the mind. It has ontological significance in language, culture and thought.

If culture, sociality and everyday conversation inevitably take on metaphoric forms we should expect this to be reflected in the discourses of the social sciences, and indeed this is the case. All sociological theories of life embody what might be termed root metaphors, fundamental images of the way the world is. In functionalist theories society is variously conceived as an organism, or like a machine. In structuralist positions culture and society are conceived as languages. Notions of cultural evolution are bound up with ideas of an evolution of the species. In ethnomethodological and other interpretative approaches social conduct is viewed as drama, or as a game. People are actors following rules, life is like a theatre. All use of models in the social sciences is metaphorical in nature. Analogies are forms of metaphorical reasoning in which the formal implications are spelled out so that Society X or social practice X may be said to be like Society Y or social practice Y. Photographs, employed as 'evidence', act as metaphors for the reality they portray. All maps are metaphors for the towns or landscapes they represent. In this manner it is possible to claim that metaphors structure social scientific thought from the most general to the most specific levels (see Brown 1977 for a detailed discussion). They are essential and lie at the heart of the transmission of theories and their replacement. Metaphors establish links between language use in the social sciences and the worlds that are described and discussed (Kuhn 1993).

Metaphor and Language

Attempts to theorize the metaphorical process in language have been many and various. In this section I want to discuss briefly some of the most influential perspectives. According to a traditional *substitution* view of metaphor the process of understanding a metaphorical statement requires translating out of the metaphorical terms into a literal language. So metaphors of the kind 'John is a fox' can simply be expressed literally as 'John is crafty'. A metaphor, in effect, says one thing and means another.

According to the *comparison* view, basically a variant on the substitution view, the literal paraphrase imputed by the metaphor is a statement of some similarity or analogy. The essence of metaphor is that it is a condensed or convoluted form of simile. The statement 'John is a fox' is a compressed comparison between the behaviour of John and what we know about the behaviour of foxes. In both these views metaphors are expendable forms of discourse, embellishments of an originary literal language (for detailed discussion see Black 1962; 1993). There are two major problems with these views. First, it is often impossible to provide a literal translation for metaphorical statements except in well-chosen simple cases, such as those given above. Providing a literal gloss to substitute for statements such as 'Crazed through much child-bearing, the moon is staggering in the sky', the opening two lines of Yeats's poem 'The Crazed Man' (Kittay 1987; Gibbs 1994: 214), is an altogether different matter. Second, many metaphors cannot be 'converted' into similes without a loss or reduction in meaning. The power of many metaphors may be held to reside in the fact that they are not similes. A statement such as 'the interviewer hammered the prime minister' is not particularly well expressed by stating that 'what the interviewer did to the prime minister was like someone hammering a nail into a piece of wood'. Black cogently puts it this way: 'in discursively comparing one subject *with* another, we sacrifice the distinctive power and effectiveness of a good metaphor. The literal comparison lacks the ambience and suggestiveness. . . . In a metaphor as powerful as Pascal's, of man as a 'thinking reed' . . . the figure's effect depends . . . very much on the ambience' (Black 1993: 31). A statement about human frailty and weakness is produced in the metaphor in a particularly vivid manner impossible by the conversion of the statement into a simile or a literal statement of comparison. The traditional view of metaphor is that it is a type of trope in which a figurative word is simply substituted for a literal word on the basis of an apparent resemblance. From this substitution-theory perspective metaphor can only be an embellishment to language. It is not strictly necessary and we could get along very well without it. Metaphor can only be assigned a decorative role and/or an emotional import. This perspective is inadequate because it is incapable of providing an account of the processes by means of which novel metaphors get produced.

Does the poetic or the literal dominate?

> Whereas literal knowledge aspires to the inert status of information, metaphor works with indeterminancy to keep meaning safe from the final clarification that is its obituary. (Game and Metcalfe 1996: 50)

Linguistic tropes are, of course, part of the poetic use of language and are so defined by reference to literal language that is often thought to be dominant in our culture: special cases, special expressions. But on closer examination this does not prove to be the case. Our everyday use of language is filled with metaphor. It is just that the metaphors are so normal and so commonplace that we simply do not acknowledge or recognize this. Quantitative research by linguists, reported by Gibbs, underlines the ubiquity of metaphor in speech, literature, poetry and scientific writing. One study examined metaphoric language in transcripts of psychotherapeutic interviews, various essays and the 1960 Kennedy–Nixon presidential debates. The researchers counted only phrases sufficiently non-literal to be easily recognized, and distinguished between frozen or dead (usually unrecognized) and novel metaphors (see below). The results were 1.8 novel and 4.08 frozen metaphors per minute of discourse. Another analysis of metaphor in TV debates found one unique metaphor for every 25 words used. Novel metaphors were used every two to three minutes of discourse by US senators (Gibbs 1994: 123–4). This research reveals, admittedly in a rather crude way, both the ubiquity of metaphor in speech, and that its use is neither particularly esoteric or gifted.

The most unusual, profound, and novel metaphors undoubtedly occur in poetry and literature, where the poet or novelist consciously works to produce metaphors, but they also form a routine, normal and standard component of everyday communication. There is thus little empirical basis for any claim that language is first literal in nature and only secondarily metaphorical. Both the literal and the figurative form equally important fundamental components of language use in everyday speech.

Perhaps the most popular or dominant view of metaphor in the contemporary philosophical literature is the *interaction* view developed by Black (1962; 1993) on the basis of Richards's seminal work which did so much to revitalize metaphor theory from the 1930s onwards (Richards 1936). Richards provided the basic terminology and conceptual framework for discussing metaphor that has subsequently been modified or reacted against. He argued that metaphor consists of two terms, the *tenor*, or topic, and the *vehicle*, and the relationship between them. The tenor is the underlying idea which the metaphor expresses, while the vehicle is the analogy used to carry or embody the tenor. Tenor and vehicle *interact* to create the meaning. Black (1962; 1993) substitutes the terms *focus* and *frame* for Richards's tenor and vehicle. The metaphorical statement's focus is the word or words used non-literally in relation to a surrounding literal frame, or context. Black argues that metaphorical statements have two distinct subjects, the 'primary subject' and the 'secondary one':

> In the context of a particular metaphorical statement, the two subjects 'interact' in the following ways: (a) the presence of the primary subject invites the hearer to select some of the secondary subject's properties; and (b) invites him to construct a parallel implication-complex that can fit the primary subject; and (c) reciprocally induces parallel changes in the secondary subject. (Black 1993: 28)

This perspective on metaphor usefully emphasizes that metaphorical statements actively produce similarity because of the manner in which the words 'interact' in the mind of the reader or listener. In the metaphors 'people are wolves' and 'society is a sea', we do not directly compare persons or societies (the topic or focus of the metaphors, and wolves or the sea, the vehicles or frames) for similarities that actually exist, but instead view each in a new manner so as to create the similarities which reside in an active system of relationships.

Ricoeur builds upon the work of Richards, Black and others to produce a *tension* theory of metaphor (Ricoeur 1978). Metaphors have to be understood not at the level of a simple word substitution but from the contextual perspective of the statement (sentence). Metaphors perform their work through the establishment of a tension between two or more terms in the sentence through the *violation* of established linguistic codes. The metaphorical utterance then serves to reduce this tension by means of the creation of a novel and striking semantic pertinence within the sentence as a whole:

> Metaphorical meaning is an effect of the entire statement, but it is focused on one word, which can be called the metaphorical word. This is why one must say that metaphor is a semantic innovation that belongs at once to the predicative order (new pertinence) and the lexical order (paradigmatic deviation). In its first aspect it depends upon a 'dynamics' of meaning; under the second, upon a 'stasis' or non-dynamic state of the system. (Ricoeur 1978: 156–7)

For Ricoeur metaphor is the process through which the inherent polysemy of words becomes expanded and transformed, a capacity attributed to the referential dimension of the metaphorical statement or its power to redescribe reality. Meaning is created and reality becomes redescribed by means of the sentence supporting a metaphor. Metaphor shatters and increases our sense of reality by simultaneously breaking down and increasing the referential and transformative capacity of language. Metaphors produce semantic innovations by means of which new information about the world is created. They perform the role of teasing our minds into having new thoughts by stimulating us to perceive resemblances which were previously not noticed and not thought. Novel metaphors help us to break with ordinary everyday vision and enable us to comprehend something new and unexpected. This is a process in which 'language divests itself of its function of direct description in order to reach the mythic level where its function of discovery is set free' (ibid.: 247). For example, in the poetic statement 'nature is a temple where living columns' the tension that metaphor sets up and then resolves is between what are alternatively referred to in the literature as

1 tenor and vehicle or focus and frame, principal subject and secondary subject, source and target domains (i.e. in this case, between 'nature' and 'temple');
2 the literal meaning of the statement that is patently absurd and a figurative understanding in which 'sense emerges through non-sense';
3 in the relational function of the copula in terms of identity and difference in the play of resemblance (ibid.).

To reach an understanding of the statement the meaning of the copula 'to be' has to be reversed. Literally, 'is' should be taken as meaning 'is not', but in the figurative sense 'is' means 'is like'. The outcome is a tension in the relational function of the verb 'to be'. The metaphorical statement 'works' and creates something new through the process of creating meaning out of literal non-sense and through forging novel connections between tenor and vehicle. Nature becomes apprehended as a temple, a new insight, eliciting the image of trees as living columns supporting, perhaps, the roof of a sacred place. The literal meaning must be abolished for the metaphorical meaning to work. Ricoeur argues that in metaphoric language the openness of language to the discovery of possible being, the ability to make fresh connections between things and understand them in a novel way, occurs because of a core image functioning of language allowing us to conjoin linguistic sense with the materiality of a cognized image (in the example given above the sacred grove of trees). The emergence of metaphorical meaning going beyond literal meaning can be considered to be an ontological characteristic of language itself, the way language is, what it permits. So metaphor is not something 'external' to linguistic communication, but of its very essence. Language has a 'doubleness' at its core manifest in the duality of the literal and the metaphorical (ibid.: 313).

The traditional substitution theory of metaphor degrades the term.

Metaphors tell us nothing new, they merely provide an embellishment of literal meaning. By contrast, Ricoeur shows us that metaphors are fundamental in creating new insights and forging new links between things. A basic condition for metaphors to work at all resides in the polysemic character of words in natural languages, that they have many meanings and cannot be reduced to a single strict and 'proper' sense. Polysemy then provides the foundation for the creative extension of meaning produced through metaphor. The actual operation of polysemy, like metaphor, can only be understood at the level of the statement or sentence, in the manner in which words interact with others to create meaning and sense.

One of the problems with Ricoeur's tension theory resides in the manner in which he opposes literal to metaphorical or figurative meaning, from which 'tension' arises. The implication of his approach is that a reader expects literal meaning first and when this expectation is not fulfilled the tension arises. The reader then translates, in his or her mind, from a literal frame of reference to a metaphorical one. Literal meaning still seems to be granted a priority in Ricoeur's position. But it can be argued that normally we do not have the problem that Ricoeur describes: we simply and immediately read and understand the statement directly as being metaphorical without first passing through a literal stage of confused reading. The implication is that metaphor is more than a mere matter of language use.

Metaphor and Thought

Cognitive psychologists and linguists have presented a detailed body of work demonstrating that metaphor and metonymy are fundamental tools which allow us to understand both abstract concepts and abstract reasoning. Avoiding a mind/body dualism the mind is effectively put back into the body, conceived as embodied. Metaphorical understanding is grounded in non-metaphorical preconceptual structures arising from everyday bodily experiences (Lakoff and Johnson 1980; Lakoff 1987; Johnson 1987).

Metaphor is not so much a matter of language in general, and literary use of language in particular, but a matter of *thought* (Lakoff and Johnson 1980; Gibbs 1994). We do not just employ and construct metaphors but live through them. Our ordinary conceptual system by means of which we live, think and act is fundamentally metaphorical in nature. Metaphorical concepts structure perception, action and social relationships. Because of the routinized character of the vast majority of social life we simply do not realize the extent to which our conceptual system or thought processes are metaphorically structured. Communication through language is, of course, based on the same conceptual system guiding thought and language. By analysing language use we can obtain a good idea of the form and character of the conceptual system that produces it. The kind of scenario Ricoeur describes is, in fact, only likely to arise when we are confronted with particularly striking novel metaphors in poetry and literature, precisely the kinds of metaphors that the majority of critics have discussed rather than the normal everyday metaphors guiding our ordinary conceptual system.

Lakoff and Johnson define the essence of metaphor as *understanding* and *experiencing* one thing in terms of another (Lakoff and Johnson 1980: 55). While poets and literary writers may be masters of metaphor they only take to a 'higher' or more 'refined' level what everyone does every day — think in a poetic or figurative manner. Virtually all everyday talk reflects the ability of people to think routinely in ways that are not literal. The implication of this position is that while metaphors may help to create new insights and interpretations the fact that these processes take place at all reflects underlying schemes of thought that have a fundamental figurative quality. Even if we wished to do so we could not evade metaphor and the meaning and construction of human culture would be impossible without it. This position, a 'poetics of mind' (Gibbs 1994: 16–17), involves the following main propositions:

1   The human mind is inherently non-literal in character.
2   Language reflects the human perceptual and conceptual understanding of experience.
3   Figuration is not just a matter of language but provides much of the foundation for thought, reason and imagination.
4   Figuration is not ornamental but commonplace.
5   Figurative modes of thought motivate the meanings of many linguistic expressions typically viewed as having a literal interpretation.
6   Metaphorical meaning is grounded in non-metaphorical aspects of recurring bodily experiences or experiential gestalts.
7   Scientific theories, art, music, myth and material culture exemplify many of the same figurative schemes found in everyday thought and language.
8   Figurative language does not require special cognitive processes to be produced or understood.
9   Children's figurative thought motivates their significant ability to both use and understand many kinds of figurative speech. A whole series of experiments by cognitive linguists, reported by Gibbs, has

demonstrated that no special processes are required to understand metaphors. They are readily comprehended by young children, so an ability to cope with metaphor seems to be as normal and everyday a part of thought processes as is its use. No unique or special decoding processes are required.

For Lakoff and Johnson metaphor involves a mapping from a source to a target domain. The source domains are familiar, often of the physical world. They are easy to think with because the thinker can readily conceptualize relations among the elements in such domains and changes in these relations when the elements are set in motion conceptually. The target domains are abstract conceptual domains, frequently of the internal mental and emotional world or unseen and unknown domains of the physical world. Lakoff and Johnson argue that a small number of schemas of physical world relations, termed *image schemas*, underlie metaphors and are based in bodily experiences and the manner in which the body interacts with the physical environment. Spatial concepts are a primary example:

> Our spatial concept UP arises out of our spatial experience. We have bodies and stand erect. Almost every movement we make involves a motor program that either changes our up–down orientation, maintains it, presupposes it, or takes it into account in some way. In other words the structure of our spatial concepts emerges from our constant spatial experience, that is, our interaction with the physical environment. (Ibid.: 56)

Our understanding of containment is based on looking into and taking things out of containers, going into and out of containers like rooms, and comprehending our bodies as containers of – fluids, sensations, organs. Our understanding of the physical world of containers and containment then becomes mapped onto abstractions so that theoretical arguments can be understood as containers. Our lives are filled with pathways, routes of movement to and from places. A human understanding of pathways develops soon after birth when a child starts to crawl around so that it is not perhaps surprising that human purposes become described in terms of destinations that we try to reach, and so on (Johnson 1987: 113ff.).

In his analysis of the word 'anger' in American English Lakoff argues that in common expressions such as 'You make my blood boil', 'Don't fly off the handle', 'He blew up', 'They were having a heated argument', 'He went over the top', 'He got red with anger', the 'ANGER IS HEAT metaphor, when applied to fluids, combines with the metaphor THE BODY IS A CONTAINER OF THE EMOTIONS to yield the central metaphor of the system: anger is the heat of fluid in a container' (Lakoff 1987: 383). In the central metaphor coolness and calmness correspond to a lack of anger in such expressions as 'keep cool' and 'stay calm'. The central metaphor has a rich series of metaphorical entailments, e.g. when hot fluids start to boil the fluid goes upward, hence it is possible to make a statement such as 'her pent-up anger *welled up* inside her', which is conventionally understood by everyone. Lakoff's basic argument here is that metaphor governs rather than facilitates reasoning and constitutes understanding. An important part of Lakoff and Johnson's project (Lakoff 1987; Lakoff and Johnson 1980; Johnson 1987; Lakoff and Turner 1989) is the systematic undermining of objectivist and empiricist accounts of language and the world. Underlining the significance of metaphor in thought and language provides a direct challenge to objectivist accounts in which only literal statements, concepts and propositions can describe and explain the world. They successfully demonstrate that even basic concepts such as anger do not exist as literal objective descriptions of reality, and that these cannot be understood apart from their metaphorical grounding and entailments. A language that is non-metaphorical in nature could logically only consist of proper names. But natural languages do not have proper names. To name something is to ascribe it properties, to perceive similarities, to engage with metaphor. This is an assertion of the cognitive value and respectability of figurative language in an analysis of the social. Culler notes that 'the act of grouping distinct particulars under a common heading on the basis of perceived or imagined resemblance, which is the central act in any narrative of the origin of language, corresponds to the classical definition of metaphor: substitution on the basis of resemblance' (Culler 1981: 203). The historical implications are clear. If language originates in tropes then literal language is a language whose tropic origin has been forgotten through cultural convention. Through time a figurative understanding of the world becomes converted into literal understandings and this process runs in tandem with the development of an abstracted 'scientific' knowledge. Scientific terms represent a last stage in the mummification of language. They *appear* to express something about their discursive objects completely and exactly but are in fact a residue of conventional or frozen metaphors.

Deconstructing the Literal/Metaphorical Divide

> The appeal to the criteria of clarity and obscurity would suffice to confirm [that] ... this whole philosophical delimitation of metaphor already lends itself to

being constructed and worked upon by 'metaphors'. How could a piece of knowledge or a language be properly clear or obscure? (Derrida 1982: 252)

Any attempt to maintain an absolute distinction between the literal and the metaphorical inevitably breaks down. The binary opposition is far too crude. The literal, the privileged term in many discussions of metaphor, is supposedly the opposite of an 'ornamental' figurative language but, as has already been noted, by an ironic twist a literal expression can be argued to be a metaphor whose figurality has been forgotten. Metaphor, traditionally regarded as secondary and derivative, can now be regarded as basic. However, this does not necessarily lead to the claim that *all* contemporary use of language is metaphorical because metaphors typically rely on some basis of comparison with an entity in a different conceptual domain. We do not conventionally understand a sausage, or a dog, by mapping them in relation to something else. We can have a metaphorical understanding of a dog. The dog's tail might be understood as a flag, but this does not mean that the tail cannot be understood simply as a physical attribute of the dog, as a tail. Despite this, it may often be misleading to try and rigidly divide concepts and statements into those that are metaphorical in character and those that are not, because metaphoricity is bound up with aspects of conceptual structure and the polysemy of words. While descriptions of the world may or may not be metaphorical in nature, interpretations of the world almost inevitably *are* since they typically involve the mapping, or understanding, of one unfamiliar and poorly understood domain in terms of another. To deconstruct the literal/metaphorical opposition is to displace it and situate it differently, to undermine the 'common-sense' priority and status granted to the literal in our culture. It should not result in a monism in which only metaphor is left. This position recognizes that literal language is a language in which key elements of figurality have been forgotten instead of considering figurative speech as a deviation from a supposed norm of literality.

Dead and living metaphors

In a consideration of the difference between dead and living metaphors we can distinguish between statements such as 'I *see* (i.e. understand) what you mean' and 'he's almost *gone*' (i.e. died), which are elements of ordinary metaphoric expression in English, and isolated metaphors which are idiosyncratic and are not used systematically in our language and thought, such as the *face* of the clock, the *legs* of the table, the *mouth* of the tunnel, the *belly* of the pot, etc., which are far more specific (Lakoff and Johnson 1980: 54).

One claim is that all these dead metaphors are no longer properly metaphoric, so that to say 'I "see" what you mean' merely suggests that 'see' has, historically, come to have 'understand' as one of its meanings, or, similarly, that one of the meanings of 'gone' is died. While this is undoubtedly the case, *seeing* as a metaphor for understanding has profound effects on the structuring of our unconscious and the routine habitual actions we carry out in the world. In Western culture, since the Enlightenment, the sedimented importance of the visual in language is linked with a culture that can be called 'ocularcentric', dominated by vision (Jay 1993: 4), in which vision becomes the 'noblest of the senses' (Descartes 1965: 65) and knowing becomes indelibly connected with seeing. Dead metaphors, apart from the isolated idiosyncratic descriptions of specific things mentioned above, which cannot be claimed to play a major role in our conceptual system, are not so much dead in the sense that they are inactive or unimportant to us. They are only dead in so far as they remain hidden rather than recognized, and indeed, because of their loss of strangeness this may be a fundamental component of their very power and veracity in our culture. The whole notion of dead metaphor, implying the metaphor has become so conventionalized as to become literal and essentially passive in our thought, depends on setting up an opposition between the literal and the metaphorical in which the former is granted primacy in so far as it is claimed that ordinary conventional language is in *essence* not metaphorical. This is mere presupposition. The ubiquity of dead or conventional metaphors in fact leads to the opposite conclusion (Lakoff and Turner 1989: 130; Gibbs 1994: 276). Dead metaphors remain dead only in so far as the user *does not think of them*, i.e. they are part of the unconscious, of the mind.

Metaphor and Culture

Jakobson (1956), in a famous paper, put foward strong arguments for the centrality of both metaphor and metonymy in language use. Discussing *aphasia*, a loss or impairment in the ability to speak or understand speech, he argued that aphasia affects either the paradigmatic or the syntagmatic axis of language. The former is the selective dimension of language use (relating to Saussure's *langue*), the latter is the combinative dimension (relating to Saussure's *parole*). Any particular utterance or message involves

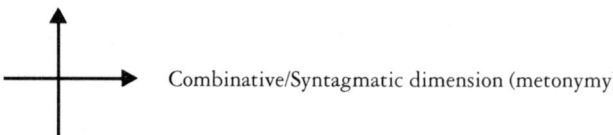

Figure 1.1 'Horizontal' (metonymic) and 'vertical' (metaphoric) components of linguistic messages according to Jakobson.

a combination of constituent parts (e.g. sentences, words, phonemes) *selected* from the repository of all possible parts. Any utterance can, therefore, be understood in terms of a 'vertical' movement selecting the parts to be used from the inventory of language as a whole, and a 'horizontal' movement in which the parts get combined together to form a particular message or sentence. The combinative or syntagmatic process manifests itself in *contiguity*, one word being placed after another; the selective process expresses itself in similarity, one word or concept being 'like' another. Jakobson further argued that the mode of the former is metonymic, the latter metaphoric (Figure 1.1). These two distinctive poles of language use, according to Jakobson, are such that aphasia may result in *either* a 'similarity disorder' (metaphor) or a 'contiguity disorder' (metonymy). Aphasics suffering from the similarity disorder showed a marked inability to use alternative words for the same object or to reason analogically – in other words, the inability to use metaphor. Those suffering from the contiguity disorder did not have the ability to use the 'syntactical rules organizing words into higher units' (Jakobson 1956: 85).

The general distinction that is drawn here between metonymic and metaphoric modes of thought forms the basis for Lévi-Strauss's (1966) discussion of the workings of the 'savage mind' in relation to totemism and myth. Opposing a 'civilized' abstract science with a 'primitive' science of the concrete (see Tilley 1990 for a discussion), the central features of his argument are that through a process of bricolage or a series of culturally contingent ad hoc responses to the environment, the primitive mind acts so as to establish a structured series of correspondences between an ordering of nature and an ordering of culture. These become, in effect, mirror images of each other and provide a means for explaining the world. This process involves the interplay of paradigmatic and syntagmatic associations, an interaction of metaphors and metonyms: metonymy celebrates the parts of experience while 'the more eloquent metaphors of the myth . . . refer back to the whole for significance' (Lévi-Strauss 1969: 242).

Myths serve to establish homologies between natural and social conditions, making it possible to equate significant contrasts found on different planes, e.g. the geographic, zoological, botanical, technical, social and ritual (Lévi-Strauss 1966: 93). The essence of savage thought is that it is analogical in character, a system of concepts embedded in images, 'building mental structures which facilitate an understanding of the world in as much as they resemble it' (ibid.: 263). Particular cultural conceptualizations of an ordering of nature provide the source of metaphors to produce an understanding of the target domain, culture: 'thanks to the myths, we discover that metaphors are based on an intuitive sense of the logical relations between one realm and other realms; metaphor reintegrates the first realm with the totality of the others. . . . Metaphor far from being a decoration that is added to language, purifies and restores it to its original nature' (Lévi-Strauss 1969: 339). In totemic thought, social differences between clans may become mapped or understood analogically in terms of differences between bird species: Clan A is to Clan B as Eagle is to Crow and so on. The particular metaphorical transformations are culturally determined by the specific series of differentiations, contrasts and oppositions and the range of analogical transformations involved. The savage mind takes the physical and concrete as its starting point and moves towards the abstract, whereas modern scientific thought works in the opposite direction.

Evans-Pritchard (1956), in a discussion of the classic Nuer metaphor 'twins are birds', reports that in order to characterize twins the Nuer employ expressions which seem contradictory. On the one hand, twins are one person, conceived in the sense that they are said to have a single personality (ibid.: 128). On the other hand, twins are not persons at all, but birds. This is because twins are manifestations of spiritual power and considered children of God.

In his structural analysis of the statement, Lévi-Strauss (1962: 79–82) argues that the sky for the Nuer is the abode of the spirit and twins are associated with it as 'persons of the above' and contrasted with other humans, 'persons of the below'. Since birds are of the sky and thus 'of the above' they belong to the same celestial order as twins (Figure 1.2). Lévi-Strauss concludes that 'Twins "are birds," not because they are confused with them or because they look like them, but because twins, in relation to other men, are as "persons of the above" to "persons of below" and, in relation to birds, as "birds of below" are to "birds of the above"' (ibid.: 80–1). They thus occupy, as do birds, an intermediary position between the supreme spirit and human beings. Terence Turner, in his re-analysis of the

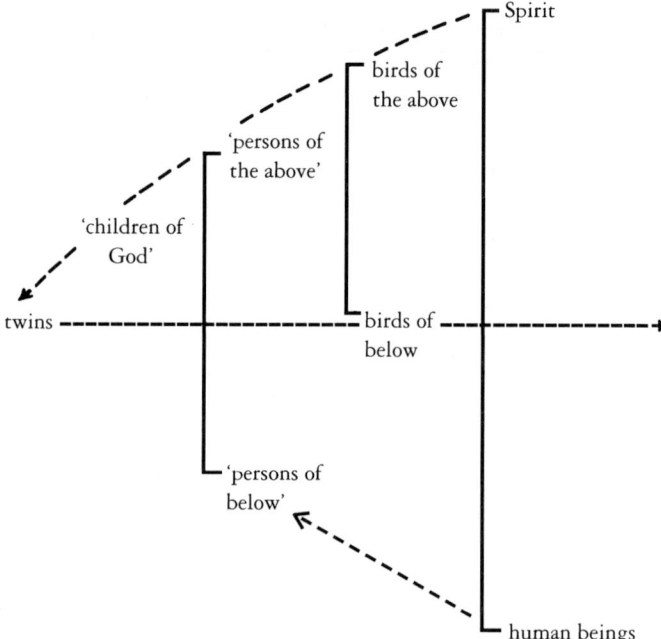

Figure 1.2 The relationship between conceptions of twins and birds in Nuer mythology.
Source: Lévi-Strauss (1962). Reproduced by kind permission of Merlin Press.

discussions of Evans-Pritchard and Lévi-Strauss (Turner 1991: 141–6), notes that birds, for the Nuer, are divided into:

1. those unambiguously of the sky: high or good fliers with bright pure colours;
2. those more ambiguously associated with the ground: birds of the below: ground-walking and dappled species such as the pied crow and guineafowl.

It is the latter, rather than just any species of birds, who are specifically likened to twins by the Nuer. Although twins are associated with the spirit world and, therefore, 'of the above', they are also humans and reside on the ground. The specific analogical relationship between 'birds of below' and twins is thus comprehensible as a metaphorical correspondence of an ambiguous combination of associations between sky and earth, above and below, spirit and human worlds.

Turner argues that the chain of reasoning pursued by Evans-Pritchard and Lévi-Strauss rests on an unanalysed Nuer category of spirit. Pointing out that twins and birds are claimed by the Nuer to have one substantial identity (i.e. they are parts of the same species of beings), he argues that the relationship between them is metonymical rather than metaphorical in nature (Turner 1991: 143).

Twins are ambiguous with respect to conventional Nuer notions of personhood. They are separate persons but share a common identity because of the circumstances of their gestation and birth. They resemble each other yet they are different. Twins are also ambiguous as both ordinary humans and distinctive extraordinary sacred beings. They combine difference and sameness in a manner contradicting usual social realities. In transcending ordinary reality they acquire the sacred quality of Spirit: a union of oppositions, a synthesis of contradictions. The sky together with birds, its inhabitants, constitutes for the Nuer a separate non-human transcendental plane. It is inaccessible and Other. It also cross-cuts the boundaries and differences characterizing normal human existence on the earth, being unconstrained and homogeneous in form. The high-flying species of birds, with light or homogeneous colours, participate in the attributes of the sky most purely. Ground-dwelling birds like the crow, having a dappled plumage, combine the colours and attributes of both the earth and sky. They, like twins, also have an ambiguous essence, being birds, and thus associated with the above, but living on the ground, and thus of the below. Consequently, they can act as effective metaphorical mediators between the two domains. So a parallelism exists between the relationship of twins to ordinary humans and crows to ordinary high-flying monocoloured birds. This forms the material basis of the metaphoric association. But, Turner points out, this is in fact a complex tropic construct combining metaphor, metonymy and synecdoche (twins and birds are part of a single continuum of spirit).

According to Turner, the problem with the way a theory of metaphor has been used in much anthropology is that it has concentrated on the analysis of individual tropes such as 'we are parrots' and 'twins are birds' in isolation, abstracting analysis from social, ritual and narrative contexts. There is a crucial need to embed a consideration of metaphor in relation to social action and other tropes – synecdoche and metonymy, a play of tropes in culture. Part of the process of making culture is the creation of a sense of totality or wholeness in which what appear to be fragmented differentiated domains of human experience and action become fused together. The play of tropes back and forth creates the fusion. An understanding of the statement 'we are parrots' involves much more than simply stating that it is a metaphor (Crocker 1977; 1985). In a cultural and ritual context it simultaneously involves metaphor, metonymy and synecdoche. The archetypal themes of myth and ritual involve the constitution of specific linkages between nature and culture or society. This involves (a) the reorganization of the object world and (b) the transformation of the subjective perspective in dialectical interplay.

Turner attempts to exemplify this position most fully in his fine analysis of the role of parrots in Brazilian Bororo and Kayapo cultures. Parrots are the preferred animal form entered and possessed by dead human souls for copulation and eating, which they otherwise cannot perform. Parrots are thus conceived as a medium for the materialization of human essence. 'We are parrots' is a statement referring to a metamorphic process following death in which the soul of a human enters into the form of the parrot. The meaning of this statement has to be considered in terms of a division between the profane and sacred domains of culture. The Bororo distinguish between male and female semantic domains in which men become explicitly identified with parrots. They are metaphors for men. According to Turner, the essence of the metaphor 'we are parrots' can be best understood as 'we make ourselves parrots' (Turner 1991: 136). Men don red parrot (macaw) feathers in communal ritual. These feathers are both scarce and prestigious. The men 'become parrots' by performing this action. They have to make themselves parrots in order to be Bororo in the context of ceremonial performance, the most important constitutive element of social reproduction in Bororo life. Since men alone perform these ceremonies they serve to constitute the essence of maleness in Bororo society. The ceremonies make and sustain men. But for men to be men (having a physical body and a soul) they need to become parrots. Turner points out that the collective or plural form of the Bororo word for plumes also means spirit or ancestor. This polysemy of words provides the basis for the subsequent metaphorical transformation. The Bororo conceive of the spirit of a thing as creating the external visible world of appearances. Red parrot plumes, especially the tail feathers, are the most spectacular ceremonial items in the Bororo world. They are difficult to obtain, a scarce resource. Hence they become emblems of the spiritual world. They are a material medium through which the Bororo men simultaneously acquire and manifest the spiritual essence of their humanity: 'by covering themselves with arara plumes, the Bororo create themselves *in the form* of creators of social form' (ibid.: 139). They create themselves as spirit beings. The men, then, empower themselves as spirit actors in the context of rituals designed to reproduce society. A linkage occurs here between the transcendental powers of souls (conceived as flying) with the lightness of feathers. Among the neighbouring central Brazilian Kayapo, ceremonial dance is likened to flight: 'the metonymic assumption by the ritual actors of feathered form as plumed "spirits" becomes the metaphoric basis of their power to reproduce the forms of society through collective ceremony' (ibid.). The act of Bororo men becoming parrots involves, therefore, metonymy, metaphor and synecdoche, in an ascending order of complexity.

At an initial metonymic level of meaning the detached part, parrot feathers, stands for the whole, the parrot. Parrot feathers signify the spiritual powers of parrots, involving flying (lightness) and the ability to grow feathers, constituting the outward form of 'parrotness', and simultaneously spirituality. There is also a metaphorical relation at work here: the lightness of the feathers metaphorically represents the capacity for transcendence associated with flight. The donning of feathers in ceremony by Bororo men allows the metonymic acquisition of the spiritual powers of parrots, simultaneously metonymically and metaphorically embodied by the manner in which feathers are conceived.

On a metaphoric level, the powers men obtain by donning the feathers are the powers of the ritual reproduction of the social order, metaphorically transformed in ceremonial performance. By becoming flying beings men separate themselves, in the ritual context, from normality. They acquire the spiritual powers necessary for social reproduction through harnessing the generative powers embodied in the feathers.

At a final synecdochic level of meaning the feathered dancers move within the patterns of village space recreating these patterns and with them key transformations in social relations that are the focus of the rites of passage being celebrated. The direction of these powers into the reproduction of social form as a whole, Turner argues, suggests that social form is itself conceived as a parrot form. The form created by the parrot dancers assumes, as a whole, the character of the parts, i.e. the parrot dancers who create it.

Turner's work, and in a more opaque fashion that of Fernandez (1986) and Wagner (1975; 1986), sensitizes us to the role of tropic interplay in the social production and reproduction of culture, so that we cannot afford the reductionism involved in an assimilation of all tropes to metaphor. It also underlines the importance of analysing tropic meaning in a performative cultural context. But there are other theoretical issues at stake. One of the most significant of these is whether a theory of tropes at work in culture offers us anything very different from a structuralist understanding of what culture means.

Metaphor in Culture: A Digital Logic or Analogic Logic?

Barth (1975), in a detailed analysis, usefully stresses that the symbolic value of elements in Baktaman (Highland Papua New Guinea) ritual depends very much on the particular manner in which metaphors become employed and the relative degree of structuring and coherence between them within different symbolic domains. The Baktaman, Barth argues, in an archetypal fashion, use the domain of the familiar (nature) in order to grasp the significance of the unfamiliar (culture) by means of metaphoric analogical reasoning. As part of this process something less clearly conceptualized becomes illuminated by the analogies made. The analogies so constructed may then also act back recursively on the more familiar element of the metaphorical relationship and also serve to clarify it by subsuming it under a more generalized cultural model implicit in the formation of the analogy itself. There is a crucial need for understanding metaphor in relation to objects and activities.

Barth makes the very important observation that the *material* metaphors at work in culture are not entirely arbitrary. In the process of making metaphorical connections there is always likely to be an inherent connection between form and meaning. The two questions: what does a symbol mean? and why is this particular symbol selected? are inevitably interconnected. So, the meaning of dew rubbing in Baktaman ritual is clarified by an understanding of how dew occurs. The meanings of pigs as symbols are linked to what pigs do, and how they behave.

Barth contrasts the analogic reasoning involved in producing metaphoric connections with a Lévi-Straussian structuralist digital logic of binary oppositions. The problem with a digital logic is its presumption of arbitrariness. The meaning of symbols can only derive from the place each occupies in the code as a whole. So in the Saussurian perspective of Jakobson and Lévi-Strauss, cat is cat because it is not dog, etc. In an analogic code if I symbolize 'humanity' with a stick-line representation, this is clearly not an arbitrary process. The meaning depends on an understanding of the transformation effected from an object to a symbol by means of a particular mode of representation, and the manner in which I actually experience reality. Consequently, it is possible to argue that the concrete symbol's objective qualities and apparent suitability to its actual meaning are vital. As Barth puts it, the 'meaning arises independently of any total code and not from the symbol's systematic place among a limited set of alternatives within such a code' (Barth 1975: 208). A structuralist binary logic involves the *weakening of contrast as source of meaning*. Complex messages, as in ritual, cast in an analogic code, are specifically suited for multiple interpretations. A ritual message can be interpreted simultaneously by different participants using different keys for decoding. The multiplicity of actors and sacred and other objects in ritual entails a relatively loose structure of messages, rather than the structuralist's presumption of a tight system in which one cultural domain is presupposed to mirror another. Precisely because there is, and can be, no tight structure at work linking together all the different domains of society or culture, the message can still communicate to the unperceptive, e.g. the initiate.

Rites not only say something, they *do* something. They are embedded in a means-to-ends context. Imagery fetched in ritual from the various domains of the mundane world through the contrivances of ritual practice creates and elaborates associations providing material for metaphor. For example, painting ancestral sacra and novices with red adds new metaphorical content to the meaning of the colour.

An analogic code involves a linking of metaphors employed in *different contexts*, particularly in myth and ritual. There may be various degrees of coherence between the elements. There is no presumption of a totalizing systemness linking everything in a culture into a tight structuralist fit, where one domain mirrors another and analysis is concerned with making all the pieces fit. We can expect various degrees of fit and coherence. A key point here is the improvised nature of culture, that it is a contrivance. This position avoids a 'simplistic assumption of total logico-deductive integration in culture' (ibid.: 213). Various natural species may have characteristic features or qualities, making them apt for abstract thought. This is a rather different position to regarding relations between the species in a taxonomic structure as being in some way isomorphic with the relations between other social and cultural categories, providing a vehicle for their expression, as in the work of Lévi-Strauss (1966) and Douglas (1970). Metaphor is part and parcel of cultural creativity for which structuralism has no role. It allows an understanding of ritual in its performative and social context, and in terms of the individuals who take part in them and their improvised and contingent transmission of knowledges.

As an example we can consider the symbolic role of pandanus (a variety of palm) in Baktaman life (Barth 1975: 188–9). The most valued species of pandanus is the one that develops a scarlet red fruit up to 50 cm long. It has a tangy flavour. Plants are carefully guarded, personally owned, and the fruits harvested, cooked and eaten. The cooking process is hedged around with taboos. The fruit must be hollowed out with the femurs of cassowary (the largest ground-dwelling bipedal bird in the Baktaman universe) and cooked with cooking stones used for cassowary, and not those used for cooking pig or marsupials. The cooked fruits are only shared between men of close initiation rank, and not with women. They thus become associated with men. The association made between the pandanus and the cassowary is based on an empirical association, as well as constituted in ritual: cassowaries, like people, also seek out and feed on pandanus fruits. The pandanus fruits are phallus shaped and this similarity in shape to the penis is a premise for the metaphorical symbolism linking them to men. Penis gourds, worn by men, are attached by plaited bands made of pandanus leaf fibres. These fibres are taken from the leaves that cover the developing pandanus fruit. The metaphoric identification between the penis and the red pandanus fruit thus becomes quite explicit. The same pandanus fibres are only used by the Baktaman in one other context: to attach arrowheads to their shafts. The identification of the arrow and the male organ is expressed through the metaphorical medium of red pandanus. Red is the pre-eminent sacred colour signifying, in an expressive and generalized way (see the discussion of summarizing symbols below), descent and the ancestors. Red pandanus fruit is also used to colour 4th-grade initiation novices, and in the ceremonies explicit associations are made between pandanus and fertility in general. An artifical wig of pandanus leaves is worn by the initiates. Here another set of associations is created between sexuality and hair as symbol of fertility and growth, puberty and male fertility. The Baktaman make further associations between pandanus and fire making. Pandanus leaves are also used to wrap sacred relics linked with the ancestors.

Here there is no overall coherent code linking pandanus into a totalizing system of symbolic linkages between different domains of thought and action. Rather, pandanus enters individually into larger ritual contexts and messages. The implication of this example is that the kinds of integration that result from the subsumption of several meanings under the same material symbol are almost inevitably loose and partial, but they do become cognitively and emotionally linked by the associations created in performative contexts which, in themselves, may pose an intellectual problem to the actors involved. Core symbols, such as the pandanus, have different *independent* sources of meaning in the separate metaphorical linkages which cannot be conceived as being connected in a tightly structured way, as symbols operating within a digital code would be. An analogic code needs to be understood in the context of its praxis. Ritual builds on metaphors and may transform their original understanding. In the

Baktaman world only material objects persist while linguistic communication is, by definition, ephemeral. Thus, only those messages which are constantly recreated and used will be transmitted and persist as part of the tradition, those metaphors that catch on and are re-used as part of the corpus of material codes. This is the structure that persists – 'not exemplified paradigms with an almost infinite productivity of the "sayable"' (Barth 1975: 229). The material symbols serve as anchors not only of abstract thought but of ephemeral communications in general.

Key Metaphors

To argue that there is no necessity to presume a totalizing cultural coherence produced through metaphorical linkages does not imply the converse, a completely fragmented view of culture. What it suggests is that different symbolic, cultural and social domains will be linked together in different ways. Sometimes they may mirror each other, in other cases they will be contradictory. Some metaphors will be more inclusive, others more exclusive. Ortner (1973), Victor Turner (1974), Barth (1975) and others have all referred in various ways to the presence of core symbols with a condensation or multiplicity of meanings. One and the same symbol can serve as vehicle for several distinct metaphors. There may or may not be a contradiction between alternative metaphoric imageries, or ways of seeing. For the Baktaman, water has certain 'objective' properties from which metaphorical understandings and elaborations 'flow': cold in a mountain environment, it puts out fire, washes away substances and appears out of thin air as dew. Any one of these referents or aspects of water can be used to create metaphorical meaning without compromising its other perceived qualities. Water as a concrete symbol can have its metaphoric meanings elaborated and used differently among different Mountain Ok groups in Highland Papua New Guinea or it can take on different meanings in different ritual contexts (Barth 1987). Victor Turner (1967; 1969; 1974) similarly stresses the multivocality of symbols in ritual contexts. Despite this quality, he argues that their referents tend to polarize between physiological phenomena (e.g. blood, milk, semen, birth, death, coitus) and normative values (e.g. reciprocity, generosity, obedience, respect), which are themselves linked to principles of social organization (matriliny, patriliny, age-grade organization, kinship, etc.). The drama of ritual action metaphorically links the poles of physiology (the 'orectic' pole) and cultural norms and values. In the process the normative referents become charged with emotional significance and the biological elements ennobled.

Ortner (1972) distinguishes between what she terms summarizing and elaborating symbols. The former have focusing power, drawing together referents, intensifying experience. They are synthetic and collapse experience into a perceived sense of wholeness. Most traditional sacred symbols such as the cross in Christianity or emblems such as a national flag are examples. The metaphorical meanings invoked may principally be of an emotive kind (e.g. the flag as invoking senses of patriotism and national unity). Elaborating symbols permit the ordering or sorting out of experience and action, linking together disparate domains through an analogic logic. They are vehicles for sorting out complex feelings and ideas so that they may be communicated to others: 'they may have primarily conceptual elaborating power; that is they are valued as a source of categories for conceptualizing the order of the world. Or they may have primarily action elaborating power; that is, they are valued as implying mechanisms for successful social action' (Ortner 1972: 1,340). Ortner terms symbols with a capacity for conceptual elaboration as root metaphors. Their mode of operation is likening many aspects of experience through the symbol itself providing common sets of categories for conceptualizing different experiences. These root metaphors may be contrasted with symbols that facilitate particular patterns of social action (in Ortner's terminology 'key scenarios'). This distinction between thought-directed core symbols and action-directed ones, and that between elaborating and summarizing symbols is, of course, relatively arbitrary. Any particular symbol may have different degrees of synthetic or elaborating power and the capacity to link together different areas of thought and life, or to direct action.

To return to the Baktaman case, dew, pig fat, fur and hair are all metaphorically linked as symbols of growth and increase. Growth and increase are processes whose significance the Baktaman try to grasp through these material metaphors and through repeated ritual acts such as dew rubbing and fur burning. Dew (a miracle: water that grows spontaneously on the leaves of the forest) and pig fat (a symbol of wealth and wellbeing) are rubbed on the body of the initiate. Fur that grows on marsupials is identified with taro growth. Hair is identified with vegetation in general, and taro growth in particular. Through a linkage of these material metaphors, growth in pigs, taro and boys is conceived as one and the same process. The deeply physical aspects of concrete symbols are isolated by the Baktaman and given occult significance. There is a high degree of coherence. In initiations a substance or object with a widely recognized significance provides a metaphor for the transmission or conferment of this quality (in this case, growth, increase and fertility) and acts so as to embody an understanding of the real and hidden nature of things to the initiate.

By contrast, the conceptualization of pigs in Baktaman thought is highly ambiguous. Wild pigs are an obsession for the Baktaman. They ravage gardens and are dangerous. Baktaman men are constantly at war with them. Yet the boars impregnate domestic sows and are symbols of sexual potency and masculinity. Their meat is considered delicious and is highly valued. Pigs, because of the damage they create, are opposed conceptually to garden fertility. There are numerous taboos on entering gardens after eating pig meat. In Baktaman thought they become highly ambivalent and potent symbols with multivalent meanings and ambiguous metaphorical associations. They are models of forces both promoting and threatening fertility. Here the meanings of pigs, and the metaphors employed, clearly do not have the coherence shared by conceptualizations of dew, fat, fur and hair.

Conclusion: Metaphor and Ontology

> The domain of metaphor is constituted by these problems: the unstable distinction between the literal and the figurative, the crucial yet unmasterable distinction between essential and accidental resemblances, the tension between thought and linguistic processes within the linguistic system and language use. The pressure of these various concepts and forces creates a space . . . that we call metaphor. (Culler 1981: 207)

From the point of view of an empiricism and an objectivism that would deny the power of metaphor in the construction and interpretation of the social we apparently require the maintenance of a linguistic hygiene so that we can express ourselves clearly and unambiguously. But there is the essential irony that any attempt to *remove* that which Culler refers to as the 'space of metaphor' from our discourses can only be accomplished by metaphorical means. The only sensible alternative to a futile attempt to banish metaphor is to appreciate its significance in our writings, and as a mode of interpreting and understanding the world.

One of the very real problems for the interpretative social sciences has been the persistent tendency, in the majority of writings on the subject, to produce an analysis of metaphor on the basis of the often highly unusual and novel form it may take in literary and poetic works. These may well be the most interesting of metaphors, in so far as they stretch the mind to understand them. A burgeoning cottage industry of literary critics and philosophers has much work to do in order to understand these peculiar metaphors. The resulting convoluted analyses may, however, do little to aid an understanding of the manner in which metaphor operates as part and parcel of the structuring of everyday life, the social world as mediated through language and material culture and cultural norms and values.

For Lakoff and others we have seen that metaphors become systematically linked in the functioning of the human mind, which – avoiding the mind-body dualism set up in empiricist positions – is itself embodied, i.e. directly implicated in bodily experience and action. Yet metaphors are culturally specific. There are relatively few universal quintessential human experiences of the world that can embody the mind. The alternative position put forward by Quinn (1991), amongst others, is that metaphors do not so much constitute understanding but instead become selected to fit into pre-existing and culturally shared models:

> metaphorical systems or productive metaphors typically do not structure understandings de novo. Rather, particular metaphors are selected by speakers, just because they provide satisfying mappings onto already existing cultural understandings – that is, because elements and relations between elements in the source domain make a good match with elements and relations among them in a cultural model. (Ibid.: 65)

It would seem most sensible to develop an analysis of metaphor in language and culture in an ontology of bodily experience and perception that is understood as being dialectically linked to cultural understandings. Merleau-Ponty's phenomenology emphasizes the mediational character of the somatic dimension of human cognition and existence, explicitly developing a parallel between physical embodiment and the 'incarnational' quality of linguistic meaning in and through the metaphoric use of speech (Merleau Ponty 1962; see discussion in Gill 1991). The body is the ground or anchor by means of which we locate ourselves in the world, perceive and apprehend it. The centre of our own existence is always our body, as an axis from which spatiality and temporality are orientated: the human body *inhabits* space and time (Merleau-Ponty 1962: 138). Rather than mirroring the world, speech can be conceived as an extension of the human body in the world, a kind of artefact, by means of which we extend ourselves in the world, gain knowledge of it and alter it. Metaphor is an essential part of this process. Cognition is essentially a process of seeing something *as* something and this is the core of metaphorical understandings. Seeing something as something is grounded in culturally mediated bodily experiences. As Johnson puts it, 'concrete bodily experience not only constrains the "input" to the metaphorical projections but also the nature of the projections themselves, that is, the kinds of mappings that can occur across domains' (Johnson 1987: xv). Structures of bodily experience work their way up into abstract meanings, embodied imagination. The body, culture and metaphor act so as to constitute each other. Contextualizing both metaphor and a metaphorical human mind in this manner, it may be possible to avoid the inherent danger of what Culler refers to as the 'tropological inflation of tropes' (Culler 1981: 202), an unhelpful form of idealism in which the entire world becomes a tropic form in which both culture and language become reduced to nothing more than an endless play of tropes.

There is no necessity to grant analytical primacy to either an originary metaphorically structured human mind, or to sets of non-metaphorical cultural understandings adapting metaphors within a pre-existing framework functioning somehow prior to metaphor. Lakoff, Johnson, Gibbs and others have argued convincingly for a natural reflex to think metaphorically. Accepting this as an attribute of the human mind, the most interesting questions are those to do with the way in which a mind, with this propensity, becomes articulated, through cultural experience, to produce particular kinds of metaphorical links within historically determinant and determined social circumstances.

An analysis of metaphor grounded in the solid domain of material culture, the subject of the next chapter, may go some way to redress the ever-present tendency towards an idealism present in a great deal of contemporary metaphor theory. By taking metaphor out of language and into artefacts, we may hope to appreciate its significance in a rather different manner.

2

Solid Metaphor: The Analysis of Material Forms

This chapter is intended as a review of some of the principal anthropological studies of metaphor in relation to material culture. The process of writing it recalls Borges's celebrated *Book of Sand* (Borges 1977): as one opens the book the pages keep on growing, and a page once seen is lost. Since metaphors are as pervasive in culture as in language, there is no immediate hierarchy of subjects or an order to follow, apart from the obvious starting points of the human body, the house and the landscape, all comprising fundamental aspects of dwelling in the world. Landscape metaphors are discussed separately in Part III of the book. The topic of metaphor constantly threatens to fragment into all the other topics that have been written about by anthropologists and get lost in the process (Fernandez 1986: 6). Like all discourses, anthropological discourses are metaphorical. Key concepts, such as culture, are both polysemous and metaphorical, simultaneously definable and defying definition (Wagner 1975: 21ff.). Metaphors thus provide both the medium and outcome of anthropological analysis. Texts structure them and are, in turn, structured by them. The question then inevitably arises: whose metaphors are they, the analyst's or the informant's? In the following account I simply want to accept Wagner's (ibid.: 10) putative solution to this problem, that the anthropological monograph is the outcome of a dialogue between anthropologist and informant in which the pre-existing understandings of both are brought together and mediated as an interactive construction, creating something new through dynamic interchange. A case, then, of mixed metaphorical sources stimulating the imaginative invention of culture in which the interpretative endeavours of any anthropology and archaeology reside.

Since this chapter attempts to cover a wide range of studies it is inevitably selective and cannot hope to convey the rich descriptive detail and subtlety of the analyses which are discussed. It runs the risk of stripping details out of ethnographic context, and reducing them to a series of vignettes. The text, perhaps, then, evokes rather than represents.

The Body

The human body has long been recognized as a potent source of metaphors for understanding and ordering the social world, an argument originally elaborated by Mauss (1973) and extended by Douglas (1966; 1970). The human body is the most accessible and ready-to-hand image of the social system, providing a potent source of metaphors for society as a whole. Cultural conceptualizations of the body are intimately linked with bodily experience and perception and thus appear natural and basic. It is this perception of the 'naturalness' of the body which allows it to be thoroughly engrained, or embodied, in the collective consciousness. The general theme in Douglas's work is the manner in which the body system (its anatomical structure, orifices or exits and entrances, the substances it secretes, its postures, etc.) provides sets of analogies for understanding the social system and the manner in which there is a continual exchange of meanings between the experience of the physical body and the social body (society): 'the social body constrains the way the physical body is perceived. The physical experience of the body, always modified by the social categories through which it is known, sustains a particular view of society' (Douglas 1970: 93). The human body is metaphorically intertwined with the social body and itself patterned and constructed through this integration. Everywhere the natural symbols and images of the body encode social and cultural forms. The body is both the Same and Other, an object and a subject of practices and knowledges, a tool and a raw material to be worked upon. If the body is society, then its parts may represent different parts of that society, so that anatomical parts of the body, as among the Dogon of West Africa, may express marriage and kin or political relations (Griaule

1965). The widespread dualism of left- (evil) and right- (good) hand symbolism may be elaborated as part of a ramifying system of categorizations (Hertz 1960; Needham 1973) in which linkages may be set up between the left and the profane, darkness, death, weakness, and the cardinal directions west and north, and between right and the sacred, birth, light, east or south, fertility and strength. Anthropomorphism is one of the primary metaphorical processes in small-scale societies in which terms for body parts act as an enormous reference system and are extended to describe houses, artefacts, animals and plants, as the many examples given in this chapter indicate. Basic spatial and temporal categorizations such as inside/outside; near/far; centre/periphery, etc. are based on bodily organization. In most cases the skin and the orifices serve as media for the exchange and separation between the individual and society, the inner and the outer self. The orifices, and the substances imbibed and ejected through them, differentiate between upper and lower, front and behind, before and after, permit or prevent passage or contact. Bodily emissions such as hair, nails, urine, faeces, saliva and sweat all come from the body but may be separated from it. They can thus serve as metonymical substitutes for the body in rituals as a means of bodily protection and provide the raw materials for sorcery. The kaleidoscopic connections between body imagery and sociocultural orientations can scarcely be overemphasized. Ideas about the body metaphorically inform ideas about conception, gender, growth and nurturance, colour, food and food taboos, fertility, maternal and paternal roles, sexuality, death, production, exchange, consumption and cosmological schemes (for example, see Knauft 1989 for a recent review of the myriad forms body metaphors take in Melanesia). The values internalized by the body through dress and decoration, movement and gesture and interiorized conceptualization are both profound and difficult to express in words, for we are dealing with a multidimensional and multisensory field. Through the *hexis* of the body – the way persons carry themselves through stance, gesture, ways of walking, ways of standing, ways of looking – the principles of the differentiation of the social world may be both read and enacted (Bourdieu 1977: 90). Becker's (1995) analysis of the Fijian body and self in contrast with the body-self in Western society shows how in the case of the former the body is situated within a socio-cosmic matrix and embodies the collective. Body experience transcends the individual self and is diffused to other bodies or the collective. By contrast the body in Western society has become a medium for the staging of an individualized self through its discipline, cultivation and management. The Fijian imperative is towards the cultivation of social relationships, not directed towards an intensified disciplining of an individualized personalized body (Foucault 1977; Bourdieu 1984: 192). Regulation and cultivation of the body, its aesthetics, etc., are part of a collective domain rather than a progressive embodiment of the self (Becker 1995: 129).

The body as metaphor may reflect society and social values or vice versa, but in ritual practices operating on the body a space may be opened out for its reconstitution and re-identification, a body that is no longer a kind of reflective (or inverted) mirror of something beyond itself but acts as a source of cultural creativity and innovation. Devisch (1993), in a subtle and rich account, has analysed the manner in which body metaphors in the healing rituals of the Yaka of southwestern Zaire are highly sensuous and transactional in nature, encouraging the senses, emotions and dispositions of the participants in a culture in which (unlike that in the West) conceptual borderlines between the physical, social, ethical and spiritual are only very weakly demarcated. Rituals release forces and disclose meaning but go beyond mere representation:

> A ritual metaphor is a performance and transaction in a field of meanings and forces . . . a productive and metamorphic process grounded in corporeal capabilities and skills that search out and develop beyond linguistic expression. . . . Ritual metaphor is basically a bodily enacted method for the innovative production of synesthetic meaning and empowerment. It makes a ritual into a morphogenetic, hence cosmogenetic art. In its creative move, ritual metaphor does not know beforehand how its ingredients should cohere or commit to one another. It does not point to facts in terms of other facts but rather establishes 'facts of experience' and webs of relationships mostly through confluence. (Ibid.: 43–4)

The various sensory fields involved in healing practice – the visual, olfactory, tactile and the verbal – are drawn together in new constellations in a multilayered and multisensory contact and engagement with the world. The metaphors, drawn from the ordinary realms of day-to-day experience, become reworked in the ritual process to have a cathartic effect. Ritual, for Devisch, is a form of praxis that produces meaning and power in and through bodily action enhanced and reinforced by images, metaphors and forces. Corporeal praxis shapes, 'expresses, and reembodies a particular bodily and social order, and a particular view of, and relation with, the lifeworld or cosmos' (ibid.: 46). The healing of a patient thus develops from specific kinds of metaphorical integration of the bodily experience of the patient, his or her family life and life-world. The performative dramatization and mobilization of the metaphors operates largely beyond a conscious level of representation and spoken discourse. Ritual becomes more of a weave of elements or a musical oeuvre than a narrative form: 'weaving is rhythm, and rhythm underscores the weave of life. The participants' experiences are rhythmically interwoven with the ideals and norms of the community. Health is interwovenness' (ibid.: 160). The basic forms the healing rituals take is as rites of passage in which the patient is led symbolically to die from illness and be reborn into a new condition. Ritual form is given to the death and expulsion of illness through cult-specific metaphors and metonymies drawn from the wider cosmological and social fields. Yaka cults and ritual activities depict seasonal, lunar and life-cyclical changes in the cosmos and in the plant and animal worlds as fundamental processes of life transmission, which become played upon in healing rites. Initiation into the arts of healing are ways of weaving the patient into the vital forces of the life-world.

Devisch (1993) argues that the dramas of ritual healing are acted out within the fabric or drama of culture (ibid.: 48). Culture, however, is not text or narrative but simultaneously a transmitted and inventive production. In this drama whole layers of experience are simply felt and acted out rather than verbally discussed, yet participants actively engage in the symbolic practices, drawing on layers of meaning and mobilizing them. The body, conceived as a surface of separations and contacts, allows for 'the mediation between fusion and separation, corporeality and language, subjective images and shared symbols' (ibid.: 49). The human body establishes homologies and communication between its own physicality, the social group and life-world or culture of the individual. The healing cults and therapies, largely mobilizations of practical and preverbal knowledges, position the body as a fabric and weaving loom, an agent of intertwining between the body shell, orifices, sensory and communicative functions providing exchanges between initiate and healer, husband and wife, parent and child, patient and group, patient and cosmos. The ritual house, in which the healing cults take place, is 'a hen laying an egg, a human and cosmic womb in gestation' (ibid.: 49). The Yaka healing act is not a scripted plot or play, but a generative act. Healing rituals offer a space for constituting and transforming rather than acting as manifestations of wider cognitive structures.

Metaphor in Architecture

The house, a home for and extension of the human body and the social body, has long been noted as a principal model generating spatio-temporal metaphors for, of, and in the world. Bourdieu has cogently emphasized the role of the house in providing a coherent language with which to organize reality:

> In a social formation in which the absence of the symbolic-product-conserving techniques associated with literacy retards the objectification of symbolic and particularly cultural capital, inhabited space – and above all the house – is the principal locus for the objectification of generative schemes; and through the intermediary of the divisions and hierarchies it sets up between things, persons and practices, this tangible classifying system continuously inculcates and reinforces the taxonomic principles underlying all the arbitrary provisions of this culture.
> (Bourdieu 1977: 89)

Architecture and its metaphoric relationship to principles of social order, as a structuring structure, has been extensively analysed in the literature (recent collections of papers include Carsten and Hugh-Jones 1995; Kent 1990; Waterson 1991; Parker-Pearson and Richards 1994). In the following discussion I outline the role of the house as source and focus for metaphors through considering the superbly documented case of Batammaliba architecture as analysed by Preston Blier (1987).

The Batammaliba live in the border region between the West African states of Togo and the Benin Republic in an area dominated by the Atacora mountains. In this area with a great deal of rainfall land is divided between wooded expanses sheltering game and cleared areas with fields and settlements. The Batammaliba are patrilocal and patrilineal but the matriline that is still maintained is an important focus of religious ceremony. The age grade organization delimits types of works, marriage and ritual prerogatives, dress, cicatrization forms and participation, for men, in hunting and warfare. In Batammaliba religion the omnipotent solar god Kuiye, both male and female, corporeal and spiritual, is at the top of the pantheon. Lesser deities are associated with particular activities and powers, e.g. Butan with the earth and the underworld. Priesthoods identified with the gods are widely distributed in the village community, each house serving as a religious sanctuary for one or more deities and for ancestral and wild-game powers.

The Batammaliba live in impressive and architecturally complex multi-storey earth houses built by individual male architects. Each structure has a compact symmetrical design format and individual houses are basically variations on a generic theme. House size varies between 6 and 18 metres in diameter and 4 to 5 metres in height. Each house is built from mud

42 METAPHOR AND THE CONSTITUTION OF THE WORLD

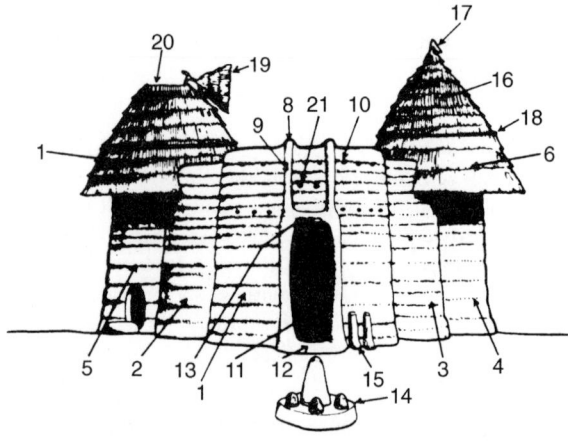

1 House entrance, *kunakwanku*
2 Female joining wall, *kulotiniku*
3 Male joining wall, *kulotilaku*
4 Male granary support, *libotolaku*
5 Female granary support, *libotoniku*
6 Male granary, *libolaku*
7 Female granary, *liboniku*
8 Entrance horns, *linakwanyeni*
9 Feet of the horns, *silaca*
10 Beam ends, *kuminlo*
11 Doorway, *liboli*
12 Door sill, *liwatali*
13 Lintel, *takanabeta*
14 Mound, *lisenpo*
15 Resting place shrine, *liboloni*
16 Granary cover, *tibutimuti*
17 Granary handle, *taboluta*
18 Granary vine, *babokwatibi*
19 Granary cap, *kubokakli*
20 Granary mouth, *libonli*
21 Wall eyes, *falotinonfa*

Figure 2.1 Diagram of Batammaliba house façade parts.
Source: Preston-Blier (1987)

courses, a new layer being added each day. They consist of a rhythmic series of curvilinear supports and joining walls covered with plaster and decorated with incised lines when wet by women of the family. When the plaster is dry the house is stained with a maroon or brown fruit and water solution which helps protect the walls. The centre of each house has a single west-facing doorway. Above the portal are usually two upward-thrusting entry horns. The corners of the façade are marked by two elevated straw-covered granaries, one male, to the north, one female, to the south (Figure 2.1). The ground plan is made up of a grouping of round or oval rooms and support structures enclosed on the outside by a series of semi-circular joining walls. The most significant of these are the female joining wall to the north of the entrance and the male joining wall to the south. Centrally placed on the western side is the entrance chamber and behind this the 'cattle room' serving as chapel, barn and sleeping place for elder men, with the main house altar to the back. Above the ground-floor rooms are the house terrace areas with a wider variety of different uses.

There is a complex relationship between cosmogony and building design. In effect, the house translates cosmogonic narratives into a material, spatial form. The architectural representations of cosmological themes work both as mnemonic aids and as permanent and concrete expressions of the underlying principles of Batammaliba cosmological order. The houses express cosmological ideas in visual form. Key Batammaliba cosmological acts – building the earth, fabricating humans, setting the sun in motion, shaping the sky, constructing the underworld, and the creation of various deities which control these realms – are given metaphorical expression through architectural form. The house is a condensed visual metaphor encapsulating essential characteristics of the cosmos. Preston Blier (ibid.: 36–7) identifies a diversity of themes at work:

(1)   Directional affiliation is materially translated by metaphorically identifying a particular form on the basis of its orientation and direction. The direction of openings and the positioning of parts in relation to each other provide a frame of reference to the world and the cosmos. The orientation of the two horns above the entrance along the sun's east–west axis reinforces, through the metaphor of directional affiliation, the importance of Kuiye as the Earth's creator and source of life. The crosspieces of the house terrace also resemble those of the Earth in that they are placed with their large butt ends orientated east and their smaller ends to the west, paralleling the direction of the sun's daily passage, reinforcing the idea of Kuiye as creator both of the Earth and humans. The repetitive movements of the sun are reflected in the repetition of the architectural elements.

(2)   Silhouetting, in which an object is identified by its distinctive profile, metaphorically translates important themes. Circular silhouettes, found in the shapes of houses, tombs and village designs, are of vital significance, because they represent a miniaturization of the large Earth structure. The ceremonial recreation of Kuiye's original building of the Earth is reflected not only in the circular form of the houses but in the perceived circular (actually oval) form of the village. Every four years the village borders are redrawn by pulling a goat around the perimeter.

(3)   Nesting, or the transposition of a series of elements or ideas into parts. In many Batammaliba architectural and ritual forms the main ideas of a cosmological narrative are presented by means of the positioning of one element inside or superimposed on another. This metonymic nesting may materially represent the sequential ordering of ideas in a narrative.

The upper areas of the house are associated with the heavens, the terrace region below recalls the structure of the Earth, and the ground floor, with its dark and damp interior and inclusion of aquatic animal and ancestor shrines, parallels the underworld. The house, like the cosmos, is a multi-storeyed structure organized into a series of carefully delimited parts.

(4) Skeuomorphs, in which a material other than the original is used to convey an idea, are translated by substituting one material for another to represent changes in place, time or status. The material Kuiye used to build the Earth was taken from a sacred stone mound in front of this deity's house in the sky. This is represented visually by the construction of earthen *lisenpo* mounds in front of the house portals, earthen skeuomorphs of Kuiye's stone mound (see Figure 2.1).

(5) Key ritual actions, architectural elements or the entire house may be used synecdochially to suggest essential features of the cosmos. In the context of human creation Kuiye is said to have formed humans from earth balls. Balls of earth form the basis of house and shrine construction. Special sanctified earthen balls are also incorporated into each house foundation to protect it and provide it with a sacred identity.

(6) Through reversal metaphors ideas of transition are given concrete visual expression. For example, the house-half to the north of an imaginary line that runs east–west between the horns is associated with women, that to the north with men, and gender activities are frequently linked to one or other of the house sides:

> The basis for this north–south division in the house derives partly from gender distinctions associated with the creative solar god, Kuiye [who] . . . is androgynous. This god's vagina is positioned under the right arm, and the penis is under the left. Kuiye's right hand in this way is identified with women; Kuiye's left hand is associated with men. To translate this aspect of Kuiye's identity into house-gender symbolism, one must use the perspective of the house's western orientation as the house faces Kuiye and Kuiye's sky village. From this position, the right (female) house side is found to the north, and the left (male) house side is located to the south: when one is on the outside looking toward the façade, the left–right gender identity is reversed. There is in this way a symbolic inversion in gender–spatial symbolism that occurs when one makes the transition from exterior to interior. (Preston Blier 1987: 145–6)

Batammaliba houses are anthropomorphic forms and are metaphorically identified with humans through parallels in language and structural components. Like a person, each house is made from flesh (earth), bones (pebbles) and blood (water). Its outer skin, the plaster, is incised with the cicatrization patterns of women. The various parts of the house are given human-related names and associations (head, eyes, lips, tongue, penis, etc.). Forms of house ornamentation portray skins, hats and cloths. Symbolic behaviour directed towards the house points towards and reinforces its symbolic qualities (greeting the house, feeding the house, drinking with the house, etc.). Houses, like humans, also have their own discrete psychological identity. Medical treatments and passage rites focus simultaneously on the individual and the house as a means of restoring order and balance. In Batammaliba ontology both houses and humans share the same essence. Metonymically they are parts of each other.

Human metaphors in architecture are grounded in the use of the body as a model for comparable structural, decorative and symbolic forms. The male architect who designs and constructs the house and the female plasterer and wall decorator have similar roles to the deceased male and female elders who are said to model and plaster every Batammaliba baby from an earth ball in its mother's womb. The basic element of construction is thus the same for babies and houses. Each step of the construction process also parallels human development. Each grows according to a standard pattern. From its inception and throughout the process of its construction and use the house is fed in human fashion. Every house receives its first nourishment at the foundation laying, when it is given beer to drink and special *titati* materials (balls of special clays wrapped with the leaves of plants) are incorporated into the foundations. The clay comes from a spring said to have been brought from the primordial village. In this way part of the first village is incorporated into each structure. The leaves and plants are identified with the gods of geomancy, death and fertility, and the plants used have an important place in the curing and initiation ceremonies associated with these deities. A completed house is like a new-born baby. Both house and baby must be bathed in rich fruit and oil solutions so that their skins will be toughened. Properly cared for a house will live, like humans, for at least 56 years or ten initiation cycles. When old, both house and human become dry and brittle. Each dies to give birth to a successor built partly out of the fabric of the old. The anthropomorphic house when viewed from the exterior is conceptualized in a vertical or standing position. When defined by its ground plan it is regarded as in a horizontal posture. Tiny façade windows of the house are its eyes. The front doorway is compared with the human mouth – the means of entry to the interior. Stones for grinding corn just inside the entrance are the incisors of the house, used to chew the grain into flour. The granaries are the stomach of the house because they store the food. Drain-

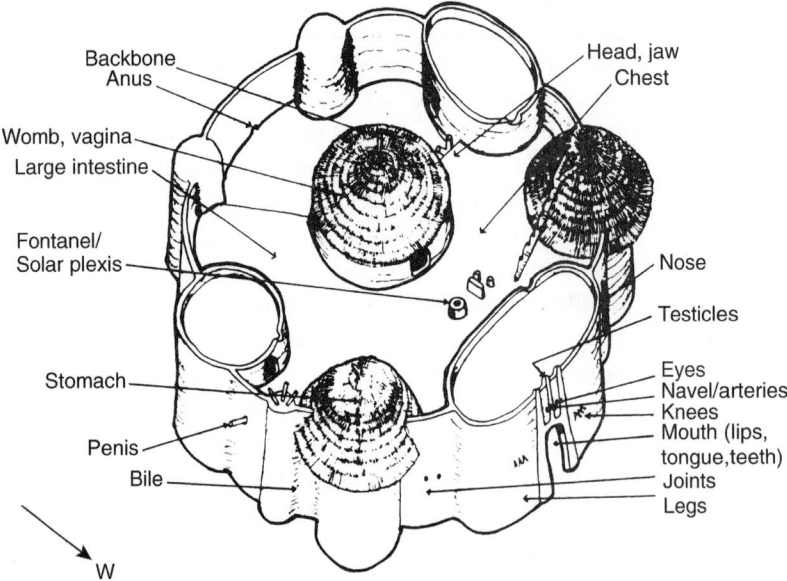

Figure 2.2 Diagram of the Batammaliba house with its human parts.
Source: Preston Blier (1987)

pipes on the side of the house are its penis through which it urinates and so on (Figure 2.2).

At another level of meaning the house is the family: the same word is used for each. Houses are categorized in relation to each of the major kinship distinctions. The largest category of village houses consists of residences associated with the nuclear family. Other houses are identified both as nuclear family houses and as representing the extended family, lineage clan and/or village 'family' as a whole. These great houses are known as foundation houses, differentiated from the others by the incorporation of a third horn over the doorway dedicated to the extended family, lineage or clan. There are generally two clan houses in each village and one village great house constructed near the symbolic head of the community. The house is again both of ontological import – it has its very basis in the family – and is a metaphoric model for diverse family identities. Without the house (or family) an individual is without support. The house also represents the family in time through the incorporation of resting places for deceased elders and in its association with the tomb. Spatial divisions into left and right, front and back, upper and lower parts underscore the complementarity and opposition between men and women who dwell in the house. The female part of the house is to the right, the male to the left, as mentioned above. Upstairs space is generally associated with women, that downstairs with men and this determines the locations of internal male and female house shrines. This inverts the spatial association of men with the male sky deity and women with the female earth deity in an analogous manner to the left/right and inside/outside inversions previously discussed. The front and outside of the house are generally associated with men, the back and interior with women. This spatial division parallels cosmological ideas. Things that are regarded as being in front are linked with the future, those that are behind are associated with the past. Although in the symbolism of the architecture men are identified with the world outside the house and women with the interior, in this patrilocal society the outsiders, who are brought to the house, are women. In Batammaliba cosmological thought the actions and images associated with the ancestors are inversions of the everyday world. They extend their left rather than their right hand, walk backwards rather than forwards. They have an invisible body and visible soul. Ordinary humans have a visible body and invisible soul. The inverted house symbolism thus metaphorically links the house with the ancestors and the deities. Only secondarily is it identified with its inhabitants.

This is reinforced by the role of the house as the resting place for deceased elders. House doorways are orientated west, both to face the deity Kuiye and the village of the deceased ancestors that is nearby. The resting places of the ancestors in the house are aligned along the east–west path of the sun. The north entry horn above the portal is associated with female ancestors, the south one with male ancestors. The stone doorsill is an important seat of ancestral power and should never be replaced, marking a transition between living and dead, exterior and interior, male and female. The ideal is for every house to be built on the foundations of a previous one belonging to a previous family or village member. Previously occupied sites are thought to be free of underworld spirits causing misfortune. In the case of very ancient and sacred houses, primarily those of village and lineage founders, this is especially important as they are focal points of village history and ceremony. Each deceased family elder is associated with corporate resting places such as the horns and the doorsill and is represented by individual oblong clay resting places that are fixed, or planted, to the house façade or interior walls. Each has an incised central line (the path of the ancestor) and a portal hole. Every afternoon at dusk they are illuminated by the rays of the setting sun. Deceased elder resting places conform to the gendered division of space in the house, female ancestors having places on the terrace, male ones on the ground floor.

The symbolism of house and tomb among the Batammaliba is complementary. Each serves to analogically reference the other. In the centre of each house is a flat circular tombstone, which on the death of the elder is taken to the cemetery to serve as the tomb closure. Each tomb is a multi-level structure, like the house, but it is carved into the earth as opposed to being built on top of it. Like the house it has a raised and plastered terrace, a circular roof (defined by an overturned jar), a west-facing portal, an auxiliary room and an interior sleeping chamber. Tombs are positioned in the cemetery in a manner roughly imitating the position of houses in the village. Houses recall tombs while villages resemble cemeteries.

The houses take on important theatrical and dramaturgical roles during the staging of ceremonies, especially funeral performances, which are simultaneously celebrations of life while marking the passing of a life. Through these performances essential aspects of architectural meaning and metaphoric symbolism become reinforced. The house becomes a theatre for the play of death, life and cosmos. The circle is the most significant primary shape in Batammaliba architecture. Actions of circling are frequent in ritual life and in the course of these actions 'the circle's inherent identity with enclosure, definition, protection, and identity is reinforced. The manner of circling the house, tomb, and cemetery in the funeral parade or of circling the village earth in the periodic goat-pulling rites encloses and defines the boundaries of related forms' (Preston Blier 1987: 208). Batammaliba cooking, eating and storage vessels also have circular form, emphasizing the association of the circle with ideas about nourishment and life, the focus of the provision of which is the house itself.

The key metaphors in Batammaliba architecture are ontologically grounded in human experience and specifically derived from (1) an anthropomorphic mapping of the human body onto the house: this mapping is drawn from the physical and psychological experience of the body, its parts, secretions and actions; (2) the notion of the path and life, both sacred and profane, following a path. The house itself, once conceptually mapped in this way, acts recursively as a source domain for a diversity of metaphors associated with Batammaliba culture as a whole. Every being, animal, human or spirit, has a house. Key features of the cosmos are given concrete expression through the medium of the house. The house both expresses the metaphorical symbolism derived from other domains and serves to recontextualize this symbolism. It provides a context for the metaphorical understanding of things and actions in relation to other things and actions. It is not the cosmos, a deity, a human, a family or a tomb, but provides an objectified model for understanding all these things. It is an ordered and ordering device, structured and structuring fundamental principles of social life and the cosmos.

Animal Metaphors and Human Worlds

Lévi-Strauss's (1962) observation that animals 'are good to think' inevitably forms the basis for an understanding of the manner in which human social categories and animal categories are metaphorically linked. One may be mapped in terms of the other. This position has stimulated the production of a large number of studies (e.g. Bulmer 1967; Douglas 1966; Leach 1964; Sahlins 1976: ch. 4; Tambiah 1969; Willis 1974). Willis argues that the profound significance of animals derives from the fact that the animal is

> both within us, as part of our enduring biological heritage as human beings, and also, by definition, outside and beyond human society. The image of the symbolic animal is therefore necessarily a dualistic image, structurally homologous with the duality in human society and the self between the real and ultimate ideal, the actual and the longed for. (Willis 1974: 9)

Animals being similar to humans and yet different are able to alternate in a particularly salient manner between the contiguity implied by metonymic thought and the analogic mode of metaphoric thought (ibid.: 128). For Lévi-Strauss (see Chapter 1), Willis and many others, human categories are thought of as being mapped in terms of perceived differences in the natural world so that they become mirror images of each other. Humans use animals in order to draw elaborate pictures of themselves. Douglas in her later work and others have maintained that it is the other way round: animals are brought into human categories by an extension to them of the principles that serve to order human social relations (Douglas 1996: 143; contributions in Willis 1990). It would seem to be quite inappropriate to posit any universal cultural principle as regards the directionality of the symbolism, whether human beings turn 'naturally' to each other to derive analogies with animal species, or use animal species to understand themselves. By far the most significant point is that the construction of principles of metaphoric analogy between the domains of humans and the domains of animals forms a fundamental basis for self-understanding and the construction of meaning in all known societies. Animals are key source domains and target domains of metaphors through which culture is constituted. The specific meanings depend on the manner of their engagement or coupling, and either domain may provide a model for the other. Differences between socio-economic activity and narration and myth cannot be simply collapsed into a distinction between the material and the mental. Both arise from forms of dwelling and engagement with the world. Put another way, observations of the characteristics of animals inform the metaphorical workings of the human mind, providing it with raw materials for processing and informing an understanding of human society. Such a self-understanding then further informs conceptualization of the world of animals. Animal–human metaphors are thus in a constant process of structuration. The metaphors employed are both the medium and outcome of thought. And once one set of metaphorical understandings has been built this provides a frame for their referential extension.

Conceptions of the culture of nature may play a key metaphorical role in thinking through the nature of culture. Bird-David (1990; 1992) has made the fascinating argument that for forest-dwelling hunter-gatherers such as the Nayaka of south India, the Mbuti of Zaire and Batek of Malaysia, perceptions of the environment are organized by the primary metaphor 'the forest is parent'. Among neighbouring cultivators the primary metaphor is trransformed so that the environment (the land) becomes ancestor rather than parent. This in turn structures an entire series of values and attitudes that pervades the manner in which these people live. The forest as parent gives unconditionally. It shares its resources with people just as people share with each other. Ancestors, on the other hand, only give things in return for prestations. These key metaphors of parenting and sharing enable people to understand their environment and their own actions. Whether such metaphors are ultimately derived from the human experience of parenting and sharing or from the equally human experience of living and foraging in the forest and constantly interacting with plants and animals is a chicken and egg question, and has no meaningful answer. Ingold (1996) has recently emphasized the dynamism of the relationship: 'action does not serve to translate pre-existent form from one domain (the mental) to another (the material); rather, form arises and is held in place *within* action: it is movement congealed' (ibid.: 146). The phenomenological process of *dwelling* in an environment, which Ingold usefully stresses, is not however somehow prior to metaphor, as he argues;

rather, metaphors provide the ontological basis *for* that dwelling and for reflecting on the process of that dwelling. The outcome of metaphorical thought is that, once the process starts, it transcends any duality between 'culture' and 'nature' and makes them one. In Fernandez's (1986) felicitious phrase (see Chapter 1) it 'returns us to the whole', a whole that is cognized rather than inchoate. Metaphorical thought is grounded in an ontology of human existence in which a culture/nature divide becomes meaningless. When humans are metaphorically compared to animals or vice versa both are then understood as sharing a common existential status. The forest, or the animals within it, or human social relations, may be either the source or target domains, focus or frame, tenor or vehicle (see Chapter 1), depending on the metaphors used. Which metaphors are actually chosen is ultimately contingent on the cultural tradition and environmental context.

In some cultures a wide variety of different animal species may provide source or target domains for metaphors. In other cases one particular species may have a key or dominant role in a metaphorical hierarchy. For the Nuer and the Dinka pastoralists it is clearly the ox. The intimacy of connections between the human and bovine worlds can hardly be overemphasized (Evans-Pritchard 1940; Lienhardt 1961). Cattle provide an inexhaustible set of categories for understanding experience. For example:

> The Dinkas' very perception of colour, light and shade in the world around them is . . . inextricably connected with their recognition of colour-configurations in their cattle. If their cattle-colour vocabulary were taken away, they would have scarcely any way of describing visual experience in terms of colour, light and darkness. Other Nilotic peoples, who have lost many of their cattle and much of their material dependence upon them, have yet retained a colour vocabulary based upon cattle-colours, and develop poetic images on the basis of these cattle-colour names. (Lienhardt 1961: 12–13)

Such is the intimacy of personal connections between men and cattle among the Dinka that boys take the colour names of oxen in addition to personal names on initiation into manhood. Men imitate cattle and this self-identification with the ox is exhibited in customary body postures (ibid.: 17). Dinka words for social groupings refer equally to cattle. A beast which has been killed for no good reason and without ceremony may haunt its killers as may the ghost of a human similarly unjustly slain. In the division of sacrificial meat when a beast is killed 'the people are put together, as a bull is put together' (ibid.: 23; Figure 2.3). To have rights in a herd is to have rights in a descent group. The same is true of the Nuer,

52 METAPHOR AND THE CONSTITUTION OF THE WORLD

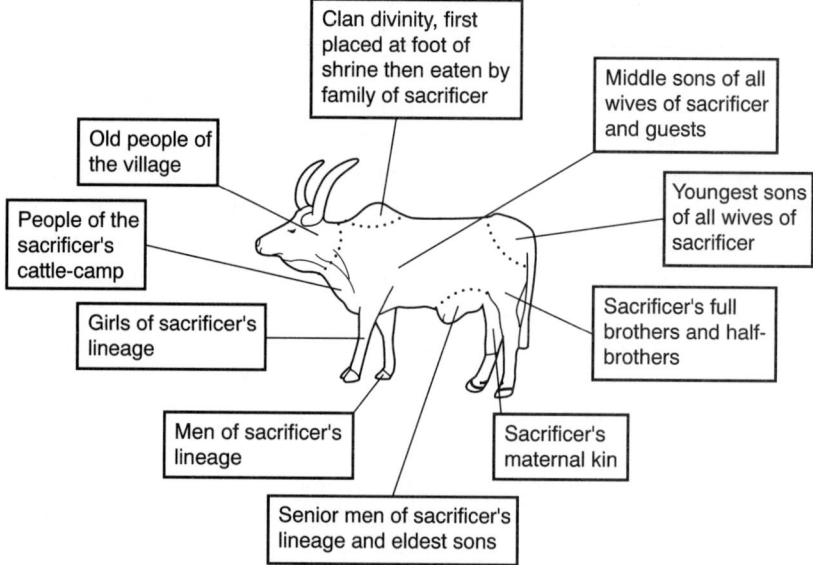

Figure 2.3 Distribution of the Dinka sacrificial beast.
Source: Lienhardt (1961). Reproduced by kind permission of Oxford University Press.

who conceive of cattle as socially identical with their own lineage system, and only permit themselves to eat cattle as a sequel to ritual sacrifice. Nuer have ten principal colour terms for cattle (Evans-Pritchard 1940: 41) which, in combination, provide several hundred named colour permutations. Further names describe horn shapes and, as amongst the Dinka, boys take on the names of oxen. A Nuer genealogy is like the inventory of a kraal and cattle cause men to quarrel and slay each other (Evans-Pritchard 1956: 41). In contrast to the intense interest in cattle the Nuer have little interest in hunting or wild animals, which are thought to inhabit a realm apart from human society, and this distance forms part of the basis for the conception of twins as birds (see the discussion in Chapter 1). By contrast, the Lele (Douglas 1957; 1963) regard domestic animals with disdain, while wild animals provide them with the primary sources of metaphors (for a detailed comparison of Nuer, Lele and Fipa beliefs see Willis's excellent (1974) account).

Throughout Melanesia it is the pig that has pre-eminent ritual significance. Nowhere was this complex of pig symbolism more developed than in the northern islands of the Vanuatu (former New Hebrides) archipelago. Here intersex or hermaphrodite pigs were reared and the practice of artificially inducing the growth of tusks was widespread, through knocking out the upper canines so that the tusks would have nothing to bite against and so continue their upward growth unimpeded. The natural curve of the tusk growth results in it circling through the cheek and jaw. Such tusks may attain three complete circles. Boars with such tusks were the prime sacrificial animals. It was only through their sacrifice that men could move up through the ranks of the graded society, achieve holiness, and attain life after death (Layard 1942; Funabiki 1981; Jolly 1984). Just as the names of men engaged in *kula* transactions (see Introduction to Part III) cannot be remembered without the shells, so men could not attain rank and spiritual essence in northern Vanuatu without pig sacrifice.

In the Small Islands of northern Malekula tusked boars were graded into four main categories according to the length and curvature of the tusk and there were a host of other terms recording intermediate stages of growth (Layard 1942: 246–7). Time could be measured in a pig's tusk. Tusked pigs were principal items of exchange and the tusks were ceremonially displayed after sacrifice, but since the boar was the sacrificial animal it and its tusks had little or no exchange value after death. Layard comments that 'the tusk symbolises the spiritual essence of the boar, that part of the boar which does not decay, and is the nearest thing to what we call a "jewel" that the Malekulan can possess' (ibid.: 310). Through pigs a man acquired prestige and rank, acquired wives, a soul necessary for the journey to the dead, and an ability to communicate with spirit beings. Sacrifice in the fifteen- to twenty-year cycle of *Maki* rites involved the identification of the victim, the sacrificer and the mythical being to whom the sacrifice was directed. A man advanced through the graded society by 'following a boar', a material carrier of his own spiritual essence. This boar must be reared by the man himself and cared for until the communal sacrificial rites. The sacrificer did not eat the flesh of the animal he had reared (it was anyway virtually reduced to a bag of skin and bones due to the severe difficulty it had in eating, the pain caused by tusk growth and its age). No man could sacrifice, in the *Maki* rites, a boar that he himself had not reared from his own sow because he would die or be killed by the spirit of the boar (Layard 1955: 288). The relationship between men and these boars is thus clearly metonymical. Sows were never sacrificed, nor could they be eaten by men because they were female. Women could not eat pig flesh at all (ibid.: 242). The boars, according to Layard, metaphorically represent sexual and reproductive relations between men and women in which the evulsion of the incisors of the boars is the equivalent of boys' circumcision initiations.

Layard suggests that boar sacrifice replaced earlier rites involving human sacrifice. Boar sacrifice is designed to satisfy a female devouring ghost, Le-hev-hev, who would otherwise devour men's souls on their way to the place of the dead (located in a volcano on the island of Ambryn): the deity accepts the pig's soul in lieu of that of the man. The volcano, Layard argues, symbolizes male and female sexuality, with its raised orifice ejaculating lava. Pigs, metonymically and metaphorically related to men, are essential to make persons in life and to the continued existence of their souls in death.

In his rich account of Thai animal symbolism in the village of Baan Phraan Maun, Tambiah (1969/1973) attempts to demonstrate a series of structural homologies between rules of etiquette in house space, eating rules and marriage and sex rules. House categories are understood in terms of a scale of spatial distance, marriage and sex rules in terms of social distance, and rules that apply to eating domestic and wild animals as edibility distance (Table 2.1). Read horizontally the table shows the distance gradient, read vertically the metaphorical transformations. So, for example, column 4 can be understood as: marriage with other people (non-kin) is acceptable; visitors entering the house and cleansing their feet on the house platform; eating edible animals of the forest. Each shares an equivalent spatial distance in relation to other kin, house and food categories, and in terms of the three different symbolic domains being represented are roughly isomorphic metaphorical transformations.

Animal classification takes the form of a complex series of differentiations and oppositions (Figure 2.4). Insects and birds are separated off into inedible and edible categories and are regarded as distant to humanity. Land animals are differentiated from water animals and are divided in terms of whether they are domestic or wild. It is the latter that are most conceptually elaborated and it is primarily in relation to these that attitudes of affinity and separation, opposition and integration are metaphorically thought through in relation to kin and sex rules and rules of house space. The dog living in the house has a close association with its residents. It has a metonymical relation with human society and hence eating it is taboo. Yet at the same time

> the dog is considered degraded and incestuous and thus stands for the antithesis of correct human conduct. This degradation to a subhuman status is used by the villager to perform a metaphorical transfer on the basis of an analogy. Man imposes on the behaviour of the dog the concept of incestuous behaviour, thereby attributing a human significance to the sexual behaviour of dogs. This then allows man to copy the behaviour of dogs metaphorically, e.g. eating food from a tortoise shell, in order

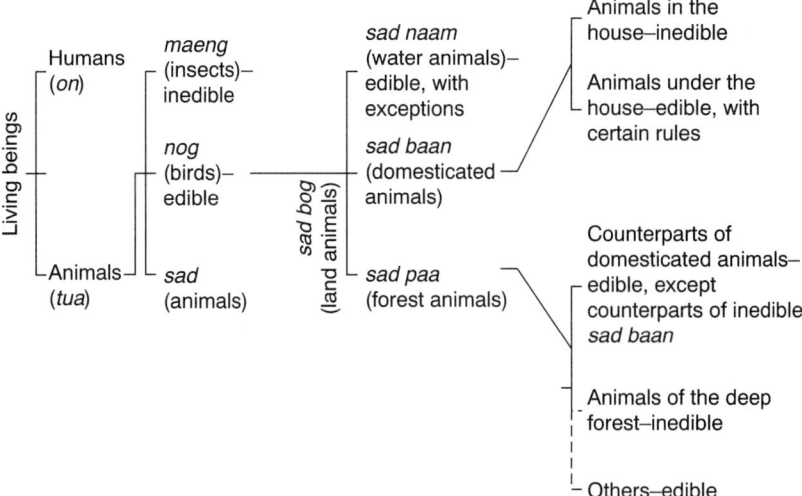

Figure 2.4 The classification of living creatures among Baan Phraan Maun villagers in Thailand.
Source: Tambiah (1969/1973)

to correct the moral consequences of his own improper incestuous marriage. (Tambiah 1969/1973: 163)

The ox and the buffalo have a metonymical relation to humanity but are evaluated highly positively. Humans must act ethically towards them. They are edible provided certain rules are followed. Their metaphorical relation to humanity is an inversion of that of the dog. An impure act of an ox (e.g. straying into the dirt of the washing place at night) is a bad omen for humans, corresponding to improper sexual relations by the inhabitants of the house. The taboo on eating the meat of the ox or buffalo at a wedding feast is a metaphorical statement of a proper marriage in which rules about eating and sex become conjoined. Wild animals of the forest are inedible because of their extreme distancing from humanity, but they provide metaphoric imagery for social and anti-social heroes. Anomalous wild animals that do not easily fit into the general classificatory scheme derive their significance either from being regarded as imitations of domestic animals or as intruders into the orderly life of the house and village. Vultures, toads and snakes are prone to enter the village and establish unwanted contact. They become omens of misfortune. Otters resemble dogs but are distant from humanity. They are anomalous within the

Table 2.1 The relationship between marriage and sex rules, eating rules and rules of etiquette concerning house categories.

	Blood siblings	First cousins (second cousins are ambiguous)	Classificatory siblings beyond second cousins	Other people	Outsiders
Human series					
Marriage and sex rules	Incest taboo	Marriage taboo; sex not condoned	Recommended marriage (and sex)	Marriage and sex possible	No marriage
House categories Rules relating to house space	Haung phoeng and baung suam Sleeping rules separating parents from son-in-law and married daughter	Huean yaai (sleeping room) Rights of entry but not sleeping	Huean naui (guest room) Taboo to cross threshold into huean yaai	Saan (platform) Visitors wash feet if invited in	Compound fence Excludes outsiders
Animal series	Domestic animals that live inside the house	Domestic animals that live under the house (and have been reared there)	Domestic animals belonging to other households	Animals of the forest: counterparts, deer, etc.	1 Powerful animals of the forest 2 Monkeys
Eating rules	Inedible and taboo	Cannot be eaten at ceremonials	Eminently edible at ceremonials	Edible	Inedible and taboo

Source: Tambiah (1969/1973).

class of water animals eaten and are thus doubly hated and rejected as a food.

Technology and Metaphor

In small-scale societies technology is inseparable from ideas of spiritual or ancestral involvement in the production process. The appearance and technique of manufacture of cloth, for example, can readily evoke ideas about connectedness or tying. Cloth as a metaphor for society, and weaving as an analogue for social relations, can express ideas about basic social processes (see Weiner and Schneider 1989). Homer's description of Penelope, weaving Laertes's shroud by day and then unravelling it by night, seeking to halt time and not be forced to choose a suitor, is a powerful evocation of the richness of weaving metaphors in the production of symbolic statements. Cloth is often associated with funerals as shrouds, coffin linings, gifts to mourners, etc. This may be linked to the protective functions of cloth, guarding the body against harm, but also relates to ideas about weaving and the making of cloth as linked to procreation and social regeneration. Analogies can be drawn between weaving and dying, the implications being that what is done (death) can be undone (i.e. cloth making is a reversible process and regenerative in time). So cloth can metaphorically give expression to basic ideas about death and the regeneration of life and can stand for the life-cycle of birth, maturation, death and decay. Participants in life-cycle celebrations and in death rituals often emphasize the gift of cloth as a continuous thread that binds kin groups, ancestors and the living, thus showing that the processes of making things and making people are part of the same seamless order of things.

There is also a constant tendency in which the logic of production is metaphorically expressed in terms of the logic of procreation and reproduction. Different techniques can inspire different interpretations of a basic theme concerned with regenerative and degenerative life processes.

Traditional iron making in most southern African societies is metaphorically linked to ideas about human procreation and childbirth: 'The furnace . . . was regarded as the smelter's wife for the period of the work and to sleep with his wife meant . . . adultery . . . to commit adultery whilst the wife is pregnant means . . . that the child will die, and so by analogy the furnace would not produce good iron' (Brelsford 1949, cited in

Collett 1993: 502). The link between smelting and human reproduction was frequently explicitly made by the decoration of the furnace with breasts or other female attributes. The process of smelting itself, generating heat, is like sexual intercourse making a couple hot. The process of cooking in a pot also generates heat and so a link exists in many societies between women, furnaces and pots (ibid.: 505). The cooking of food, the smelting of ore and the making of a foetus all share the common material characteristic of being irreversible transformations. One cannot reconvert the things produced to their original states. This provides a strong metaphoric link between them.

In the Cameroon Grassfields of west Africa, iron technology is linked with dual notions of fertility and violence. The smelting process is likened to pregnancy and delivery. Charcoal and 'male' and 'female' ores are fed into the furnace. These have very different sources and characteristics. The male ore is a ferralitic gravel, hard, dry, derived from a hillside, and never washed. The female ore is a clay collected in the banks of a stream, soaked and pounded and mixed with crushed slag and iron dust. The male ore is likened to semen and perceived as dry and powerful, the female ore is wet and weak, 'like a woman' (Rowlands and Warnier 1993: 524). The male and female ores produce a foetus, the bloom in the furnace, delivered when mature. The furnace is female, but in this case has no obvious iconic attributes signifying this, but participates in the attributes of fertility associated with women: 'dampness, humidity, water, "coolness", and with a lower position consistent with the women's lower position during sexual intercourse, as streams and water are found downhill' (ibid.: 524). Into this female furnace the dry male semen ore is fed from the top, the child of iron being delivered from below. Apotropaic plant medicines collected young when the plants are fresh and full of sap (water), and thus associated with women, are buried under the furnace. These are the 'spear of the workshop' designed to trap people with ill feelings, part of a taboo on violence in the smithy. Herbs used in curing rites for a spoilt smithy are the same as those used in treating women who have suffered a miscarriage (ibid.: 526). Iron production, like pregnancy, should be a non-violent process. The smith should abstain from sexual intercourse before the night of the smelt. Blood should not be spilt in the workshop and no one should quarrel, since that is the beginning of violence. Iron production, while likened to a process of fertility, is also very dangerous because iron can be used to kill and is antithetical to the reproduction process. If violence is not avoided the manufacture of iron will be out of control and cause the destruction of the community.

Every step in the production process draws on metaphorical links which are part and parcel of the magical process of iron production. In Grassfields cosmology a common theme emerges in the concept of a person, in birth and funeral rites, and in the metaphors associated with iron production. Birth involves an irreversible transformation from inanimate to animate foetus to moral being. This is accompanied by a reversible process of giving breath or spirit to the child 'which at death returns to be reborn as a future spirit whilst the corporeal form, buried on compound land, continues as an ancestor to be summoned by striking a bell and giving libations when required by living descendants' (ibid.: 539–40). The important point here is that transformations of both persons and things form part of a single continuum, both are equally animate or inanimate, depending on context and circumstances. As Rowlands and Warnier argue, the rituals surrounding iron production are not superfluous, something that could be stripped away to leave us with a technically 'rational' process. Rather, the analysis implies another mode of metaphoric thought in which smiths

> regarded themselves as facilitators in what we would call a *natural process* by which certain materials in nature transformed themselves into a substance which could be adapted to culturally useful ends. Humans were there to facilitate this process and help remove impediments, and protect against sources of danger to the natural process. By achieving these ends, humans could direct a natural process into a socially useful direction, i.e. could come to believe that they were participating in a natural process of transformation, which was equally their image of the relations of persons to things in general. (Ibid.: 541)

The 'economic', 'social', 'ritual', 'magical' and 'political' dimensions of technological processes cannot be meaningfully separated out and put into discrete boxes (Pfaffenberger 1992; Lemonnier 1993). They form part of a process in which metaphors originating in one domain are activated to make sense of another, and vice versa, in continual dialectical interplay. This is what Gell (1992a) refers to as the 'enchantment of technology' and it requires that we consider the other side of the coin, 'the technology of enchantment'.

Metaphor and the Arts of Memory

The *malangan* sculptures of New Ireland, Papua New Guinea, with their intricate engraved images (Plate 2.1) are cognitively sticky, a technology of

60   METAPHOR AND THE CONSTITUTION OF THE WORLD

Plate 2.1   A wooden *malangan* sculpture. (Source: Wilkinson 1978)

enchantment. They form an essential part of mortuary ceremonies, and part of the process of the construction of social memory (Küchler 1987; 1988; 1992). The accessibility of the sculptures to participants in the ceremonies, however, only lasts for a few hours between their public display and disposal to rot in the forest (or to be sold to collectors). While in some cases images act as memory work through their relative visual permanence as object, in this case the sculptures, made to be absent through destruction, produce memory as image in the mind. The named images of the sculptures, rather than the objects themselves, are objects of exchange:

> the sculpture is a reconstruction involving practices of recollection and transmission, and thus carries the imprint of social memory work: a given sculpture is interpreted in terms of the relation between the carved image and a template or framework for the selection of motifs and motif combinations. The sculptured image, however, is not a copy of the template which is, as it were, impressed upon the mind. Rather it is actively reconstructed in the light of the relationships which it is anticipated its transaction will engender. Sculptures are thus a record of the reproduction of images for transaction, and are both visually and conceptually a trace of the relationships that are established or reaffirmed in the process. (Küchler 1992: 97)

The word *malangan* is polysemous, meaning 'likeness', 'heat' and 'notation'. Likeness refers to the formal properties of the sculptures which may be carved in wood, woven from fibre or moulded from clay. These raw materials come from parts of the environment associated, respectively, with the social, ancestral and spirit realms. The wood used for the wooden sculptures is taken from the garden area separating the coastal villages from the mountains in the New Ireland interior, 'the place of the skin'. The garden area is also former or prospective settlement land and referred to as 'place of the womb' (ibid.: 100).

On the sculptures the carved planes refer to the exchange history of the image, its outer or public identity, while the painted patterns signify the current ownership or its inner identity. The carving of the wooden sculptures is called 'the making of skin' and can take up to three months. The carver is told in detail about the image to be carved by the eldest member of the clan responsible for the production of the sculpture, prior to dreaming induced by a magical potion of leaves, which further aids in the production of the image, and is held to be responsible for the success of the work. In the dreaming the carver 'recalls' an image, made perhaps twenty years previously, which he has not seen. The memory work involved in producing it is thus an active process. An image forgotten is reconstructed in memory in the process of its representation. The image produced is not in any sense to remember what has been forgotten. Rather, it metaphorically embodies energy or life force. The *malangan* images allude to the human body and the process of sculpturing them is conceived as one analogous to conception. This culminates in the coming to life of the sculpture and its subsequent death. In the climax of the mortuary ceremonies the image comes alive, becomes hot, and into it the soul of the deceased enters. The carving, as skin and container, now replaces that of the body of the deceased. Küchler comments:

> metaphorically, the visual inseparability of painting and carving, or of the 'skin' as both container and envelope, alludes to the practice of transforming house sites (or the place of the womb) into garden land (or the place of the skin). This transformation is instigated by the death of a person, and culminates in the making of an ancestor through *malangan*. The making of ancestors mirrors the process of merging the categories of inside and outside in both carving and land use. (Ibid.: 102)

The life-force of the deceased through the carving and subsequent killing of the image becomes rechannelled to the living in the form of power which is derived from the control over the re-embodiment of the memorized image into new sculptures, rights over which become transacted between individuals and groups through ceremonial exchanges accompanying the display of the carving immediately prior to its death. The decomposing sculpture, deposited in the forest, decomposes in order to set free the forces that can be reintegrated into other sculptures and forces. Thus, the *malangan* sculptures act as metaphorical model and medium for social reproduction.

Artefacts as Metaphors: Netbags, Basketry and Axes

The New Guinea looped string netbag (*bilum*) is much more than a useful container. MacKenzie (1991), in a rich and detailed analysis, demonstrates the way in which 'through the medium of metaphor its imagery is used by men and women to model, and thus confront, dissonance in the paradoxical nature of their relationship' (ibid.: 1). Netbags (Plate 2.2) are used throughout most of Papua New Guinea, from remote villages to suburbs, in virtually every domain of day-to-day and ceremonial life: for transport, shelter, to store and contain a wide variety of things – food, firewood, utensils, personal belongings, babies, piglets, puppies – and as a material representation of knowledges. At a time when indigenous craft production is declining, except to serve tourism, netbag production is thriving by assimilating imported raw materials such as died yarns. They are, in the

Plate 2.2 Two women with *bilums*. (Source: Mackenzie 1991)

process, acquiring new cultural value as a medium of personal innovation and emerging as neo-traditional symbols of post-independence Papua New Guinea unity. The looping techniques, raw materials, design features and embellishments vary, such that each group produces unique forms of *bilum* still serving as markers of cultural and social identity. Men, women and children may each have more than one *bilum* for different purposes, and old ones may be recycled and reused. Women may carry as many as five at once hanging from their heads, lower ones filled with garden produce, the middle one cradling a baby, outer ones shading the child. Women are not properly dressed without a *bilum*. Babies nestle horizontally in the string bag, spending most of their first year of life cradled against their mother's back or breast. In the gardens netbags may be hung on a stick as a hammock. In traditional beliefs ancestral powers residing in the land creep up the stick to enter the child, precipitating growth and imposing an obligation to care for the land in adulthood. The netbag is an artefact laden with social significance. Here it effects a material link between growth, nurturance, ancestral transformations, generational continuity and land rights. Slung over their shoulders (as opposed to women's netbags carried with a band around the head) men's netbags typically contain implements for the hunt, personal items, heirlooms, ritual paraphernalia, and are a means of storage for household items.

In traditional belief systems spirit beings are said to possess netbags. Small miniature amulet *bilums*, worn round the neck, provide supernatural protection. As exchange items netbags are used to mediate between different social groups and between men and women. In some areas of Papua New Guinea they formed an essential part of bridewealth payments. Today, the *bilum* serves as a traditional indicator of ethnic identity through the recognition of different looping techniques, shapes, textures and decorative elaborations. Within social groups the style of the *bilum* signifies its owner's social identity. Transitional stages in the life-cycle are marked by wearing different kinds of netbags. The *bilum* is a key item of gender differentiation. There is a universally recognized relationship between the *bilum* and the womb. This is manifested in the visual and functional similarity between expansive *bilum* and a pregnant woman's belly and the use of a *bilum* like an external womb, as cradle and the fact that a *bilum* is a woman's constant accessory in fulfilling her productive and reproductive roles.

MacKenzie reports that the pidgin English term *bilum* refers not simply to the string bag, but also to all indigenous looping techniques, to the various products made by these technical processes, to introduced Western functional equivalents such as pockets, and to natural objects including the marsupial pouch, human placenta and afterbirth (ibid.:18–19). Thus, the pidgin term is analogically extended so that the social product, the string bag, is linked to the fecund female belly and wider cultural notions of nurturance, encompassment and protection. This lexical link between the *bilum*, the placenta, womb and marsupial pouch is common in the vernacular languages of many *bilum*-producing Papua New Guinea cultures. According to Schieffelin, the Kaluli do not have a term for childbirth. The term they use meaning 'to give birth' means literally 'to put a child in a netbag' (Schieffelin 1976: 124). To summarize: the *bilum* as artefact is itself intricately woven into the centre of social life. The *bilum* protects and nourishes life. If an infant dies it is often buried in its *bilum* cradle. It marks transitions in the life-cycle, individual achievements and clan membership; it is used to establish and maintain kinship and ritual relations; it serves as a practical tool, wealth item and vehicle for creativity; and is an expression of cultural values. The young, old and the sick are carried in it. At death a woman's *bilum* may be buried with her. *Bilums* may be used as symbols substituting for the deceased, as a memorial effigy of the dead person or a resting place for bones: on death one returns as one was born into its universal protection.

MacKenzie's (1991) analysis of the use of the *bilum* among the Telefol of Highland Papua New Guinea begins with its initial production and follows the way it moves through different transactions and social contexts, how it acquires new functions, meanings and value. This biographical approach allows a detailed understanding of how indigenous conceptions of what a *bilum* is and what it means may become continuously extended as it enters into different contexts, usages and performative associations. The more flexible the range of functions the more associations become attached to the *bilum*, creating metaphoric resonances which are as much a part of the bag as its material form (ibid.: 26). The meaning of the netbag is not fixed but polysemous and transformative.

There is a marked division of labour among Telefol in the production of *bilums*. Women monopolize the looping technology and generate the principal form, the netbag itself. Men then take some of the netbags produced by women as their 'raw material', creating forms of netbags differentiated from the female product by application of additional features. These male elaborations are contained inside the bag or hang on the outside of the looped female product, an embellishment and transformation of female labour. Men then reclassify these *bilums* as a product of their own labour.

MacKenzie points out that while women's *bilums* are made in open settings, the male embellishments take place in the secrecy of the men's house from which women are excluded. The women's *bilums* are open. One can see through the string loops to see what the bags contain. By contrast, the male embellishments, principally feathers, both hide the basic female labour product and conceal the contents. This is consistent with the general principle of secrecy and an aura of taboo surrounding men's activities in Telefol society. It results in a curious inversion of the association of men with the public sphere and women with the private and domestic sphere so common in Melanesian societies: a male is to female as public is to private stereotype.

Bilums have considerable utilitarian value, but they also have aesthetic value as ornament, enhancing the wearer. Men claim that the women's *bilum*, unornamented with shimmering feathers, cannot create the same heightened intensity of aesthetic emotion as theirs. However, women gain enormous satisfaction in making a string bag that pleases them. This is linked to moral notions of goodness. A good *bilum* speaks volumes about a producer's ability to fulfil culturally expected roles. A good *bilum* is referred to by the same terms that mean 'correct', 'good', 'beautiful' and 'happy'.

An excellent *bilum* enhances a woman's appearance. It also displays her prowess – looping skills – and advertises her productive abilities. It becomes synonymous with a good woman who works hard. Its production is all about transforming elements from the natural world into an aesthetically pleasing cultural product. The manufacture of *bilums* is also a primary locus for socialization and the inculcation of gender roles. Making a netbag is all about being female. The relationship between a woman and her netbag is metonymical: the *bilum* stands for detachable aspects of a woman's identity that are still indelibly linked to her. When women give away *bilums* they give away part of themselves: their labour, creativity and energy. In the same way men become identified with one of their principal manufactured products: arrows. But there is a fundamental difference in the metaphorical associations at work. The *bilum* is linked with nurturance and has life-giving connotations, whereas arrows signify destruction and life-taking (ibid.: 142).

MacKenzie points out that there is an obvious visual similarity in mental images of women and *bilums*. The flat skin of the belly and the formless loops of an empty *bilum* both manifest a potential for expansion and growth. The netbag swells and so do pregnant women. Both women and the *bilum* swell in order to contain, protect and nurture and bear. The verb used by the Telefol in 'to take something out of the *bilum*' (as opposed to taking something out of other containers) is the same as that used in 'to give birth to a girl'. The verb 'to put things in the *bilum*' also means to bear fruit, reproduce, or pay back a gift as part of an exchange.

The Telefol say 'the *bilum* is our mother'. Motherhood is the most central attribute of womanhood. The metaphor 'the *bilum* is our mother' refers also to the ancestor Afek, the primal mother who established the male/female division of labour to reproduce Telefol society. An association is thus established between the *bilum* and all the qualities and activities associated with Afek's primal mothering activities (ibid.: 147). The netbag links the male and female domains together in a more general theme of social reproduction.

Men's *bilums* are the products of multiple authorship. A man receives a bag indissolubly associated with the woman who made it. To this he adds feathers as signs of male identity. While the feathers differentiate between male and female the set of distinctive bird species from which the feathers are acquired serves to distinguish man from boy and initiate from non-initiate. The qualities and behaviour of each bird species used draws attention to analogical similarities and equivalences between the bird and the initiate. MacKenzie (ibid.: 169) points out that these are elaborations on a *bilum* already carrying a heavy metamorphic and metonymical load in which the female contribution is fundamental. The feathers are adjuncts to wider associations of the netbag with female fecundity and biological motherhood, themes expressed through the *bilum* and elaborated in male ritual. Mackenzie argues that the netbag is an amalgam of the creativity of men and women. While apparently hiding women's work, and making it appear as male product, the use of men's feathers elaborates on the metaphor 'the *bilum* is our mother' in the context of ritual practice. One thing distinguishes the bird species such as the hornbill and cassowary, the principal feathers used on *bilums* for men's ceremonial practice, from other birds for the Telefol and that is that the male of the species is responsible for the activities of incubation, nurturance and protection of the young. These birds are male mothers. A number of procreative themes pervade male secret ritual cults in which the netbags are used. The verb used to describe putting a boy through an initiation ceremony also means to give birth to a boy. In so doing the male initiator becomes the 'mother' of social reproduction. Senior male initiators are referred to as the mother and father of the initiates. The cult house in which the ceremonies take place is known as the mother house. The male cult is itself centred on the primal mother figure of Afek, who gave birth to Telefol culture and all the significant items of Telefol material culture, including the netbag. In the rites links are established between biological motherhood, ritual motherhood, social motherhood and primal motherhood, effected metaphorically through the use of the *bilum* as androgynous object. It becomes manipulated in ritual so as to effectively blur the oppositional separation between men and women:

> The *bilum* represents both initiatory status of the male initiate *and* woman's biological fertility and Afek's extraordinarily potent creative forces. In male ritual it is used to host the union of female and male sexual fluids, and provide imagery of the powerful forces of fertility which are released through the synthesis of male and female. . . . Through the metaphor 'the bilum is our mother', maternal and paternal care, male initiation, taro fertility, the primal mother Afek – mythic source of all that is significant in life, and access to ancestral power are analogically interconnected. . . . The metaphorical associations between the bilum and motherhood link women and men in the joint task of reproducing society, thereby

confirming an identity of interest between the sexes at a cosmological as well as sociological level (Ibid.: 193)

The efficacy of the bilum as a means through which

> the inconsistencies of sexual autonomy/opposition and sexual cooperation/integration can be explored and confronted draws on its capacity to model the situation, to embody the interconnectedness of separation and integration. Through its imagery problematic situations are rephrased and reframed.... For example the way the bilum is used within male rituals reorientates initiates towards women.... The participants experience meaning as part of the process of the rituals, and understanding occurs in the interaction between the individual and his uses and observations of the bilum. The process of achieving new understanding in this way is aided by the understanding that nothing is really as it appears to be on the surface, and that the most important connections in the world are those which are initially concealed, which are then hinted at, and finally demonstrated in ritual form. (Ibid.: 206)

Yekuana basketry

In the Amazon region of lowland South America basketry is a fundamental vehicle of cultural communication. Beautifully woven and decorated baskets are an essential part of the technology and are an 'art' form. Basket-making is the principal activity of the male Yekuana of the upper reaches of the Orinoco river of southern Venezuela while in the village. In his superb ethnography Guss shows that the process of making baskets orchestrates dialogue: 'conversation simply did not occur without someone making a basket' (Guss 1989: 2). Basket-making and myth are, for the Yekuana, parallel symbolic systems which inform each other. Each activity, Guss argues, is determined by the same underlying configuration of symbols and meanings. To tell a story is to weave a basket, and vice versa. Baskets provide a prism through which the Yekuana universe is reflected: 'cast in a metaphor of endless dualities, the symbols in the baskets, like those elsewhere, confronted the most elemental oppositions between chaos and order, visible and invisible, being and non-being' (ibid.: 4). The process of basket-making is one of a constant metamorphosis of reality into a comprehensible, coherent and *legible* order.

The Yekuana distinguish between traditional objects and those that arrive from the outside. Indigenous objects (termed *Tidi'uma*, from the verb 'to make') such as houses, canoes and baskets are what distinguish their culture from everything acquired through trade and exchange from the outside (*Mesoma*). These objects, such as tin cans and plastic buckets, have none of the symbolic power or meaning associated with things that are made. They are insipid alien objects, perhaps functionally useful, but they incorporate none of the symbolic powers enabling the Yekuana to survive and maintain their cultural integrity. Meaning and making are thus linked and through them culture is reproduced. Through the symbolism accompanying the making, design and use of things indigenous material culture takes on a metaphoric significance far more essential and fundamental than any utilitarian function hand-made objects might have:

> In learning how to make the various objects required for survival, one is simultaneously initiated into the arrangements underlying the organization of society as a whole. Just as ritual actions may be said to necessarily accompany all material ones, the symbols incorporated into the manufacture of all *tidi'uma* require that every functional design participate in a greater cosmic one. (Ibid.: 70)

Those that create the most skilfully crafted objects are also the most ritually knowledgeable members of the community, and nowhere more so than in the manufacture of their intricate baskets.

Virtually all material activities require baskets, from the hunting of game to gardening, to processing poisonous yuca into cassava, to items only intended for ceremonial use. Skill in basket-making becomes a means of evaluating both individuals and members of a village community. It is used to chart practical knowledge, status and identity. A man cannot support a wife without being able to make the baskets that enable her to work. Yekuana state that a boy is not ready for marriage until he has mastered the art of making every different kind of basket. Following marriage and a change of residence in this matrilocal society, a man must weave his wife a series of baskets in a strictly prescribed order. The completion of a cycle of basket-making represents the conclusion of a year-long marriage ritual. The first basket that a man weaves for his wife is a plain form called *waja tıngkuıhato*. The manner in which it is woven serves to produce a pattern of radiating lines known as the 'frog's bottom'. This basket is made from a sacred cane with heavenly origins. It is considered a pure and safe substance. It is from this basket that the couple eat during the first year of their marriage. At the end of the year the man weaves a painted basket with a pattern marked out by black and white plaits that alternate. The painted basket is made from two varieties of cane that are associated with dangerous and powerful spirits that are potentially life-threatening.

People who are in a weak and spiritually precarious position should avoid eating out of such a basket. Put in this context the use of the plaited vessel to mark the end of the marriage ritual is a clear sign that the marriage is well established, the potential dangers of its establishment over.

The symbolism incorporated into the design of each basket metaphorically refers to that which is signified by its origin, name, physical properties and use. The baskets are visual metaphors, the meaning of which is sustained through analogical reference to other structurally similar cultural and mythological objects of knowledge. The concentric-circle dualism present in the designs replicates circular imagery found in the house, in dress and in the gardens. They share a common and fundamental spatial symbolism. Each individual design has powerful affective properties. Guss maintains that 'through the aesthetic organization of woven elements, emotional and psychological responses are induced to reify the same symbolic constructions erected elsewhere' (ibid.: 121).

Examining individual designs on the baskets in relation to the origin story of the *waja* (circular serving trays for serving cassava), Guss shows how they are all related to death and the toxic properties of a natural world that have to be culturally absorbed. This is a key metaphor about cultural creation and reproduction told in myth and materially translated in the basketry designs. *Awadi*, the venomous coral snake (Figure 2.5), like all snakes, is an ever-present danger for the Yekuana. Snakes represent a world of death and poison. New-born children have chants sung for them to ward off the dangers and a special herb is mixed with water and used to bathe the child and so avert the danger. Throughout life herbs, paints, chants and gourds are employed as defences. Through the design's name and form, a deadly association with snakes is ascribed to the baskets, which themselves are said to resemble the markings of a snake skin. Through the act of basket-making the dangerous wild, toxic and unpredictable powers of the snake are transformed to become a safe and usable part of culture. The generic metaphorical meaning of the imagery of the painted basket is that of something which extracts foreign and toxic elements and makes its contents safe. For people who are in a spiritually strong state the painted baskets are a positive force, symbolically purifying. Such ideas become readily explicable in a culture in which toxic properties have to be controlled in all the three main subsistence activities. In gardening poisonous yuca needs to be converted through the medium of basketry into edible cassava. Hunting is associated with the curare of poisoned arrows, fishing with the use of barbasco which deprives the fish of oxygen and leaves them stunned.

Figure 2.5 Yekuana *waja* representing *Awadi* the poisonous snake.
Source: Guss (1989)

Part of the meaning of designs is related to context of use, how they are seen and 'entered':

> like the house, the basket is also round. When it is used, it is laid flat on the ground, a circle of hungry people around it, consuming the cassava it contains. As the meal progresses, the images start to appear from beneath the food. Yet, according to where one is sitting, each view of them will be slightly different. For unlike a Western painting that stands rectangular and upright against a wall, the *waja* has no one perspective. It is meant to be entered (like the culture) from any point, a work of art which sits inside its circle of viewers. (Ibid.: 121)

The meanings of the baskets are physically and unconsciously internalized through their repetitive use and this does not require verbalization.

The metaphorical meanings of the designs are materially present *in* the designs and unconsciously transmitted through the mind.

The basketry symbols are informed and produced through metaphorical reference to wider cultural principles which, in turn, are formed and reproduced by them. The ability of the symbols to evoke these principles depends on their polysemous multi-referential nature. In Yekuana culture the concentric-circle floorplan of the round house is a model of the cosmos, a model reproduced in the structure of the garden (consisting of two concentric circles, an outer one dedicated to the material production of food and an inner core, a preserve of women's ritual knowledge and herbal magic – in this sense an inversion of the round house in which the sacred core is male) and in human body decoration encircling the torso, and is a model reproduced in the design of baskets. The round house has a sacred inner space, reproduced in the central square design of the baskets (a limitation of the plaited medium) surrounded by a profane outer ring. The centre of both house and basket refers to the centre of heaven, the outer ring of the basket is similarly equated with the edge of the known world and the lines of rain that run from it. Guss further suggests that 'the ability of the basket to contain the image of the universe, as translated through the house, is itself but a metaphor for the entire process of cultural creation. For if every action has the power to reproduce the whole, it also has the power to incorporate all of its parts' (ibid.: 168). The round house is itself a woven form, twined with cane. Both house-making and basket-making are part and parcel of the transformation of the world into a coherent and ordered reality, making a sum, a whole, out of seemingly disparate parts.

Axes: bodies and the finishing of the dead

The ceremonial stone axe is one of the key object valuables in the southern Massim area of Papua New Guinea. Battaglia (1983; 1990) presents an excellent interpretation of the significance of axes in relation to concepts of personhood in the context of mortuary ceremonies which serve to reproduce and recreate social life. The axe (Figure 2.6) takes its name from the triangular stone blade, *tobwatobwa*. The blade is the *hinona* or 'content' of the axe. This word also means 'genitals' and 'right hand'. A wooden handle or 'arm' displays and 'supports' the blade. Its form is suggestive of bones (*titiwa*). The handle is carved from a red wood associated with maternal flesh and the matriclan. The 'head' of the handle is carved in the form of a bird's head in profile, signifying clan member-

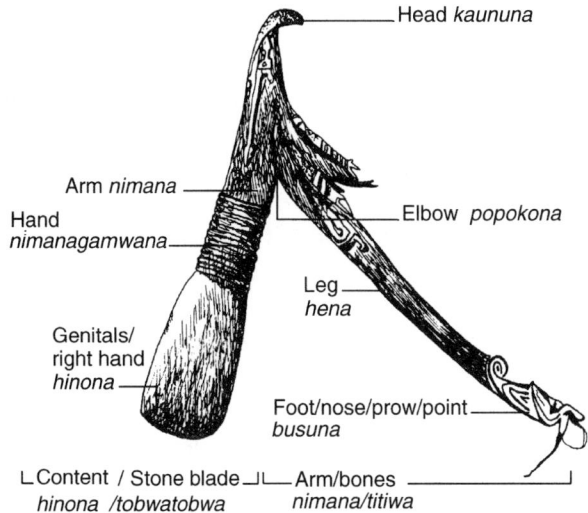

Figure 2.6 Sabarl ceremonial axe showing named parts.
Source: Battaglia (1990). Reproduced by kind permission of Chicago University Press.

ship. Battaglia points out that 'as "bones", "flesh" and clan "head" the wooden haft is a representation of the "body" of the corporate person – the person as a clan member. The greenstone blade, as *hinona*, broadly represents the singular person and the reproductivity of the individual' (Battaglia 1983: 295). The axe blade thus serves to unify two different aspects of the individual, as person and as member of a clan. *Hinona* in relation to a person is a substance that resides within the body, a material life force that enables the body to breathe and continue to exist. Witchcraft is said to eat the *hinona* away. As the term for the genitals *hinona* also refers to reproductive energy. In this manner *hinona* is a term that provides the metaphorical connection between persons and ceremonial axes (ibid.: 293). The axe becomes identified with the very essence of the physical existence of a person. *Hinona* as relating to biological reproduction is a force associated with heat, the heat of sexual intercourse generating conception. This heat is also manifested in the heat of aggressive labour associated with axes in their use as utilitarian implements and as weapons. The axe blade is thus described as heat-generating or 'greasy' in particular social contexts. *Hinona* as a metaphorical concept links economic productivity: making new objects; biological productivity: making new persons; and social productivity: making new social relationships effected through the exchange of axes (Battaglia 1990: 134). The arm of the axe contains this heat. It both provides support and complements the blade.

Although the hafted axe appears to be a static triangular shape it is in fact dynamic, an image of action and directed movement. The Sabarl islanders maintain that the axe shares the shape of mortuary feasts. These involve the lateral movement of wealth items from the father's side (the left side or 'arm' of the person) to the mother's side (the right 'arm') and then back again. This is a commemoration of the support given to a person by kin during life.

The bend in the handle of the axe (*popokona*) is referred to as the elbow. Elbows are the parts of a person's arms that make him or her strong. The elbow of the axe represents 'the joint in the socially vital movement of reciprocal giving (as rendered in the *tobwatobwa* arm); also the point in an individual's existence where primary clan tensions articulate. This same movement is perceived as the ideal route of valuable objects away from the person, clan or village, and, importantly, back again' (Battaglia 1983: 297). The elbow of the axe thus metaphorically refers to the turning point of social action in the mortuary feasts. The axe is a materially embodied image of mobility. Sabarl thought and action places a high premium on mobility as an index of personal and group viability and success. Things must be turned to one's own advantage. Durable circulating items such as the ceremonial axe provide 'evidence' about the course of a social relationship, 'thus the arm of a ceremonial axe may be seen as the representation of the body of a person or as the bidirectional "path" of exchange between cousins and as the dispersal and reclamation of wealth' (Battaglia 1990: 135).

On the head of the axe haft is a bird head signifying the clanship and a place for the matriclan at 'the armature of exchange' (Battaglia 1983: 297). It metaphorically refers to the support given to individuals by their clan groups. But it is a condensed polysemous symbol with other meanings. The bird is a reef heron which, in myth, is a male fisher married to a woman. In the axe handles a snake is depicted in the heron's beak, not a fish. The bird and the snake represent the mythical creators of the archipelago of islands of which Sabarl is a part but also signify sexual opposition. Battaglia argues that relationships of support between kin are transformed at death into individualistic conflict over inheritance, etc. This is visually encoded by the bird and snake sign set and conceived in terms of sexual opposition. The metaphoric symbolism of the axe thus simultaneously expresses ideas about support and conflict, reciprocity and personal appropriation. The imagery is dualistic. One 'covers' or obviates the other (ibid.: 298).

In the Sabarl *Segaiya* or mortuary feast the paternal clan of the deceased publicly presents five axes to the maternal clan heirs, having paraded them through the village to the house of the deceased. In secrecy, the axes are then used to construct an effigy of the 'corpse' of the dead. The house is made hot through magical spells and the corpse of axes is made by propping the handles against each other so the axes rest on their blades. These become metaphorical substitutes for the dead person resembling the body reclining in the grave. The axes as corpse take on the form of the traditional L-shaped grave shaft. The effect is dramatic, a representation of the dead person as if raised from the grave. This symbolizes a transformation from being a living member of the community to the status of an ancestor. This ancestral corpse is draped with red shell necklaces and other valuables arranged around it. It is then induced to produce more axe blades. Finally, the axe corpse is deconstructed. Axe blades are thought to be capable of parthenogenesis because they are persons rather than objects, linguistically classified as animate. In the context of the mortuary ceremony they become associated with paternal substance. The axe corpse metaphorically kills and finishes the memory of the dead, effecting a transformation to the status of an ancestor. The ceremony kills the dead person and breaks clan links. In the process it makes new ancestors and memories through the creation of absence. The materiality of the ceremony is crucial: 'understandings gained from participation in public performances, whether passively or actively, are more trusted than anything conveyed through the mediating sight and talk of others' (Battaglia 1990: 197). The objectification of fundamental cultural values is not conveyed in words but in performances in which material forms are metaphorically put to work to effect the social transformations required. Memory and meaning are linked to the performance and become attached to the artefact. The power of the artefact to create meaning resides in its very materiality, a materiality that is recontextualized in ceremonial performance.

Conclusions: Persons and Artefacts, the Social Lives of Things

As Appadurai notes, contemporary Western common sense characteristically opposes things to words. Things are regarded as mute and static, only set in motion and animated by persons and their words (Appadurai 1986: 4). Yet in the majority of small-scale societies, past or present, this is simply not the case. Things create people as much as people make them. From a *theoretical* point of view it is obvious that people do encode metaphorical meanings into things which would themselves have no meaning. But from the point of view of *methodology*, of the analysis of material forms, things once created work themselves to reproduce or transform the social contexts in which they are encountered and move. They are active rather than passive and dialectically related to their social conditions of existence. Things, as Kopytoff (1986) usefully emphasizes, have biographies, or life-phases, like persons. We can ask such questions of things as: what are the socially constrained biographical possibilities of the object (as, for example, bulk commodity or prestige valuable)? What is the usual or ideal biography of a thing? What are the recognized 'phases' in a thing's life? How does its use and meaning change with age? What happens when it moves from one cultural context to another? How is it redefined and put to use? What happens when it is no longer useful as a utilitarian item? How is its meaning related to the manner of its production and the sources and qualities of the raw materials from which it was manufactured? Such biographies of things inevitably work in terms of other categories, whether we are concerned with the social, economic, technical or religious use of the thing, and all the interlinkages between relating to an artefact's production, exchange and consumption, its birth, movement, use and death through deposition (as grave good or votive deposit) or destruction. The biographies of things are obviously intimately linked to whether they are commonplace or widespread, their exchange is restricted or generalized, whether they move in discrete spheres of exchange as in the case of the *Kula* armbands and necklaces, whether they represent alienable or inalienable wealth and so forth. Kopytoff (1986: 89–90) suggests that one can draw a direct analogy between the ways in which societies construct persons and the way they construct things. One provides a metaphorical model for the other. In most small-scale societies a person's social identities are relatively stable and changes are normally effected by cultural rules rather than biographical idiosyncrasies. Drama in an ordinary person's biography results from being within a certain status (as initiate or non-initiate, male or female, elder or junior, married or unmarried, etc.) Things are similarly modelled, acquiring their biographical status in a relatively clearly structured system of exchange values and spheres. Things that do not fit the usual categories are anomalous – either cast out or sacralized. The biographies of things and persons are intimately linked to broader sets of shared metaphoric collective understandings, a theme which I further explore in Parts II and III of the book and in the conclusions.

Part II

Text, Artefact, Art

Introduction

Part II consists of three substantive case studies in which I consider the linguistic work of metaphor in text, one supposedly utilitarian artefact form – the canoe – as solid metaphor and interpret the metaphorical meanings of a series of prehistoric rock carvings in their landscape setting in southern Sweden. This last chapter, while primarily considering 'art' and its metaphorical significance, is also integrally linked with the general perspectives on landscape put forward in the introduction to Part III of the book.

In Chapter 3 I consider the term 'megalith' as a key archaeological metaphor and the effect the use of the term has had on discourses about the European past for over one hundred years. While it will be of little surprise, on the basis of the discussions in Part I, that all archaeological texts work metaphorically both to produce the past and the meaning of that past, I consider a much wider issue. This is the manner in which 'megaliths' as discursive objects serve to structure and constrain a particular reading of the past which remains peculiarly constant despite apparent theoretical changes radically altering conceptualizations of that past. Running beneath the surface theoretical froth I argue that the dead, frozen or unrecognized metaphor 'megalith' still performs active work in the minds of archaeologists. Concomitantly, the manner in which the past is understood is unconsciously structured by a particular metaphorical way of thinking. This constrains the forms in which thought becomes textually manifested. The power of the megalithic metaphor on the archaeological imagination is such that to attempt to abandon the term becomes unthinkable, threatening discursive chaos. Yet the ambiguity and uselessness of the term also causes confusion and dissatisfaction. This discursive ambiguity and polysemy results both in a freedom to write and research (is productive of knowledge), yet sets the terms of the discourse in which nothing radically new is possible to say. The metaphor both produces and restricts discourse.

In Chapter 4 I consider solid metaphor, discussing in detail the social lives of Wala canoes. On the basis of field observation and ethnohistorical information I attempt to demonstrate that they entangle, or draw together, dense layers of metaphorical meaning. This meaning is both sedimented from the past and continually being produced in the present, and no layer can be considered to be primary. The canoe, as utilitarian object, is linked to virtually every aspect of daily life. The canoe as metaphoric object also meaningfully links together radically different domains of action, sociability and meaning through its silent non-verbal discourse. The material form of the canoe as solid metaphor permits that which has never been said to be said and to mediate between different domains: ideas about gender, the land and the sea, rootedness and journeying, subjects and objects, the past and the present.

In Chapter 5 I move from a single portable artefact to consider a static 'artwork': Swedish Bronze Age rock carvings and their placement in the landscape. I consider in particular metaphoric and metonymic associations between depictions of the human body and human body parts such as hands and feet. I attempt to demonstrate that the metaphorical meanings of these depictions of humanity cannot be understood apart from the metaphorical meanings of the network of different images carved on the rocks. Furthermore, an essential element in their meaning is where they are located in the landscape and the sequential 'narrative' sequence of these rocks involving relationships between land and water, high areas and low areas, visibility and lack of visibility. I argue that the meaning of form is contextually dependent on spatial location. Building metaphor on a metaphor I undertake a narrative journey describing the process of walking through and phenomenologically encountering the carvings in order to construct a contemporary account of the significance of body images from the past.

INTRODUCTION

These three studies have been chosen in order to attempt to demonstrate and exemplify the richness of a concept of metaphor for the understanding of texts, objects and artworks, an understanding of all of which remains one of the core concerns of material culture studies. Metaphors, as discussed in Chapters 1 and 2, can never provide self-sufficient devices for an understanding and interpretation of textual, object or art worlds. They form part of a nexus of cognized relations involving the body and the mind in socially constituted space-time, providing a point for departure and a point for return in a dialogic process of question and answer, part of a never-ending hermeneutic circle drawing together subject and object, observer and observed.

3

Frozen Metaphor: Megaliths in Texts

Introduction

The term 'megalith' is a key word in the archaeological literature concerned with the prehistory of Europe. In this chapter, I want to perform a genealogical analysis of the use of the term in archaeological discourse, investigating the manner in which it has grown, developed and transformed. The main questions I shall address are: to what ends has the term been employed? Why? Has its meaning shifted through time? To what extent does the term 'capture' the reality of the stone monuments it is used to discuss – does it illuminate or obfuscate an understanding of the past?

The Genealogy of a Conceptual Metaphor

As is well known, and indeed repeated constantly in the literature, the term 'megalith' is derived from the Greek *megas*, meaning big, and *lithos*, meaning stone. According to Daniel (1958: 14) it was first used to describe stone monuments in Europe and other parts of the world in the period 1840–60. It had its birth, then, at the same time as other key words in contemporary archaeological discourse, such as 'Palaeolithic', 'Neolithic',

'Bronze Age' and 'Iron Age'. Like them, the term was generated during the formative years of archaeology as a 'scientific' discipline aiming to achieve a systematic and 'objective' study of the past. It is of interest to note that the use of the Greek automatically provides the term with a certain aura of scientificity, part of the technological jargon of a fledgeling discipline. Unlike many other archaeological key words coined around the same time it was not originally used to refer to a putative temporal phase but a specific class of archaeological remains. Today, after 150 years of usage, the term has a particular and unique resonance in the archaeological consciousness. There is no equivalent 'scientific' term applied to any other specific class of archaeological remains from the prehistoric past in Europe. For example, terms used to describe other widespread types of material remains found over large areas of Europe such as 'cave art', 'beaker', 'barrow', 'cairn', 'midden', 'rock carvings' and 'long house' are quite ordinary everyday words, or the precise terminology varies locally, or is used infrequently. All archaeologists 'know' what the term megalith means and it is used habitually to organize sessions in conference proceedings, in books, university courses and in reading lists. A term like this one, then, might be claimed to reside at the discursive heart of an archaeology of Europe, which is why it is particularly fascinating to analyse its meanings and usage in texts. A *disciplinary* archaeological consciousness constructed the term to bring order and control to a set of disparate remains. I want to try to make the case that the term has now taken over and structures the archaeological consciousness. Its use, whether explicitly in texts or in the mind sets of archaeologists carrying out research, structures what may or may not be said or written about a chunk of the prehistoric past. The term creates a particular form of discourse and – such is its power – there appears to be an inability to reinscribe the past in a fresh manner, despite quite radical changes in theoretical ideas and methods of analysing archaeological information.

The sample of literature used in this analysis consists of sixteen texts. These include all major published works in the English language specifically devoted to the subject of megaliths (Fergusson 1872; Peet 1912; Daniel 1958), the English translation of Joussaume's *Dolmens for the Dead* (1988), originally published in French in 1985, and Montelius's classic work *Orienten och Europa* (1905). In addition to these books some general surveys on the prehistory of Europe were analysed, all of them published between the 1920s and 1990: the first and sixth edition of Childe's *Dawn of European Civilization* (1925 and 1957) and works by Hawkes (1940) and Hodder (1990). A number of papers and book chapters on megaliths published at different dates and representative of different styles of archaeological thinking were also used (Forde 1930; Renfrew 1973; 1976; Chapman 1981; Jarman, Bailey and Jarman 1982; Hodder 1984 and Thomas 1991). The sample thus comprises a period of 120 years' writing about megaliths and includes examples of work chosen as representative of 'traditional', 'processual' and 'post-processual' archaeology (Table 3.1).

In these sixteen texts the word 'megalith', the plural 'megaliths' or the derivative term 'megalithic' are employed on no less than 1,648 occasions. In all cases the word has a generic usage. In other words it stands and is used as a classificatory term supposedly replete with meaning in itself. The extent of this generic usage, of course, varies widely from author to author, but there is a clear general trend to an increase in the relative frequency of generic usage through time (Figure 3.1). The term is rarely used on its own prior to the 1920s and it is interesting to note that the first three books in the sample, all of which are specifically devoted to the subject of megaliths, do not employ the term in their titles. Montelius uses the word on only a few occasions and in his text always inserts it within inverted commas.

Table 3.1   The sample of texts used in the analysis of 'megaliths'.

James Fergusson (1872) *Rude Stone Monuments* [532 pp.]
Oscar Montelius (1901) *Orienten och Europa* [252 pp.]
T. Eric Peet (1912) *Rough Stone Monuments* [161 pp.]
V. Gordon Childe (1925) *The Dawn of European Civilization* First Edition. Parts or all of chapters 6–9, 13, 18–19, Epilogue [76 pp.]
Daryll Forde (1930) 'Early cultures of Atlantic Europe', *American Anthropologist* [82 pp.]
Christopher Hawkes (1940) *The Prehistoric Foundations of Europe*. Chapter 5, pp. 158–99; Chapter 6, pp. 205–17 [56 pp.]
V. Gordon Childe (1957) *The Dawn of European Civilization* Sixth Edition. Chapters 10: 221–38; 12: 260–70; 13: 277–88; 14; 15: 315–32; 17; 18: 373–81; 19 [109 pp.]
Glyn Daniel (1958) *The Megalith Builders of Western Europe* [136 pp.]
Colin Renfrew (1973) *Before Civilization* Chapter 7: 'The enigma of the megaliths' [28 pp.]
Colin Renfrew (1976) 'Megaliths, territories and populations' [35 pp.]
Robert Chapman (1981) 'The emergence of formal disposal areas and the "problem" of megalithic tombs in prehistoric Europe' [11 pp.]
Jarman, M., Bailey, G. and Jarman, H. (1982) *Early European Agriculture*. Chapter 7: 'The Megaliths: a problem in palaeoethology' [20 pp.]
Ian Hodder (1984) 'Burials, houses, women and men in the European neolithic' [16 pp.]
Roger Joussaume (1985) *Dolmens for the Dead* [315 pp.]
Ian Hodder (1990) *The Domestication of Europe*. Chapters 6–9 [131 pp.]
Julian Thomas (1991) *Rethinking the Neolithic*. Chapters 3, 6, 7 [102 pp.]

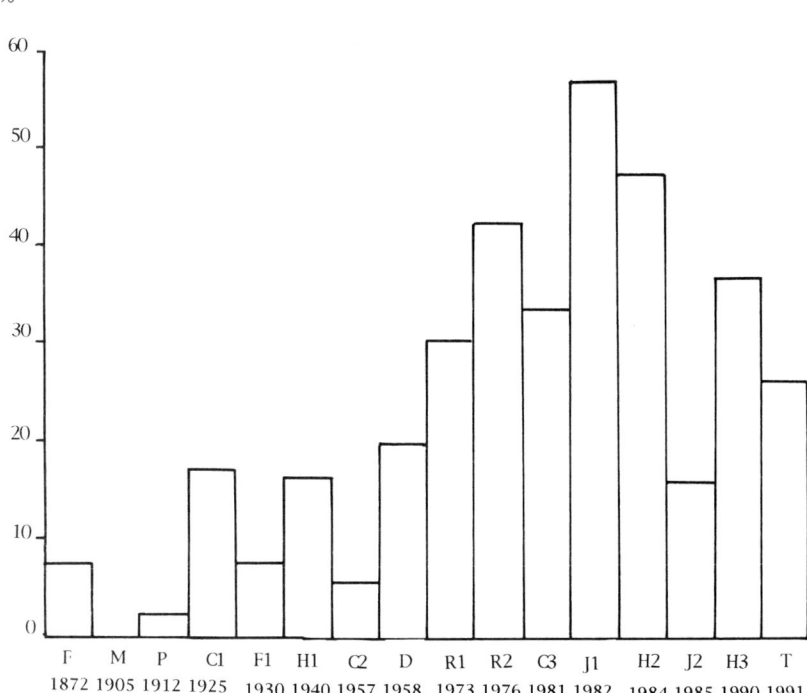

Figure 3.1 The relative frequencies of generic usage of the terms 'megalith(s)' and 'megalithic' in the texts analysed in relation to author and publication date. F: Fergusson (1872); M: Montelius (1905); P: Peet (1912); C1: Childe (1925); F1: Forde (1930); H1: Hawkes (1940); C2: Childe (1957); D: Daniel (1958); R1: Renfrew (1973); R2: Renfrew (1976); C3: Chapman (1981); J1: Jarman et al. (1982); H2: Hodder (1984); J2: Joussaume (1985); H3: Hodder (1990); T: Thomas (1991).

While Fergusson and Peet use the term infrequently, the equivalent 'monument' – sometimes qualified with the words 'rough' or 'rude' – is clearly more important to them. With the advent of 'processual' archaeological writing (Renfrew 1973, 1976; Chapman 1981; Jarman et al. 1982) generic usage increases significantly, a trend which continues with 'post-processual' works (Hodder 1990; Thomas 1991), although the absolute frequency of usage is in some cases very low. This general trend towards an increase in the frequency of generic use through time indicates the manner in which the term has become relatively unproblematic and has so thoroughly pervaded the archaeological consciousness that its use has become standard practice. Hodder and Thomas deliberately use the word 'monument' very frequently, presumably because it has less clearly defined connotations, but in many cases this amounts to a simple synonym for 'megalith', as is also the use of the term 'tomb' in their texts. This has clear similarities with the writing styles of Fergusson and Peet, with their constant references to 'rude stone' and 'rough stone' monuments, except that the rude and the rough have been deleted!

Looking at the absolute frequency of usage, expressed in terms of the mean number of usages of the term per page of text, a slightly different picture emerges (Figure 3.2). The term is infrequently used in the earliest and latest texts, achieves great significance in the work of 'traditional' archaeologists, in particular that of Forde and Daniel, and enjoys a short renaissance in some 'processual' texts. We seem to have here a growth and dying away of the term, at least in a simple quantitative sense of the frequency of use. However, it is worth noting that the mean frequencies are necessarily artificially depressed in those works discussing a wider range of archaeological evidence than just 'megaliths', such as those by Hodder and Thomas.

As well as occurring on its own the term 'megalith' has always (and necessarily) been consistently linked to others. Taking the sixteen texts as a whole it is employed in combination with 151 other words by the various authors. These can be broken down into a number of general categories (Table 3.2). Table 3.2 might be contextualized by considering it in relation to another alternative using terms never conventionally associated with 'megaliths' (Table 3.3). Bearing in mind what the word 'megalith' actually means, i.e. *big stone*, why is it that we might laugh at 'megalithic' (big stone) vegetable when it is apparently quite normal and unproblematic to refer to big stone evolution, big stone people, big stone territories, big stone rituals, etc? The answer is, of course, the deeply metaphorical, yet unrecognized nature, of the entire discourse used to discuss and describe the past. The term 'megalith' is a classic example of a frozen metaphor whose meaning is now taken as being literal. This emphasizes the point that all archaeological texts are primarily *literary constructions* and can be analysed in an analogous manner to literary texts, bracketing aside the questions of truth, falsity, adequacy or inadequacy in relation to the physical artefact world that are normally asked from the outset. The concern might rather more pertinently be to do with the manner in which the language itself is structured and mobilized to create meaning and sense. The discourse structures what and how we think. In turn, that which we think and say serves to restructure the discourse used.

If we examine the frequency of different words connected with the word 'megalith' in terms of author and data (Figure 3.3) and the rank order of

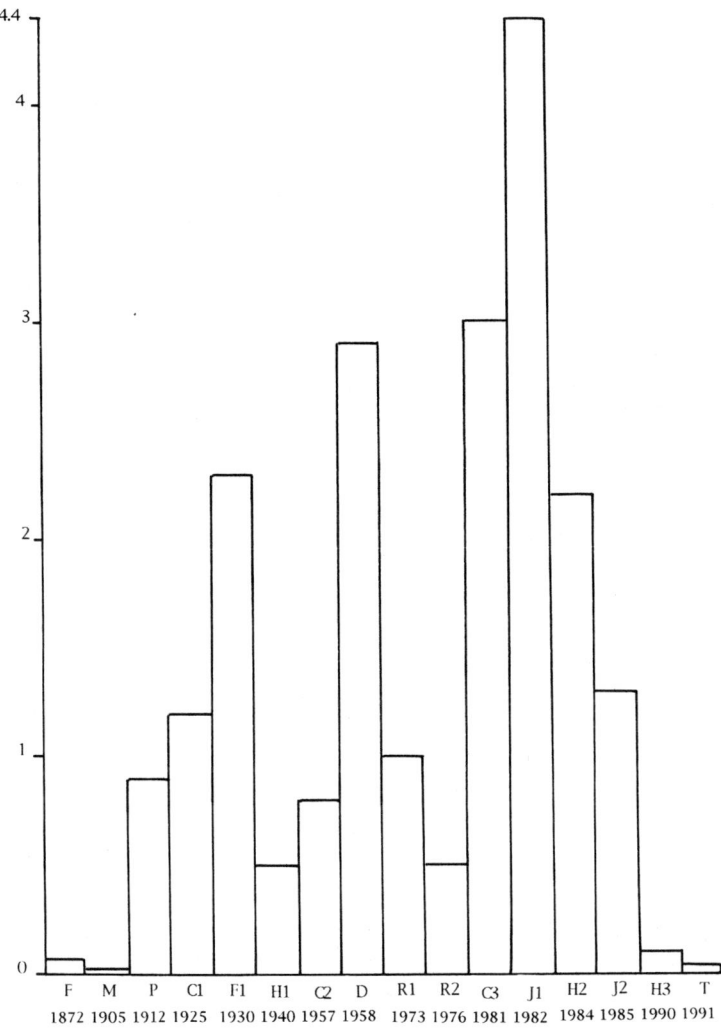

Figure 3.2 The mean frequency of occurrence of the term 'megalith'/page of text analysed according to author and date of publication. For key see caption to Figure 3.1.

usage (Table 3.4) we see a discourse that is at first extremely restricted, then grows and develops and reaches a fluorescence up until the 1960s, and finally becomes restricted again with the advent of so-called 'processual' and 'post-processual' archaeologies. Fergusson (1872) usually confines the word to simply describing sets of architectural remains and the sense

Table 3.2 The words linked with the term 'megalith' in the sample of analysed texts.

1 *General* (no. = 18)

ensembles	components	manifestations
aspects	style	feature
character	examples	elements
homology	type	form
complex	phenomenon	intermediate
versions	contexts	'paramegalithic'

2 *Space* (no. = 14)

districts	areas	regions
territories	concentration	centre
group	province	seaway
spread	sites	distributions
density	Brittany	

3 *Time* (no. = 11)

times	period	phase
evolution	tradition	series
branch	origins	chronology
facies	epoch	

4 *Types of monument* (no. = 9)

circles	huts	passage-tomb
gallery	passage-grave	dolmen
allée	chamber-tomb	gallery-grave

5 *Architecture* (no. = 35)

remains	work	monument
chamber	cist	rude stone
monument	blocks	structure
uprights	construction	galleries
architecture	capstone	building
slabs	walling	wall
slab-cist	extensions	lintel 'table'
pillars	stones	chests
façade	vault	passage
'yard'	'fathom'	roofing-slab
architectural type	keystones production	

6 *Art* (no. = 2)

art	rude-stone-art

7 *Artefacts* (no. = 3)

pottery	pendants	axes

8 *Death* (no. = 18)

burial-chambers	burial-places	funerary monuments
grave	funerary structures	coffers
grave chamber	grave goods	tombs
burial	cemeteries	mortuary practices
collective tomb	collective burial	tomb-practice
funeral-practice	funerary usage	skeleton

Table 3.2 *Continued*

9 *Ritual* (no. = 12)		
sepulchral chamber	sepulchral architecture	temples
faith	religion	burial
ritual	rites	cult
sacred sites	superstition	ideological megalithicism
10 *People* (no. = 22)		
people	builders	civilization
populations	building-traders	navigators
building-ancestors	man	settlers
folk	race	culture
civilization	colonization	influence
creativity	diffusion	idea
creativity	occupation	chiefs
aristocracy		
11 *Work of archaeologists* (no. = 7)		
'problem'	problem	controversies
antiquities	specialists	studies
literature		

Table 3.3 Some alternative words to associate with the term 'megalithic'.

megalithic vegetable
megalithic sago pudding
megalithic horse
megalithic Volvo
megalithic spaghetti
megalithic buttercup
megalithic mouse
megalithic cheese
megalithic underwear
megalithic hat
megalithic brain
megalithic psychotherapy
megalithic undergraduate
megalithic politician

intended remains on a more or less literal level. Subsequently, metaphorical usage dominates and the meanings of the word become almost infinitely extended to link with radically different terms such as 'race', 'region' and 'culture', although in terms of ranked orders of usage there is

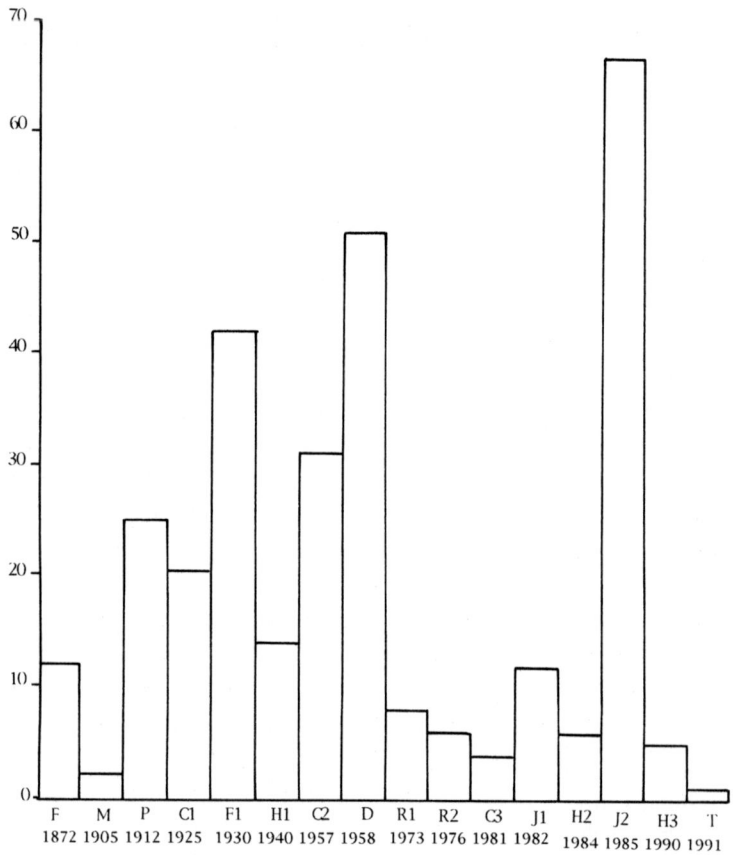

Figure 3.3 The frequency of different words linked with the term 'megalith' in relation to author and publication date. For key see caption to Figure 3.1.

remarkable consistency through time, with 'monument' and 'tomb' used more frequently than others. In 'processual' and 'post-processual' accounts metaphorical extension of sense is mainly restricted to the categories of architecture and death, but is also used to refer to the work of archaeologists themselves. So, at one level, 'processual' and 'post-processual' archaeologies return us to the meanings ascribed at the origins of the discourse, an example of manner in which exactly the same word – rather than having a consistency of usage and sense – changes its meaning and has

Table 3.4 The three most common words used in combination with the term 'megalith' by author and date of publication. The words used are ranked according to their order of frequency and the percentages of usage noted for each rank. The percentage of the total number of combinations accounted for by the three most commonly used words is also given.

Author	Date	Rank 1 Word	%	Rank 2 Word	%	Rank 3 Word	%	Total %
Fergusson	1872	remains	46	monument	20	art	9	75
Montelius	1905	grave	100	–	–	–	–	100
Peet	1912	monument	36	people	11	area	8	55
Childe	1925	tomb	24	culture	21	builders	14	59
Forde	1930	tomb	20	culture	16	architecture	6	42
Hawkes	1940	tomb	28	religion	20	pass. grave	8	56
Childe	1957	tomb	33	builders	9	culture	8	50
Daniel	1958	tomb	28	monument	15	builders	11	54
Renfrew	1973	tomb	50	construction	10	architect	10	70
Renfrew	1976	tomb	27	monument	18	builders	18	63
Chapman	1981	tomb	86	'problem'	5	'area'	5	96
Jarman	1982	monument	24	tomb	18	area	18	60
Hodder	1984	monument	67	burial	5	problem	5	77
Joussaume	1985	monument	35	building	21	tomb	4	60
Hodder	1990	tomb	40	burial	30	monument	10	80
Thomas	1991	tomb	100	–	–	–	–	100

different connotations through time in relation to different styles of analysis and understanding.

Little Discursive Treasures

As is well known, at a general level an explanatory discourse has moved from a stress on diffusion and megaliths as part of a spatial transmission of culture around the Atlantic seaboards of Europe, to a 'processual' emphasis on population and territory, to a 'post-processual' concern with symbolism, gender, power relations and the nature of a megalithic space. The historicity of a megalithic discourse would appear, then, to be characterized by changing interpretations, while at any one time generations of archaeologists appear to be in broad agreement as to what megaliths mean and how they may be best understood. Considering the literature at a more finegrained level, despite apparent changes of theoretical orientation, it remains peculiarly restricted and constrained. The same types of statements tend to be repeated over and over again, evidently too good to be lost. To exemplify the point I want to consider one more recent example in some detail.

In 1984 Ian Hodder published 'Burials, houses, women and men in the European neolithic', the main claims of this article being subsequently repeated in his *The Domestication of Europe* (1990). Part of the explicit authorial position taken in both texts is their representation as a radical break with previous (especially 'processual') discourses on megaliths. Hodder's innovation is to argue that megaliths symbolize or mean houses. In attempting to substantiate this argument he draws eight points of similarity between the form of central European Linearbankeramik long houses and long mounds on the northern and western European periphery. He reflects on the argument put forward in his 1984 paper in the context of a recent collection of papers (Hodder 1992). He writes that since the initial publication of the 1984 paper the idea has been proved more and more plausible to archaeologists, and cites as evidence of this Sherratt's (1990) adoption of it (Hodder 1992: 21). Now this idea that tombs might be connected to houses was well known to the 'traditional' archaeologists of the 1920s to 1950s, who did not emphasize it too much except in so far as it was used to back up a general diffusionary framework purporting to account for the spread of megaliths from one area of Europe to the next, and their work is cited by Hodder. If we were to trace an origin for the idea itself it would have to be to one of the first scientific studies undertaken of megalithic tombs in Sweden by Sven Nilsson. It was one well known to Montelius, a fellow Swede, who used it as the foundation for his interpretation of megaliths in 1905, which also argued that they were derived from house forms. Through the translation of Montelius's work into German it became known more widely in European archaeological circles. Nilsson's book *The Primitive Inhabitants of Scandinavia* was published originally in four parts between 1838–43 and translated into English in 1868. In it Nilsson systematically compares the ground plans of houses (Eskimo huts in Greenland and North America) with those of Swedish passage graves (Figure 3.4). He explicitly draws seven points of morphological similarity in his discussion of form; proportions; height; size; direction of the long narrow side gallery; the division of the vault into stalls (Nilsson 1868: 139).

Hodder's argument is similarly based on a style of analogical argument adducing morphological similarities. Nilsson concludes his discussion by stating: 'One cannot but be astonished, when reading the description of

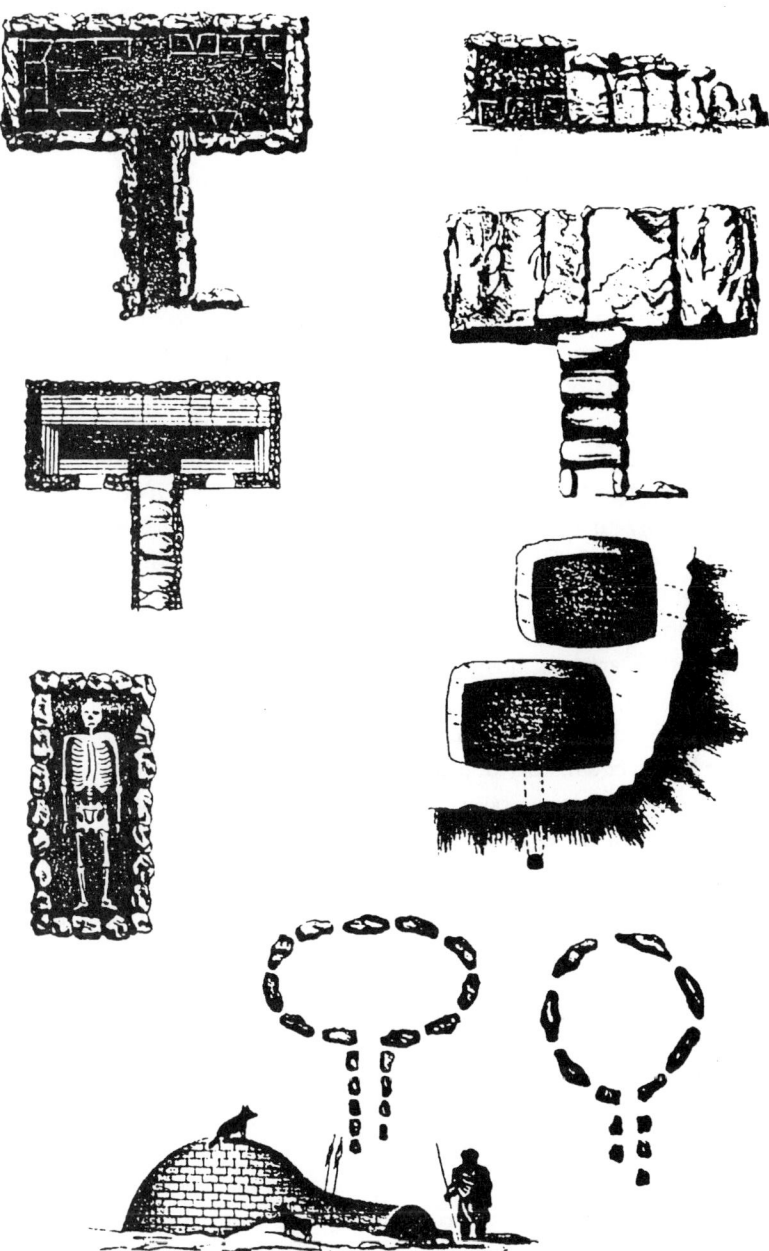

Figure 3.4 Reproduction of plate XIV from Nilsson's *The Primitive Inhabitants of Scandinavia* showing ground plans of Swedish passage graves and a reconstruction diagram of an Eskimo house.

our Scandinavian gallery graves, to find it applicable, almost word for word to the Greenland huts' (Nilsson 1868: 135). He also comments that 'during the years which have elapsed since I first discovered and pointed out this resemblance . . . I have carefully examined many of the Eskimo huts and found my former statement more and more confirmed' (ibid.: 141). So Hodder in 1984 comes to exactly the same general conclusion as Nilsson did 146 years previously, bases his argument on the same type of analogical reasoning, and later states, like Nilsson, that he is more and more personally convinced of the plausibility of the general position. From antiquarianism to post-processualism a megalithic discourse has turned full circle and returned to its own origins, backing up its claim on the basis of drawing points of formal similarity and reaffirming the power of the argument on the archaeological mind. Of course, there are important differences: Hodder compares different classes of archaeological data, Nilsson is involved in drawing ethnographic analogies; Hodder socializes his account by making reference to power relations between men and women and control of the land, while Nilsson does not. But the point at issue here is not whether Hodder's or Nilsson's interpretations are right or wrong, convincing or not, or that the basis for the idea and the mode of argumentation are not novel but form one of the *earliest* explanatory accounts of megaliths, but why this notion of a connection between tomb and house has had such power over the archaeological imagination. It does not merely reflect a history of ideas in archaeology and the routes by means of which these are filtered between and transformed by individual authors. I want to suggest instead that the implications of this repetition are more profound. 'Good' ideas, such as this one, get recycled, reused and reappropriated; they are little discursive treasures that are too valuable to be forgotten. But why?

These are not personal criticisms, but criticisms of a tradition of thought, an interrogation of a discourse rather than that of an individual who necessarily operates within its terms of reference. What may be said is clearly constrained by a discourse of writing about megaliths in general, a code for producing knowledge which is *out of control* because it is not understood, or even suspected to exist. The implications are that if we are, or want, to write in a radically different manner about megaliths, or indeed anything else from the past, a first requirement would seem to be to attempt to understand exactly what the discourse is that we inhabit and how it operates. There is a need to begin to excavate what determines an archaeological consciousness to think in one way rather than another. The chief point at issue is: given that megaliths *might* be interpreted in so many different ways, why is this clearly not the case? Why do we tend to think about them in such a limited number of ways? What constrains the archaeological imagination? The response that it is because we have arrived at a kernel of truth and therefore have no alternative but to repeat ourselves, is surely too glib and self-congratulatory to be entertained.

Some Principles of the Genre

The grand narrative

All accounts of megaliths are narrative constructions and all the authors considered in the survey, from Fergusson to Thomas, *assume* that there is something linking these stone monuments together, either at a regional or a European level: battlegrounds, people, ideas, races, chiefs, critical resources, house symbolism, ideology or power. In books about European megaliths the reader follows the author on a journey around a textually constructed continent. The lines of movement in the text between different European nation-states are often integral to the argument being made. So with Montelius we embark on a journey that begins in the Orient and ends in Scandinavia. The dolmens and passage graves metaphorically take on the roles of peoples and their journeys. Joussaume's *Dolmens for the Dead* (this time on a world rather than continental scale) reads like a travel guide with Joussaume himself as personal narrator: 'We cannot leave the Near East without a word about . . .' (p. 258), 'We will not linger over the megalithic monuments of the Balearic islands . . .' (p. 220), 'This journey through the world of dolmens' (p. 295) and so on. The reader, in effect, becomes his anonymous travel companion. The spatial and narrative flow and organization of Joussaume's text (and other texts as well) is as vital to the message and arguments as is the discursive content. They frequently exist in a relation of tension and systematically act so as to deconstruct and undermine each other. Renfrew (1973; 1976) in his 'processual' position claims a series of independent centres for the 'invention' of megaliths. Similarly, for Hodder (1984) no necessary connection exists between megaliths in different areas of Europe. Yet the 'routes' taken in their texts to describe and discuss the evidence are exactly the same as in traditional archaeological discourse (Figure 3.5). We begin on the fringes, in the Aegean or Scandinavia, and go round in a prescribed direction. There is no logical reason for this. The texts could, on the basis of their theoretical grounding (independent origins), begin and go anywhere, trace new routes

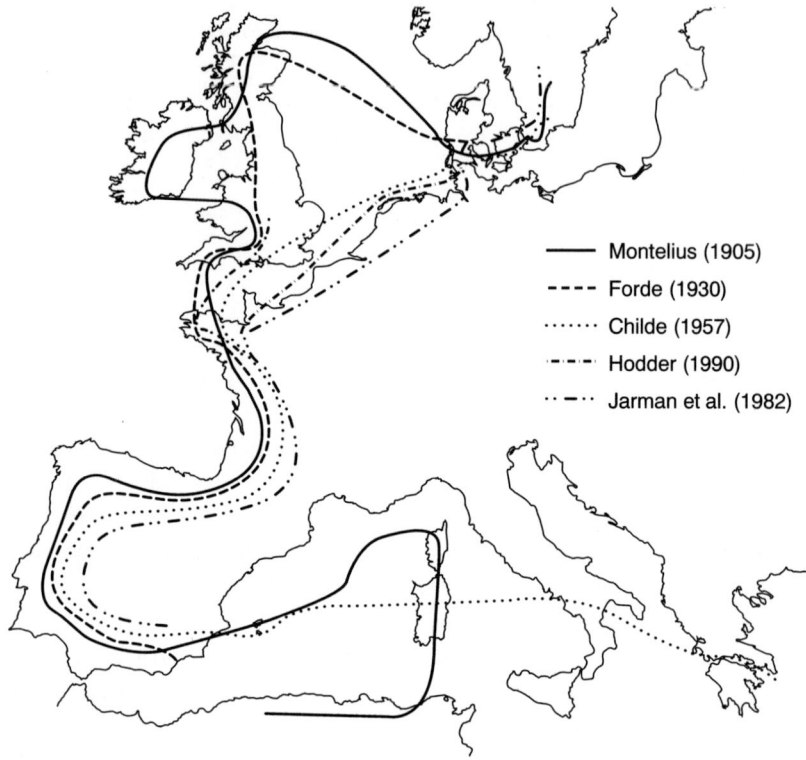

Figure 3.5 Some 'megalithic' textual journeys around Europe.

and directions. The fact that they do not implies the operation of a powerful subconscious discursive constraint on the 'correct' manner in which to construct an 'acceptable' text.

The subsumption of particularity

The notion that what are termed megaliths have nothing whatsoever to do with each other has constantly threatened archaeological discourses ever since the category was first invented. The history of archaeological writing about megaliths is one of a continual definition and redefinition of the terminology. In the early works of Fergusson and Peet, stone circles, menhirs and alignments are all included in the accounts. The category of the megalith is kaleidoscopic and threatens to explode. From Childe onwards the discourse is more restricted, revolving around stone chambers.

Then what counts as a true megalithic chamber becomes problematic. Time and time again attempts are made to save the discourse and impose unity. The monuments of Sardinia and the Balaeric islands get dropped from the discussion by Daniel, who distinguishes between 'cyclopean' and 'megalithic' architecture. For Renfrew, the Maltese megaliths do not fit the category and become temples instead. There are sometimes queries about how big a stone should be to be a big stone, i.e. a megalith, and whether a rock-cut monument can be properly included in the category. Is Newgrange really the same kind of thing as a Pembrokeshire dolmen? The category 'megalith' unifies what are disparate things. The more archaeologists pay attention to empirical detail the more the analysis shatters the category that it sets out to investigate and that supposedly unifies, but this cannot be accepted. Megaliths are frequently labelled as tombs, but are they? Is a single functional attribution adequate? Might this provide a basis for unification? Renfrew (1973; 1976) thinks both that they are and are not, sometimes referring to 'tombs'. A typical line from Thomas's book reads: 'as with the Cotswold–Severn tombs, then, the passage-grave tradition integrates temporal control into the control of access to the chamber' (Thomas 1991: 45). The totally different tomb morphology of Cotswold–Severn tombs and passage graves is explained as part of a desire to control the movement of the body through space. Difference is recognized (there are different megalithic 'tombs') but is simultaneously denied in a desire to create a narrative structure and an explanatory account that can work with and embrace different categories of monuments. But why should totally different cultural arrangements of stones be forced into the same narrative? Why is this natural? Why is it needed? Why might it not be suggested that a Cotswold – Severn tomb and a passage grave have completely different meaning sets and associations? Perhaps this is a failure to think and allow for difference, a desire to tame and domesticate the difference of the past within a single narrative structure. The unthinkable of the archaeological discourse that controls us is to suggest that all megaliths, or different typological groups of megaliths, have nothing whatsoever to do with each other. Difference is, then, the unthinkable. Why? The answer resides in that discursive object of knowledge archaeologists themselves have created, 'megalith', which by its very objectification in discourse as a separate entity leads us to expect that we *should* be dealing with a unitary phenomenon.

Not only is there a textual reductionism at work in the manner in which megaliths are operated upon, but also a particular manner to illustrate and represent them – generally as small postage-stamp line diagrams or line plans, set side by side for comparative purposes. The illustrations which occur in recent texts are frequently exactly the same as those used by Montelius ninety years or more before. Like the written message, the illustrative message is constrained by the 'right' way to depict these things.

An obsession with origins

Hawkes opens his *Prehistoric Foundations of Europe* with a quote from Aristotle: 'he who thus considers things in their first growth and origin, whether a State or anything else, will obtain the clearest view of them' (Hawkes 1940: 1). The notion of a single origin is a leitmotif running throughout discourses on megaliths, despite assertions to the contrary. We all know that the earlier work of Montelius, Childe, Daniel and Piggott attempted to trace this origin to the Orient and/or the Aegean. With the advent of 'processual' and 'post-processual' archaeologies we apparently get a totally different perspective. Renfrew suggests independent centres of development (as does Chapman), Hodder stresses local sequences. But this does not in fact result in the abandonment of a concern with origins, but merely displaces it somewhat. For all his independent centres of development Renfrew still has a single origin in a postulated movement of farmers to an Atlantic façade where the megaliths mushroom up. Hodder's point of origin is in the central European long-house tradition, Jarman's in a pastoralist economy, Thomas's in a need to assert ideological control over populations. What we have here are an origin in movement, an origin in the house, an origin in the economy, an origin in political structure. The theoretical emphasis has of course shifted somewhat, but only in terms of substituting a conceptual or a more geographically diffused 'beginning' for one located rather more precisely, in a geographical sense, in south-east Europe.

Discourses that Deconstruct

A close examination of all works concerned with megaliths shows that, time and time again, the texts embrace an uneasy agglomeration of contradictory relations, so much so that they deconstruct their own striving for meaning. In *Orienten och Europa* Montelius puts forward the case for an Oriental origin of megaliths. He is quite unequivocal on this. He also discusses at length the Scandinavian monuments and puts forward a typological sequence for their development. This is a four-phase sequence from simple box-like dolmens to gallery graves (Montelius 1905: 183). In so doing he clearly wanted to order the Scandinavian remains into an evolutionary sequence. The implications of this, not lost on other archaeologists, is that here we might have an independent Scandinavian origin, or at the very least an internal development from dolmen to passage grave. Montelius is unable even to entertain the thought, arguing for separate waves of Oriental inspiration introducing first dolmens and later passage graves (ibid.: 187). Why then does he introduce transitional typological forms between dolmens and passage graves, why all the detail?

In Childe's work there is a systematic tension between wanting to provide a single grand narrative for the megaliths, based on a notion of eastern 'inspiration' and realizing that there may be nothing that links them together, that the category is completely vacuous. In the first paragraph of chapter 12 of the 1957 edition of *The Dawn of European Civilization*, entitled 'Megalith builders and beaker-folk' he states: 'the diffusion of Oriental culture in Western Europe must have been effected in part by maritime intercourse. And evidence of such intercourse is supposedly afforded by the architecture of groups of tombs' (Childe 1957: 260). The significant word here is 'supposedly'. Why should Childe use it at all? He explicitly considers certain features which might be argued to be common factors linking earlier European prehistoric monuments. First he considers the application of the word 'megalith' to describe the monuments and finds it inadequate because European tombs may be built of big or small stones, or may be cut out of rock. Second, he considers other potential classificatory devices in which archaeologists refer to passage graves, long cists, etc., but considers these terms equally arbitrary and useless because there exists such a bewildering variety of forms. Third, he examines whether collective burial might provide a unifying thread but notes that it 'can hardly represent the unifying idea, since collective burial in natural caves was practised even in mesolithic Palestine' (ibid.: 266). Grave goods are of little help either because they differ so radically throughout Europe and the presence of exotic imports or metals, in some cases, does nothing to clarify the situation. So, going systematically through various categorizations and types of archaeological evidence, Childe is forced to acknowledge its particularity and the difference between various 'tomb' types. In so doing he effectively destroys any reason to believe in European Neolithic 'tombs' or megaliths as a unitary archaeological class or entity for which a single explanation might suffice. Yet he is also unable to accept this. Having stressed architectural difference he then denies it: 'No new typology need be attempted here. The architectural agreements cited reveal the megalithic province as a cultural continuum' (ibid.: 269). The only 'agreements' Childe in fact mentions are 'seemingly arbitrary peculiarities of plan and in accessories such as porthole slabs and forecourts' (ibid.: 267), yet as he also points out these are only found in a few of the monuments.

It is my suspicion that Childe wanted to accept difference but was unable to do so. The evidence for difference was, and is, overwhelming, but Childe inhabited a discourse that would not allow him to accept this as an intellectual possibility, for to do so would be to fall into a terminological and explanatory abyss. This is repeated again and again in the literature. Variability is stressed, recognized, and then almost immediately suppressed. This is also manifested in the obsession with origins; for Renfrew and Hodder the origin of megaliths in different areas is independent, and yet it is not. For Thomas the megaliths are polysemous texts, and yet they are not, because the same story is encountered in the interpretation of each 'text'.

Conclusion

The word, and the discursive object of knowledge, 'megalith' is one that has surfaced throughout 120 years and more of texts. *Rarity* (repetition) is a primary characteristic of this megalithic discourse. Given that there is so much that might be said or written it is surprising how constrained the discourse appears to be. From the very beginning the value of such a discursive object has been questioned and its appearance and use in the literature have created as many problems and confusions as have been solved, yet it continues to be employed and has almost taken on a life of its own. The concept is acknowledged as useless and yet it remains so apparently valuable that it cannot be thrown away and must be retained. As the discourse extends and ramifies through time the meaning of the term changes in various ways and its ability to unify that which is a disparate collection of archaeological remains weakens, yet the notion of a unity – embedded in the concept itself – between various stone monuments is so strong that it cannot be denied. That would require a fresh fold in thought, a rethinking of every archaeological assumption. This unthinkable of archaeology surfaces recurrently to deconstruct the texts in which the discursive object is employed, undermining their claim to make sense or meaning of the data. I suppose the question becomes this: do we want to try and think what to us is the unthinkable, that the primary characteristic of these European megaliths is difference rather than sameness? Could we think there might be as enormous a gulf between a Cotswold–Severn cairn and a portal dolmen, or between a passage grave at Los Millares and one in Denmark, as between a Beaker and an Acheulean hand axe? An archaeological discourse on megaliths has been productive of knowledge and understanding, of texts and lectures that purport to represent some prehistoric realities. It has similarly restrained and restricted thought so that we have an endless series of textual repetitions with our knowledge going round in circles. Discourse has always begun and ended at the monument. An alternative might be to stop thinking of these monuments as pivotal in any sense and inscribe them in a discourse which is *topological* in form, i.e. so that they become points for discussion among many others — non-privileged sites for discursive articulation. In this short chapter I have written the word 'megalith' or 'megalithic' 64 times, excluding the use of the word in tables and captions! Is it useful for us now to start to cross the word out in our texts, in a classic Derridean move, and accept that megaliths do not exist, while realizing they will almost certainly continue to do so?

4

The Metaphorical Transformations of Wala Canoes

Strathern (1988) has argued that Melanesian people differ from Europeans in understanding relations between producers and products in multiple and divisible terms. She produces an analytical fiction, contrasting an 'ideal type' of a Western body, which is unitary and sexed, with a Melanesian 'ideal' body, which is partible and has both masculine and feminine elements. Bodies become 'male' or 'female' not because of observable biological sexual characteristics but by virtue of the nature of their positioning in social acts. Men and women have both male and female elements which become activated in different social contexts. Gender construction is much more than a simple articulation of difference on pre-existing male or female bodies. It becomes something endowed on persons and their bodies, artefacts, events, architecture and spaces. 'Male' and 'female' are two principles that constitute society; not distinctive attributes of different bodies, but forms of action.

While we may be uneasy with the contrast Strathern draws between Melanesian and Western bodies (cf. Butler 1990) and the associated notion that work or objects cannot be alienated (Thomas 1991: 57), what is valuable here, and that which has been cogently stressed in the writings of other Melanesian anthropologists (e.g. Battaglia 1990; Keller 1988; Jolly 1991a; 1991b; MacKenzie 1991; Munn 1977; 1986; Thomas 1995), is a way of thinking about the relationship between producers and their products centring upon *activity*. It is this that produces meanings and serves to gender both persons and artefacts. Objects are created not in contradistinction to persons, but out of persons. A conceptual separation of subject from object (with the latter regarded as inert 'dead' matter) is usefully avoided. Production becomes a performance through which persons and objects create and define each other. The artefact is as crucial and as active a participant in this performance as the person. Production is a practice in which relations with kin, affines and others may be acknowledged, created or marked through a realm of material things. The work of men or women may not necessarily be identified as the work *of* men or women, and the meanings of the artefact may not necessarily be grounded in the person of an individual, or in terms of a simple binary opposition between male and female.

In the field of cultural production and reproduction it is the case that an order of artefacts performs its symbolic work of socialization and the creation of social identities silently, continuously and, therefore, relatively unremarkably. Through creating, exchanging and ordering a world of artefacts people create an ordering of the world of social relations. Such a process of objectification is about the construction of meaning and values about social relationships and self-understandings of those meanings and values through material forms. Social images are constructed through the material media of artefacts.

These images and forms of presentation and representation in which persons 'present themselves to themselves' (Strathern 1990: 26) may not be, and often cannot be, articulated in spoken language. The meanings created through artefacts and words cannot be exchanged for each other, and thus the material object forms a powerful metaphorical medium through which people may reflect on their world in a way simply not possible with words alone. Through the artefact, layered and often contradictory sets of meanings can be conveyed simultaneously. The artefact may be inherently ambiguous in its meaning contents precisely because it acts to convey information about a variety of symbolic domains through the same media, and because it may perform the cultural work of revealing fundamental tensions and contradictions in human social experience. In other words the artefact, through its silent 'speech' and 'written' presence, speaks what cannot be spoken, writes what cannot be written, and articulates that which remains conceptually separated in social practice (Tilley 1991). It is a multiple site for the inscription and negotiation of social relations, power and social dynamics. The artefact is both interwoven with and recursively engaged in the production and constitution of society.

In this chapter I consider the metaphoric meanings of the construction of canoes on Wala island, Vanuatu, in the past and in the present, from the general perspective of objectification processes, and as polysemous objects in which notions of place and landscape, rootedness and journeying, exchange, gender and historical meanings become layered and entangled together, drawing on ethnohistorical information and personal field observations.

Canoes as Dominant Symbols

Wala is one of six coral islands, known locally as the Small Islands, situated just off the coast of north-east Malekula, Vanuatu (Figure 4.1). It is barely 1 km in diameter, fringed by reef and low coral cliffs except for a white sand beach in the south-west facing the mainland of Malekula across a narrow strait. The population of around 200 persons, divided into five exogamous patrilineal clans, is concentrated in one village, Serser, by the beach. People moved to this site, under missionary influence, about sixty years ago. Wala has always been noted as the navigational centre for north-east Malekula, the name 'Wala' meaning 'to run before the wind', 'to sail' or 'to go on an ocean voyage' (Layard 1942: 455). The canoe has always been the largest portable artefact made by Wala islanders and everyone owns or has access to one. Early ethnographers remarked on the sophistication and degree of elaboration of the canoes built on the Small Islands of northern Malekula compared with most of the rest of Vanuatu (Speiser 1990; Haddon 1937). The scene on the beach today with scores of canoes drawn up on the sand is still very similar to that depicted in photographs from the early twentieth century in ethnographic works.

Canoes still remain the principal means by which people reach the mainland, supplemented only very recently by a single small motor boat. Early in the mornings children paddle across the narrow strait to go to the mission school. Catholics paddle over to the church on the mainland for Sunday morning service. People leave for their gardens on the mainland, returning in the evening with the canoe laden with produce: yams, manioc, coconuts and citrus fruits. Wala has no running water and only limited amounts of rain water are collected. In the past fresh water was brought over to the island by canoe in bamboo shoots, nowadays in plastic containers. Two wells sunk in the village of Serser have water of dubious quality

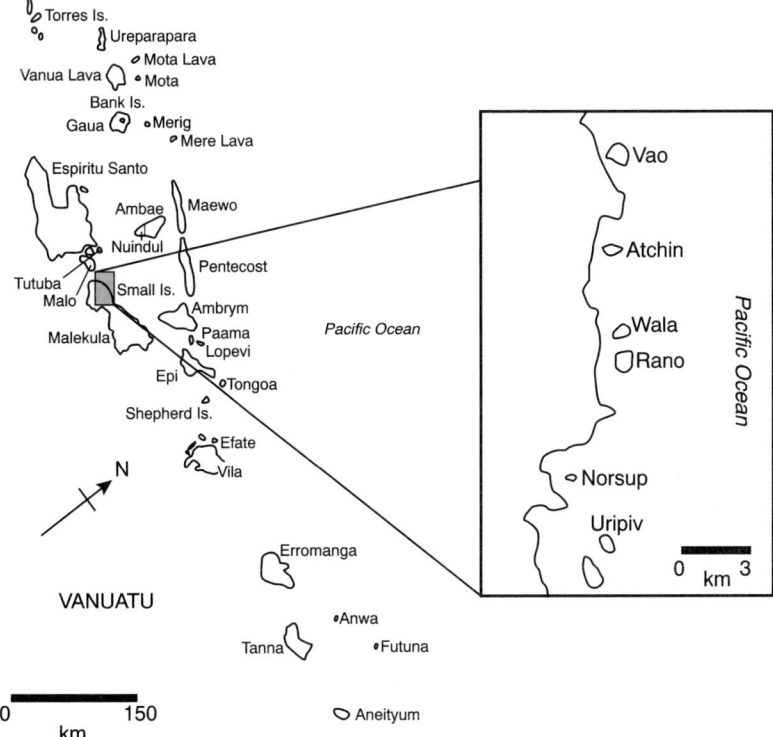

Figure 4.1 The location of Wala and the Small Islands of north-east Malekula, Vanuatu.

subject to salt-water contamination, and are largely used for washing. Old canoe hulls protect the ridge poles and palm thatch of the houses from the rains. When a person dies the corpse is placed in a canoe during the period of mourning. Paddle dances tell the story of the arrival and departure of canoes. Canoes are used extensively for inshore fishing along the coral reefs and for offshore deep-water fishing. In the past canoes were used to transport smooth stones taken from along river courses on the mainland, to erect along the dancing grounds in the centre of the island. Magic stones, slit drums, pigs, building materials, adzes, indeed most of the resources needed to sustain life and ceremony were, and are, brought to Wala by canoe. With the exception of fishing expeditions, the canoes today are only used for the twenty-minute journey to and from the mainland. In the past they were used in warfare and long voyages were undertaken along the coasts and between the major islands forming the northern part of the

Vanuatu archipelago to exchange gifts and acquire tusked pigs. The canoe today has become a living symbol of tradition, of *kastom* (see Chapter 8).

It is no exaggeration to state that there is hardly any part of life on Wala that is not intimately connected with the canoe. It represents tradition, sustains life, protects dwellings, provides the medium for social contacts, material and spiritual exchange. Precisely because the canoe operates in all these different domains and links them together, it is an artefact invested with considerable symbolic potency: a condenser and transformer of signs, a metaphorical vehicle for transmitting fundamental beliefs and values.

Today, there are three basic types of canoe, all named after the principal tree from which they are constructed (the *rav*). They all have single outriggers. Three basic forms are distinguished and named after different prow forms:

1 *Rav Msore*: canoes with extended prows with figure-heads.
2 *Rav Solip*: canoes with attached prow figure-heads.
3 *Rav Res*: simple canoes without prow figure-heads.

Virtually all of the approximately 200 canoes which I saw drawn up on the beach on Wala were of the simplest form without prow figure-heads and were undecorated. During my stay on the island I was fortunate to be able to observe six examples of the more complex canoes being built. This was in preparation for the greatest event in the recent history of Wala island: a Sunday afternoon visit by the 'Melanesian Spearhead Group': the ninth annual general meeting of the presidents of the different Melanesian countries. They were to have lunch and conduct a seminar in the small newly established (July 1993) tourist resort on the island, part of a three-day conference being held in northern Malekula. The six traditionally designed and crafted canoes were being built to carry the politicians over to Wala island from the mainland. The canoes had to be 'correct' in every detail and conform to the dictates of *kastom*. The fame of Wala was at stake.

A floating forest

In her paper on Gawan canoes of the Massim, Munn (1977) stressed the manner in which fabrication is never simply technological construction, but instead 'developmental symbolic processes that transform both socially significant properties or operational capacities of objects, and significant

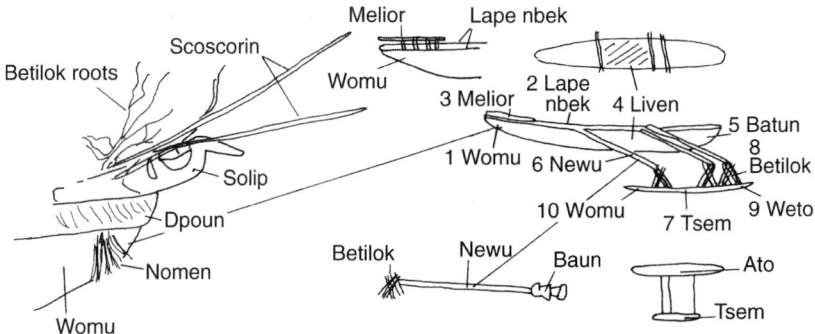

Figure 4.2 Named parts of the Wala canoes (Wala/Rano language). *Ato*: hull. 1: *Womu* (bow). Top of the *rav* ('canoe tree'). A soft whitewood. 5: *Batun* (stern). Base of the trunk of the 'canoe tree'. 7: *Tsem* (outrigger). Young branch of the 'canoe tree'. 2: *Lape Nbek* (beading around the canoe hull). Roots of the 'female' banyan tree. 3: *Melior* (carrying attachment at the bow). Melior tree. Hardwood. 4: *Liven* (central part of hull between outrigger booms). 6: *Newu* (outrigger booms). *Bauer* tree. A hard wood with a red hue. 8: *Betilok* (outrigger attachments). Betilok tree. 9: *Weto* (rear end of outrigger boom). Nomen (tassel made from edible white coconut fibres). *Dpoun* (casing at bow end of canoe from base of coconut leaf where it is attached to the trunk). *Solip* Prow figurehead. Bauer wood. *Scoscorin* (protective branches of the Neor tree over the prow figurehead).

aspects of the relations between persons and objects' (ibid.: 39). This provides the specific starting point for the present analysis. Munn points out that canoe construction, at the most basic symbolic plane, involves taking heavy wood from the bush and converting it into a mobile artefact whose most desirable qualities are lightness and buoyancy. I was told that a canoe should be like a flying fish skimming the ocean waves. Figure 4.2 shows the major named parts of the Wala canoes. Wood and materials from a remarkably wide range of trees and plants are used to construct and decorate canoes. The hull, – about 4 m long with a maximum width of 45 cm – is made from the hollowed-out trunk of the *rav*, 'canoe tree' (*Gyrocarpus americanus*). The single outrigger – about 2 m in length – is made from a branch of the same tree. It provides a soft whitewood, easily dug out. Today, metal adzes are employed. The traditional technique was to burn out the trunk and cut it with a shell adze. The canoe tree is unmistakable during the dry season, between May and August, when it loses all its leaves. It is largely confined to low-altitude coastal strips up to 150 m. Trees with a suitable trunk shape and size are not found on Wala today and must be taken from the mainland.

The rim of the canoe hull is finished with the addition of a narrow strip of wood taken from the aerial roots of the *nbek* or banyan tree (*Ficus benghalensis*). These utterly distinctive and massive trees, growing to a height of 30 m or more, are the kings and queens of the forest. Aerial roots develop from their branches, descend and take root in the soil below to become new trunks. In this manner the tree can spread laterally almost indefinitely and may, in time, assume the appearance of a dense thicket as a result of the tangle of roots and trunks. They shade all the ancient dancing grounds on Wala (see below).

All canoes have three outrigger booms, about 2 m long and asymmetrically placed, one at the front and two at the back. All three outrigger booms and the attached carved prow figure-head (about 50 cm long) are made from the wood of the *bauer* tree (Callophyllum inophyllum). This is a massive seashore tree, growing up to 30 m high, with a crown extending up to 25 m across. Confined to the littoral strip, just above the high-water mark, it has long, spreading branches (the lower ones often horizontal and leaning over the water) and large fleshy leaves. This wood is hard, with a reddish hue.

The prow end of the canoe has two attached carrying handles made from the wood of the *melior* tree (*Dysoxylum gaudichaudianum*). This is a large canopy tree of the lowland forest, resembling a European ash, providing a hard and resilient wood. The outrigger booms are attached to the outrigger by means of strips of wood driven diagonally into holes bored into the float so that the sticks cross one another. The attachment is secured by lashings of coconut rope. The sticks used for this attachment are from the *betilok* (*Myrsine* genus), a birch-like shrub growing in areas of disturbed regenerating forest. The roots of the same tree are attached over the top of the carved prow-head, together with two long wispy branches (the *scoscorin*) from the *neuru* tree (*Casuarina equisetifolia*). This is a tree common to the coastal strip with pendant, needle-like foliage, similar to a conifer and giving it a feathery appearance. It has the ability to grow on the most barren land, such as exposed coral platforms virtually devoid of soil (Wheatley 1992).

The outrigger booms are lashed to the hull and the outrigger with rope made from coconut fibres. These brown fibres are taken from *long* coconut shells. Other appended tassel decorations at the front and back of the canoe (*nomen*) are taken from the edible fibres of the shell casing of smaller, *rounded* coconuts. The carved prow-head is lashed to the canoe after the wood of the canoe prow has been covered with sheet-like fibre taken from the casing of the coconut leaf at the point where it joins the trunk of the tree.

On special occasions the entire canoe may be beautified with brightly coloured cycas leaves attached to the boom lashings and tucked in around the prow-head. These leaves are widely used as ceremonial body decoration, attached to arm bands and belts.

Thus, no less than eight different plants and trees were used to construct the canoes. There is no functional or utilitarian reason which could explain such a wide choice. Heartwood and sapwood is employed, softwoods and hardwoods, woods of contrasting colour, grain and degree of suppleness, aerial and underground tree roots, young branches and older branches, different fruits from the coconut. The plants and trees employed grow in a wide variety of different environments: in areas of bare coral, in the litoral zone overhanging the sea, on Wala island, on the mainland, away from the beach in the interior of the tropical forest, in areas which are freshly regenerating and in others with long-established growth. The leaves, fruits, bark and other physical characteristics of the trees used (from the deciduous *rav* to the conifer-like *neuru*) are all different. Although people on Wala do not, to my knowledge, make the connection explicitly, the canoe brings together, in one artefact, all the different environmental and physical characteristics of the major trees of the forest, and unites or marries them together as a floating forest. The hull may be beautified with leaves which 'sprout' from it, just as fresh leaves sprout from the canoe tree, at the end of the dry season. The top of the trunk of this tree forms the bow end of the canoe, the base, the stern. Thus, the movement of the canoe on water, bow first, can be regarded as a symbolic transformation of the upward growth of the canoe tree. Both extend themselves in space, sprouting leaves. At one level of symbolism the canoe is a material metaphor for the forest which surrounds and envelops people throughout their daily lives. It is a forest transformed into motion. Houses and villages are rarely visible from the shoreline in Malekula. To an observer standing on the mainland, Wala and the other Small Islands along the coast of Malekula appear uninhabited. From Wala the only visible trace of habitation on Malekula is the large and recent clearing around the Catholic mission and school. The canoe unites the trees of the forest just as it unites people and their life experiences from the moment of birth to the moment of death.

Birds and roots

The bow of the canoe has a carved figure-head (*solip*) lashed to its tip with coconut rope. The standard Wala island form of this design now consists of two main elements: a bird figure-head with outstretched wings curving backwards embracing a fish. Two canoes being built on the neighbouring island of Rano had variants on this form. One consisted of a bird design only. The other, occurring on the bow of a canoe with an extended prow (*Rav Msore*), consisted of two birds with heads facing away from each other over the top of a pig mounted on another bird. The bird form always occurs and senior men have individual rights to carve variants on this design. The only other design element, carved today, to occur in conjunction with the bird, is the flying fish or the pig. Extending above and out beyond the prow design, over the bird head, two long wispy twigs are affixed and above them again, a tangle of tree roots. The decorated canoe prow-head of hard, red (*bauer* tree) wood contrasts with the creamy yellow-white soft wood of the canoe hull. Traditionally, this figure-head would be blackened by smoking before being attached to the canoe. I saw a number of examples of these blackened bird prow-heads in the houses of senior men, but none were employed on the canoes I saw being built.

The bird design represents the frigate bird (*Fregata ariel*). This bird has a number of fascinating physical and behavioural attributes combining to make it most apposite as the primary, invariant and most significant element in the design of the carved prow. It is a huge sea bird, the largest to occur in Vanuatu, and ranges all over the Pacific Ocean. It keeps mostly out to sea, nesting on small and remote islands. It is mainly black in colour with white patches on the flanks, a great wing span and forked tail. The male has a bright red throat patch which is inflated like a balloon during courtship (Harrison 1983; Bregulla 1992). Frigate birds are superb fliers, soaring magnificently in thermals with little perceptible movement of their wings. They can hover and glide with ease in updrafts along sea cliffs. They have been known to brave cyclones. One of my informants reported seeing them soaring effortlessly over Wala during a violent storm. Another term for the frigate bird is the 'man of war bird' because of its piratical attacks on other fish-eating sea birds. They mob other species, forcing them to disgorge their fish in order to lighten themselves and escape. The fish are swooped up in mid-air by the frigate birds.

The frigate bird thus combines qualities of superb agility, the ability to weather the worst of storms, and voracious habits, terrifying other species. It would be difficult to imagine a more appropriate image for the carved canoe prow-head metaphorically effecting a transference of these desirable qualities to the canoe itself and its crew. The choice of the flying fish design in combination with it reinforces aspects of the same symbolism in relation to the canoe: its desired qualities of buoyancy, being able to glide over the water, and weather storms. The redness of the wood chosen for the prow design strongly indicates that it is the male frigate bird (with a red throat pouch) that is being represented and its aggressive characteristics valorized (see the discussion below).

The frigate bird prow-head is covered with two tentacle-like *neuru* branches and *betilok* roots. The reason for these attachments, I was consistently told, was to protect the carved prow, the most important part of the canoe. Speiser notes that 'it is a gross insult to damage such a prow, and people are said to have been killed for breaking off a boat prow' (Speiser 1990: 225). One informant likened the *neuru* branches to the tentacles of a lobster, protecting it from harm. Such was the almost obsessive concern with the protection of the prow-head that in one case I observed, on the island of Rano, the branches and roots were deemed insufficient and the whole prow end of the canoe had a cage structure of coconut palm branches woven around it which had to be cut loose before the canoe could be launched.

Given that the front of the canoe hull is the part of the tree trunk closest to the sky, the addition of roots in this position, rather than at the stern of the canoe, in effect represents an *inversion* of a literal ordering of nature: roots in the sky, protecting the frigate bird, positioned below. Root imagery carries a heavy symbolic load in north-east Malekula. Roots support, protect and hold up the tree, stimulating growth, making it firm and strong. Their protective powers are clearly being transferred to the canoe and its forward movement. The canoe, unlike the tree, is not anchored to the ground. It is a mobile force which the roots protect as it moves forward. Canoes are always drawn up on the beach with their prows forward, facing the land. The roots are thus highest up on the beach, preventing the canoe from slipping back into the water and being carried away by the waves and the tide. It is interesting to note here that the major reason given for people settling on Wala and the other Small Islands, in the historical past, was the protection this afforded them from attack by inland peoples who were not accustomed to the sea, and who had no means of reaching the islands when the canoes of the inhabitants were all drawn up and 'rooted' on the beach.

In men's traditional club houses on Vao and the other Small Islands of north-east Malekula, as documented by Speiser in 1910, some of the bamboo cane purlins are left with their rootstocks intact, projecting beyond the front edge of the roof (Speiser 1990: 105). Ancestor houses lining the dancing grounds also had a ridgepole consisting of a trunk, complete with roots. The root end pointed forward toward the interior of the dancing grounds. The roots on both the club houses and the ancestor houses represent the opened wings of a bird. The body of the bird is formed by the ridgepole itself (ibid.: 348). Root imagery is thus connected both with height and birds. It links canoe prows, the highest part of the canoe, the gable ends of men's club houses, and the ridgepoles of ancestor houses. The ridges of the club houses were themselves covered by the hulls of old canoes (ibid.: 105), as houses are today. And all these are built exclusively by men. The ridgepoles, with their bird-roots, hold up and protect the men's club house and houses containing the ancestors and ancestral powers, just as the canoe protects those using them. In turn, the canoe covers and protects the ridge of the club house. Height is connected with spiritual power, a dominant theme in Wala culture. The bird depicted by the rootstocks of the houses is the soaring hawk. So the roots over the canoe prow may also be interpreted as representing a hawk soaring over the frigate bird. The hawk is the most ritually important and symbolically significant bird connected with the land. Just like the frigate bird it has ferocious habits, killing other birds. The frigate bird and hawk symbolism of the canoe prow-head thus connects the domains of land and sea and links them to the communal club house in which men sit together, as if in a canoe. The prow adornment is a metaphorical vehicle of meaning that synthesizes, through metonymic association, non-human and human domains, rootedness and movement, land and sea.

On Tanna island in the south of Vanuatu, Bonnemaison (1994) has shown that the canoe is both a metaphor for society and sociality: 'the individuals who meet daily make up the core of a local group, a "canoe" or *niko* as it is called on the island, which itself is linked to a larger "canoe" made up of several patrilocal clans sharing the same territory and mythical heritage' (ibid.: 108). Munn has argued in relation to the island of Gawa, Milne Bay province, Papua New Guinea, that a basic contrast exists between the body-house and the body-sea. These represent opposite poles along an axis of the spatio-temporal extension of the self. The body-sea, in the form of the Gawan canoe, is an exterior self-extending dynamic pole of social being because the canoe establishes social connectivities. The house, on the other hand, is an interiorized bounded world, statically rooted in the heaviness of the ground (Munn 1986: 79).

On Wala the canoe, the club house and its society of men appear to be fundamental metaphorical transformations of each other. The canoe is a floating communal men's house with its roof turned upside down on the water. The club house is conversely an inverted canoe which can no longer float. The spatio-temporal transformation of the self and the move from the interior social world of the men's club house outwards to establish relationships with persons on other islands requires that the club house be 'opened out' with the men now sitting in its roof.

A basic contrast between rootedness and journeying is at the heart of much Melanesian thought (Munn 1977; Battaglia 1991; Bonnemaison 1994: 122). Ultimately, on Vanuatu, the strength of custom or tradition is symbolized by the firmly rooted banyan tree (Bonnemaison 1994: 122; Jolly 1982). Personal identities are rooted in the land. The person who abides and stands straight will take root just like the tree. Conflicts occur because people leave their roots. A place provides persons with roots, the canoe forges alliances and relationships necessary for social and spiritual reproduction. Thus, on one symbolic plane the prow imagery of the Wala canoes unites the *duality* of the construction of social identities which are both permanently rooted in the land and established through movement over the sea. The land is the terrain over which the hawk soars and the ocean is where the frigate bird has its domain.

Canoes and the body

Below the carved prow design, and attached through holes bored into the canoe hull, two fan-like sets of coconut-fibre decorations are suspended. These are also suspended from holes bored in the bow end of the canoe hull, which has no other decoration. On three of the six canoes I observed the coconut-fibre decorations used at the prow end of the canoe were white in colour, contrasting with the red-brown of the coconut rope lashings. Those at the bow of the canoe were the same colour as the rope lashings (Plate 4.1). These two types of coconut-fibre decorations, with white/red colour contrast, are derived from different coconuts. Those attached to the bow end of the canoe are derived from small, round, sweet coconuts whose fibres are edible. Those at the hull are derived from long coconuts whose inedible fibres are also used for the canoe lashings and bindings. The white fibres at the front are white and old, those at the back fresh and young. The coconut fibres dry out from the centre of the coconut. Those used at the front come from the inside of the husk, next to the kernel, those at the back from the outside. So there are a series of structured contrasts at work here:

white	red
old	young
dry	wet
inside	outside

Plate 4.1 Wala canoe prow figure-head.

edible   inedible
short   long
CANOE BOW   CANOE STERN

The tassels at both the bow and the stern were consistently described to me as being the 'moustache of the canoe'. The term 'moustache' may thus refer to the canoe as being both double-headed and gendered as male. Layard records that large sea-going canoes which were constructed formerly (see below) had bows at each end and two carved prow-heads. In addition, these canoes had two subsidiary figure-heads, one on each side of the main figure-head (Layard 1942: 460). It is possible that the moustache tassels on either side of the bow and stern and below the prow figure-head are transformations of this arrangement on the large sea-going canoes.

When I asked why the fibres were white at the bow and red at the stern of the hull, I was told by the group of men making the canoes that this would make the bow end appear 'flashy' and 'stylish'. I asked whether the presence of the 'moustache' at both ends meant the canoe had two heads or faces, and meant that the canoe was a double-headed male. This suggestion caused much amusement. The explanation given for the canoe 'moustache' was that it was a traditional *kastom* element. On long sea journeys the moustache would be used for lighting fires when people reached the land.

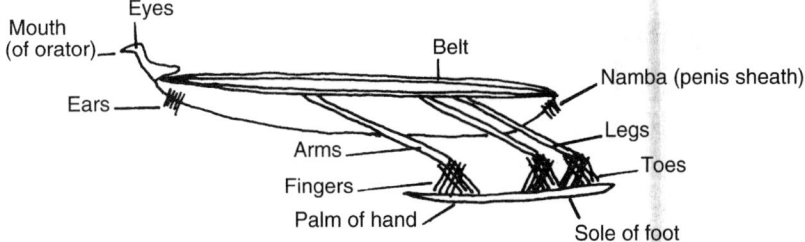

Figure 4.3 The canoe as a big man.

It became quite apparent that such an explanation could not be given much credence. In motion both canoe 'moustaches' were continuously drenched by even the slightest of waves and would hardly provide effective tinder. Apart from the reference to *kastom* and the 'stylishness' of the moustaches no other explanations were offered to me by the group of men building the canoes.

One informant living on the mainland opposite Wala gave me an altogether different explanation. The canoe represented a big man. The moustache at the front was the ears of the big man, who listens to others, that at the back his *namba* or penis sheath. The outrigger booms were his arms and legs, their attachments to the outrigger his fingers and hands. The outrigger itself represented the sole of the foot and the palm of the hand. The bird prow beak symbolized the mouth of the big man, his skill as an orator. Finally, the banyan root lashed around the rim of the canoe hull was the belt of the big man holding his namba at the stern end in place (Figure 4.3). Why, I asked, if this was the case, did the canoe only have three rather than four outrigger booms, two at the back (two legs) and one at the front (one arm)? And why was the big man's mouth (bird beak) closed? Two explanations were provided: large sea-going canoes, built in the past, would have four outrigger booms. This was not possible in the case of the smaller coastal canoes being constructed today, as four booms would interfere with paddling. Bird prow designs, which could only be carved by senior men, who jealously guarded these rights, were double, with the beak opening extending down the gullet. I had previously been shown these double bird prow-heads in the house of one of the five Wala 'chiefs' who owned the rights to carve it. Speiser (1990) also provides an illustration of one example from eastern Malekula, collected *c.* 1910 (Figure 4.4). Layard (1942: 456) states that the larger sea-going canoes constructed in the past had four booms (see below). This interpretation of the canoe as

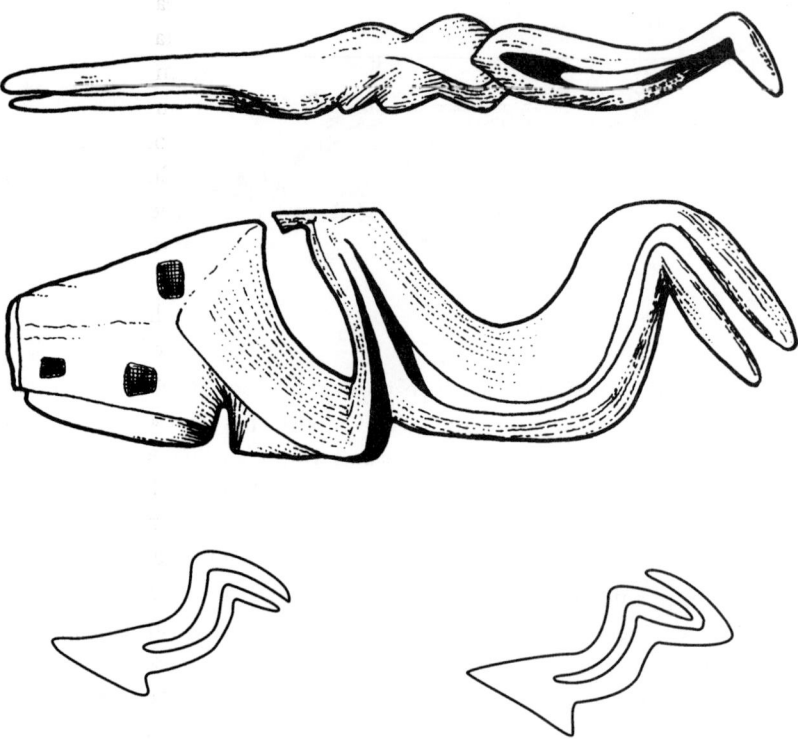

Figure 4.4 Top: traditional carved prow-head collected from Vao island *c*.1910.
Source: Speiser (1990: plate 64). Bottom: sketches of elaborated bird figure-heads from Atchin island (*c*.1914).
Source: Layard (n.d.)

a dressed male body makes good sense of the two 'moustaches' and their different colours. It also provides an explanation of the contrasts noted above: the 'edibility' of the moustache (ears) hanging beneath the prow (in the historical context of a culture with a strong element of cannibalism) and the 'inedibility' of the moustache (penis wrapping) at the bow. The white fibres at the prow end may be further understood as signifying the age of the big man (white facial hair). The 'ears' at the bow end are shorter than the '*namba*' (penis sheath) which was traditionally dyed red (Layard 1942: 42), with wood frequently preferred to bast for the belt (Speiser 1990: 175). Today, *nambas*, red or purple in colour, are still worn on ceremonial occasions and in dance displays for tourists. Cycas leaves are tucked into the belt and under arm rings and leg rings. These same leaves were stuck under the banyan wood 'belt' of the canoe to beautify it during the journey taking the Melanesian heads of state to Wala island. The canoe, in this interpretation, is a heavily anthropomorphized form, the body of a big man. It directly projects an image of the big man adorned. For ceremonial occasions, both the human body and the body of the canoe are decorated to create the best possible impression on guests. Such impression management is essential to create the desired effect: the seduction of persons with whom one wishes to maintain links and from whom one wishes to extract gifts and favours.

When the Melanesian heads of state had landed on the island, they were led from the beach into the dining hall of the Wala resort by a group of male dancers dressed in *nambas* with leaf decorations in arm and leg rings. They performed a traditional welcome dance: the paddle dance. One man at the front held a canoe prow-head and moved forward away from the beach. Two parallel rows of male dancers followed, holding brightly decorated paddles representing each side of the canoe. A man at the rear symbolized the canoe rudder. Having arrived by canoe the heads of state were 'carried' by the canoe of men into the dining hall of the tourist resort. This was built in the form of a men's club house (i.e. an inverted canoe). Afterwards the paddle dancers carried them back to the water. While they had set foot on land, they had never left a canoe. The canoe, as decorated artefact, metamorphosed into the canoe as a decorated body of men, into the canoe of the dining hall, and back again.

An androgynous object

From the discussion so far the Wala canoe would appear to be an artefact entirely gendered as male. Its exclusive construction by men, the vicious and violent frigate bird (and hawk?) imagery, references to moustaches and *nambas*, would all seem to indicate that the canoe is masculine labour objectified, acting as an icon of male power and virility. Yet there appears to be another less obvious and more subtle level of meaning, quite literally *embedded* in the choice of wood and canoe shape. One informant told me that the best wood to use to construct the hull would come from the female *rav* tree at the time that it fruited. Such a canoe would be stronger, last longer and not be so heavy. The outrigger should be made from the younger branches of the tree. The hull and the outrigger, then, connote imagery of lightness, fertility and femaleness. A cultural distinction is made by Wala islanders between male and female banyan trees. The aerial roots of the male banyan are said to grow down parallel with the trunk, those of the female to grow outwards so as to create cave or womb-like hollows. It is wood from the *female* banyan root that is wrapped around the canoe hull. While roots representing the hawk protect the frigate bird prow-head (both embodiments of an aggressive masculinity), it is the elastic female banyan root that is wrapped around the hull, protecting the people contained within it. The canoe, long, narrow and vulva-shaped, contains people like a womb containing the child. At a more abstract level a female principle holds up both men and women. It is this that is fundamental, while the overt male imagery of the prow-head is merely an appended form. Traditionally, if a man and a woman travel together in a coastal canoe the woman should sit at the back, at the stern (stump/root) end of the hull, and steer. The man at the front may propel the canoe forward, and be most visible, but the woman *governs* its course.

MacKenzie (1991) has discussed in detail the manner in which string bags constitute a subtle medium for Telefol people of the New Guinea Highlands to articulate views and images of relations between men and women. She argues that the *bilum* is used in the construction of identity to *both* reinforce and blur, or neutralize, an obvious oppositional separation between men and women. It points '*beyond* the polarities associated with the contrasted concerns of the sexes to an identity of interest between them' (ibid.: 193). The androgyny of the Telefol string bag becomes a material metaphor for reflecting on society and the cosmos (see discussion in Chapter 2).

Something similar seems evident in the case of the Wala canoe, but the female elements are far less obvious and far more understated compared with the overt and brash male prow imagery. The female elements in the canoe constitute a silent unremarked complementary material discourse which nevertheless remains fundamental to the ontological significance and value of the artefact. Although the canoe itself is exclusively fabricated by men, its manufacture is continuously nurtured by women who cook on a daily basis for those involved in its construction. In the past women also plaited the sails which propelled the large ocean-going canoes forward (see below).

Ethnohistory of the Wala Canoe

In the past two kinds of canoes were constructed on the Small Islands of Malekula: (1) the smaller coastal canoe, still used and constructed today and (2) large sea-going canoes used for exchange and ceremonial expedi-

METAPHORICAL TRANSFORMATIONS OF WALA CANOES 119

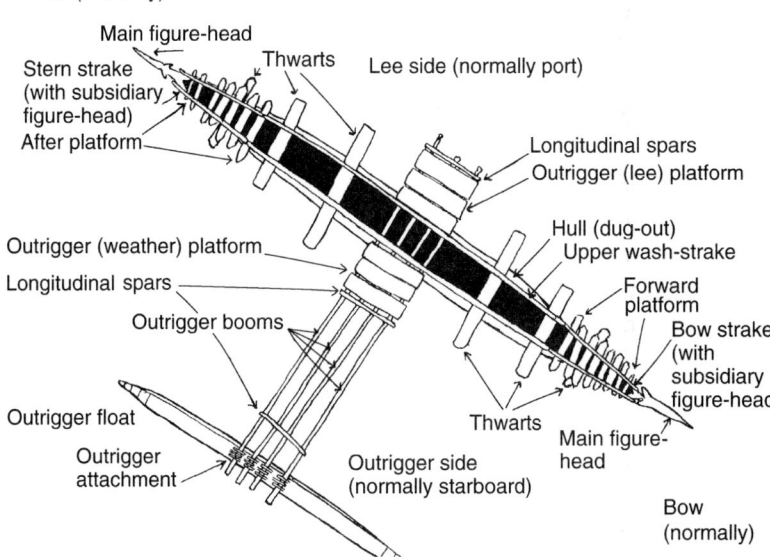

Figure 4.5 Sketch of large sea-going canoe showing main constructional details. *Source*: Layard (n.d.)

tions. These were already being replaced by whalers purchased from white traders in the first two decades of the twentieth century. Speiser's (*c.*1910) and Layard's (*c.*1914) descriptions of the smaller coastal canoes of northeast Malekula match well the manner in which they are constructed today in terms of size, number of outrigger booms and bird prow-head, for example (Speiser 1990: 225; Layard 1942: 458; Layard n.d.). The coastal canoe, single-ended and with a single figure-head on the bow, could sail in one direction only, whereas the sea-going canoes, double-ended with main and subsidiary figure-heads at either end, were constructed so as to be able to sail in both directions. While the coastal canoe had three booms, the two aft booms being close together and at some distance from the fore-boom, the sea-going canoe had four equidistant booms close together amidships. This symmetrical arrangement (see Figure 4.5) was clearly required by its reversible direction. The large sea-going canoes usually had two wash strakes while the coastal canoe was usually a simple dug-out with a rail along each gunwale to which the booms of the sails were lashed. Layard states with regard to the coastal canoes: 'I have no special notes regarding the construction of these small craft, nor of the rites accompanying it, save that, trees large enough being found on all the Small Islands, all the work is done at home ... the work on the canoe is a purely family affair' (Layard n.d.: 67–9). Speiser's and Layard's descriptions of large sea-going canoes from Vao island do not mention the presence of roots above the prow-head, or 'moustaches' at both ends of the hull, or the different types of wood used in canoe construction. Layard's unpublished manuscript (Layard n.d.) about canoe construction on Atchin island (a short distance to the north-east of Wala) mentions that 'sticks of the *nilak* plant pulled up by the roots and attached root-forward are made fast, for magical purposes, alongside the subsidiary figure-head' (ibid.: 4). I have already noted that it is possible that the 'moustaches' of the contemporary canoes represent the subsidiary figure-heads present on the large ocean-going vessels of the past, but since all the other details of the canoes conform to Speiser's and Layard's descriptions this seems unlikely. Layard records that the small coastal canoes from Atchin island had bird figure-heads divided into two main classes. One was a plain figure-head with an ordinary beak ending at the throat. These could be made and used by any man without payment and, consequently, were rare since virtually every man desired something more elaborate. These are the usual form carved today (see Figure 4.2 and Plate 4.1). The second was a bird figure-head of the same form but with the split forming the beak extending right down the neck. The right to carve this design had to be purchased from someone already possessing it (see Figure 4.4). Additional features such as a pig or pig's snout, or rarely, a human face might be carved behind the neck, each entailing payment to a previous owner. Another form Layard describes as a 're-entrant-tusker figure-head', of the same form as the elaborated figure-head, with extended beak, but with the addition that the upper portion of the beak itself, at its extremity, is extended backwards over and above the upper portion (Layard n.d.: 72; see also Figure 4.4). There are clear parallels here between the degree of beak and neck elaboration of the bird figure-heads and the practice of producing tusked boars by knocking out the upper incisor and allowing the lower to grow unhindered, spiralling through the jaw (see Chapter 2 and below). Bird-beak and boar-tusk imagery become conjoined. Neither Speiser nor Layard record the bird species represented by the figure-head. The contemporary presence of a flying fish behind the plain frigate bird prow figure-head, carved today without an extended throat slit, seems to be a recent innovation, and is related to the carving of prow-heads as pieces of tourist art: a single bird design not being considered sufficiently elaborate to satisfy this market.

Speiser mentions three features not present on the small canoes observable today on the Small Islands, and those examples I watched being constructed on Wala. The first is the double bird prow-head. The second is the presence of small cross-boards fixed 'on the bow-like little seats. They have nothing to do with navigation but simply indicate the *suque* [*maki*] rank of the owner. The higher his rank, the larger the number of boards he may display on his boat' (Speiser 1990: 225). The third is the occurrence of sails on the small coastal canoes. These were made from the leaf sheaths of the coconut palm sewn together with fibres forming a triangular surface stretched between two crossed bamboo poles. The upper edge was curved.

> Each bamboo is stayed by three coconut ropes. From one bamboo a rope runs to the rear outrigger spar, the second to the front one, and the third to the bow. ... If the sail is not being used, it is rolled up and tied with broad tapes of bast. When the sail is in use, these tapes then hang down fluttering from the bamboos and are an additional adornment to the boat. (Ibid.: 225)

Layard records that the Vao word for sail means 'wing' and each upper angle of the sail was referred to as the 'tip of the wing' (Layard 1942: 461). From these observations it would appear that the canoe sail represented a large bird with outstretched wing tips, either a frigate bird or a hawk. The redness of the sail might indicate the former.

These canoes could not tack against the wind because of their shallow draught, but they could move at an extraordinary speed with the wind. As is the case today, they were owned by individual men or families and were not used as items of exchange. Layard notes that some large coastal canoes were heightened by planks lashed to either side of the hull with a special bow piece added in the form of a short piece of hollowed log (ibid.: 458). A hollowed log was used to heighten the bow end of two of the canoes (*Rav Msore*) that I saw being constructed, but planks were not added along the sides of the hull.

Canoes today are only intended for short trips between Wala and the mainland. The much larger sea-going canoes constructed in the past were used for voyages between Wala and the other large islands in central and northern Vanuatu: Ambae, Espiritu Santo, Pentecost, Ambrym, Maewo and Malo. The distances involved were up to 80 km, generally involving island hopping. The scale and duration of these voyages always seems to have been rather limited compared with other areas of Melanesia and Polynesia, with long-distance voyages not being undertaken, and rarely by night. From the 1870s onwards the frequency of these contacts was progressively reduced as a result of frequent blackbirding (canoes provided an easy target for the slave labour ships) and the gradual introduction of inter-island steamers subsequently.

These large canoes could hold up to forty persons. Somerville (1894: 375) reports that they were built of three or four planks each about 30 cm wide, lashed together with tough fibre, caulked with tree gum and painted with lime. The bow ends were formed by the keel foundation log, sharply pointed off. The planks did not overlap and were sewn at their ends to a thick heavy end board extending to 30 cm or so above the planking, narrower at the base and wider at the top, 'forming a sort of trough with spreading sides'. These canoes had a mast:

> it is generally a stout, moderately straight piece of bough with a fork or 'yaws' (as on a gaff or boom) at the foot which rests on a stout transverse stick like a thwart, so that the mast does not touch the bottom of the canoe. It is supported on this thwart by the fibre guys fore and aft, and the sail is hoisted on it, the halliards reeving through a hole burnt in the head. By this means, the mast can be 'stepped' at any part of the boat, there being several of these thwarts, acting as strengtheners, and can be inclined at any angle towards bow or stern, and lowered quickly in case of a squall. (ibid.)

The large sea-going canoes were used exclusively by men and were both communally constructed and owned. For Vao, Layard notes:

> if a *maki* is in progress, the canoe belongs exclusively to the officiating 'line' of Maki-men, that is to say, to the officiating matrilineal moiety. ... Though the canoe belongs to the whole 'line' ... one man is spoken of as the 'owner.' It is he who performs the main sacrifices and directs operations, and it is with his personality that, after the consecration rite, the canoe itself becomes identified. ... This man is probably the leader of the Maki. (Layard 1942: 462–3)

Women could not touch or enter these canoes. Codrington (1881: 293) records that the large canoes had proper names, like a person. By the turn of the century these were replaced by European whaleboats, bought from white traders. On Vao the first such boat was bought in 1906 and the big outrigger canoes left to rot on the beach (Speiser 1990: 223). The main purpose of these voyages to the other large islands of northern Vanuatu was to acquire tusked boars for the great *Maki* (grade-taking ceremonies). Another essential item, turmeric (used to dye clothing), was obtained exclusively from the island of Malo and southern Espiritu Santo. Because of frequent fighting they were also known as war canoes (Layard 1942: 456). As regards the sails, Somerville comments that 'all down both of the outside edges of the sail long graceful fringes hang down, with extra large bunches at the tips' (Somerville 1894: 376). Layard records that the sails were of plaited pandanus leaves, dyed red. The plaiting was done by the women, and the sail-strips sewn together by the men (Layard 1942: 460). Layard also records that on Atchin island the task of sewing the strips together was performed by the men in the dancing ground in secrecy (Layard n.d.: 35), transforming an undifferentiated female labour product into the finished form of the sail, which was attached to booms and displayed in the dancing ground before being carried down to the beach and erected on the canoe. These accounts provide further evidence for the complementarity of male and female labour in canoe construction, and confirmation that the sail symbolized a large bird's wing, the fringes representing the frayed plumage of the primary feathers on the wing tips.

Elaborate rites and magic accompanied various stages of canoe construction from the initial tree felling to its consecration when completed. These rites were most elaborate for the large sea-going canoes. They varied in their details between each of the Small Islands of north-east Malekula, and from one village to another. The general pattern and purpose appears, however, to have been similar: (1) to provide payments to those involved in the work and to the owner of the land on which the tree was felled; (2) progressively to transform an *object into a subject*. As the canoe was successively constructed the rites accompanying the process became increasingly more elaborate, culminating in the consecration rites accompanying its launching.

Proceedings opened with a feast in the dancing ground. A small initiatory sacrifice, usually of a fowl, was performed at the foot of the tree to be felled, almost invariably on the Malekulan mainland. After the tree felling, pigs were killed and presented along with yams to the workers. The log was then dug out and payments of pigs, including tuskers, made to indemnify the owner of the land on which the tree grew. The dug-out was then transported to the island and more pigs were sacrificed (but no high-ranking tuskers). Bow and stern pieces were cut and fitted but not made fast, accompanied by more feasting. The exact placing of the outrigger booms on the hull required a ritual specialist, who worked in secret, cast spells and placed the booms where they were to be attached. The rest of the canoe was finished. After completion another rite followed involving the ritual specialist placing a sow in the canoe and forcing it to run up and down from one end to another, symbolizing the fertility of pigs and auguring success in pig exchanges. The sail was then assembled, followed by an all-night inauguration dance ('the dance of the sail') in the dancing ground. More pigs were sacrificed at either end of the canoe below and around the figure-heads, and a taboo put on women entering the canoe (Layard 1942: 464ff.). Accompanying the entire process of canoe construction, presentations of cooked food, provided by women, were made to the workers and divided between the different village segments involved in canoe construction. Godefroy records that for the consecration of a whaler in 1926 the rites performed were 'similar to that of one of the great chiefs' (i.e. men of high *Maki* rank) (Godefroy, cited in Layard 1942: 468). Separate rites were performed to consecrate the hull, the sail, the mast and the rudder. Through these rites, in particular pig sacrifice, the canoe acquired a *subjective* identity. It was given a proper name, like a person. Through the sacrifice of boars it acquired a high rank, like a big man and a 'soul', and was gendered as male.

It is interesting to note that the initial sacrifice at the base of the tree to be felled was of a fowl, the sacrificial bird used for female grade-taking rituals. Once the tree had been felled, pigs and tusked boars, quintessentially associated with men and male grade-taking ceremonies, were used: female substance was converted into male essence. Special houses were built on the beach to protect the canoes and, subsequently, the whalers. These vessels were considered not only to live like human beings of high rank (in a large house), but also to die, and mortuary rites appropriate to the status of a high-ranking big man were performed for *wrecked* vessels. Those which were not wrecked during their lifetime were allowed to die a 'natural' death, i.e. to slowly rot away in their tabooed boat house. Timber was never taken away for firewood or any other use (ibid.: 470–2). One of my informants remarked that it was 'taboo to sleep in a canoe'. From the above account the reason for this seems fairly evident. The entire process of canoe construction converts inanimate materials into an embodied subject. In the process fixed trees, rooted in the ground, are converted into a mobile subject. Thus, it is only possible to sleep in a canoe when dead.

Model mortuary canoes in the Small Islands were used to finish the memory of the dead. As a final act in mortuary ceremonies, the body of the dead was metamorphosed into a gift of food to maternal affines. A model canoe, loaded down with a pig, yams, bananas, coconuts, puddings and fowl, is sent away across the water to maternal relatives on a neighbouring island or on the mainland as the final act in mortuary ceremonies. One of my informants remembered having picked up such a canoe, sent over to Wala from Rano island in 1977. The food was used by the maternal relatives, the model canoe itself left to rot on a small, rough-stone platform on the beach.

Dancing in canoes

In the centre of Wala island there are five great *namel* (dancing grounds). They are all built high up on the island, out of sight of the sea. Long parallel lines of megalithic structures consisting of rows of stone tables and monoliths line the dancing grounds, the rows of monoliths representing genealogical depth: successive generations who have taken part in the *Maki* or grade-taking ceremonies in which individuals acquired new names and statuses, involving the sacrifice of tusked boars (for men) and fowls (for women) to ancestral spirits said to enter the stones once sacrifice had been performed. Each *namel* was associated with a communal *nakamal* (men's club house). Enormous banyan trees still shade these places. Each of the dancing grounds belonged to a neighbouring village. One side of the dancing ground, the upper side, marked by large coral and stone monoliths (up to 2 m high) was the men's, the other marked by much smaller monoliths, the lower side, was the women's. These places were the centres not only for the *Maki* rites (which have not taken place in living memory), but also for the entire ritual life of the village community and were of paramount significance.

What is of great interest here is that the dancing grounds on Wala are all shaped like canoes. Figure 4.6 shows a sketch plan of Lowo *namel*. It is long (about 140 m) and linear in form, and widest (about 24 m) in the centre. At the western end this dancing ground even has a prow-like

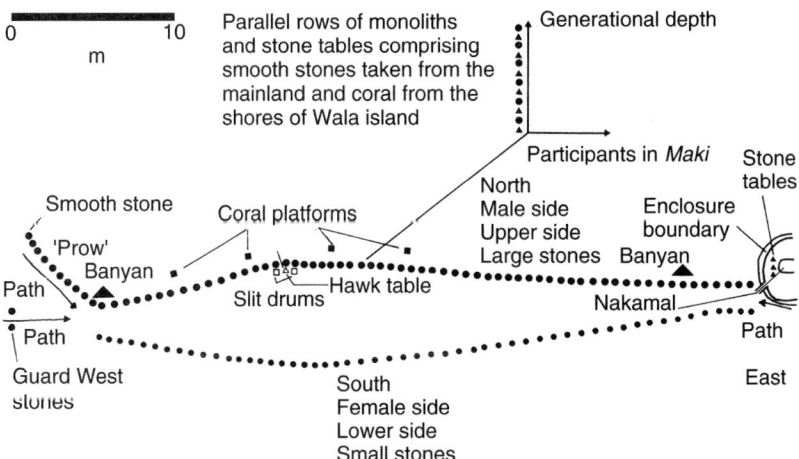

Figure 4.6 Sketch plan of Lowo *namel* (dancing ground), Wala island.

structure, diverging to the north of the main line of stones on the men's side at an angle of about 45 degrees, consisting of two parallel lines of monoliths and stone tables and terminating with a single large monolith of smooth stone taken from a river channel on the mainland.

Layard does not mention the overall canoe-like morphology of the dancing grounds with reference to Vao island (and here they may very well be a different shape), but notes other connections between their spatial organization and canoes. In the great *Maki* ceremonies the arrangement of stone monuments and tuskers was likened by his informants to a large sea-going canoe. Circle tuskers were added to represent bird figure-heads at either end of the hull. Tusked boars on the upper or men's side of the dancing ground were likened to the body of the canoe, while gelded tuskers on the lower or women's side represent the outrigger float. Special high-grade tusked pigs on stone platforms behind the stones on the upper side were likened to piles of food, principally yams and bananas, placed on the lee platform of the canoe (Layard 1942: 428) (Figure 4.7). Symbolic weight is thus placed on the male side of the dancing ground, laden down with high-grade tusked pigs and yams. In this manner the canoe hull and prow-heads become identified as male, the outrigger as female. The androgynous nature of the canoe as an indissoluble mixture of male and female elements becomes even more apparent through this symbolism. It is also possible to understand why a ritual specialist was required secretly to bespell and precisely position the outrigger booms on the hull, because it was not just 'arms' and 'legs' that were being attached but 'male' to 'female' in complementary opposition.

The culminating parts of the Maki grade-taking ceremonies were likened to the approach of a canoe, and Layard notes a general similarity in the ceremonial pattern for the *Maki* rites, canoe inauguration and gong raising. Layard suggests that in the past a new canoe might have been constructed with each successive *Maki* (Layard n.d.: 16). The chief use of the canoes was to obtain pigs and the chief use of the pigs was in *Maki* sacrifice. Pig sacrifice was essential to all the main stages in the production of the canoe. Pigs made canoes just as they made men's souls. An entire *Maki* rite would cover about thirty years, or the length of a generation, and the life of a canoe would have been about the same.

Another feature of the dancing grounds is of interest in this connection. At Lowo and at the other *namel* on Wala, it is the 'female' banyan tree that dominates. These huge trees shade and protect the dancing grounds under which the grand ceremonies were performed. The enormous root systems of these trees wrap themselves around and incorporate the ancestral stones. In an analogous manner the roots of the female banyan

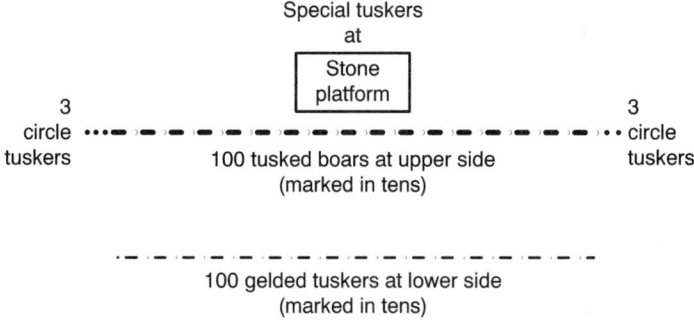

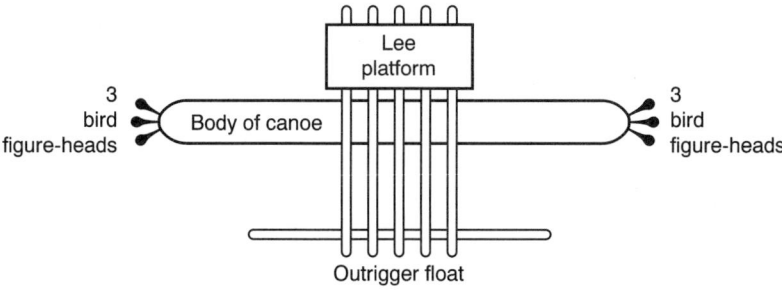

Figure 4.7 Diagram illustrating the comparison made by Layard's informants (c.1914) between the arrangement of sacrificial pigs at the *Maki* ceremonies and a large sea-going canoe.
Source: Layard (1942: Figure 52)

are wrapped around the hulls of the contemporary Wala canoes. While Wala islanders make a cultural distinction between the male and female banyan, in practice it is rather difficult, especially for an outsider, to tell the two apart. More to the point, the 'gender' of these trees is highly ambiguous. Through time, with the continued growth of aerial roots, a 'male' banyan with roots growing parallel to the trunk, will transform into a 'female' banyan: its gender is both inherently mobile and open to various interpretations.

Slit drums and canoes

In the centre of the men's side of the dancing ground huge slit drums were erected, some twice as tall as a person. The rites accompanying the erection of these drums were 'just like those for gong raising' (informant cited in Layard 1942: 464). The same hardwood trees were traditionally used to make both the large sea-going canoes and the slit drums, and both were dug out in similar ways with shell adzes. Like the canoes, the drums are considered the exclusive property of men. These drums, some of which have now been freshly erected in the centre of three of the dancing grounds on Wala (of the 'wrong' kind of wood – soft whitewood of the same tree used to construct the coastal canoes today), are slit longitudinally with solid sections at the top and bottom, with a face carved at the top. Traditionally, the slit forms the mouth of the face, with lips on either side. The sound which the drums emit is said to represent the voice of the ancestors.

Clausen interprets these drums as 'hermaphrodite':

> the slit now held in the patrilineal small islands to be a mouth with its two lips may originally have represented rather a vagina with its two lips. Such an interpretation would, in fact, be more consonant with the vertical position of the slit which extends right down near the base of the drum representing the human figure than with its interpretation as a mouth which physiologically should be at right angles and not vertical to the body of the instrument. (Clausen 1960: 18)

It seems clear that the slit drums, like the contemporary canoes and the dancing grounds, are *androgynous* forms: both penis and womb-like, with male 'lips' and a female 'vulva' combined into one. And, like the canoes, they are conceived as subjects rather than objects, their voices called to speak by the drummer.

The intimate connection between these drums and the canoes in terms of mode of construction, type of tree used, rites performed, and their androgynous nature is striking. There is another connection. The canoes transport people over the ocean. The slit drums are

> like canoes on the ocean of the spirit world, connecting mankind with the otherwise unknown world of the ancestral ghosts whose voices they represent and who live on – literally, feed on – the psychic essence of the boars that are sacrificed to them. Slit-drums thus constitute a psychic medium of communication with the spirit world corresponding to the trading voyages of the canoes in external life. (ibid.: 19)

Clausen, following Layard (both he and Layard regarded the canoes as embodying exclusively male symbolism), interprets the 'female component' in the slit drums in terms of an evolutionary developmental sequence on the Small Islands from an originary matrilineal social organization to a patrilineal and patrilocal one, which already existed when Layard carried out his research in 1913–14. The overt male ideology of the canoes and the slit drums was all to do with men freeing themselves from women and their powers and asserting their own dominance. The 'hermaphroditic' nature of the slit drums was thus a kind of relic of a previous social order. Abandoning this evolutionary framework, another potentially more insightful interpretation is that the female connotations of the slit drums, and those identified above in the contemporary canoes, are part of a discourse about both male and female essences or powers, which are being brought together and combined in the silent discourse of material culture, a discourse which is not and cannot be articulated in language but is nevertheless made continuously present through the objects themselves. The canoes, the dancing grounds and the slit drums are ideal objects for this purpose, since none could be, or were, exchanged. They constituted permanent markers of the inalienable wealth (Weiner 1992) of Wala islanders.

Conclusion: From Tuskers to Tourists

I have argued that contemporary canoe building involves the material surfacing and articulation of a series of material metaphors bound up with the creation of social identities and intertwined male and female essences. A hierarchy of male power is implied by the overt canoe imagery, the distinction between the upper and lower sides of the dancing grounds and in the slit drums. Yet at a base metaphorical level the canoe hull and outrigger are female, the female banyan tree protects the dancing grounds, its root is wrapped around the canoe hull, ancestral voices issue from the vaginal mouth of the slit drums. Wala canoe imagery, past and present, combines both male and female metaphorical imagery, male and female work. They are ambiguous artefacts in which various levels of meaning appear to contradict each other: the overt male imagery of the canoe is quite literally wrapped around with female forms.

Among the traditional beliefs of Wala islanders was the notion that the human body was made up of a hard, dry, male component (the bones of the skeleton), wrapped around by wet female flesh and blood. Layard notes that in this body image symbolism

> in which the body symbolises the whole psyche, the matrilineal line of flesh and blood symbolises, or is the carrier of, the soul which is female. The bones and patrilineal line of descent symbolise the spirit which is not only incubated in the soul, but, like a skeleton, upholds it and gives it form, and subsequently outlives

the soul, which, having performed its incubating function, dies, giving way to the male spirit which is at once its father and its child. (Layard 1972: 321)

The combined male and female imagery of the canoe may thus ultimately be a material metaphor for marital bonds and procreation, with the canoe representing the reproduction of society as much as an individualized body-subject.

The men doing the work of constructing contemporary Wala canoes often preferred to give practical and 'functional' explanations for even such obviously symbolic items as the canoe 'moustaches'. A reluctance to talk about the meanings of material forms has both been noted by, and frustrated, many Melanesian anthropologists (e.g. Forge 1979; Keesing 1987). This refusal to verbalize is perhaps because the artefact as material does the talking in a much more profound, succinct and vivid manner. The canoe is 'good to think' precisely because its meanings are not verbalized. Discourse occurs at the silent level of the artefact and is continuously presenced in the world as such. It is a discourse which is not, and cannot be, articulated in speech, in a social world constituted, as elsewhere in Melanesia, by extreme male/female sexual antagonism. The symbolic work the canoe does is to 'resolve' or contain, within the image of the largest and arguably the most important portable artefact, contradictions in social life, relations between men and women, which cannot be discussed in language or negotiated in social practice.

Today, none of the traditional rites, described above, linked with the construction and consecration of the large sea-going canoes, are performed. I was present at the launch of one of the new canoes and was invited to sit in the front. The canoe was pushed off the beach, with one of the five Wala chiefs in the rear steering. We followed the coast of Wala for about ten minutes and then returned to the launch site, dragged the canoe up on the beach, and then left to drink kava. It would be easy to describe the coastal canoes constructed on Wala island today as empty vessels of custom. They have been decontextualized from the ritual practices surrounding their construction and consecration. Mortuary ceremonies are no longer performed for them. None of the canoes on Wala island, except for the six I watched being built, even had carved prow-heads, although these were being carved as tourist art in limited numbers for a growing tourist market.

The reason for these canoes being constructed at all was the visit of the Melanesian heads of state to the island. Subsequently, they were to be used to ferry tourists over to the new resort. The knowledge of the meanings of the details of the canoe design has an entangled history. Coastal canoe construction on Wala island has been continuous (whitewood canoes only last for four to five years). We are not simply dealing here with a reinvented tradition of canoe manufacture, but the metaphorical meanings of the artefact have clearly not remained constant, nor are they consistent. They invite reinterpretation by Wala islanders and by myself.

The enduring symbolic and social significance of the canoe for Wala islanders has always principally resided in its use as a vehicle of power, and in the social *relationships* that it engenders. The process of constructing canoes today brings forth and acts so as to negotiate social relationships between men. Those building the Wala canoes (up to ten being involved at any one time) belonged to all five patriclans on the island, among whom in the past warfare took place, and between whom in the present, disputes over land and resources are a recurrent element. The project of building the canoes was bound up with a perceived need to both preserve and revive *kastom*. It forged a remarkable sense of solidarity and community spirit between the men engaged in the act of construction. It is of interest to note here that the old traditional *personal* insignia of rank, such as special carved prow-heads or wooden boards lain across the hull, were not used, and indeed would have been most inappropriate in this communal venture. In the process of making the canoes new sets of social relations were negotiated and made visible.

On another and more abstract plane of meaning the canoes are a dynamic symbolic manifestation of the strength and *power* of the past in the present. But this interest in the past by Wala islanders is not for its own sake. It is stimulated by a desire to direct this power of the past – metaphorically, to steer a course for the future. In a canoe one does not travel alone. A canoe is only ultimately important in terms of the wealth and relationships it elicits. The evident pride the men took in the traditional form of the canoes was all about the way these artefacts would empower the community to change their lives. The *kastom* in the canoe is thus a medium for the social and material regeneration of the local community today.

The outward appearance of the canoes constructed today on Wala is similar to those built one hundred years ago. The primary symbolic directionality of canoe movement has always been *towards* Wala rather than away from the island. In the manufacture of these canoes a decision has to be made on which side to attach the outrigger. The prevailing trade winds blow from the south-east, or to the left of Wala as one stands on the beach at Serser, facing the sea. Placing the outrigger on the left-hand side of the canoe means that it is easier to travel to the mainland, because the outrigger breaks the force of the waves. Virtually all canoes, however, have their outriggers attached to the right, making it easier to reach Wala. Emphasis is thus placed on the fleetness and buoyancy of the canoe on the journey home, of their return laden with goods. Canoes have always transported sustenance, wealth and fame to Wala island. Today, they no longer carry tuskers for the *Maki* ceremonies. Instead, they bring sacrificial cargo of a rather different kind: tourists are substituted for tuskers, dollars for ivory.

5

Body Metaphors in Southern Scandinavian Rock Art

Prehistoric rock art constitutes one of the richest resources we have to hand to enable us to begin to read cosmologies and their relationship to the structuring of social relations. In this chapter I want to try and provide an interpretation of the metaphorical meanings of a particular set of Bronze Age rock carvings from the west of Sweden, concentrating on the carving site of Högsbyn in Dalsland (Figure 5.1) and in particular on the form and character of the depiction of the human body and body parts in space. The carvings at Högsbyn form the only substantial concentration of rock art in this region of Sweden, being separated by a distance of around 70 km from the major concentration of carving sites along the west coast of Sweden in Bohuslän. The carvings themselves were probably all executed in a relatively brief 300–400 year period towards the end of the Bronze Age (Montelius IV–V on the basis of the ship depictions (Kaul 1995)). The carved rocks are located on the north-east shore of the Råvarpen lake and form a roughly linear series running from the small Ronarudden peninsula jutting out into the lake in the south, up a gentle slope to the north, through pasture to arable land. The very special landscape setting of these rock carvings and the obvious linearity in their arrangement must constitute a significant element in their meaning. No contemporary Bronze Age settlement sites are known in the vicinity of the carvings, but there are a

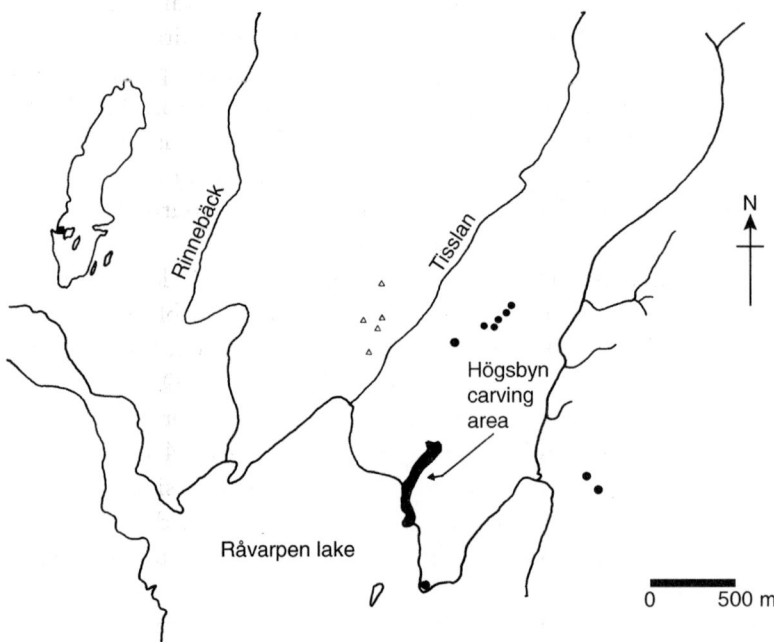

Figure 5.1 The location of the Högsbyn rock-carving area in Sweden. Large and small cairns in the vicinity marked by dots. Other important rock carving sites to the west of the Tisslan marked by triangles.

series of larger and smaller cairns set away from them at distances varying between 300 and 800 m (Figure 5.1). These include, to the north of the carvings, one of the largest and most impressive Bronze Age cairns in Dalsland. Other rock carvings occur in the region, notably in a wooded area of higher land to the north-west of Högsbyn and separated from it by the valley of the Tisslan. Like the cairns, they are set apart from the carved rocks at Högsbyn and are also later in date.

The gently undulating terrain of Högsbyn, bounded by the lake to the south, is surrounded to the north, west and east by much higher rocky, heavily wooded hills which also stretch round to the south of the lake, creating the impression of a very special place, an isolated, interiorized, cultural 'island' by the lake. Its location, more or less in the centre of a network of waterways and lakes to the west of lake Vänern, implies that it was a site that was visited and left, as it may be today, from the water.

The lack of contemporary settlements, contrasting with the situation in Bohuslän (Bertilsson 1986; 1989), and the relative isolation of the Högsbyn carving site from others in this part of Sweden, together with the presence of probably contemporary cairns, suggest that this was a special cult site, possibly only seasonally visited and used. My initial proposition is that the linearity in the arrangement of the carvings provides a key element in attempting to understand them. I will argue in this chapter that the arrangement of types of carvings in the landscape is structured in a definite sequence and metaphoric order. Understanding the manner in which this order unfolds enables the construction of a narrative that makes sense of the spatial arrangement of the carvings.

The rock carvings at Högsbyn have been known since at least 1718, but they have only recently been recorded, documented and published in detail (Svensson 1982: 10–57). Svensson's excellent publication, supplemented with recent research and documentation by Andersson (1992; 1994; 1995 and unpublished documentation), provides the basis for my research. Svensson (1982) provides illustrations of all but 6 of the 34 known carved rocks. Of those not illustrated in her book one only had a single cupmark (rock number 2) and could not be located at the time of documentation (1981). The other five rocks (numbers 8–12) were entirely overgrown and not recorded. Andersson has recently recorded these rocks (results as yet unpublished) and provided additional details, incorporated into the present analysis, for rocks 25, 19, 4, 3 and 5.

Högsbyn has a minimum number of 1,245 individual motifs executed on 33 discrete rock areas, which for the purposes of this analysis were subdivided into 60 carving surfaces (Figure 5.2). The following criteria were employed to define these carving surfaces:

1 Large natural fissures demonstrably present at the time of carving demarcate a discrete carving surface on a single large rock area.
2 Viewing angle: carving areas which are not intervisible on different slopes of the same rock (e.g. west, east) or carvings on a rock slope as opposed to those on the crown of the same rock.
3 Distance: large gaps of 2 m or more separating carving areas on the same rock surface.

I have followed Svensson's numbering system using lettering to define individual carving surfaces on the same rock, e.g. 25A, 25B, etc.

Design Classes

Twelve different major design types can be distinguished (Figure 5.3). Of these, six are geometric or abstract in form. The others can be clearly

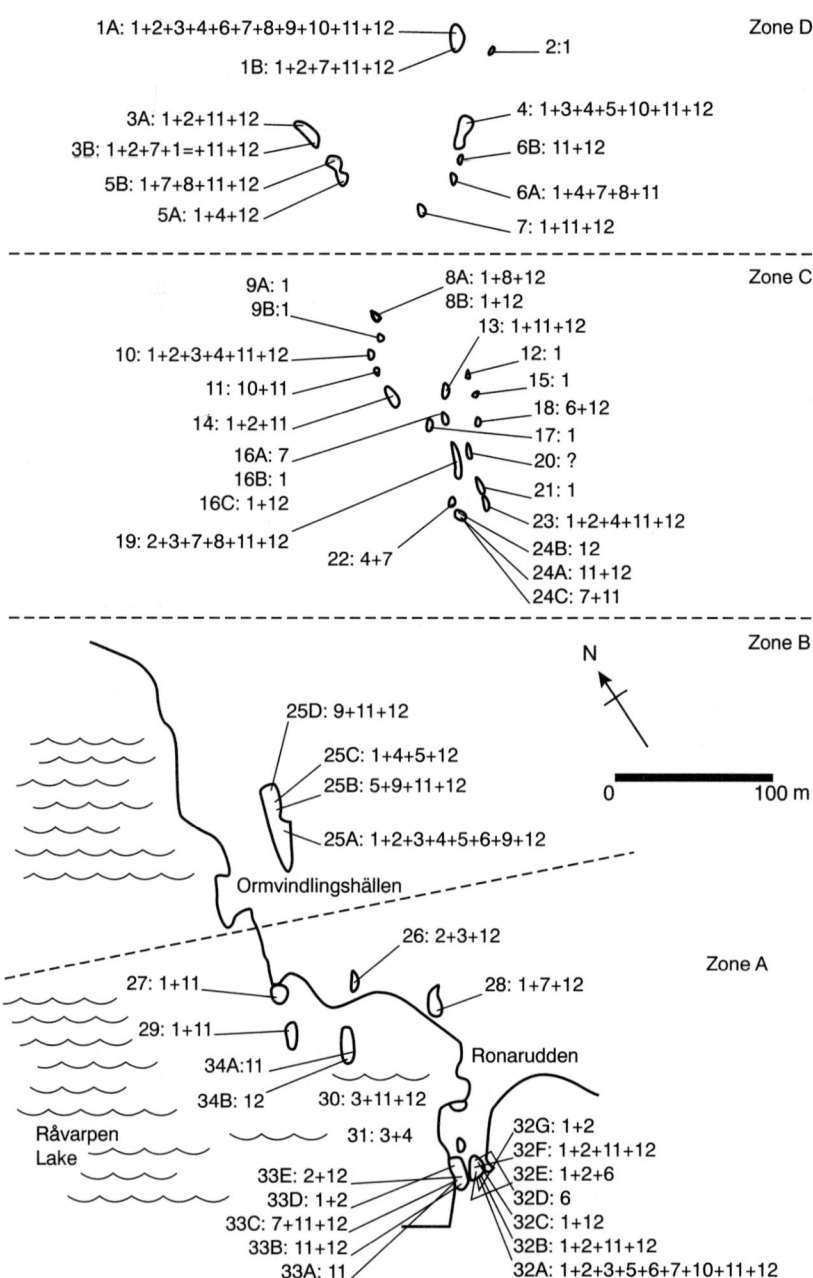

Figure 5.2 The distribution of the carved rocks at Högsbyn showing the occurrence of different designs on individual rock carving surfaces. Carving surfaces on the same rock are differentiated by letters. A four-fold spatial zonation of the site from south to north (A, B, C, D) is shown. *Key*: 1: Cupmark; 2: Circle cross; 3: Circle; 4: Wavy lines; 5: Cross; 6: Infilled motif; 7: humans; 8: Animals; 9: Feet; 10: Hands; 11: Boats; 12: Shoe-soles.

BODY METAPHORS: SOUTHERN SCANDINAVIAN ROCK ART   137

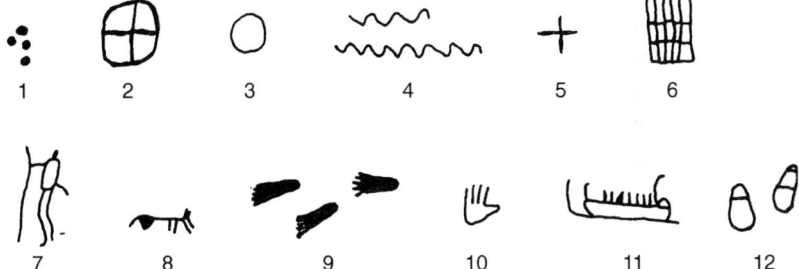

Figure 5.3   The twelve major design classes present at Högsbyn.

Table 5.1   The motif types at Högsbyn in terms of number and relative frequency of carving surfaces on which they occur: total numbers of motifs and relative frequency (A%) and relative frequency excluding cupmarks, rare or unique, and unidentifiable designs (B%).

Design type	No. of carving surfaces	%	Number	A%	B%
Cupmarks	37	61	568	52	–
Circle cross	17	28	41	4	8
Circle	9	15	19	2	4
Wavy lines	10	16	66	6	13
Cross	5	8	11	1	2
Infilled motifs	7	11	10	0.9	2
Humans	12	20	35	3	7
Animals	5	8	6	0.5	1
Feet	4	6	16	1.5	3
Hands	5	8	9	0.8	1.5
Boats	28	46	80	7	15
Shoe-soles	34	56	187	17	36
Other	4	6	36		
Unidentifiable	30	50	161		
Total	60		1,245		

identified as human beings or body parts (hands and feet), animals, boats and shoe-soles. In addition, a few rock surfaces possess unique or very infrequent design forms (e.g. a double spiral, U markings, bird/razor and plant or tree branch designs). The frequency of the major design forms and their occurrence on individual carving surfaces is shown in Table 5.1.

Cupmarks, as in all rock-carving areas in southern Scandinavia, are quantitatively dominant both in terms of the numbers of motifs and the carving surfaces on which they occur. Otherwise the abstract designs most common at Högsbyn are the circle cross and wavy lines. Boats and shoe-soles are most frequent among the representational designs. The majority of rock-carving surfaces possess representational designs (73 per cent) in varying frequencies. Excluding the cupmarks, rare and unidentifiable designs, 31 per cent of the motifs are abstract in form.

Design Combinations

In order to investigate the meanings of the designs it is crucial to consider their relationship with each other, as part of the meaning of a design is likely to be constituted through its relationship with others. In this section I will attempt to determine whether there is any design grammar governing the relationships and associations of designs on individual carving surfaces, regarding each design as a unit of meaning in an overall structural and structured system, adopting a methodology discussed at length elsewhere (Tilley 1991). The analysis is only concerned with identifiable 'free-standing' designs rather than those forming parts of others (e.g. people in boats). The first stage in the analysis is to investigate which designs occur on their own and not associated with others on a carving surface, and then consider the manner in which combinations of different design types are built up. At Högsbyn only 14 (23 per cent) of the carving surfaces possess solely one design type (Table 5.2).

It is of great interest to note that only four of the twelve major design classes occur on their own. The others have a purely relational significance, i.e. part of their meaning is actively constituted in relation to others. The number of carving surfaces with two different types of designs is restricted.

Table 5.2 Carving surfaces with only one identifiable design type (e.g. one cupmark or a number of cupmarks).

Design type	Number of carving surfaces	%
Cupmarks	9	15
Shoe-soles	2	3
Boats	2	3
Infilled	1	1.5

Table 5.3 The frequency of carving surfaces with two different identifiable designs.

Design combination	No. of carving surfaces
Cupmarks and shoe-soles	2
Cupmarks and circle cross	2
Boat + shoe-sole	3
Circle cross and shoe-sole	1
Circle and wavy line	1
Boat + cupmark	2
Human + boat	1
Shoe-sole + infilled	1
Wavy line + human	1
Hands + boats	1

Only 10 combinations (15 per cent) (see Table 5.3) occur out of a total of 66 theoretical possibilities. However, only three of the designs (feet, the cross and animals) do not occur in these combinations and all are quantitatively infrequent. Three of the combinations are made up of representational designs, two of abstract designs and three of a combination of representational and abstract designs.

A further eight carving surfaces have three different designs. The same design combination is only repeated twice. All other carving surfaces with three different designs are unique. This situation of non-repetition of design combinations is repeated for all carving surfaces with more than three designs with one exception, the occurrence of cupmarks, circle cross, boats and shoe-soles twice (see Table 5.4). On no carving surface do all design types occur together. The most complex surface has eleven design types, the cross not occurring. The design grammar or permitted numbers of different combinations is extremely restricted. There is a lack of repetition such that beyond surfaces with only two design types each surface, with only one exception, has a unique design combination. These combinations in all except one case (humans + hands + boats + shoe-soles) include both abstract and representational designs.

It is possible to investigate the structure and sense of this design grammar in more detail by considering the representational and abstract designs separately. Table 5.5 details combinations of representational designs.

Shoe-soles and boats, the most common representational designs, are the only ones to occur with any frequency on their own. Again, the number of

Table 5.4 The frequency of design combinations on carving surfaces with three to eleven different designs including both major design classes and rare designs.

Design combination	Number of carving surfaces
Three designs	
Human + boat + shoe-sole	1
Circle + boat + shoe-sole	1
Cupmark + human + shoe-sole	1
Circle cross + circle + shoe-sole	1
Feet + boat + shoe-sole	1
Cupmark + circle cross + boat	1
Cupmark + boat + shoe-sole	2
Cupmark + animal + shoe-sole	1
Four designs	
Boat + cupmark + circle cross + shoe-sole	1
Cupmark + circle cross + infilled + plant	1
Human + hand + boat + shoe-sole	1
Cross + feet + boat + shoe-sole	1
Cupmark + wavy line + cross + shoe-sole	1
Cupmark + wavy line + shoe-sole + plant	1
Five designs	
Cupmark + circle cross + circle + cross + infilled	1
Cupmark + circle cross + infilled + boat + shoe-sole	1
Cupmark + circle cross + wavy line + boat + infilled	1
Cupmark + circle cross + human + boat + shoe-sole	1
Six designs	
Circle cross + circle + humans + animals + boat + shoe-sole	1
Eight designs	
Cupmark + circle cross + circle + wavy line + boat + shoe-sole + plant + bird	1
Cupmark + circle cross + circle + wavy line + cross + infilled + feet + shoe-sole	1
Nine designs	
Cupmark + circle + wavy line + cross + hand + boat + shoe-sole + U design + double spiral	1
Ten designs	
Cupmark + circle cross + circle + wavy line + infilled + human + feet + hand + boat + shoe-sole	1
Eleven designs	
Shoe-sole + foot + hand + boat + human + circle cross + circle + cupmarks + animal + infilled design + wavy lines	1

Table 5.5 The frequency of carving surfaces with different combinations of identifiable representational designs.

Design combination	Number of carving surfaces
One design only	
Shoe-soles	7
Humans	2
Boat	5
Two designs	
Shoe-sole + boat	10
Shoe-sole + human	1
Human + boat	2
Shoe-sole + foot	1
Boat + hand	1
Shoe-sole + plant	1
Three designs	
Shoe-sole + boat + hand	1
Shoe-sole + boat + foot	2
Shoe-sole + boat + human	2
Human + boat + animal	1
Four designs	
Shoe-sole + human + hand + boat	2
Shoe-sole + human + boat + animal	2
Boat + shoe-sole + plant + bird	1
All designs	
Human + foot + hand + boat + shoe-sole + animal	1

combinatorial possibilities is severely restricted and five of the six representational designs occur together just once on one carving surface, rock surface 1A in the extreme north of the carving area. The abstract designs present a similar situation. The only design to occur on its own in any frequency is the cupmark, the most common design at Högsbyn. Combinatorial possibilities are again severely restricted. Virtually all surfaces with more than two designs possess unique combinations and only one carving surface has all the abstract designs represented, surface 25A in the middle of the carving area, the 'Ormvindlingshällen' (Table 5.6).

Merging Designs and Superimposition

There are a considerable number of cases of design superimposition and designs which join or merge into one another at Högsbyn (Table 5.7). It is

Table 5.6 The frequency of carving surfaces with different combinations of identifiable abstract designs.

Design combination	Number of carving surfaces
One design only	
Cupmarks	19
Cross	1
Circle	1
Wavy lines	1
Infilled design	2
Circle cross	1
Two designs	
Cupmark + circle cross	7
Cupmark + wavy line	2
Circle + wavy line	1
Circle cross + circle	1
Three designs	
Cupmark + circle cross + wavy line	1
Cupmark + infilled design + circle cross	2
Cupmark + wavy line + cross	1
Four designs	
Cupmark + wavy line + circle + cross	1
Cupmark + circle cross + wavy line + circle	1
Five designs	
Cupmark + circle cross + circle + wavy line + infilled	1
All designs	1

assumed here that this was both intentional and constitutes part of the meaning of the designs through physical association.

Merger or overlap between identifiable designs occurs on carving surfaces throughout the carving area, but is more frequent on the northern rocks in which merger or superimposition includes a greater number of different individual designs. Spatially, the nature of this overlap changes. On the southern rocks most cases involve boats; in the middle wavy lines; and in the north boats, wavy lines and shoe-soles. The latter merge or overlap with all other designs except the cross and animals, both of which are quantitatively insignificant. The shoe-soles may thus be claimed to articulate together other designs in an overall system of meaning, which I shall argue is metonymically linked to the human body.

Table 5.7 Cases of design superimposition or merging between different identifiable design classes.

		Design numbers											
No.	Design type	1	2	3	4	5	6	7	8	9	10	11	12
1	Cupmarks		+	+	+							+	+
2	Circle cross	+			+							+	+
3	Circle	+											+
4	Wavy lines	+	+				+	+	+	+		+	+
5	Cross												
6	Infilled				+								+
7	Humans				+							+	+
8	Animals				+								
9	Foot				+							+	+
10	Hand												+
11	Boat	+	+		+			+		+			+
12	Shoe-sole	+	+	+	+		+	+		+	+	+	

Making Sense of Högsbyn: Design Form

Up to this point in the account a simple distinction between representational or iconic and geometric or abstract designs has been maintained and the crucial question of the meaning of design form has not been addressed. It is now necessary to ask: why these designs and what relationship is there between them? It is simplest to begin with the six designs that can clearly be identified as representing something in the world. These fall into three groups:

1   human beings and body parts of humans: feet and hands;
2   animals;
3   cultural objects: shoe-soles and boats.

Only six depictions of animals occur on five carving surfaces. The species in question are not readily identifiable. They all appear to represent horses or dogs, with no other certain representations of wild or domestic animals (one other possible animal depiction, perhaps representing a deer on rock 33 recorded by Svensson (1982: 56) is probably modern). Since these depictions are quantitatively so few they do not appear to be an important element in the Högsbyn carvings. Humans and body parts of humans never occur on their own on individual carving surfaces, whereas shoe-soles and boats do, thus further serving to differentiate between these classes of designs and their significance.

Hands and feet only occur together with humans on three carving surfaces: that in the extreme south of the carving area on surface 32A and two in the extreme north on surfaces 3B and 1A (see Figure 5.2). On the southern surface and on 3B they are separated from the human bodies, while on surface 1A the humans occur in close relationship to the depictions of their body parts. Why are hands and feet detached from the human body as separate depictions and not other body parts? A number of reasons can be suggested: (1) they are more or less identical extremities of the body: (2) they move in a manner far more complex than the joints of the arms or legs; (3) they are the primary means by which the human body is able to sustain itself physically. The feet carry the body through space; the hands actively permit the grasping and manipulation of the external world. The hands are the most expressive part of the body used to signal, command and complement verbal discourse. They are the primary medium through which humans work on, interact with and transform the world. The rock-carving surfaces themselves are, of course, transformed by the hand producing designs. Both the hands and the feet are in continuous contact with the external world beyond the body in a manner in which other body parts are not. Feet, carrying the body, represent its lowest point; hands raised upright on the arms are higher than any other part of the body.

The carving area may be subdivided into four spatially distinct zones, from the south to the north (see Figure 5.2). Looking at the sequencing of hand and foot depictions in relation to those of the human body throughout the Högsbyn carving area, an interesting pattern emerges. On the southernmost surface humans, hands and feet occur together. On rock 28 two stick-line humans occur together along with ambiguous feet/shoe-soles. In the middle zone of the rock-carving area only feet occur on Ormvindlingshällen. On the next series of carved rocks depictions of humans and hands occur on *separate* surfaces but feet are absent, only occurring together with hands and humans on rock 1A. The human body, then, is being broken down and separated into its extremities, which are in turn separated, only to be associated again on rock 1A. The major distinctions may be summarized as follows:

Zone A (South): humans, foot, hand (spatially distant on carving surface)
Zone B: humans separated from feet and hands
Zone C: humans separated from hands

BODY METAPHORS: SOUTHERN SCANDINAVIAN ROCK ART 145

Zone D (North): humans, foot, hand (spatially close together on carving surface)

A logic of similarity and difference thus connects hands and feet. They are both to do with movement, but while hands are high, feet on which the body walks are low. A number of properties connect hands and feet with boats and shoe-soles. Like hands and feet, boats and shoe-soles are intimately connected with movement, boats on the water, shoe-soles on the land. Shoes worn on the feet enable the body to move on land more efficiently; boats permit more efficient movement on water. They both enable the body to travel further and faster in time and space. But while shoe-soles are beneath the feet, boats ride high on the water. So a contrast between low and high links shoe-soles and feet, hands and boats:

Shoe-soles : Feet :: Boats : Hands :: Low : High

or shoe-soles are to feet as boats are to hands as low is to high. The above structural sequence may be rearranged as follows:

boats (water) ⟶ shoe-soles ⟶ feet (land) ⟶ hands

LOW_____⟶HIGH

given that water is lower than land and that people stand in boats and on the land. High and low are, in turn, connected with north and south as:

High : North :: Low : South

Such a linkage is suggested by a number of observations: the southern rock carvings by the lake are physically low. One moves up a slope towards the highest carvings of all, which are in the north of the carving area. In the course of this movement the human depictions become larger, bolder and 'higher' (see below). The largest and most elaborate boat depictions, reaching an overall length of over one metre, by contrast, occur on rock 32 in the south. The boats carved on carving surfaces in the rest of the Högsbyn area are generally smaller and less elaborate. It is only in the middle and north of the carving area that boats 'carry' and/or are superimposed on human figures, many of which are larger than the boats with which they are associated.

    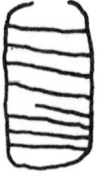

Figure 5.4 Examples of infilled designs taken from different carving surfaces at Högsbyn.

Three features may, then, be held to link the representational designs:

1   an intimate connection with the human body in *movement*;
2   a high/low contrast;
3   a south/north contrast in the character of the depictions.

Six 'abstract' design types make up the rest of the carvings at Högsbyn. As with the more obviously representational forms we can ask: why these designs? Is there any structural logic connecting them together and with the representational design classes?

Three of these designs – the circle, the cross and the circle cross – may be regarded as connected inasmuch as a combination of the first two, as basic elements, is sufficient to constitute the third. The other three – cupmarks, wavy lines and infilled designs – are heterogeneous in character. The last category, in particular, has no real unity including a disparate set of forms (Figure 5.4) and together with the cross is quantitatively insignificant. What does appear to link the other five design forms is a concern with numeration, temporality and the subdivision of space. I shall argue that they are intimately connected, like the representational designs, with movement – but in this case the movement of celestial bodies – and in particular the passage of the seasons.

On a number of carving surfaces the cupmarks are clearly arranged in sequences and multiples of six and twelve (Figure 5.5). It is not hard to suggest that this may be related to lunar cycles or years, given the common preoccupation with the passage of the seasons and solar and lunar observation in small-scale agricultural societies. Farming is quintessentially a seasonable task defined in a definite rhythm and correlated with the passage of the seasons. The agrarian calendar is an extremely important means of orchestrating group activity, whose time is usually marked by

Figure 5.5 Examples of sequencing and a concern with temporality in relation to cupmarks and wavy lines. 1: These cupmarks (bottom row numbering 12) are the only carvings present on rock 17; 2: Double sequence of six cupmarks from surface 25A (Ormvindlingshällen); 3: Cupmarks marking changes in the curves of the wavy lines on carving surface 25A.

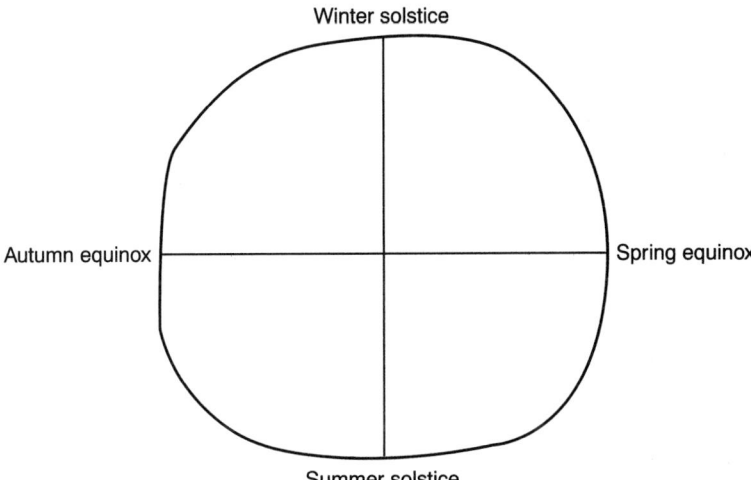

Figure 5.6 The circle cross as seasonal marker.

ritual practices intimately connected with the sacred tasks of ploughing, sowing and reaping (Bourdieu 1990), as well as other seasonal practices such as hunting. The circle cross, long interpreted by archaeologists as a solar symbol or sun wheel, is divided into four segments. These segments may perhaps represent the summer and winter solstice and the spring and autumn equinox: fundamental natural markers of the passage of the year and the seasons (Figure 5.6). This would explain why this design is so common at Högsbyn and throughout those areas of southern Scandinavia with rock carvings, otherwise it is particularly hard to account for its frequent occurrence and specific design form. A few of the circle-cross designs at Högsbyn are more complicated. The initial design form is further subdivided into eight, ten or sixteen segments. Some are extended

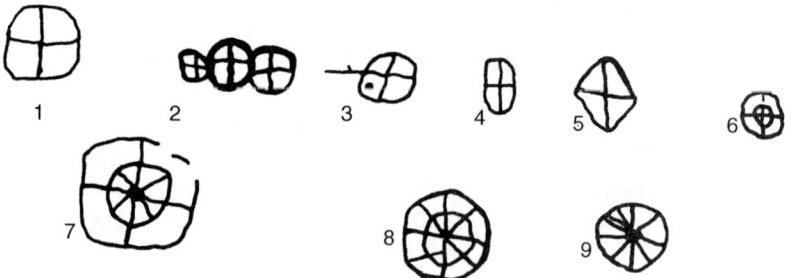

Figure 5.7 Varieties of circle-cross designs taken from different rock-carving surfaces at Högsbyn.

in shape: longer or shorter seasons or periods of light? On one carving surface three circle crosses are conjoined in a series suggesting years or different agricultural cycles (Figure 5.7). Given the concern with numeration demonstrated with the cupmarks, it is of interest to note that a cupmark occurs only once within a circle cross at Högsbyn on carving surface 1A, which I have already noted has other distinctive characteristics. It marks the third quarter (autumn or harvest?) and this design occurs at more or less the centre of the carving surface (see figures 5.7 and 5.15). The wavy lines or 'snakes' (they are certainly unlikely to be the latter, lacking heads) can be understood in a similar manner as marking the passage of time, and perhaps in particular lunar motion. The moon, viewed from the earth, is the largest celestial body in the sky. It has a regular 28-day cycle, waxing and waning, changing its shape, size and brightness every day. Lunar motion and its phases must have been noted as correlating with the seasons, in turn linked with agricultural activities. The moon's cycles involving growth, death and rebirth have always provided a metaphor for the life-cycles of human existence. Brennan (1983) has convincingly interpreted the prevalence of the wavy line in Irish megalithic art as representing lunar cycles, noting that

> in many cultures the moon is symbolized by a snake or dragon because of its motion in the sky, weaving above and below the ecliptic (the sun's path) each month. During the year the moon meanders in a wavy line above and below the celestial equator. (Brennan 1983: 137) (see Figure 5.8)

The wavy lines at Högsbyn may represent, then, days or months with each turn of the line representing a unit. Which unit is unclear, as breaks in some of the wavy lines may be a result of weathering of the rock surface

BODY METAPHORS: SOUTHERN SCANDINAVIAN ROCK ART   149

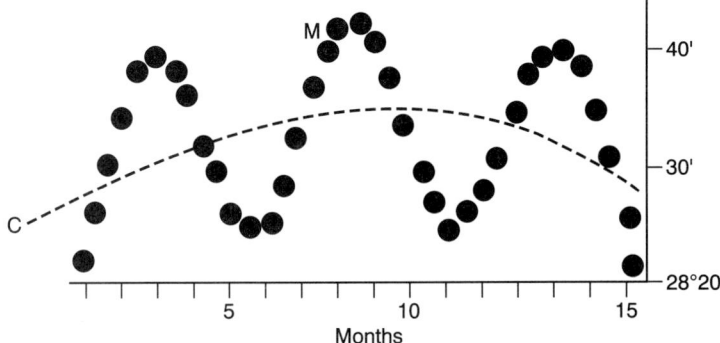

Figure 5.8 The consecutive monthly maximum north and south declinations of the moon during a year. The path of the moon carries it in an ascending and descending motion above and below the celestial equator through the year.
Source: after Brennan (1983)

while in other cases it is likely that these lines were added to and extended over the years as part of a process of reckoning time. It is interesting to note that the main carving surface on which the wavy line occurs at Högsbyn has the largest number of circle crosses (ten) and that changes in the wavy lines are sometimes marked with cupmarks which, as has already been noted, do occur in linear sequences of six and twelve. These wavy lines are also superimposed on, begin or terminate with shoe-soles (linked with movement) (Figure 5.12). One of the wavy lines on surface 25A begins or ends in an infilled figure that from its shape may represent the waxing and waning crescents of the moon. Out of this design the wavy lines 'emerge'.

The 'abstract' designs at Högsbyn can then be argued to be linked together as an expression of seasonal, solar and lunar cycles. In the most abstract sense the concern is with movement and change. And it is this concern with movement that logically links them with the representational designs discussed above and the oppositions between high and low and south and north.

Looking at the entire rock-carving areas, there are two oppositional axes structuring the spatial organization of the most frequent designs. One axis is shared by boats and wavy lines, the other by shoe-soles, feet and humans. Most boats and wavy lines are orientated in one direction, north–south along the rock surface. Almost invariably the humans, shoe-soles and feet are orientated west–east. The particular orientation may be reversed in some cases, but the relative orientation, in terms of horizontal and vertical planes, will usually be maintained. If boats point in one direction, shoe-soles point in another. Some of the abstract designs, notably the cross, circle cross and infilled types with a chequered pattern, effectively combine both orientational axes on various carving surfaces. A spatial logic of orientation thus also links and opposes particular design classes. Such a pattern can be taken further.

The relationship between the human depictions and the living is clearly denotative and metaphorical. While the human depictions stand for human beings in a direct manner, three other representational designs, namely hands, feet and shoe-soles, are connotative signs with a metonymical significance: the part stands for the whole; they signify but substitute for humanity at a second order or level of meaning. This is reinforced by the fact that the human depictions, shoe-soles and feet are usually orientated on the same axis opposing the ships and wavy lines. Just as feet connote human beings in a relationship of metonymy, it can be suggested that wavy lines on some carving surfaces either substitute for or supplement boats. The relationship in both cases is a transformative one: from humans to feet; from boats to wavy lines. Here the notion of motion can be introduced again. While shoe-soles and feet are obviously connected with normal human motion and activity on the land, the movement of boats on the water is of a different order and in a different medium. The close connection between the ships and the wavy lines suggests that the former may in fact be celestial signifiers rather than real boats and connected with celestial motion. Their significance goes far beyond being just something people ride in on the water. This connection of the boat with cosmology has long been pointed out by archaeologists. One suggestion has been that the boats may be conveying the dead to another world or connected to agricultural rites. Marstrander, in particular, has noted that

> the ship figures may well have been intended to represent fertility ceremonies in which the vessel of the god of vegetation was drawn ashore and across the fields in order to arouse the powers of growth and make the land yield good crops. ... In the folklore of both Scandinavia and western Europe there are traces of ceremonies in which ships were borne over fields in the spring as part of fruition rites. (Marstrander 1963: 454)

The Zonation of the Carving Space at Högsbyn

Since all the carving surfaces with the more complex design combinations are unique and only two surfaces possess respectively all the abstract and all the representational designs, it is pertinent to examine their spatial distribution in relation to each other in some detail.

As noted above, the entire rock-carving area can be subdivided into four groupings of carved rock surfaces: those around and in the lake in the south, those on the isolated Ormvindlingshällen and a group of rocks to the north, today on pasture land, and those in the far north (Figure 5.2). The progression today is one from water to grazing land to arable land, but during the Bronze Age the majority of the carvings were probably located in and around arable land. This close association between rock carvings and fertile agricultural land has been well documented by Bertilsson (1986) in relation to the Bohuslän carvings further to the west. To see all the carvings requires upward movement on a slope. The further the rocks are to the north in the sequence, the higher they are. Looking at the overall frequency of the representational and abstract designs from south to north, an interesting picture emerges. Abstract designs, excluding or including cupmarks in the analysis, are most frequent in zone B. By contrast, numbers of representational designs are most frequent in the south (46 per cent) and north (zone D) (30 per cent) and it is only the most northerly rock of all (1A) that has all the representational designs on it. Looking at design combinations, of the twenty carving surfaces in the south only two (10 per cent) have combinations of more than four different designs. In zone B with four carved surfaces, only one has complex combinations, while in zone C there are three complex surfaces (12 per cent) and in the northernmost zone, with eleven surfaces, six (60 per cent) have four or more different designs present. Overall the trend is towards a greater complexity of design combinations in the north of the carving area.

Figure 5.2 shows design combinations on the carving surfaces. The general picture is one of movement from more complex representational design combinations in zone A to simpler ones in the middle to more complex ones, again in the north. No such trend is apparent for the abstract designs, with more complex and simpler carving surfaces roughly evenly distributed through the four zones.

For individual classes of representational designs some interesting trends emerge. Animals are only found in the northern zones, C and D. Only one hand occurs in zone C, the eight others in zones A and D. Feet only occur in zones B and D. The frequencies of human depictions increase from south to north, but such depictions are absent in zone B. Shoe-soles are by far the most frequent in zone D. Frequencies of boats are virtually identical in zones A and D, but much more infrequent in zones B and C (Table 5. 8).

Table 5.8 The absolute and relative frequency of different designs according to a four-fold zonation (see Figure 5.2) of the Högsbyn carving site.

Design type	Zone A		Zone B		Zone C		Zone D	
	N	%	N	%	N	%	N	%
Cupmarks	61	11	91	16	148	26	268	47
Circle cross	17	41	10	24	5	12	9	22
Circle	7	37	2	10	4	21	6	31
Wavy lines	1	2	33	50	6	9	26	39
Cross	2	2	6	60	–	3	3	11
Infilled	5	50	3	30	1	10	1	10
Humans	5	14	–	–	14	40	16	45
Animals	–	–	–	–	2	33	4	66
Feet	–	–	13	81	–	–	3	19
Hands	3	33	–	–	1	11	5	55
Boats	29	36	2	3	16	20	33	41
Shoe-soles	44	23	44	23	23	12	76	41

Generalizing from these statistics three distinct patterns emerge:

1 Designs increasing in frequency from south to north (humans; shoe-soles).
2 Designs only common in zone B (feet).
3 Designs absent or infrequent in zones B and C but occurring in roughly equal frequencies in the south and north (boats; hands).

There are clear trends apparent for three of the classes of geometric designs. Circle crosses steadily decrease in frequency from south to north. Only one wavy line is present in the south zone, 50 per cent in zone B middle zone and about 40 per cent in zone D in the north. Cupmarks steadily increase in frequency from south to north. I can now begin to express some of these spatial relationships of representational and abstract designs in terms of a number of generalized generative principles:

1 As shoe-soles and humans increase from south to north, circle crosses decrease in frequency.
2 Where feet are common in zones B and C, so are cupmarks and wavy lines.
3 Where boats are common in the south and the north, hands occur.

4 Where abstract designs dominate in zones B and C, surfaces with complex design combinations are more infrequent.

Towards a Phenomenology of the Högsbyn Carvings

Today, a visitor coming to Högsbyn by road experiences the carvings in entirely the wrong direction: from north to south walking down the slope to the lake. This is also the sequence in which they are documented in Svensson's (1982) book. This means that some of the carved rocks are only visible *after* one has passed beyond them. It has been the contention in this chapter that the sequencing of the designs on the rocks only makes sense from south to north and that they were meant to be experienced in this way.

The relationship between land and water in this part of Sweden has not altered significantly since the Bronze Age. Both the lake bed and the surrounding rocks have risen up at the same rate. What has changed is the degree of variability in the water levels in the Råvarpen lake, since these are now regulated. In the past there would have been much greater fluctuation in water levels, perhaps by as much as 5 metres or more, meaning that at certain times of the year some of the designs on the southernmost rocks would have been submerged by water. Old photographs from the 1930s show the Ronarudden peninsula as an island (Andersson pers. comm.). A progression from a series of rocks partially or completely surrounded by water in the south to those situated high up in dry agricultural land in the north appears to be a very significant element in any narrative of Högsbyn. Another is the degree of visibility between the carved rocks. In the south–north sequencing of the site one can normally see the next carved rock in the distance, but the detail of what is actually carved is not apparent until an observer is a few metres or less away. Consequently, the encounter with each carved rock, by which one must pause to look, becomes a process of revelation. The visibility of the carvings also alters according to the qualities of the light in accordance with the east–west movement of the sun, and the time of the day. Another rather different feature of light at Högsbyn is that this area is particularly prone to lightning strikes during the summer months, adding to the cosmological significance and power of the place.

Excavations below two of the carved rocks at Högsbyn (Svensson 1985) have revealed a stone platform in one case, at the foot of rock 19 (Figure 5.14). This rock has a series of human depictions associated with boats and shoe-soles. In the platform there was a charcoal concentration and a deposition of quartz waste was placed immediately below the centre of the carving panel. Despite the radiocarbon dates (far later than the carvings) the stone platform and the quartz deposition may very well be connected with the ritual use of the carvings, especially in view of evidence from Østfold in southern Norway, where platforms and depositions of smashed pottery are clearly associated with the carvings (Johansen 1979).

The entire carving area of Högsbyn was almost certainly a focus for ceremonies involving processional movement between individual carving surfaces acting as a focus for specific ritual events. The designs occur on rocks in a 'consecrated' space whose meanings would be manipulated as part of a choreography of movement. I want to suggest specifically that the site was utilized as a symbolic resource forming an important focus for the ordering of calendrical and initiation rites. The carved surfaces, their inspection and interpretation, form a kind of scene-setting for ritual events. We know that virtually all rites of passage and ritual events more generally occur through a tripartite organization of experience involving rites of separation from the profane world, the seclusion from this world in a liminal space, and rites of reincorporation. In virtually all societies, including our own, individuals move through different socially recognized statuses as a series of discontinuous leaps. Each period takes various lengths of time with rituals marking the transitions: puberty rite, wedding, funeral, healing ritual, etc. The hallmark of all these rituals is their social timelessness and the crossing of boundaries is always marked out by rites, a passage from x to not-x, not-y to y. These ceremonies have three purposes: (1) they proclaim a change of status; (2) they magically bring it about; (3) they are interval markers in social time.

A few basic and invariant elements of rites of passage may be summarized (Turner 1967; 1969). The first phase involves a separation from normal life, removing the initiate from normal existence and who becomes abnormal in space, time and appearance. The second phase is one of social timelessness, a liminal phase. The essential thing is that the initiate be removed from normal activities and kept physically apart, sent away or secluded. During this period of separation the initiate undergoes all kinds of prohibitions and proscriptions involving clothing, food, movement. For ordinary people the initiate is in a state of holiness: sacred, contaminated, dangerous, 'dirty'. During the liminal phase the characteristics of the ritual subject remain ambiguous. He or she passes through a cultural realm that has few of the characteristics of the past or the coming state. The third phase involves reincorporation into normal society in a new role, a rite of aggregation. These are often similar to rites of separation but in reverse, so, for example, processions may move in the opposite direction. The special costume or state of nakedness of the liminal state is removed along with food restrictions and a new costume appropriate to the new status put on.

The second or liminal period is most crucial and may be emphasized in a wide variety of ways and always by contrast, for example: feasting/fasting; formality/informality. Birth/death symbolism is extremely common in marking out states. In initiation ceremonies involving the change from child to adult, bodily mutilation is frequent: circumcision; knocking out teeth; head shaving; scarification. These are all metaphors of purification and death. The child must die for the adult to be born. The attributes of the liminal state are frequently ambiguous, since this condition and the persons involved in it elude normal social classifications, statuses and positions. Liminality involves a process of *becoming*. It is betwixt and between: a kind of anti-structure or a reversal of the structure of day-to-day social existence and statuses.

I now wish to consider the sequencing of the carved-rock surfaces in some more detail in order to reconstruct a narrative of the way in which the rocks may have been experienced and understood.

In terms of the frequency of motifs, three carved rocks stand out from all the others: rock 32 in the south with 7 carving surfaces, rock 25 with 4 surfaces and rock 1 in the far north with 2. Together, these three rocks possess roughly 50 per cent of all the carvings and the most complex design combinations, and a considerable degree of merger or superimposition on rocks 32 and 1. Surface 25A is the only one to possess all the abstract designs. Surface 1A has the greatest complexity of all design combinations and is the only rock to have all representational designs present on it. Surfaces 32A and 25A have 9 and 8 different design combinations respectively, surface 1A 11. I want to argue that these rocks, respectively, represent and encode the three crucial ritual phases of separation, liminality and reaggregation.

Zone A

The starting point for an encounter with the rocks at Högsbyn is the large sloping panels of rock 32, by far the most dramatic and crowded with designs on the Ronarudden peninsula. These panels were also the first to be recorded at the site in the eighteenth century. Rock 32 (Figure 5.9 and Plate 5.1) is situated at the southernmost point of the entire carving area. Its east-facing surface is covered with carvings and is clearly subdivided by two deep natural fissures. The carvings are not broken by these fissures,

Plate 5.1 Högsbyn: rock 32. Surface A.

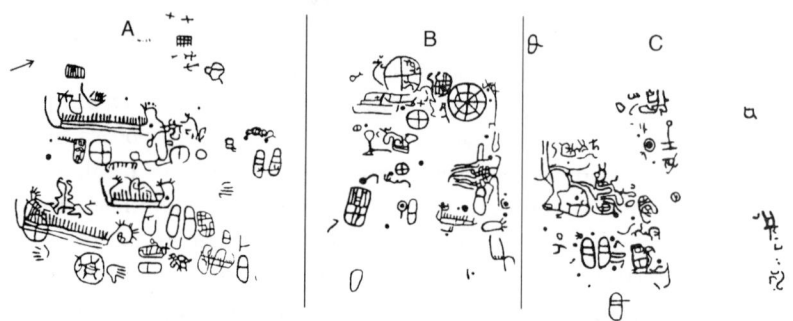

Figure 5.9 The carvings of the three eastern surfaces (A, B, C) of rock 32 in the far south of the Högsbyn carving area. Scale 1: 25.
Source: Svensson (1982)

which must therefore have been already present when the rock was carved (Svensson 1982: 49). The carving technique is uniform over the entire rock surface and provides no indication of any great temporal distinction between the carving of individual designs. The western slope of the rock, not visible from the eastern side, has a smaller number of carved designs on five different areas/surfaces.

The three eastern carving surfaces are very different and have a clear sequential order from south to north. The following regularities may be noted:

1 The frequency of representational designs decreases, as do the number of different motifs, on the same carving surfaces. Shoe-soles, boats, hands and humans all occur in the southernmost area (Figure 5.9: A). Only shoe-soles, boats and one possible foot occur in the middle, while the only clearly identifiable representational design on the northernmost part of the rock is the shoe-sole (Figure 5.9: C).
2 The frequency of cupmarks increases from surface A to C, as does the degree of merger and superimposition. There is such a high degree of superimposition of designs in area C that it is impossible to distinguish clearly any design type apart from shoe-soles.

In looking at the three surfaces we move from south to north from clearly distinguishable representational and abstract designs to a tangled mass of carved lines, from structure and order, to what might be termed anti-structure and disorder. Humans and body parts of humans (hands) are only present at the beginning of this sequence in which the boats are largest, most prominent and frequent. The circle cross only appears in areas A and B and a very elaborate spider's web-type form of it occurs in area B internally subdivided into fifteen spaces, as opposed to the normal fourfold division. Elaborate infilled designs (some resembling the form of shoe-soles or boats with crew strokes in area A) occur on all three carving surfaces. A net figure on the western slope of rock 32 (defined here as being on surface 32D) is clearly set apart from the other carvings in area C, rather than being integrated with the other designs as in areas A and B. One must move around the rock to the north to see it and the other simpler design combinations on the western slope of the rock (surfaces 32 E–G). The large panels on the eastern slope of rock 32 may represent a process of separation from the normal order of the world, involving the dissolution of representations of humanity. Rock 33 consists of a series of small panels depicting boats, shoe-soles, circle crosses and one possible stick-line human. Rock 33 introduces a new design, the wavy ('snake') line not previously encountered, but one that dominates later in the sequence in zone B. Rock 30, the next in the sequence, depicts a simple boat, shoe-soles and a circle, and is not visible from the carved rocks to the south. From it the next carved rock, 28, is visible but the carvings themselves cannot be distinguished until one has approached the rock by crossing an area of land that would have been seasonally inundated with water. Two stick-line humans occur together with two cupmarks and three shoe-soles. All carving surfaces after 32C lack the extreme degree of design superimposition present on that surface. They depict a few design elements in selective combinations while maintaining their separate identity. Rock 28 is the last on which humans occur before reaching the rocks in zone C much farther to the north and higher up the carving site. Rock 26, the last in the carved rocks of zone A, depicts an elaborate infilled circle cross, a single shoe-sole and circle designs. Other carved rocks to the west by the lake shore or situated on rocks surrounded by water depict a few isolated boat, shoe-sole and cupmark designs only and do not appear to be part of the main sequence of depictions at Högsbyn.

Standing looking at the southern carved rocks one is constantly aware of the water. It forms a backdrop to the depictions: water is always beyond them. One is also constantly aware of the odour of the lake and the sound of the water lapping against the rocks. Visiting the rocks involves moving around or across water-filled areas and here the boat designs tend to be both visually dominant and most memorable.

Zone B

Rock 25 ('Ormvindlingshällen', the snake meander rock) in the southern part of Högsbyn (zone B) is the only one in the carving area to be spatially separated from all other carved rocks by a considerable distance: approximately 140 m away from the nearest carved rocks to the north and about 80 m from those to the south. Its very separation from other rocks suggests liminality, as does the degree of abstraction of the designs. The rock itself is also utterly distinctive in character when compared with all the other carved rocks at Högsbyn. It is a huge 40 m-long and 3 m-broad curved dome, dipping down at the southern and northern ends, with well marked north–south striation lines running along its surface (Plate 5.2). Virtually all the carvings must be seen from the eastern side of the rock (as on rock 32), to the left of someone approaching from the south. The western face of the rock, unlike that of rock 32, has no carvings on it whatsoever. This means that an observer facing the designs also looks towards the water of the lake beyond to the west. The carvings, then, are 'framed' by water in much the same way as those on the Ronarudden peninsula, but with the difference that Ormvindlingshällen is much further away from the lake

Plate 5.2 Högsbyn: Ormvindlingshällen.

shore. The water here is thus both present and absent at the same time. Directly to the east of the rock the slope of the land gently rises away, today as arable fields. To the west it drops sharply down to the lake. From rock 26, the last in the southern sequence of carved rocks, the presence of carvings on Ormvindlingshällen can be noted, although nothing of their specific form. Similarly, from most of the carved panels on Ronarudden others can be seen. By contrast, from Ormvindlingshällen no other rock carvings are visible either to the south or the north. Rock 25 can be subdivided into four panels (Figure 5.10: A–D) on the basis of gaps separating the main series of depictions. The largest of these, 25A, is at the southern end and dominated by meandering wavy lines. (As suggested above, connected with time reckoning and as possible symbolic transformations of boats. They perhaps represent water too: the waves on the lake?) These wavy lines are orientated along the south to north longitudinal axis of the rock. By contrast, the majority of the depictions of feet and shoe-soles are orientated west to east pointing down the slope of the rock towards the east, away from the water and towards the land. This repeats the pattern on rock 32 where the shoe-soles also point east down the rock slope in opposition to the north–south orientational axis of the boats. But

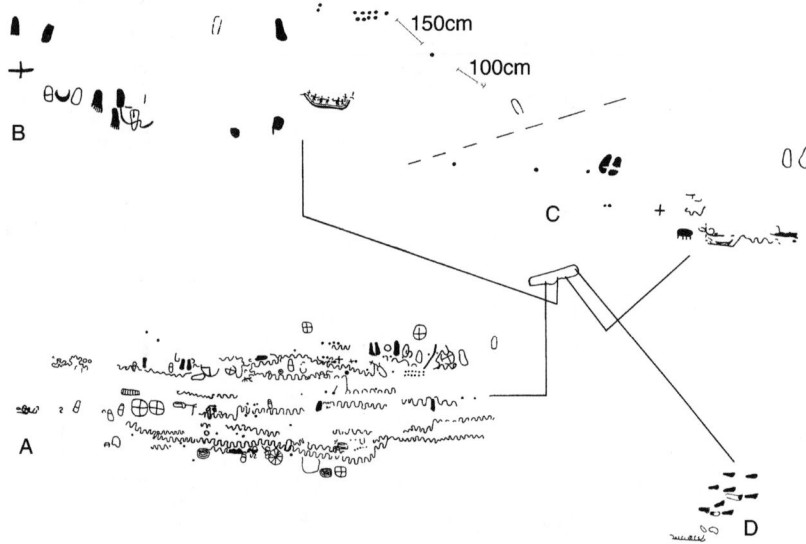

Figure 5.10 The four rock-carving surfaces on Ormvindlingshällen.
Sources: Surfaces 25A and D: Svensson (1982): scale 1: 25. Surfaces 25B and C: Andersson (unpublished): scale: 1: 10

here they nevertheless point towards the water, as this rock is surrounded by water on three sides. Rock 25 contrasts in an interesting manner with rock 32. As one moves from south to north the character of the designs changes from predominantly abstract and geometric to entirely representational. The movement is from surface 25A dominated by wavy lines, circle crosses and cupmarks, to a series of panels with feet, boats and shoe-soles. Superimposition occurs frequently on the large southern carving surface, but is infrequent on the three surfaces at the northern end. In effect this reverses the sequence encountered on rock 32. We move on Ormvindlingshällen from the abstract to the representational. Human beings here are entirely absent, only being represented metonymically by the feet and shoe-soles. Boats are also absent, with only two exceptions on panels 25B and 25D. On the former, an exceptional boat design occurs with a crew of up to seven human figures. Elsewhere at Högsbyn the boats only possess crew strokes or the character of the human figures is out of all proportion to the boats themselves, being superimposed on them rather than constituting an integral part of the boat design. The main feature of surface 25A is the dominance of the snake-like wavy lines merging with or superimposed on circle crosses, shoe-soles and internally divided designs. These wavy lines, I have argued, suggest a concern with time, the seasons, solar and lunar cycles, all of which are powerful symbolic referents in many rites of passage. The only other representational designs present are a pair of feet. The sequence of representational designs on the four panels, and their orientation, is as follows:

25A feet and shoe-soles orientated west–east
25B boat with seven clear human figures as crew orientated north–south; feet and shoe-soles orientated west–east
25C shoe-soles orientated west–east
25D feet, shoe-soles and boat orientated north–south

The three different representational designs present, feet, boats and shoe-soles, only occur together at the end of the sequence and here they also all share the same orientational axis. The feet and shoe-soles on the final surface of rock 25 are all orientated to point to the north, i.e. in the direction of the next series of carved rocks. This represents a clear reversal, or inversion, of their west–east orientation on panels 25A–C and on rocks 32 and 1 at the most southerly and northerly ends of Högsbyn. It is interesting to note in this connection that this final and most northerly panel on rock 25 is not intervisible with the three others to the south.

The feet on panel 25D, as we have seen, point in the direction of the next series of carved rocks, situated up the slope. Some of these rocks are visible but not their carvings. The north-facing feet designs clearly act here as a directional pointer for movement towards the next series of carved rocks. The present-day path followed by visitors is, again, in the wrong place, in that it is located within the Högsbyn nature reserve and runs a little to the west of what would seem to be a normal course of movement, up a gentle slope from rock 25 to the centre of rocks 24 and 23, marking the beginning of zone C of the carving area.

Zone C

The carved rocks in zone C form three rough south–north rows on land now very gently sloping up to the north. Rocks 24, 22, 19, 16 and 13 and rocks 23, 21, 20, 18, 15 and 12 form two parallel series, while a more northerly series is made up of rocks 14 to 8. These carved rocks have a very different character to Ormvindlingshällen and the southerly rocks of zone A. The carved surfaces are small and the rocks themselves low and not very distinctive in character, with the exception of rock 19. The carvings on rocks 24–13 and 23–12 occur either on flat tops or on low exposed eastern faces. For an observer this means that one is generally looking down on the carving surfaces rather than across and at them, which is the case for the large southerly panels (25A–C) at Ormvindlingshällen and many of the carved surfaces in zone A. There is also a comparative lack of visual clues to movement among these rocks. While movement from rock 23 to 21 is obvious, rocks 20 (now entirely overgrown), 18, 15 and 12 (also overgrown) have a flat and hidden character. The lack of any visual clues as to their presence – these rocks cannot be seen except from above – means that a novice would have had to be led to them and shown their location. The designs on the two panels of rock 24 are not intervisible, nor can those on rock 22 be seen from rock 24. Movement from rocks 24 and 22 to 19 is obvious, although the content of the designs on rock 19 cannot be seen from them. From rock 19 the presence of designs on the eastern face of rock 16 is clear (although not their specific form) and from rock 16 the presence of designs on rock 13 is apparent.

Moving up-slope from Ormvindlingshällen (Plate 5.3 and Figure 5.14) one enters into what resembles a theatrical space bounded by carved rocks to the west and east. The designs on those rocks to the west (24 and 22) can

Plate 5.3 View of the carved rocks at Högsbyn in zone C seen from the south.

be clearly seen, those to the west are hidden, their presence only suggested by a few cupmarks on the western part of rock 23. Looking at these carvings the backdrop of water beyond is now almost entirely lost. A small north–west arm of the Råvarpen lake is now only visible in the far distance to the west, but has little visual impact. By the northerly end of the rocks in this zone water has entirely vanished as part of the visual experience of the carvings. The rocks in zone C are definitely of, and part of, the land and its heaviness and static character, as opposed to the fluidity and buoyancy of the water very much associated with the rocks in zone A.

The sequence of designs on rocks 23 to 12 is simple. They appear to have a secondary and supplementary significance to the main south–north series of carved rocks at Högsbyn, much like rocks 27, 29 and 34 in and around the lake in zone A. No superimposing or merging of designs occur except on rock 23, which is the only rock to have more than two different identifiable designs (shoe-sole, five small and simple boat designs, cupmarks and a circle cross). Rocks 12 and 15 are only decorated with a few cupmarks, those on rocks 20 and 21 are indistinct, while rock 18 has an infilled design and a pair of shoe-soles. There is a fading away of design complexity to the north.

By contrast, the eastern series of carved rocks (numbers 24–13) is a much more complex, visually impressive and important series. Human figures occur on surfaces 24C (now covered), 22, 19 and possibly 16, although here they are indistinct and highly ambiguous in form. It is only on rock 19, however, that they are large and more than stick-line representations. This panel, by far the most important in zone C, shows quite clearly a cult procession with two boats (Figure 5.11), that to the left (south) possibly driven forth on a wheel, with two acrobats (one on each boat), helmeted lur and spear bearers and a horse (Andersson 1992). Rock 16, to the north, has three surfaces, an eastern facing panel with ambiguous human designs, a mass of cupmarks on its flat top (more than on any other carved surface at Högsbyn) and a pair of shoe-soles on its western face which point towards the small flat rock 17, on which there is a series of cupmarks in rows (see figure 5.5, no. 1). Rock 13 has shoe-soles, cupmarks and simple boat designs.

I have already noted that the designs on rocks 24–13 and 23–12 must be seen either from above or from the east. Approaching from the south one must pass to the *right* of the rocks. This repeats the pattern found on Ormvindlingshällen and in the southern zone A. This becomes particularly interesting when it is appreciated that most of the foot and shoe-sole representations portray the right side except when pairs are clearly

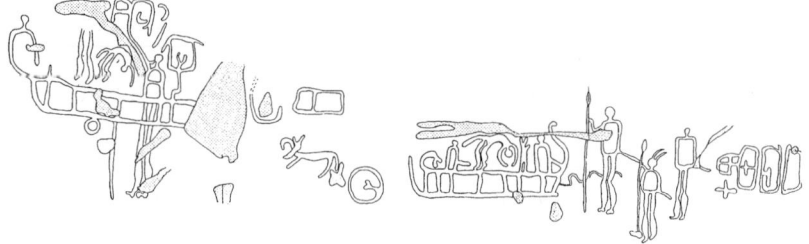

Figure 5.11 The rock carvings on rock 19.
Source: Andersson (1992): scale: 1: 10

depicted (see below). Right is thus associated with the east and with land rather than water, as there is no water visible to the right or east of the rocks once one has moved beyond the Ronarudden peninsula. So a double series of symbolic oppositions is apparent. The first, previously noted, is between north and south, low and high, water and land. The second is between west and east, left and right, water and land.

This is of great interest in relation to what happens next in the series of carved rocks as one moves from south to north at Högsbyn. Rocks 14 to 8 have an entirely different character to the ones previously discussed in zone C. The rock outcrops occur here on a steep slope to the west, as do rocks 5 and 3 to the north. The carvings mainly occur, therefore, on the western faces of these rocks or to the *left* as one moves between them from south to north. Following the break of the slope one is naturally led along between rock 14 and rock 3. From any of the rocks in zones C and D, the designs on rocks 14 to 8 and 3 to 5 are entirely hidden. Again, as a novice one would have had to be led to them. Rocks 14 to 8 and 3 and 5 are best seen in the morning before the sunlight shines on them directly, whereas the majority of the other rocks in zones A, B and C are best seen in the mid-afternoon when the sunlight shines on them obliquely.

Rocks 14 and 11 have a few simple designs (boat, circle cross and cupmarks and boat, hand and cupmark respectively). Rock 10, by contrast, has a mass of designs with a great degree of overlap, merger and superimposition. These include a circle cross, circles, a pair of shoe-soles, wavy lines, cupmarks, a plant-like figure and bird/razor designs. On rock 9 a series of cupmarks is depicted and on rock 8 shoe-soles, a horse and cupmarks. Surface 5B stands out from the others in the occurrence of at least six human depictions, a large number of paired and single shoe-soles, elaborate boats and two animals. There is perhaps here the representation of a hunting scene. One of the humans with a bow is associated with a dog. Two human depictions, including the archer, are phallic. The paired shoe-soles on this carving surface are unusual in being orientated both west–east and north–south, directing movement towards rocks 3 and 1 to the north. Rock 3, with two carving surfaces, has no human depictions, but shoe-soles and a hand are present, together with unelaborated boat designs, cupmarks, circle crosses and infilled figures. The fingers on the hand on surface 3B point to the north as if directing one towards rock 1.

Zone D

From the rocks in zone D any view of the water when looking at the carvings is completely absent. They are all high up on the slope and surrounded by arable land. The eastern carved rocks of zone D (nos 7-1: see Figures 5.2 and 5.14) form a clear sequence and the most obvious direction towards them is from rocks 12 or 13 at the northern end of zone C. From rock 13, rock 6 is visible but not the designs on it which occur on its eastern face. Rock 7, small and completely flat, remains hidden until one approaches it. A boat and a series of cupmarks form parallel series orientated north–south. Two shoe-soles occur. One superimposed on the boat is orientated towards the north and rock 6, another approximately west–east pointing towards rock 5. This rock may then mark alternative courses of movements towards the most northerly carved rocks in zone D. Rock 6 is rather similar in shape to rock 19 in zone C. The two human spear carriers depicted on it are also very similar to those on rock 19 and the same artist may have carved both these rocks. An animal depiction also occurs and a very simple boat design. The long sequences of wavy lines occurring above the human depictions make this panel very distinctive. Elsewhere at Högsbyn wavy lines are not combined on the same panel as human depictions, except on surface 1A. This surface combines human depictions with the dominant design form (wavy lines) found on Ormvindlingshällen (surface 25A), completely lacking in depictions of humanity. Rock 6B with a boat and shoe-sole design is probably a continuation of the carved surface of rock 4. This is a rounded, low rock with depictions around and on top of it. Two isolated hands occur, wavy lines, boat depictions, crosses and cupmarks. At the eastern end of the surface a wavy line, orientated north–south, is superimposed over a series of west–east orientated shoe-soles, a replication of the relationships between these two classes of designs on surface 25A. At the north-east side parallel rows of U designs occur, interpreted by Andersson (1995) as animal tracks, together with a unique double spiral design. Animal designs and human depictions are entirely absent. Rock 2 has an isolated cupmark.

Rock 1, in the far north of the Högsbyn carving area, is situated at a point of transition. It occurs at the very top of the south–north slope. To the north of it flat arable land stretches away. From it (the view is now blocked by a house), directly to the north, the largest and most impressive cairn in the Högsbyn area would be visible just over half a kilometre distant. The designs occur on the western slope of the rock, approached from the south, on its left-hand side, connecting it with the series of carved rocks (14, 11, 10, 9, 8, 3 and 5) situated along the break of slope to the west in the north of the Högsbyn carving area. From these rocks one looks at the designs in the direction of the rising sun. From all others at Högsbyn one looks down at the rock or facing towards the setting sun.

Divided by a large crack into two distinct carving surfaces, rock 1 combines a series of abstract and representational designs in a similar manner to carving surface 32A in the far south (Figure 5.12), but has a number of unique features. As already noted, surface 1A possesses the greatest combination of different designs at Högsbyn and is the only carving surface to include all representational design classes. More depictions of humans occur here (at least seven) than on any other carving surface. Not only that, six of the seven depictions cluster at the northern end of the carved area (surface 1A), but these human depictions are interspersed, overlap and merge with hands, ambiguous feet/shoe-sole designs,

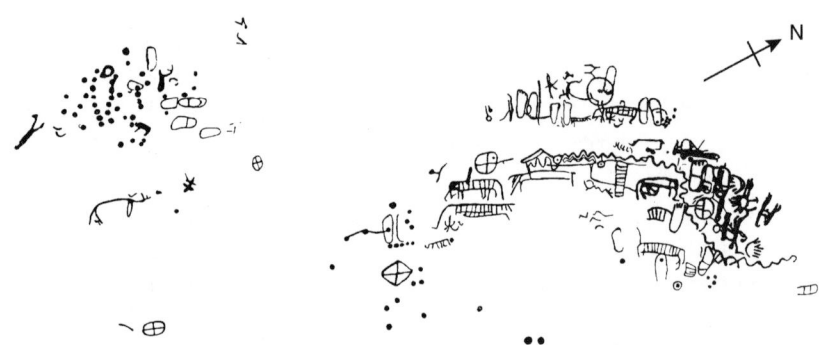

Figure 5.12 The rock carvings on rock 1.
Source: Svensson (1982): scale: 1: 25

shoe-soles and a circle cross. The group of human figures is bounded by a series of wavy lines separating it from a contrasting design field dominated by boats and cupmarks. This rock, the only one in which all the representational designs are brought together, is clearly a culminating (reaggregational) terminal point in the sequence of carved rocks at Högsbyn. That this is so is crucially confirmed by the character of the human depictions, which will now be considered in more detail.

Human Bodies at Högsbyn

A minimum number of 35 human depictions occur at Högsbyn on 12 carving surfaces scattered throughout the rock-carving area. These change substantially along a south to north axis. On the three southern carving surfaces with humans only one or two depictions occur. They are all small, ranging in size from around 10–25 cm in height. The figures on these rocks are all simple incised stick-line representations with no discernible thickening in the torso or elsewhere in the body. None of the bodies have sexual organs, carry tools or do anything. The human depictions are diminutive in comparison with the boat designs on the same rocks and are about the same length or shorter than the hand and shoe-sole depictions. Humanity is simply present and certainly not a key element in the design structure of these rocks, one element among many that disappears just beyond the Ronarudden peninsula to be metonymically replaced by the shoe-soles and feet on the carving surfaces of Ormvindlingshällen (rock 25). The only other presence is in a unique series of seven members of a boat crew on surface 25B, the only boat at Högsbyn to depict humans as opposed to crew-stroke markings.

Depictions of humans occur again on four carving surfaces in zone C. Three of the rocks with human depictions portray, again, simple stick-line figures. On the other surface, 19, the imagery is substantially different. The figures are much larger (25–50 cm in height). They are more numerous, with up to eight figures appearing on the surface, including two acrobats (see Figure 5.11 and the discussion above), and they are clearly the key element on the carving surface for the first time. In zone D with five rock surfaces portraying people, the torso is now marked out in a variety of techniques. On surface 6A the human bodies appear in outline technique as on rock 19. On surface 5B they are entirely scooped out of the rock. The torso is substantial in some cases and two figures are depicted with a thickening of the calves. The contrast between the representations of humanity on surfaces 5B and 6A is quite striking. One of the humans on surface 6A has a head-dress, both carry spears. On surface 5B one figure holds a bow, another perhaps an axe. More simple stick-line representations occur again on surfaces 3B and 1B. On both surfaces they are closely associated with boats and animal representations appear (very rare at Högsbyn). Phallic figures appear on surface 5B.

On rock 1A, the most northerly, the representations of humanity are substantially different from those appearing on any other rock-carving surface. At least six large (approx. 40–50 cm) figures are tightly clustered and interspersed with hands, feet and shoe-soles. These are the most substantial human figures at Högsbyn, being entirely scooped out of the rock surface. Two figures probably carry swords, others objects of a ceremonial nature. This is one of only two carving surfaces (both in zone D) on which sexual identity is clearly marked: three or four figures have a phallus. On this rock a 'marriage scene' (see the discussion in Yates 1990; 1993) occurs between two figures who may both be male.

The majority of the human depictions at Högsbyn are orientated east to west with the head to the west. The exceptions occur on carving surfaces 32A, 5B, 1A and 1B at the extreme southern and northern ends of the carving area. On surface 32A both stick-line human representations on this surface are orientated north–south. One appears to have the head facing south, the other to the north. On surface 5B two of the figures are orientated north to south with the head to the north and four west to east with the head to the east, thus reversing the orientation found elsewhere. On surface 1B one human figure occurs with the head to the south; on surface 1A five are orientated east–west, with the head to the east, one north–south with the head to the south.

This sequence of changing human depictions (Figure 5.13) can be understood as a process of becoming, a growing formation and development of the human body involving an increase in stature, frequency and substance. On the final rock sexual identity becomes firmly established. The movement is from depictions with a minimal human identity to the creation of fully fledged social actors. The human designs thus represent a process of the coming into being and objectification of the self; the self or individual as formed through a ritual discourse.

The narrative of the human depictions literally embodies the theme of becoming fully human in terms of roles, statuses and gender identity. The human body is something on which a definite identity is gradually inscribed, as the neutral, sexless and child-like bodies of the southern rocks are dissolved into the shoe-soles and feet of rock 25 to re-emerge carrying

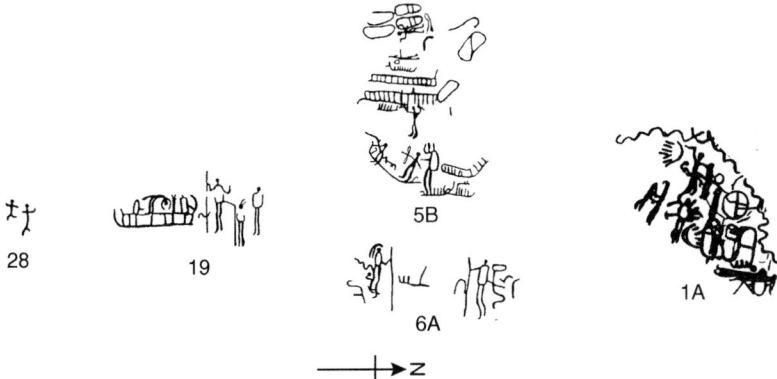

Figure 5.13 The changing character of the human depictions at Högsbyn from the south to the north of the carving area. Scale: 1: 25. Numbers refer to carving surfaces marked on Figures 5.2 and 5.14.

tools, instruments and weapons in ceremonial procession on rocks 19 and 6, as phallic bow-carrying hunters on rock 5B, finally to be locked in a sexual embrace on surface 1A. The body is initially present, 'dies' and is submerged in a liminal state on surface 25A, before appearing again in a fundamentally different form in zones C and D. This new state appears at a point in which a transition from water to land has been made. The point of transition occurs on rock 25. The shoe-soles on surface 25A point away from the water, down the rock surface and towards the land. At the end of the rock the feet point towards the north. It is pertinent, in this respect, to note that rock 25 ends in the depiction of *twelve* feet with toes pointing north towards the rock surfaces on which humanity appears again. Two of these surfaces, including carving surface 1A, have *six* human figures. The self and the body are being transactionally created through a ritual process establishing its social and sexual identity. A social body is being fashioned out of the simple and undifferentiated 'organic' body appearing on the southern rocks. The body is acknowledged to be a *constructed* product of a ritual discourse: a sociopolitics of becoming.

It is interesting to note the difference in the *scale* of the designs. The hands, feet and shoe-soles are the same size as real hands, etc. (contrasting with the human, boat and animal depictions) and of a standardized size. All other design types vary considerably in size from one carving surface to another and are not in the same sense 'realistic' depictions. There is not, however, a consistent emphasis on pairing. The foot design is relatively infrequent, occurring sixteen times on four carving surfaces, three of which are on Ormvindlingshällen (zone B) and the other on the most northerly carved rock (1A). The depictions on 1A are rather ambiguous in that they resemble shoe-soles but with toes marked inside them. In the two cases (surfaces 25A and 1A) where pairs of feet are represented both left and right feet are shown, but very differently. On surface 25A, where human depictions are absent, the feet are orientated in the same direction, whereas on rock 1A, where humans are present, they are orientated in opposite directions. In all other cases single *right* feet are depicted. This pattern is repeated in the case of shoe-soles. Where pairs of shoe-soles occur, both the left and the right shoe-sole occur. Where single shoe-soles occur, it is invariably the right rather than the left shoe-sole that is depicted, or determination is uncertain or ambiguous. Pairs of shoe-soles are frequent on the most southerly surfaces (32A and B), virtually absent on rock 25A (five left shoe-soles, twenty-three right, sixteen uncertain) and are frequent again in zones C and D (Table 5.9).

The metonymical depiction of disembodied extremities of human beings may perhaps be an expression of a social rather than an individual body – membership of a clan, lineage or group. If this is the case there is at Högsbyn a constant emphasis on the mediation of the individual body by the social body and vice versa. If the body parts and shoe-soles metaphorically signify a social body we may claim that they are to do with *structure*, while the individual metaphorical human depictions are bound up with the *agency* and the process of becoming of individuals through specific rites. This would explain why the human figures change while the design form and sizes of hands, feet and shoe-soles remains relatively standardized throughout the site. The directionality of the orientation of

Table 5.9 The occurrence of left and right shoe-sole designs at Högsbyn in relation to a four-fold zonation of the carving site.

Zone	Left	Right	Uncertain	Total
A	8	21	15	44
B	5	23	16	44
C	4	3	16	23
D	14	24	38	76

the shoe-soles and feet is clearly important. The majority (72 per cent) of the shoe-soles are orientated west–east pointing towards the east, the land and away from the water. Exceptions orientated north–south and facing to the north or south occur throughout the carving area. On a number of carving surfaces they clearly act as directional markers for further movement in the course of which the human depictions become transformed.

Conclusions

I have argued that there is a definite structural order linking the carvings at Högsbyn in the course of moving between the rocks in a south to north sequence. Högsbyn is, in part, a narrative about becoming human. The narrative at Högsbyn is also one to do with life, death and the regeneration of life, time, movement, the rising and setting of the sun and moon, the passage of the seasons, and relationships between land and water, their connotations and associations. The carvings encode a process by which human social and sexual identity is established and simultaneously linked to the passage of time, fertility, hunting and the agrarian cycle. Just as the human beings grow in stature, social and sexual identity as one progresses to the north of the carving area, they fade away as one moves south. Looking at the human depictions on rocks 1 and 5 an observer faces the rising sun, with all its connotations of birth and life. Looking at those on rocks 19 and all those in the southern zone, A, one faces the dying rays of the sun. In this respect it is interesting to note that the ceremonial procession depicted on rock 19, as indicated by the boat prows, appears to be moving both towards the south and the north (the southern boat, with acrobat, moving south; the northern boat, also with an acrobat, moving north). The vast majority of the boat depictions at Högsbyn, including all of the largest and most impressive examples, are orientated either exactly or approximately in a north–south direction (87 per cent). On surface 1A some of the prow ends face north, others south. On surface 25B the only boat with a human crew appears to be moving south. On rock surface 32A on which the largest and most elaborate boat depictions occur, one of which is superimposed on a circle cross which I have argued to be a marker of seasonality and the passage of time, all the large boats are moving south to the water. The rock carvings at Högsbyn can be considered to be a public statement relating to formal within-group relations and social categories, structured in space to make specific sets of statements. I have argued that individual design forms such as wavy lines and shoe-soles have

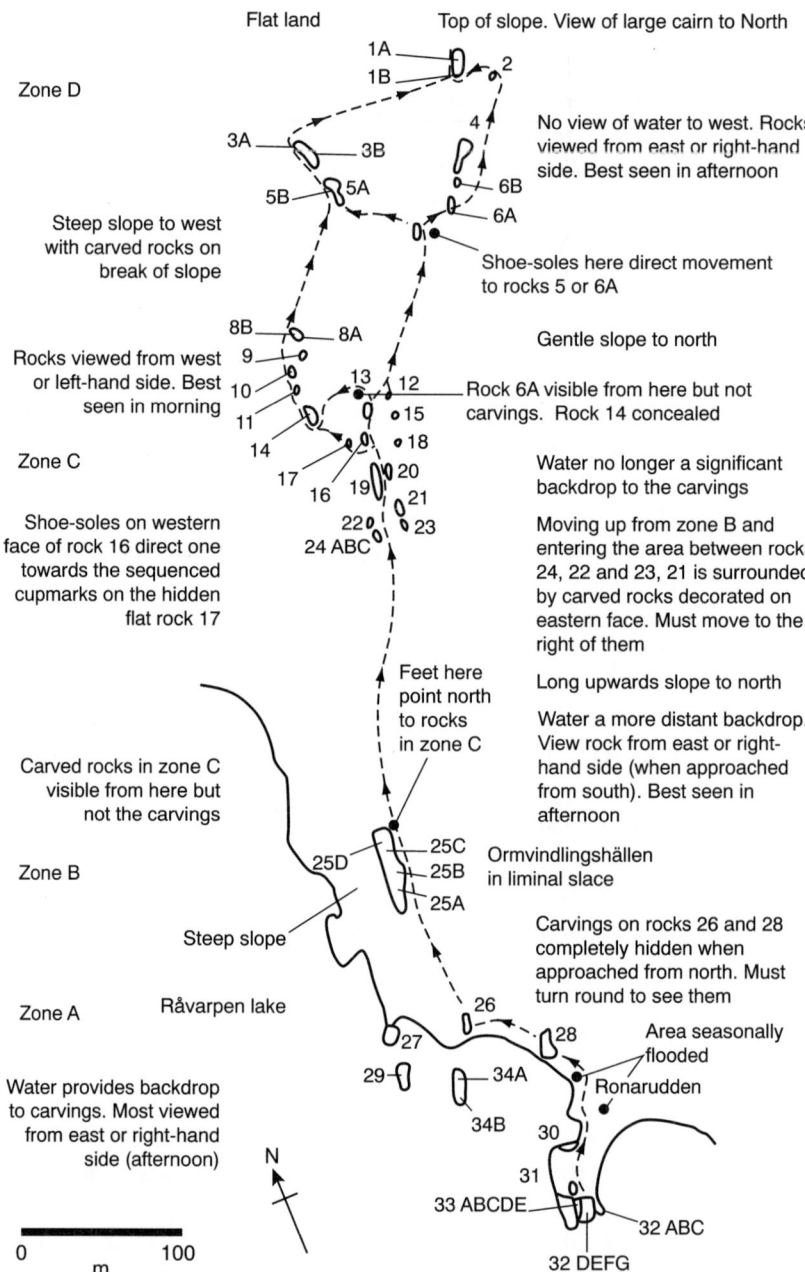

Figure 5.14 Annotated sketch plan of the Högsbyn rock-carving area. Possible paths of movement from south to north through the carved rocks are shown together with some descriptive notes.

multiple meanings. They constitute multidimensional chains with shifting and transformational relationships between signifiers whose meaning becomes contextually transformed according to their location in the series of carved rocks and their relationship to other signifiers on individual carving surfaces.

These carving surfaces formed a focus for processions and ritual ceremonies; the carvings themselves encoding ritual experiences and states that were actually acted out by people utilizing the site as a centre for initiation and calendrical rites. Alternative routes through the northern rocks may have been taken at different times and seasons. There would have been a correct way to go in order to experience the panels in their proper sequence and order. In zones C and D this may have involved passing along either the western or eastern sequence of carved rocks, in both cases the experience culminating at rock 1 (see Figure 5.14). While the rocks remained static they became set in motion through the addition of designs and the carving of new surfaces.

Högsbyn may well have been a seasonally visited cult site, possibly only visited during the spring and autumn and connected with hunting game, fertility rites and the harvest. From November until the end of March the carvings would have been buried under deep snow. The meanings encoded in the carved rocks build up a complex narrative interpreted, used and reused in ceremonial performance. The carved rocks formed a theatrical focus for schemes of perception, appreciation and action in which the meaning itself was polythetic, i.e. it was built up through looking not at one rock *after* another but *step by step*, one carving surface and its metaphoric meanings supplemented and modified through movement to the next, and so on.

Part III

Landscapes and a Sense of Place

Introduction

Landscapes, mediums for bodily actions and a home for the house, form potent sources of metaphors for the social construction and perception of reality. The two most important sources of landscape metaphors derive from places or locales and paths. Knowledge and the metaphorical understanding of landscape is thus intimately bound up with the experience of the human body in place, and in movement between places. Places form landscapes and landscapes may be defined as sets of relational places each embodying (literally and metaphorically) emotions, memories and associations derived from personal and interpersonal shared experience (Tilley 1994). They are complex and often contested arenas for social activity embracing experience and symbol. The meanings of landscapes become indelibly attached and unfolded in myths, stories, rituals and the naming of places. The social significance of places in the landscape may also find metaphoric expression in music, dance, art, song and architecture. The significance of places in the landscape and their meanings are continually being woven into the fabric of social life, and anchored to the lived topographies of the landscape. People continually perform acts that reproduce and express their sense of place and their understandings of who and what they are. Place is thus an elemental existential fact, and the social construction of a sense of place is a universal experiential medium.

Landscapes provide the frame and locales, or places, the focus in the metaphorical construction of meaning. As Casey (1996) has argued, if we want to assign any priority to the terms, a sense of place must be conceived as creating a sense of space. While space is an abstract, 'empty', analytical concept, places are always tangible and physical, their meanings bound up with the individuals who inhabit them. Places, and the stories associated with them, almost inevitably become metaphors involved in a discourse about relationships between individuals and groups. Through talking about place one can remind others of social obligations with regard to kith and kin. As such, places in the landscape forge individual and collective biographies and shared histories through processes of metaphoric construction creating meaning in the world. At a very basic metaphoric level, places, like persons, have individual names. Cultures differentially name the kinds of places (streams, mountains) and specific places that are significant to them. As Frake puts it, 'the limits of a name serve, like a verbal fence, to enclose an individual place as a spatial self' (Frake 1996: 235). Space and time are contained in places that have their own space-time rather than space containing place. There is no perception of place and landscape without memory. We mingle past experiences with those of the present. Moving in or through a place the body imports its own *emplaced* past into its present experience. Temporality is carried by the movements of the body into, out of and between places.

Paths are a frequently used metaphor in thought and ceremony. They are used to refer to destiny. Following life may be considered to be like following a path. Paths can also be used to refer to history: time is like a path. Path metaphors may also relate to personal identity. Each person follows his or her distinctive path. Paths may also refer to proper conduct: one must follow the correct path of behaviour. In Batammaliba ritual and symbolic contexts (see the discussion of Batammaliba architecture in Chapter 2) the path is the element that distinguishes and creates a sense of identity and place shared by all living forms from antelopes to humans. All things have their paths, including the pantheon of deities. The life-as-path metaphor is fundamental in giving a sense of order and coherence to the seemingly disorderly and meaningless scattering of houses in the village. Ceremonial paths, associated with men's iniation ceremonies and the image of the python deity that sponsors the ceremonies, wind back and forth between the houses, recreating in their movement that of the python. During planting ceremonies the village Earth priest and other elders trace out the body of the village Earth goddess as they walk along the village terrain. Preston Blier comments: 'the sacred images that these paths create on the surface of each village are central to the identification of each community as one comprising a terrain that is supernaturally protected' (Preston Blier 1987: 82). Signs on house façade decorations are identified with deities and sacred powers and represent the paths they are said to take in returning to the house for ceremonies. They thus identify each structure as a temple of worship to a particular deity or power. Through the architecture of the house the invisible power of each deity is made manifest.

The biographies of persons are constituted by following paths. Such paths may be weak or strong, much followed or little used, maintained or diverted (see Weiner 1991 and Parmentier 1987 for further discussion) and in an analogous way so are those of artefacts. The paths followed by persons and those followed by artefacts create each other. In the famous *Kula* exchange of necklaces and armbands in the Massim area of Papua New Guinea (Leach and Leach 1983), the shell valuables acquire very specific biographies as they move from island to island and hand to hand. The shells are persons rather than things. The most important ones have their own histories; like persons, they have bodies and the terminology used to describe named parts is heavily anthropomorphic. They have attached decoration analogous to the decorated human body; they are said to have a voice and a gender. The shells in a very real sense are as much constitutive as constituted; they act so as to create the fame and reputation of the men who have held them: 'although men appear to be the agents in defining shell value, in fact, without shells, men cannot define their own value; in this respect, shells and men are reciprocally agents of each other's value definition' (Munn 1983: 283). The names of the men engaged in the transactions can only be remembered because the shells have names and attached to the shells are the names of the men who have held them. The shells are said by some Massim communities to follow *keda* or paths. *Keda* is a polysemic concept referring not only to paths as shell routes, but also to the paths of social and political links between men and the paths by which men acquire fame, wealth and power (Campbell 1983). The concept of *keda* thus synecdochically links shells, men, fame and power. The path, *keda*, is variably constituted by reference to these parts. The *kula* men may continually manipulate the paths taken by the shell valuables to their own advantage. They may divert paths, keep paths open, or make efforts to prevent themselves from being dropped from a path, so that the movement of things enhances their own standing. The shell paths and their manipulation serve to construct the life-paths to wealth, fame or otherwise of their transactors.

The bodily sensation of perceiving things in terms of up/down; front/back; inside/outside; centre/periphery; above/below; right/left, etc. are, of course, crucial to any understanding of the metaphorical connections made between persons and landscapes. Places, pathways and human subjectivities mediate each other to create an understanding of the nature of social being. This is always a present-past because places in landscapes gather together histories, experiences, thoughts, events and associations. They are physical, cultural and historical. A phenomenology of landscape (Tilley 1994) is the process of interpreting the significance of place through the body: the hill in its physical reality, in my memory and in myths, the histories and stories told of it, the way in which I approach it, and from where. Anthropological and archaeological discourses are, in effect, part and parcel of the process of a metaphoric construction of place and movement.

Lived bodily experience of place and landscape involves constant shifts in sensory appearances, a continuous process of multisensory interactions. The body is both encultured and emplaced. Sensations are experienced presences of an embodied mind or a 'body in the mind' (Johnson 1987; see also Chapter 1, this volume).

When we consider landscape we are almost always thinking about it primarily in terms of a visual construct. The manner in which we conceptualize it in the West is dominated by visual metaphors, as Salmond (1982) among others has pointed out. In turn, visual and landscape metaphors are typically used to describe knowledges: 'theoretical landscapes', a 'landmark in thought', 'much of value was hidden', etc. Perception at the primary level of the lived body is, however, synaesthetic, an affair of the whole body moving and sensing. And this sensing is not natural or instinctive but culturally constituted. Synaesthesia, or the transposition of sensory attributes from one modality to another, e.g. sound to colour (red feels hot), like metaphor, expands knowledge. The overwhelming multisensory character of experience should lead to a multisensory conceptualization of landscape and place as heard, felt and smelt. Landscapes are not just visionscapes but also soundscapes, touchscapes, smellscapes as well (Porteous 1990; Gell 1995; Feld 1996).

Salmond (1982) argues that while the English metaphor 'knowledge is a landscape' suggests that knowledge is something distanciated and inexhaustible, based on a 'ground' that can be worked and reworked from many different vantage points, and is ultimately based in a distancing of subjectivity from objectivity, by contrast from a non-Western Maori perspective, metaphors of knowledge draw on notions of *oranga* (necessity for life) and *taonga* (cultural wealth) in which knowledge is regarded as being both exhaustible and with the potential to be destroyed (ibid.: 82). Such knowledge must be conserved and individuals may be reluctant to give it away. To keep the sacred power of this knowledge the conditions of its transmission must be deemed to be correct. The most valued forms of knowledge are intimately linked to ancestral power and efficacy. Landmarks are critical to structures of knowledge in Maori society. Knowledges are bound into them. Such knowledges could be 'talked into' topographic features, buildings and artefacts and fixed there by name. In the accounts of descent groups stories are told of how ancestors claimed territory naming landmarks after parts of their bodies, and how they travelled across the land scattering names behind them. These names relate to fishing grounds, pools, rocks, trees, streams, bushes, waterfalls, caves, hills, mountains, ridges. And a child would be taught a particular ancestral account of the significance of place, *in place*. In this manner place and knowledge were one, the name providing a guarantee of the truth of the account. Being told the story in place had the effect of bringing the past into the present, making past existence live. Hence, these places were not, for the Maori, symbols of a past time, of a dead and distanciated history, but of a past living in and informing the present.

Clearly, a metaphorical notion of a landscape that empowers the mind and acts so as to reproduce the landscapes of social life is fundamental in most small-scale societies. Basso's work (1984; 1996) among the Western Apache in Arizona provides one of the most sensitive and richly worked accounts of the significance of landscape metaphors. The land is said to 'stalk people with stories' and because of this they know how to 'live right'. Place names are likened to pictures, stories to arrows (Basso 1984: 22). For the Western Apache oral narratives have the power to establish bonds of an enduring nature between people and the landscape. As a consequence of this the stories have a moral imperative. Through the telling of stories people are forced to reflect on their misconduct and become shamed. Thus, the Apaches work in tandem the symbolic resources of landscape and language to promote compliance with standards for appropriate and sanctioned social conduct. For the Apaches place names are like pictures. All but a very few are complete sentences, e.g. 'water flows downwards on top of a series of flat rocks' or 'white rocks lie above in a compact cluster' (ibid.: 27–32). These place names are detailed *literal* descriptions of particular topographic locations picking out, pin-pointing and describing visible details. They have the capacity to evoke full and accurate images of the places to which they refer. These place names form parts of oral narratives localizing events and activities in the landscape. Historical tales about events that happened long ago begin and end with place names that localize the event, in effect demonstrating that the events did occur and that they are true. The hunting metaphor that such tales 'stalk people' works because their telling is always directed at someone who has committed a social offence to which the act of narration is a response. The act of the (literal) naming of the place is vital to the effect of the story. It grounds it in the landscape and makes it visible to contemplation. Geographical features act as mnemonic pegs for the moral lessons of history. In Basso's word's:

> such locations, charged as they are with personal and social significance, work in important ways to shape the images the Apaches have – or should have – of themselves... Apaches view the landscape as a repository of distilled wisdom... features of the landscape have become symbols of and for this way of living, the symbols of a culture and the enduring moral character of its people. (Ibid.: 45)

The metaphorical connections drawn between landscape and social action form a fundamental part of the Apaches' conceptions of themselves and vice versa. Beyond the visible reality of place there lies a moral landscape and 'it is this interior landscape – this landscape of the moral imagination – that most deeply influences their vital sense of place, and also ... their sense of self' (ibid.: 43).

Basso (1996) foregrounds the Apache metaphor 'widsom sits in places' in a discussion of the way the Western Apache conceive wisdom as residing in particular locales in the landscape. Wisdom comes into being through reflection on symbolic dimensions of the physical environment. Topographic features, their richly evocative names and the tribal narratives associated with them, are resources by means of which men and women can modify aspects of themselves, their mode of thinking and relations with others. In this manner their surroundings live in them as an interior landscape of a moral reality. A sense of place is a way of imaginatively engaging with one's surroundings and finding them significant, a personal and cultural appropriation of the world. Basso argues that this is both commonplace and unremarkable: 'locked within the mental horizons of those who give it life, sense of place issues in a stream of symbolically drawn particulars – the visible particulars of local topographies, the personal particulars of biographical associations, and the notional particulars of socially given systems of thought' (ibid.: 84).

Kahn (1996) shows, in a broadly similar way, how the Wamiran landscape of coastal Papua New Guinea provides a tangible trope for talking about social relations. Because of their potential volatility these are best addressed obliquely. Notions of the landscape are linked with the landscape as a provider of food. Stones and other features of the landscape mark the places where mythological events took place. The landscape surrounds the people with a sense of shared history rooted in the past and memorialized in the present through shared symbols. It provides a focus for common identity and a charter for social action. Events in myths are linked to places, and the place names and their associations, in turn, revolve around food and feeding, primary metaphorical idioms for talking about social relationships. A social state of 'being hungry' expresses both a physical relationship and an emotional sentiment. Social disengagement is linked to hunger.

Stones and their stories are important social anchors to the land. Clan identities are associated with named stones. They are believed to have the ability to walk around, usually at night. The stones provide tangible proof of rootedness and social identities, of the relationship of living peoples to the past and the ancestors, and their rights to land. The powers of stones ensure that the gardens give abundant food, they anchor the taro gardens in the village, and they are needed to nurture social bonds.

In Melanesia history is usually spatially mapped. It is organized in terms of spatial rather than temporal events and described in terms of migrations, myths, place names and localities which are recalled in song and story and ritual. Temporal order is thus discussed as a sequence of localities associated with events. Everywhere in Melanesia where stones are markers of past events they are frequently conceived as capable of movement. Stones can move because myth and history are negotiable and subject to revision. History is not conceived as static but as part of an ongoing relationship between past and present. Events, therefore, that are recorded in stone can be most easily brought up to date by the idea that stones like people can move (ibid.: 185). Because a stone can fix events in time it must, like time, be able to move.

The social potency and import of landscape metaphors in relation to places and paths of movement should be evident enough from the above discussion. In Chapters 6 and 7 I attempt to illustrate the value of these ideas in a discussion of prehistoric landscapes in the south of England and notions of place and social identity today in Vanuatu in the western Pacific. The studies both work from the general phenomenological perspective on landscape and place discussed above. Chapter 6 is concerned with the archaeological interpretation of long-term social change and the metaphorical meanings that may have become sedimented into the landscape through the process of monument construction. It stresses a dialectical relationship between monuments and topographic features of the landscape, both working together to create a distinctive and meaningful sense of place. Chapter 7 addresses the issue of the metaphorical significance of place and the past today. It examines this in relationship to the construction and maintenance of social identity in the context of global and local processes, the heritage and tourist industries.

6

The Beach in the Sky

Adopting as an interpretative basis the general position on landscape and metaphor and the significance of places and paths outlined in the introduction to Part III, I want now to try and provide a novel interpretation of three major and unusual aspects of the archaeological record of south Dorset which have been much discussed in the literature but little understood: (1) the widespread presence of grey Portland chert during the later Mesolithic extending from this area across a large part of southern England; (2) the unique occurrence of three massive Neolithic bank barrows which have no convincing parallels elsewhere in Britain; (3) the construction during the Bronze Age of one of the densest concentrations of burial mounds in the country, running linearly along a dramatic 16 km stretch of chalk ridge. I shall argue that the meanings of these three disparate phenomena are rooted in mythological knowledges of the powers of place and metaphoric or analogic reasoning: attempts to relate to, understand and culturally appropriate features of the 'natural' landscape which populations encountered on a daily basis. The use of Portland chert during the Mesolithic, the construction of bank barrows during the Neolithic, and the development of a linear barrow cemetery during the Bronze Age are all products of a dialogic encounter through which populations interpreted and reinterpreted the landscape in which they lived and incorporated earlier sets of understandings physically objectified in monuments and topographic features, a metaphorical restructuring of social memories.

The Landscapes of South Dorset

The study area (Figure 6.1) is a roughly 200 square km stretch of land and sea in southern England. The most striking and important inland topographic feature of the landscape is the 16 km long south Dorset Ridgeway, the southernmost edge of the chalk downlands of England. It is a windswept narrow ridge of high ground providing extensive views over the English Channel to the south and across north Dorset. The ridge top runs approximately north-west to south-east. The chalk mass is dramatically truncated to the south by the escarpment created by the Ridgeway fault, where the land drops away to the softer Jurassic clays and shales of the coastal hinterland (Plate 6.1). Looking inland from the coast the Ridgeway appears as a huge rampart dominating the surrounding area. To the north the fall of slope from the ridge top away to the gently undulating terrain of the river valleys of the South Winterborne and Frome is much gentler and less pronounced. Throughout its course, the ridge top has been cut into by small streams, now mainly vanished and below the present-day watertable, resulting in a series of northward projecting spurs jutting out towards the South Winterborne valley, creating a rolling landscape. These spurs are all lower than the top of the ridge itself and the folds in the chalk created by the dry valleys form a prominent part of the view north from the top of the ridge. Running along the base of the southern escarpment there is an almost continuous spring line. The southern line of the escarpment is indented at numerous places but there are only two prominent spurs of chalk south of the ridge top: Bincombe Hill and West Hill, both at the south-east end (see Figure 6.8).

The course of the Ridgeway can be subdivided into three sections:

1 From Broadmayne and West Hill in the east to Bronkham Hill where it runs approximately due east-west. Here the ridge top undulates between 130 and 160 m.
2 The areas of Bronkham Hill and Black Down, approximately in the centre where the overall longitudinal axis of the ridge top changes to south-east to north-west. Black Down is the highest point, rising to 237 m, with the tip of Bronkham Hill a little lower (205 m).

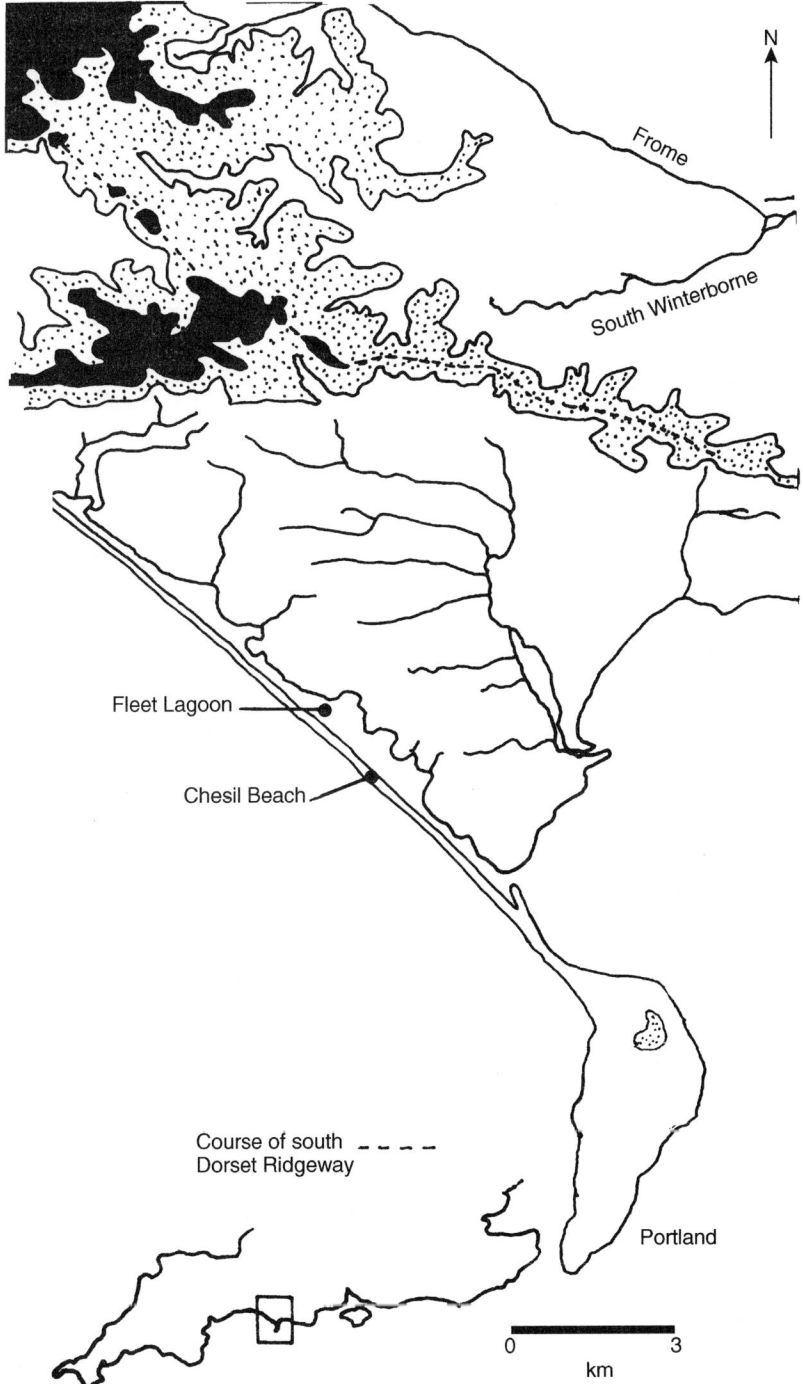

Figure 6.1 The study area: drainage and major topographic zones. Land over 200 m black; land over 130 m stippled.

Plate 6.1 The eastern end of the south Dorset Ridgeway. Crown Copyright: RCHME.

3 The stretch from Black Down to Martin's Down in the north-east, varying in height between 170 and 195 m (see Figures 6.1, 6.2, 6.8, 6.9, 6.10, 6.13).

The chalk is overlain in a number of places by deposits of tertiary and more recent date. Bagshot beds consisting of grey gravels with flint and quartz pebbles cap three areas of the Ridgeway – Bincombe Down, Bronkham Hill and Black Down – giving rise to a dark uncultivated heathland vegetation contrasting with the rest of the chalk downland, either under pasture or the plough. Small areas of clay with flints and pebbly clay with sand cover parts of the top of the ridge from Black Down to Martin's Down.

The Ridgeway is separated from the coast by a narrow strip of undulating land, mainly shales and clays. Two remarkable geological features

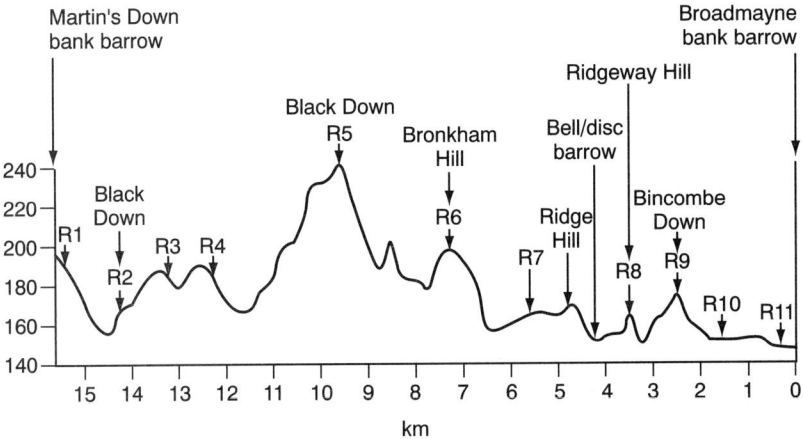

Figure 6.2 Longitudinal section along the south Dorset Ridgeway with exaggerated vertical scale. The centres of the Bronze Age barrow groups (R1–11) are marked.

mark the coast: the Isle of Portland and the Chesil Beach. Portland, 6 km long (north–south) and 2 km at the widest point juts out into the sea like the beak of a huge bird at the end of the Chesil Beach. It is utterly distinctive – the most conspicuous headland along the southern coast of England, with steep limestone cliffs towering over the Chesil Beach at the northern end. Nowhere can the flat top of the island be reached without a climb. It gently declines in height from 135 m at the northern end to 10 m at the south. Great waves scour the cliffs surrounding the island and crash like thunder. There is a dangerous race of white water just off the southern tip.

The Chesil Beach is a most remarkable geological phenomenon, the most spectacular storm beach in Britain. The western limit of the beach is essentially arbitrary. At a maximum it stretches for 28 km from West Bay in a north-west–south-east curve to the island of Portland, where it abuts the steep cliffs on the north of the island, linking it to the mainland (Figure 6.1 and Plate 6.2). The Chesil Beach is a massive curved ridge varying between 150 m and 200 m in width and progressively growing in height until reaching a maximum of 15 m where it adjoins Portland (Carr and Gleason 1971: 126). The steepness of the beach face, like its height, gradually increases from west to east. The beach is considerably wider at the Portland end than at the West Bay end. A course at right angles to the middle of the beach aligns with the Caribbean, giving an uninterrupted fetch of ocean waves for 8,000 km, directly exposing it to the full force of

190 LANDSCAPES AND A SENSE OF PLACE

Plate 6.2 The Chesil Beach seen from Abbotsbury.

the south-westerly wind and the waves from the Atlantic. It forms a protective barrier effectively preventing the soft clays and shales of this part of the Dorset coast from massive erosion. The landward site of the Fleet lagoon has been protected from marine erosion at least since the sea level reached its present height. The hills and degraded cliff lines on the landward side of the Fleet must have been shaped during one or more of the earlier inter-glacial periods and were not affected by wave action during the last (Flandrian) post-glacial marine transgression when Britain was cut off from continental Europe. As a result of the continual pounding of the waves the southern seaward slope of the beach is steep and often concave in shape. Terraces of pebbles are continuously formed and re-formed by the waves, giving the slope, through time, a mobile character. While it is occasionally overtopped by the sea in storms the beach does not appear to have been breached by the sea in historical times. On the landward or northern side the slope is far more gradual in profile, less mobile and prone to change. Canns or seepage hollows are a marked feature of the landward (Fleet) side of Chesil Beach. They are catastrophically formed under exceptional storm conditions when the waves are driven above a certain critical level on the seaward side of the beach. The porosity of the pebbles is sufficient to allow large amounts of water to pour through the canns at this time, but normally they are dry (Whittaker 1978: 79).

For 13 km the Chesil Beach is separated from the mainland by the brackish tidal lagoon of the Fleet. This varies in width between 100 and 900 m. It is fed by a mixture of fresh water from small streams draining the chalk of the Ridgeway to the north. The most westerly of these arises at a spring at Portesham just south of Black Down and runs through Abbotsbury before draining into the western end of the Fleet. Seawater continuously seeps through the pebbles of the beach, the water at high tide being markedly higher on the seaward side. The sea also enters the lagoon through the eastern mouth of the Fleet at Small Mouth. Consequently, there is a marked west-to-east (low–high) salinity gradient.

Fawn in colour, the beach is made up of yellow and white pebbles of flint and chert (98 per cent), together with quartzites, vien quartz, rare porphyries, granites and metamorphic pebbles with limestones common at the Portland end. A remarkable feature of these pebbles, which has long been noted, is their gradation in size from those the size of a pea at the western end to large cobbles where the beach adjoins Portland. Persons with intimate local knowledge are said to know precisely which stretch of the beach they are standing on through the evaluation of pebble size. The sound of the beach also varies in its course 'from the whisper of sand to the hissing of shingle and then to the hollow rattling and rumbling of down-dragged pebbles' (Treves 1906: 239). Knowledge of pebble size and the note of the sea was particularly valuable to the smugglers and wreckers of the historical past, who carried out their work by night.

Historically, this has been a beach of death, with ships tossed effortlessly upon it and dashed to pieces against its sides. The constantly mobile pebbles and steep shelf of the beach make it impossible for survivors of such disasters to gain a foothold. More shipwrecks have been recorded here than along any other stretch of the British coast. On a still day in summer the beach appears to sit calmly between the shallow blue waters of the Fleet and a line of white foam on its seaward side, but

> in a westerly gale it is a place terrible to behold. The sea roars and thunders against it with a sound that can be heard inland for miles. The ice-smooth combers crash down upon the glacis with the force of battering rams; the beach is torn at by the receding wave as if the straitened foam were a myriad of claws. (ibid.: 236)

Only about 3–7 km distant, the top of the Ridgeway is for the most part within sight, sound and smell of the sea. On a stormy day the sea can be heard crashing on the Chesil Beach below, and there is a distinct tang of salt in the air. The full extent of the beach with its remarkable continuous curve can, however, only be fully appreciated when standing on the cliffs on the north of Portland, or from the heights above Abbotsbury. Inland from the Dorset Ridgeway views are more restricted and its presence is hidden by the cliffs marking the inland shore of the Fleet, except at certain points.

The regularity of the general topographic form of the beach and the grading of the pebbles give it a remarkably *artificial* appearance, seemingly more of a work of culture than natural processes. Historically, its origin and form have been the subject of continuous speculation and debate (for a review see Carr and Blackley 1974). Portland, as a headland, was already in existence by Middle Palaeolithic times and the island played a very important part in the formation of the Chesil Beach and the Fleet lagoon. The beach itself probably originated as an offshore barrier which was progressively driven landward during the late Quaternary marine transgression. Landward recession now appears to be minimal.

The Mesolithic

Evidence for occupation of the south Dorset Ridgeway area during the Mesolithic is virtually confined to a series of sites on the southern tip of the Isle of Portland and along the inland shores of the Fleet. There are no certain finds from the chalk downlands or the course of the Ridgeway itself. Three other chert and flint scatters with a Mesolithic component are recorded just to the north-east of Maiden Castle and along the gravels of the Frome valley (Wymer 1977: 69; Woodward 1991: 129).

Settlement of Portland appears to have occurred at an early stage with the site at Culver Well giving a date of 6100–5700 cal. BC (Palmer 1970). Occupation appears to have been lengthy and a comparatively large seasonal population is likely. The Mesolithic flint scatters and occupation areas are confined to the southern tip of the island around Portland Bill. Field surveys have shown that all the lowermost fields sloping down to the cliffs on the eastern side of the Bill are 'thickly littered with artefacts of the same industry, and therefore really constitute one huge site' (Palmer 1967: 119), within which major artefact concentrations and shell middens occur.

Two of these concentrations at Portland Bill, Portland site 1 (Palmer 1968; 1977) and Culver Well (Palmer 1970; 1977) are located near to springs, and in general spring locations appear to have been particularly favoured during the Mesolithic in Dorset (Rankine 1962: 94). The Culver Well site on Portland is situated at the base of a hill slope. Debris, mainly limpet and winkle shells, formed a large mound or shell midden, over which two overlapping limestone floors, probably forming the bases of shelters, were lain down. Hearths or cooking places were found along the eastern edge of the paved area. Excavation of one of the limestone floors revealed a large triangular-shaped limestone block towards the northern end, covering a circular hole with a surrounding stone packing and loam fill. Against one side of this capstone was a large oval-shaped Chesil Beach pebble with one of its ends pointing at the large stone. Three objects formed a triangle in the hole underneath the stone: a pierced scallop shell pendant, a Portland chert tranchet axe and a round Chesil Beach pebble standing on edge (Palmer 1975: 50). Scallop shells (a deep-water species) are rare on the site and the tranchet axe is of a rare and unusual type (ibid.). This is clearly a votive deposit of a 'megalithic' nature with an unusually large pebble marking it from the outside.

Large numbers of smooth Chesil Beach pebbles are common on the Portland sites (Palmer 1977: 148) and they clearly had important ritual connotations, as the find from Culver Well demonstrates. Beach pebbles seem to have had a particular significance not only on the Portland sites but across southern England during the Mesolithic, being frequently worked to make pebble maceheads, the material of which is frequently of non-local origin. Unworked siltstone pebbles of Cornish and 'south-western' origin from the excavated sites at Farnham and Oakhanger V are the best-known examples of a much more widespread phenomenon of pebble collection, artefact manufacture and exchange (Care 1979: 98).

Artefact finds, including an unusually large number of core tools, in particular picks, from Portland Bill are dominated (around 60 per cent) by the choice of fine-grained grey Portland chert readily available in the form of pebbles from the Pleistocene raised beach at the tip of Portland or the eastern end of the Chesil Beach where it adjoins the island (Palmer 1968: 190).

Mesolithic artefact scatters also occur along the foreshores of the Fleet, along the eastern part of the lagoon, closest to Portland. None are recorded west of Herbury Point (Palmer 1963: 109). Approximately 75 per cent of the artefacts are made from Portland chert, the rest mainly high-quality brown flint (Palmer 1963: 109; 1977: 149–50). The major silting episode of the fleet lagoon appears to have begun from the earlier Mesolithic, c.7000 BC and lasted until c.5000 BC (Carr and Blackley 1974: 15) The complex ecology of developing marshes and reedbeds would have created an ideal series of habitats for fishing, fowling and plant collecting by Mesolithic and Neolithic populations.

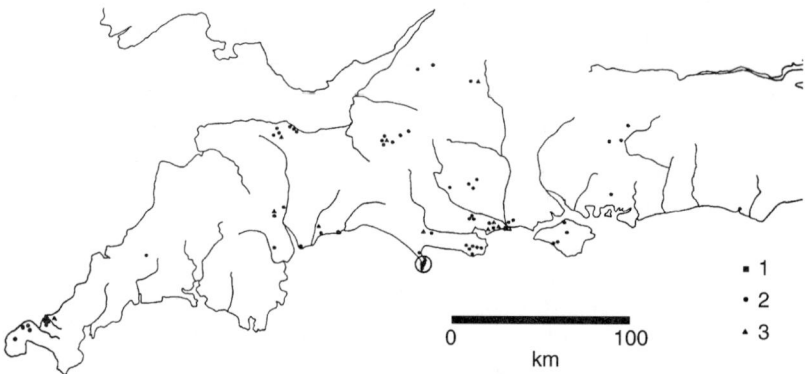

Figure 6.3 Map of southern England showing the distribution of Portland chert artefacts of various periods. 1: Palaeolithic; 2: Mesolithic; 3: Later prehistoric artefacts from the Isle of Portland (circled).
Source: Palmer (1970)

The use of Portland chert in the area around Portland Bill and from the scatters along the Fleet dates back to the Late Palaeolithic (Palmer 1970: 89). During the Mesolithic and early Neolithic its widespread coastal and riverine exchange across southern England from west Cornwall to Hampshire and Surrey (Rankine 1951; Palmer 1970) is of particular interest (Figure 6.3).

Portland chert resembles flint in its general properties and fractures conchoidally, but is distinctive in both its pale to dark lead-grey colour and frequent mottled patination. Its use provided no technological advantage whatsoever in terms of sharpness of cutting edges obtained, etc. The considerable number of picks on Portland has led Care to interpret it principally as a quarry site (Care 1979: 98). Care notes that the quantities of Portland chert found on Mesolithic sites seems to fall off with distance from the source. On some of the Mesolithic sites on Cranborne Chase, some 40 km to the north-east, the presence of picks of Portland chert indicates direct contact with the island as part of a seasonal exploitation cycle. Clearly, what was of importance, however the chert was obtained, was that it was easily recognized and came from a *known* source, a dramatic island thrust out into the sea, with important ancestral and symbolic associations. The chert embodied knowledges of *place*, of the island from which it was derived, and the populations who inhabited it.

The Early and Middle Neolithic (Figure 6.4)

Standing on the hill west of Abbotsbury looking down on the great stretch of the Chesil Beach running to the gaunt and rocky Isle of Portland, Neolithic and Bronze Age populations must have marvelled at this natural phenomenon as people do today. In the twentieth century we have various geological explanations for its formation. In prehistory it would have been similarly explained and rationalized, but in myths and stories. These myths and stories would have had an integral relationship with ritual practices (embodiments or objectifications of mythic structures) and knowledges of prior ancestral human occupation: the Mesolithic middens on the southern tip of Portland.

During the early and middle Neolithic traces of settlement are largely confined to areas to the north of the Dorset Ridgeway. These include the earliest known monument in the area, the causewayed enclosure at Maiden Castle and finds of pottery (Hembury ware), pits and worked flint and chert at Rowden, Poundbury and Flagstones, together with a series of flint

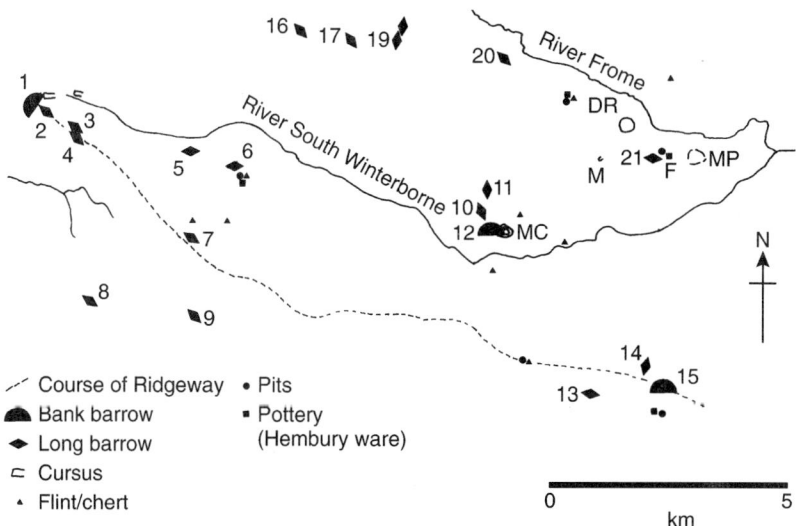

Figure 6.4 Neolithic monuments in the study area and early Neolithic 'domestic' sites (flint/chert concentrations, pits and finds of Hembury ware). Barrow numbers refer to Tables 6.1/6.2. MC = Maiden Castle early Neolithic causewayed enclosure; M = Maumbury Rings Henge; DR = Dorchester timber henge; F = Flagstones enclosure; MP = Mount Pleasant Henge.

scatters in the vicinity of Maiden Castle (Woodward 1991: 133). To the south of the Ridgeway, Hembury ware and pits are known from Sutton Poyntz and pottery and small numbers of flint and chert artefacts of probable early or middle Neolithic date are known from Portland Bill (Palmer 1968: 202–3). Along the top of the Ridgeway evidence is confined to pits with finds of flint and chert from Bincombe Down. The major focus of early Neolithic activity appears to have been in the vicinity of Maiden Castle.

The causewayed enclosure

The Maiden Castle causewayed enclosure is situated on a low but conspicuous hill island bounded to the south by the incised valley of the River South Winterborne. The enclosure, created by the digging of two concentric discontinuous ditches, covers approximately 7 ha and bounds off the higher eastern end of an oval-shaped ridge. The land drops away steeply to the Winterborne to the south, but more gently to the north. The choice of a chalk island for the siting of the enclosure is duplicated in the contemporary causewayed enclosure of Hambledon Hill in north Dorset. The monument at Maiden Castle was thus bound into the pre-existing topography and when first constructed was explicitly designed to have a striking visual effect when viewed from particular areas of the surrounding landscape. Sharples notes that

> the ditches on the western edge of the enclosure cut across some of the highest ground of the area enclosed, most of the interior slopes from east to west, and the ditches on the east side are well to the east of the break in slope that marks the top of the hill. . . . The enclosure was designed to be seen from the east, and to focus attention to the area. (Sharples 1991a: 34)

The best and most extensive views of the enclosure interior would be obtainable from the heights of the south Dorset Ridgeway, less than 2 km to the south, at the closest point. Walking from west to east along the top of the Ridgeway, Maiden Castle is first visible (the view is blocked until this point by the spur of Came Down) from the eastern slopes of Bincombe Down. It is interesting to note in this connection that Bincombe Down is the only area on the top of the Ridgeway for which there is evidence of earlier Neolithic activity. From this point onwards to the summit of Black Down, a stretch of 7 km, the enclosure ditches would have been continuously visible, but the interior obscured. Views of the surrounding landscape from the enclosure interior are very restricted to the west because they are blocked by Hog Hill. To the east there are views a short distance down the South Winterborne valley. By contrast, to the north views are extensive. To the south they are limited by the presence of the Ridgeway. The visual envelope thus created is dominated by the chalk heights of the Ridgeway to the south and by views north across the Frome valley to the chalk uplands of central Dorset.

Evidence for the use of the enclosure interior has been almost completely destroyed by the construction of a later Iron Age hillfort. A pit dug into the surface of the hill contained a large quantity of broken pottery, fragments of animal bones and limpet shells (Wheeler 1943: 86). This is almost certainly a votive deposit and the presence of the limpet shells connects Maiden Castle both with the coast and the earlier Mesolithic shell midden sites on Portland in which limpets also dominate. Excavation of parts of the inner ditch fills recovered large quantities of charcoal with oak being the dominant tree species, and a child burial, fragments of animal bones, pots and flint tools. The outer ditch seems to have been completely infilled with chalk rubble soon after it was dug. The rubble sealed a layer of material placed at the bottom of the ditch, including the disarticulated remains of two children and an adult male, scattered animal bones, flint tools, axes, carved lumps of chalk and high-quality pottery (for details see Sharples 1991a; 1991b).

Maiden Castle is situated just over 13 km due north of the Isle of Portland. Finds of Portland chert, the limpet shells from the votive pit in the interior and the many carbonized seed remains of *Atriplex littoralis* (shore orache) are direct evidence of a connection with the coast. I want to make the suggestion here that the causewayed enclosure, situated on its distinctive island hill, represented in a physical form the Isle of Portland during the earlier Neolithic, and that Portland itself, probably only visited seasonally, represented an ancestral home, a place of origins and cosmic powers. The early Neolithic enclosure of Maiden Castle tangibly represented Portland on the ground. And this ideology of the island as a place of ancestral origins may well have been widespread in the Neolithic of southern England, irrespective of whether or not it was specifically Portland that was being represented in ritual practice. The choice of hilltop 'islands' as favoured locations for enclosures is commonplace in the Neolithic of southern Britain, from the Cornish enclosures of Carn Brea and Helman Tor to Hembury in Devon, the nearby site of Hambledon Hill in north Dorset to Windmill Hill in Wiltshire, to much more distant sites such as Offham Hill in Sussex.

Long barrows and bank barrows

There are twenty-one documented Neolithic long barrows in the study area. Three are bank barrows, three chambered long barrows and fifteen earthen long barrows (see Figure 6.4). Nine are located in the north between the valleys of the South Winterborne and the Frome, the remainder along the Ridgeway and its associated northern spurs. None are known to the south of the Ridgeway. Monument construction on Portland during either the Neolithic or the Bronze Age appears to be absent, although quarrying and development may have destroyed sites in the northern part of the island. Orientation of the long axes of the mounds, their length and positioning in the landscape are variable (Tables 6.1 and 6.2). Eleven of the barrows are clearly related in associated pairs or groups, with distances between nearest neighbours ranging from between fifty and a few hundred metres. These pairs or barrow groups all have different mound orientations and lengths, as if to differentiate deliberately between them and mark out difference. The other barrows are more isolated with inter-site distances ranging up to 2 km. All three bank barrows are located on high points, a topographic location only shared by one chambered barrow, the Hell Stone, and the Bincombe long barrow along the entire course of the Ridgeway. By contrast, all but one of the five long barrows located well to the north of the Ridgeway (and all but one out of sight of it) are situated on localized high points or ridges. There is thus much greater differentiation between barrow locations along the Ridgeway than elsewhere. Inter-barrow visibility in all cases is low and confined to closely associated pairs or groups. The sea is only visible from seven (33 per cent) of the barrows all located along the Ridgeway, and looking along the long axis, from only two sites.

The chronological relationship between the three bank barrows and the long barrows in the area is problematic. Bank barrows were first defined as a distinctive class by Crawford (1938: 228–32) and Wheeler (1943: 18–24). Wheeler's major criteria were (1) a length greater than that of the normal long barrow; (2) the site crowning all or part of a ridge; (3) parallel sides with the bank of uniform height; (4) parallel side ditches that do not return around the ends (ibid.: 24). It has usually been assumed that bank barrows are somewhat later in date than long barrows (e.g. Bradley 1983; Thomas 1996: 189) and that part of their meaning and significance was derived from the long barrow construction and burial tradition. However, there is some evidence from this area of south Dorset which suggests that the bank barrows were either earlier or contemporary with the long barrows, but it is unlikely that any of them were used for burial.

Table 6.1 Long barrows in the study area: morphological characteristics and relationships to other monuments.

Name	Map	Type	HASL	L	Ort	LE	IB	RRB
Martin's Down W	1	B	190	197	NE-SW	–	2, 3, 4	2, 3
Martin's Down E	2	L	180	34	NW-SE	SE	1, 2, 3	2
Black Down N	3	L	170	92	ESE-WNW	ESE	1, 2, 4	3
Black Down S	4	L	175	76	NW-SE	SE	1, 2, 3	2, 3
Longlands	5	L	140	29	E-W	E	–	–
Coombe Farm	6	CH?	130	?	E-W	E?	7	–
Cowleaze	7	L	175	55	NW-SE	SE	6	–
The Grey Mare & Her Colts	8	CH	200	24	NW-SE	SE	–	–
The Hell Stone	9	CH	185	27	NW-SE	SE	–	–
Maiden Castle NW	10	L	115	29	NW-SE	SE	11, 12	–
Clandon	11	L	95	97	N-S	N	10, 12	3
Maiden Castle	12	B	130	546	NW-SE WNW-ESE	–	10, 11	2 2, 3
Bincombe	13	L	160	82	E-W	E	15	1
Culliford Tree	14	L	135	52	ENE-WSW	ENE	15	1
Broadmayne	15	B	140	183	ESE-WNW	–	13, 14	1, 2, 3
Frampton: Pigeon Hse	16	L	135	42	NW-SE	SE	–	–
Bradford Peverell: Red Barn	17	L	140	36	NNW-SSE	SSE	18	–
Penn Hill West	18	L	145	26	NE-SW	NE	17, 19	1, 3
Penn Hill East	19	L	145	63	NNE-SSW	NNE	18	2, 3
Longwalls	20	L	110	45	NW-SE	SE	–	2
Allington	21	L	70	75	E-W	E	?	2

Map numbers refer to Figure 6.4. Type: B = bank barrow; L = long barrow; CH = chambered long barrow. HASL = height above sea level. L = length. Ort = orientation of long axis of mound. LE = largest end of mound. IB = intervisible long barrows. RRB = relationship to round barrows: 1: Round barrow superimposed on end of long barrow mound; 2: Long axis of mound linearly continued or referenced across space by round barrows built along the same orientational axis as the mound; 3: Forms a non-linear focus for a clustered group of round barrows. ? = no information. Information on the Allington long barrow from Davies et al. (1985: 104). Sources for other barrows: Grinsell (1959; 1982) and author's fieldwork.

Two long barrows immediately north of Maiden Castle have their long axis more or less directly orientated towards the western end of the bank barrow, suggesting that these three monuments must be contemporary in date or the bank barrow earlier. Two long barrows on Black Down just under 1 km to the east of the Martin's Down bank barrow (Figure 6.4, nos 3 and 4; incorrectly labelled bank barrows on the Ordnance Survey map)

Table 6.2 The landscape settings of the Neolithic monuments in the study area.

Name	Type	Map	SV	SVAL	HP	LRT	Notes
Martin's Down W	B	1	+	+	+	–	Runs along ridge top but ends of mound do not extend to end of ridge. Steep drop west of mound cutting across Ridgeway
Martin's Down E	L	2	+	–	–	NW	NW end points up slope to Martin's Down W bank barrow
Black Down N	L	3	–	–	–	S	WNW end of long axis points to SW end of ridge top on which Martin's Down W bank barrow is located. Barrow positioned at break of slope to N so as to be skyline sited from N
Black Down S	L	4	+	–	–	SE	NW end of long axis points to NE end of ridge on which Martin's Down W bank barrow is sited
Longlands	L	5	–	–	–	SE	On sloping ground dropping away to River South Winterborne. Long axis of mound runs parallel to contours of the valley
Coombe Farm	CH	6	–	–	–	E?	Situated on steep slope dropping down to dry valley to NW running down to River South Winterborne
Cowleaze	L	7	–	–	–	SE	Situated towards head of dry valley running down to River South Winterborne. SE end of long axis points up to the Black Down summit
The Grey Mare and Her Colts	CH	8	+	–	–	SE	On sloping ground. NW end points down to the bottom of a dry valley terminating to the north of the monument
Hell Stone	CH	9	+	+	+	–	On ridge top. SE end points to Isle of Portland

Name	Type	Map no				SVAL	Description
Maiden Castle NW	L	10	−	−	−	SE	On sloping ground. SW end points to W end of Maiden Castle bank barrow running along ridge top
Clandon	L	11	−	−	+	−	On top of knoll. S end points to W end of the Maiden Castle bank barrow running along ridge top
Maiden Castle	B	12	−	−	+	−	Runs along ridge top. False crested. Skyline sited to N
Bincombe	L	13	+	−	+	−	Runs along crest of localized ridge. Land dips away steeply at W and E ends to dry valleys cutting into Ridgeway from S
Culliford Tree	L	14	−	−	−	SW	On sloping ground at head of dry valley cutting into Ridgeway from N. ENE end points down dry valley
Broadmayne	B	15	+	−	+	−	Runs along top of Ridgeway at E end. Parallels line of Chesil Beach linking Portland to mainland
Pigeon House	L	16	−	−	+	−	On localized high point. Barrow axis runs parallel to line of valley of river Frome to N. W and E ends of mound point towards heads of dry valleys running down to Frome valley.
Red Barn	L	17	−	−	−	SW	On sloping ground towards the head of a dry valley running down to the Frome to the NW
Penn Hill W & E	L	18, 19	−	−	+	−	On high point. Long axis of mounds reference dry valley running down to Frome valley
Longwalls	L	20	−	−	+	−	High point on ridge top. Long axis of mound parallels line of Frome valley to N. W and E ends of mound point towards dry valleys leading down to Frome valley from S
Allington	L	21	−	−	+	−	On localized high point. Long axis of barrow parallels ridge top running parallel with the valleys of the Frome to N and South Winterborne to the S

Map nos refer to Figure 6.4. Type B: bank barrow; CH: chambered long barrow; L: long barrow. SV = sea visible from mound. SVAL = sea visible looking along long axis of mound. HP = Situated on localized high point. LRT = Land rises to (direction noted).

have an extremely peculiar orientation to their long axes. Drawing an imaginary line across space and extending their orientational axis westwards we find that it encloses the northern and southern ends of the ridge occupied by the Martin's Down bank barrow. It is as if these barrows are mapping out the topographical parameters within which the bank barrow itself is sited. The long barrows are not orientated to the ends of the bank barrow but rather to the margins of the ridge of topographic space that it occupies.

The relationship of the long barrows and the bank barrows to features of the surrounding landscape is very different. All three bank barrows, sited on ridge tops, command panoramic views in all directions. They are massive, not only in size but in terms of the visual field of the landscape they command. By contrast, the majority of the long barrows are located on hill slopes with limited views in one or more cardinal directions. In other words the bank barrows appear to have a wider and more generalized significance in relationship to the landscape than the long barrows, where the relationship appears to be much more localized and specific. The smaller long barrows have an intimate relationship to particular locales in the landscape in their immediate vicinity, being situated at the tops of coombes running down to the river valleys, in relationship to particular hills or ridge ends, often with the long axis of the mounds pointing up or down towards these landscape features (see Table 6.2). In terms of their relationship to the metaphorical connections made in ritual, myth and cosmologies this may imply a contrast between a much more highly specific set of meanings connected with the long barrows and a more generalized and broader significance for the bank barrows. The long barrows invoked, through their particular and localized siting, the meanings of place at a much more fine-grained contextual level. By contrast, the bank barrows referenced topographic features of the south Dorset landscape of major regional significance and universal mythological importance. Precisely what they were referencing can best be illustrated by considering in detail the most massive bank barrow of all, that at Maiden Castle.

Towards the end of the early Neolithic the causewayed enclosure appears to have been abandoned and perhaps only several decades later (indicated by minimal silting over the top of the causewayed enclosure ditches) a radically new form of monument was constructed along the ridge and into the centre of the area around which the enclosure had been built: a massive bank barrow over half a kilometre (546 m) long and originally 17 m wide (Figure 6.5). It was flanked by two parallel ditches 5.5 m wide and 1.5 m deep. These do not enclose the western or eastern mound terminals. The barrow is set on a false crest, 10 m north of the summit of the ridge at the western end, increasing to 20 m at the east. The central section is situated at the top of a dry coombe running down to the south Winterborne valley. The false crest of the barrow would make it particularly prominent when viewed from areas below it to the north of Maiden Castle. It would also be an impressive landmark when seen from the Dorset Ridgeway to the south. It therefore seems to have been deliberately sited to be visible both from the north and the south. A remarkable feature of this barrow is the irregular manner of the overall orientation of the mound, with a change of axis from the western to the eastern terminals. The surviving mound can be subdivided into three sections, each with slightly different orientations: a west section 225 m long orientated approximately west to east: a central section 65 m long in which the axis shifts slightly; and an eastern section 157 m long orientated north-west to south-east (Balaam et al. 1991: 40; Sharples 1991b: 54). Seen from the south it curves around to the *right*. The easternmost (NW–SE) section runs across the ditches of the causewayed enclosure and terminates in the centre of its interior. This monument is unique in the British Isles in terms of both its sheer length and the change in orientation. Bradley (1983) suggests that it started life as a long barrow, of a fairly standard size and orientation, situated just outside the causewayed enclosure and associated with the rituals that took place within it. It was then extended to its present form after the enclosure fell into disuse. During the 1985–6 excavations Sharples found no stratigraphic evidence to either support or call into question this thesis. A point which does seem to suggest that the entire monument was conceived and constructed as a single entity is the remarkably consistent nature of the fill of the ditch along its entire length (Wheeler 1943: 86–9; Sharples 1991b: 54–5). Had the central section been constructed earlier the fill might have been expected to be different in form and character.

The bank barrow does not appear to have had a funerary use. Wheeler's excavations recovered near the eastern ends of both ditches concentrations of bones and horn cores of domestic cattle in the primary silts. The presence of post holes at the eastern end of the mound was suggested by him to be possible evidence of a concave revetment (Wheeler 1943: 88). Elsewhere within the basal ditch fills finds were rare: a scattering of animal bones, including an antler pick, and flint.

Interpretations of the Maiden Castle monument have been many and various. Sharples suggests that the bank barrow acted as a 'symbolic barrier' and territorial marker in conjunction with two other bank barrows at the ends of the south Dorset Ridgeway (Sharples 1991b: 256) (see discussion below). Woodward suggests it 'identifies the territory and resource of the Frome river and valley streams running from the north Dorset ridge' (Woodward 1991: 131). Thomas (1984) links the construction of the bank barrow with the development of an emergent local élite and ritual authority structure. In later publications (Thomas 1991: 46; 1996: 189–90) he stresses the linearity of the mound as establishing an axis of movement across the site. The presence of the cattle deposits in the ditches at the eastern end and the presence of a possible revetment there suggests that this movement was from west to east along the mound. In the course of walking alongside the mound this movement would have been directed along it, moving to the right towards the eastern end. It has been argued that there is a clear morphological relationship between the bank barrow and an (earlier?) funerary tradition associated with long barrows. Thomas suggests that although 'the long mound contained no burial... efforts were made to establish its authenticity through acts of deposition... the burial of cattle remains' (Thomas 1996: 190).

All these different interpretations of this huge monument have failed to explain two features of crucial importance: (1) its sheer size and why it should have been built in south Dorset rather than anywhere else in the British Isles; (2) its irregular orientation. Bradley's (1983) interpretation of the mound as having being constructed in stages, or explanations of it as a territorial marker or symbolic barrier, explain neither of these things. It almost certainly did define an axis of movement, as Thomas suggests, but why the change in orientation? These attempts to explain the bank barrow all have one thing in common: they try to explain it in terms of a relationship to other types of monuments and/or associated social territories. An altogether different interpretation emerges if instead we suggest a metaphorical linkage of the barrow to what is undoubtedly the *unique* and most striking feature of the south Dorset landscape, the Chesil Beach. The Maiden Castle bank barrow in its linearity, regularity and morphology – curving round to the right – is an almost exact representation of the beach: the beach converted into a cultural form and set out for display along the Maiden Castle ridge. Both the barrow and the beach have eastern 'terminals': the revetment and cattle deposits and the Isle of Portland, respectively. The Chesil Beach, bordered by water on both sides, is mirrored by the bank barrow ditches. For two thirds of its length, the westernmost section, the Chesil Beach appears to run parallel to the coast before curving round to the right to join Portland. This is similarly duplicated in the relative dimensions and change in orientational axis of the bank barrow.

The profile of Portland itself resembles a long barrow. It is the contention here that the construction of the bank barrow signals a change in the practice of ritual representation from an earlier emphasis on the Isle of Portland as an ancestral home, or place of origin, during the construction and use of the causewayed enclosure, to a later one emphasizing the Chesil Beach and the linkage it creates between the island and the mainland, stopping it from floating away: an umbilical cord or ancestral thread, a path of wandering.

But all this raises the further questions: *why* represent Portland, and then the Chesil Beach, and in what manner were these representations connected with the ritual events taking place at the causewayed enclosure and the bank barrow? The argument here is that, as centres of ritual performance, the enclosure and the bank barrow were repositories of metaphorical images of mythological structures providing both an explanation and an understanding of the world in which these Neolithic populations lived. There was a need to explain and situate these places and topographic features as part of their life-worlds in terms of origins and ancestral events. The ritual performances that took place structured and restructured understandings of mythological events. Ritual practice can be viewed as a transformation and acting out of myths, a structuring of structure. Analogies and metaphors within narrative mythic structures provide the principal means of explanation. But just as geological explanations require certain proofs, so do myths. Both crucially depend for their veracity on tangible signs. The physical form of the monuments, duplicating in miniature that which they represented, acted as key metaphorical *images* transcending individual experiences of these places to be reworked as collective socio-historical experiences in the specific language of ritual expression and communication. The monuments must have formed part of a complex compositional form including patterns of directed movement, narrative, song, dance, music, deposition of artefacts and bones, socializing persons and structuring knowledges. They were *imagenes mundi* giving form and definition to the cosmologies created by the mind and serving as tangible foci revitalizing domains of personal and social experience. In short, they were objectifications of myths which became activated in the minds of the individuals experiencing the performances which took place at and around them. Through these monuments people came to know and understand the landscape in which they lived.

Besides the Maiden Castle bank barrow, as already noted, there are two other spectacular linear monuments in the south Dorset area, at Broadmayne and Martin's Down, effectively marking the eastern and western ends of the Ridgeway, respectively. The Broadmayne bank barrow, 183 m long with two continuous side ditches, runs along the summit of the Ridgeway paralleling the highest 140 m contour and orientated ESE–WNW (Plate 6.1). Like the Chesil Beach it is slightly wider and higher at the eastern end. The Martin's Down bank barrow also runs along a ridge top along the 190 m contour, one of the highest points of the Ridgeway. It is orientated NE–SW, slightly wider at the north-east end but higher to the south-west. Again, there are panoramic views across the surrounding landscape. This is the only barrow in the area from which the sea is visible if one looks along its long axis. While the long axis of the Broadmayne bank barrow points along the east–west course of the Ridgeway, that at Martin's Down effectively crosses it at right angles, acting as a physical and visual barrier to further east–west movement (Plate 6.3). Both these monuments are still massive in the landscape, creating a lasting visual impression and contrasting with the other smaller Neolithic monuments.

From the Martin's Down bank barrow West Bay and the western end of the Chesil Beach are visible, but not the Fleet lagoon, besides which runs the visually most impressive section of the beach (arguably it can be conceived as beginning at Abbotsbury). The Broadmayne bank barrow is the only one in the area from which the Chesil Beach is visible with water on both sides of it. Walking towards the barrow from the east provides a revelation. It is *precisely* located on the ridge top so that the bulk of the Isle of Portland, and more importantly the Chesil Beach, is *first visible* only when standing on its extreme eastern end. From the site of the bank barrow the orientation of barrow and beach appear parallel, as distant transposed mirror images of each other. I have already argued that the Maiden Castle bank barrow metaphorically invoked the Chesil Beach. The Broadmayne and Martin's Down bank barrows performed a similar role in ritual practice. They also represented 'beaches in the sky'. In this respect it is of great interest to note that the Martin's Down bank barrow is located on the Ridgeway precisely 7 km due north of the point at which the Chesil Beach diverges from the mainland and the Fleet lagoon begins. This stretch of the shingle bank, where it is defined by water on both sides, is without doubt the most impressive and, indeed, might be defined topographically as the beginning of the beach as a separate entity. Just as the beach begins at this point the Martin's Down bank barrow can be regarded as the beginning of the Ridgeway in that, although higher land continues to the west, the ridge is not so well defined topographically, and immediately to the west of the ridge on which the bank barrow lies the land plunges down in a most

Plate 6.3 The Martin's Down bank barrow at the western end of the Ridgeway. Cambridge University Collection of Air Photographs: copyright reserved.

dramatic manner. The eastern end of the Maiden Castle bank barrow is located 13.5 km due north of the point at which the Chesil Beach ends when it joins the west coast of Portland, but neither Chesil Beach nor Portland is visible from here. The Broadmayne bank barrow, from which both are visible, marks the point at which the higher land of the Ridgeway drops away to the east *and* is situated due north of the eastern side of the Isle of Portland. These three barrows together thus mark the topographic limits or ends of the high ground of the Ridgeway and relate the ridge to both the Chesil Bank and the Isle of Portland. They perform the symbolic role of linking the topographies of the chalk ridge and the beach into a connected and bounded symbolic system. The form and nature of the symbolic world thus created can only be understood now in retrospect by looking at developments in this area during the later Neolithic and Bronze

Age, in which relationships between topographic features of the landscape and monuments become more pronounced and explicit.

The Later Neolithic and Bronze Age

The period from around 2900 BC onwards is characterized by a growing contrast between the character of the activities and ritual performances taking place to the north of the river South Winterborne and those to the south along the Dorset Ridgeway. Those to the north of the Winterborne are characterized by the construction of large monuments including the Maumbury henge, the Dorchester timber henge, the Mount Pleasant timber henge and enclosure, a series of other possible small henge sites along the upper reaches of the Winterborne valley, and later, stone circles. Those to the south, primarily along the course of the Ridgeway, are principally defined by the construction of round barrows. The monumental evidence and associated deposits recovered by excavation have been extensively discussed elsewhere (see Lawson 1990; Woodward 1991: 136–54; Barrett 1994: 97–107; Thomas 1996: 197–233, with references). The account here will be largely confined to developments occurring along the course of the Ridgeway.

Along the Ridgeway between the Martin's Down and Broadmayne bank barrows the most dramatic and spectacular linear Bronze Age barrow cemetery in Britain began to be constructed some time after 2400 BC (Figure 6.5). There are only two other areas with a comparable barrow density in England and these both occur around the major ritual centres of Stonehenge and Avebury in Wiltshire (RCHME 1970; Fleming 1971). Both around Stonehenge and Avebury average barrow density is considerably lower per square kilometre than that which occurs along the top of the Ridgeway, making this development in south Dorset even more unusual and impressive (RCHME 1970: 427). The bank barrows at either end effectively enclose or bound the major distribution of barrows both to the east and the west. Between the bank barrows along the course of the very top of the Ridgeway around 242 barrows are documented (Grinsell 1959, 1982; RCHME 1970: 429). The RCHME survey divided the barrows into fourteen different groups (R1–R14), but since their distribution along the top of the Ridgeway is for the most part more or less continuous some of these groupings are inevitably rather arbitrary. Only a further five barrows occur immediately to the west of the Martin's Down bank barrow and six just to the east of the Broadmayne bank barrow. A further twenty-nine

THE BEACH IN THE SKY   209

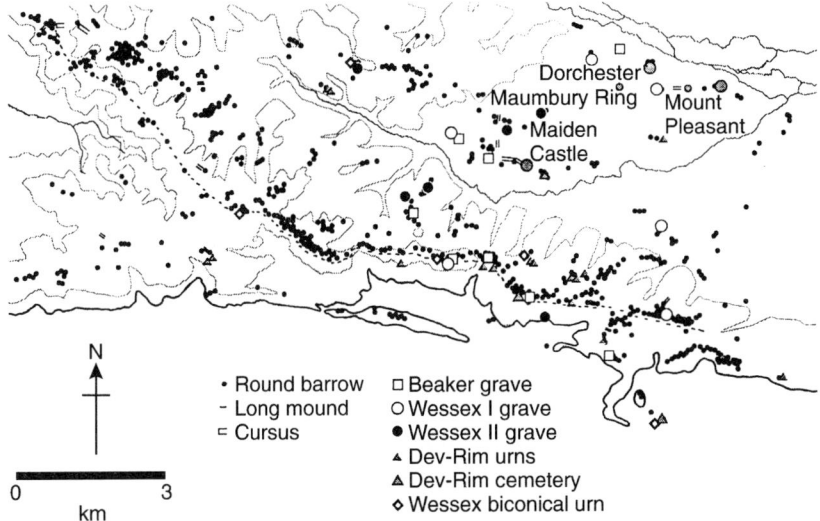

Figure 6.5 The distribution of Bronze Age barrows in the south Dorset Ridgeway area. The course of the Ridgeway is marked by a stippled line. The 130 m and 60 m contours are marked.
Source: after Thomas (1996)

barrows forming groups R12–R14 occur to the south-east of the Broadmayne bank barrow on a southern spur of the Ridgeway. Thus, nearly 90 per cent of the barrows occupy the high ground defined at the western and eastern ends by the two bank barrows.

Woodward (1991: 143) has argued for three separate 'territorial areas' along the course of the Ridgeway, each defined by barrow cemeteries: a western group, running from Martin's Down to Black Down; a central group from Black Down to Came Down; and an eastern group centred around Broadmayne and Bincombe. These divisions appear inadequate because they do not take into sufficient consideration the landscape setting of the barrows along the Ridgeway. The powers and meanings invested in the topography of the Ridgeway exerted a fundamental influence. The RCHME profitably suggest that

> the two bank barrows define the ends of a length of ridge-top which was of significance before it became studded with round barrows. . . . There may in fact be a conceptual connection between the linear aspect of long barrows and bank barrows

(apparently a local and abnormal development) and of curses and, more particularly perhaps, between the Ridgeway itself and the ridge-like appearance of the bank barrows. (RCHME 1970: 426)

This is precisely the line of argument that will be further developed here and, in particular, the conceptual connection made between the topographic form of the Ridgeway, the linearity of the Bronze Age barrow cemeteries situated along it and the presence of the bank barrows. If the latter represented 'beaches in the sky' what implications does this have for understanding the Bronze Age round barrow cemeteries and their relationship to the topography of the Ridgeway itself and that of the wider south Dorset landscape, in particular the coast and the Chesil Beach?

North of the Ridgeway, in the vicinity of the large later Neolithic and early Bronze Age ceremonial monuments, there are very few round barrows that have burials of Beaker date. By contrast, a series of such early burials is known to exist along the course of the Ridgeway (Best 1965; Peers and Clarke 1967). Thomas has argued that a number of small round barrows along the Ridgeway may be of even earlier Neolithic date (Thomas 1984: 164) and has suggested a developing zonation of the landscape with 'one area associated with large monuments and Grooved Ware, and another with funerary activities, Peterborough Ware, and the funerary use of Beakers' (Thomas 1996: 207). This broad division between the Ridgeway as principally a funerary area with the lower-lying areas to the north characterized by activities connected with the construction and use of monuments appears to continue throughout the Bronze Age (Figure 6.5). Settlement evidence during the late Neolithic and Bronze Age indicates that the primary areas utilized were to the north of the Ridgeway along the Frome and South Winterborne valleys and up along the dry valleys cutting into the northern slopes of the Ridgeway (Woodward 1991: 142). The top of the Ridgeway and its spurs became defined as a separate space of funerary practice and ritual situated closest to the sky and set apart from other ceremonial activities.

Fabulously rich grave good assemblages recovered from barrows along the course of the Ridgeway, many with exotic depositions (e.g. faience beads, gold, amber, daggers, cups, battle-axes) were used by Piggott to define a so-called 'Wessex culture' in southern England (Piggott 1938). It has been widely accepted in the literature that the Ridgeway cemeteries may be understood, at least in part, as one of the major centres of burial for a local social élite during the earlier Bronze Age of southern England. But perhaps what is far more significant is the manner in which the barrows were continuously re-used for burials throughout the course of the Bronze

Age and their meanings transformed in the process, as is documented by the variety of the grave goods and in the dates and types of burials recovered (for details see Woodward 1991: 143–54).

Woodward (ibid.) has documented considerable variation in the grave good deposits along different parts of the Ridgeway. But rather than follow him and regard these differences as simple expressions of differing ethnicities and social territories, it seems more worthwhile to follow Thomas's suggestion that 'the accrual of meanings by particular locations within the landscape (both cultural and natural) would have made them appropriate for different forms of practice in the Early Bronze Age, irrespective of any continued association with a group of people' (Thomas 1996: 225). We should take seriously the proposition that round barrow burial involved the construction of the social identities of persons in relation to the landscape which acted recursively so as to establish and define these identities. As Garwood (1991) has argued, the event of burial brought together artefacts, persons and places, relations of affiliation and descent, and dynamically transformed them in relation to each other through the ritual process. Barrett cogently argues that

> the generalized ancestral origins perceptible to the communities of the fourth and third millennia were . . . displaced during the second millennium. Lines of specific genealogical identity were constructed whose own origins then came to be fixed by mythological images of increasingly more distant times. It was in those distant and mythological ages that the inaccessible and heroic figures had lived and died who now lay buried beneath the massive turf and chalk-capped tumuli. . . . The uplands . . . [of] the Dorset Ridgeway were gradually transformed from the end of the third to the end of the second millennium. The burial mounds now emerged as the most significant, permanent points of reference to anyone wishing either to locate themselves in that landscape or to describe the setting of the plain and the Ridgeway. (Barrett 1994: 127–8)

While these arguments are well put the weakness of Barrett's position and those of Thomas and others lies in their generality. They provide us with no hint of what the mythologies might be and how they link in with the specifics of barrow location in the south Dorset landscape.

From the Neolithic to the Bronze Age: The Monumental Re-referencing of Place

It is readily apparent that the Bronze Age cemetery groups along the Ridgeway were carefully arranged and were developed in relation to both each other and earlier Neolithic monuments. There appears to be a rather close set of relationships between the Neolithic barrows and the Bronze Age barrow cemeteries throughout the study area. In some cases the round barrows are superimposed at the ends of the Neolithic mounds. In others the long axis becomes linearly 'referenced' and extended across space by placing round barrows at its ends. Or the Neolithic mound may form a focus for a non-linear group of round barrows (see Table 6.1). The two bank barrows on the Ridgeway and all but one of the long barrows (Cowleaze) form the foci around which many of the later Bronze Age barrows cluster. It is also noteworthy that a high proportion of 'fancy' types of Bronze Age barrows, disc and pond barrows, cluster towards the western and eastern ends of the top of the Ridgeway in the vicinity of the long barrows and bank barrows. These sets of relationships can be illustrated most clearly by considering in detail the Neolithic and Bronze Age barrow groups at the eastern end of the Ridgeway.

The Broadmayne bank barrow and the Bincombe long barrow both have their long axes orientated approximately east–west along the axis of the Ridgeway itself (see Figure 6.7). They are skyline sighted, making them highly visible both to the south and the north, blocking out any view of the landscape beyond them as they are approached from these directions. By contrast, from the east and west they are only visible from a short distance away, 150 m or less. The much smaller Culliford Tree long barrow is unusually orientated ENE–WSW and is not skyline sighted. In every respect it *reverses* the siting and overall form of the nearby Broadmayne bank barrow. Its orientational axis is at right angles to that of the latter (Figure 6.6). The broader and higher end is situated down-slope, whereas that of the bank barrow is situated up-slope. The bank barrow runs precisely along the top of the ridge with the land sloping away from it to the north and south. The Culliford Tree long barrow, by contrast, is situated towards the top of a south–north slope with its long axis running up-slope to the lower and narrower end. The land also slopes away from it gently to the east. It is only prominent in the landscape from the west and east, i.e. along the general axis of the Ridgeway itself rather than from off it. In the Bronze Age round barrows were built on top of both of these mounds. On the bank barrow the Bronze Age barrow was built at the lower and narrower western end of the mound itself, on the Culliford Tree long barrow on the higher and broader northern end (down-slope). It would be hard to introduce a more contrastive set of characteristics both in terms of mound morphology and landscape siting.

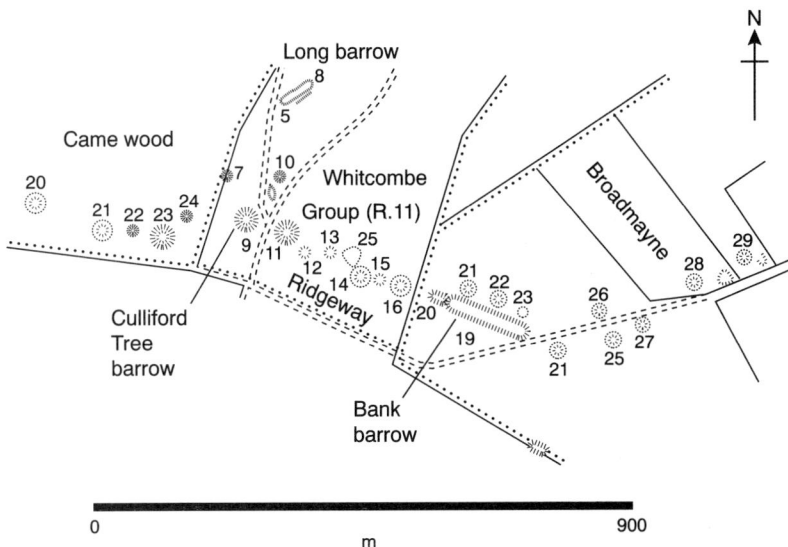

Figure 6.6 Barrows in the vicinity of the Broadmayne bank barrow at the eastern end of the Ridgeway.
Source: after RCHME (1970)

There are a number of interesting nuances at work here in relation to the manner in which the siting of these three barrows 'works' in relation to the surrounding landscape. While the Bincombe and Broadmayne long barrows are sedimented into the lie of the ridge axis itself, they are meant to be seen from off it: to the north and the south. The Culliford barrow traverses this axis but would be most visible along it. The Broadmayne and Bincombe barrows are thus *internally* positioned and *externally* sited in terms of visibility. The Culliford barrow reverses these principles.

The Bronze Age barrows completely alter the character of the Neolithic cultural landscape and the manner in which the monuments relate to the topography. This involves an attempt towards the revisualization of the world and the meanings embodied within it, while maintaining links with the associations objectified by the Neolithic barrows. The long axes of the three Neolithic barrows effectively define and mark out the general orientational axes of the area later occupied by the Bronze Age barrows stretching from Bincombe to the Broadmayne bank barrow. The positioning of the Bronze Age barrows: (1) clearly extends the directional axis of the bank barrow along the Ridgeway at both ends and (2) infills and extends the area occupied by monuments on the highest land between it to the Bincombe long barrow and beyond. However, what becomes important now is no longer the orientational axis of the ridge itself but a microtopography of place in which breaches in the ridge mass created by valleys and coombes become marked out and emphasized. In the process water sources (springs) assume great significance (see below). The area marked out by the Neolithic barrows becomes literally built upon and extended. The Bronze Age barrow builders were obviously acutely aware of the presence and significance of the Neolithic barrows and their positions in the landscape. They seem to have set out to both tap into and usurp their powers and significance. There are a number of ways in which this happens.

(1) Height was obviously of enormous ritual significance. In the Bronze Age the bank barrow and the Culliford long barrow have round barrows built on their terminal ends.

(2) The directional orientation of the long axis of the bank barrow is extended in both directions by constructing round barrows. Rows of barrows are also offset from this axis to the west and east along the course of the Ridgeway itself, thus creating a sinuous, meandering, snake-like line.

(3) The Broadmayne and Bincombe barrows are joined by a barrow arc and studded lines of barrows on Bincombe Hill and West Hill create fresh orientational long axes in the landscape related to the localized microtopography of the Ridgeway. Both of these places are slightly higher than the area of land on which the bank barrow is located and from them one can look *down* on it. The Bronze Age Bincombe Hill barrows in particular appear far more conspicuous today.

(4) The skyline sighting effect of the Broadmayne barrow becomes deliberately altered not only by the construction of a barrow on it at the western end but by placing another on slightly higher ground a short distance from the eastern end, and a whole string of barrows on the skyline due east. Two round barrows and a pond barrow were sited immediately in front of it on the northern side. Viewed from the slopes of the chalk downland to the north it is the two round barrows that stand out on the skyline and those to the west and east of the bank barrow. The latter is made as if to deliberately recede into the lie of the land, as if part of the topography itself, an order of nature rather than culture. Both of these barrows are also visible over the top of the mound of the bank barrow when seen from the south, thus creating a similar effect from this direction as well. When these round barrows were freshly constructed the visual effect must have been quite striking: gleaming white mounds contrasting with, perhaps, a dull grey-green profile of the bank barrow itself, merging as it

does today into the surrounding grass of the chalk downland. The aim must have been to usurp and tap into the directionality, height and skyline sighting of the bank barrow. Its size and position on the Ridgeway itself made this a far more significant monument than that on Bincombe Hill, which simply became incorporated into the arc of Bronze Age barrows with the addition of a small round barrow down-slope from its eastern end. The Culliford long barrow was evidently far less important since it did not occupy a high point with skyline sighting and represented much less of a 'threat' or challenge to the Bronze Age barrow constructors.

Walking the Ridgeway

The top of the Ridgeway was in historical and prehistoric times and still is an important path of movement. Much of the present-day interior stretch of the south-west coast path follows the line of the ridge and the barrows, and along substantial sections of the ridge top there are either modern or documented medieval roads. The ritually prescribed and 'correct' linear path of movement along the ridge top (which does not imply that this was the *only* path of movement) seems to have been from east to west, beginning at the Broadmayne bank barrow and ending at the Martin's Down bank barrow. This much seems to be indicated by three features: (1) the 'facilitating' orientation of the Broadmayne bank barrow running parallel with the ridge top but blocking north–south movement; (2) the 'blocking' effect of the Martin's Down bank barrow running at right angles across the west–east axis of the ridge top; and (3) the presence of two cursus-type monuments a short distance away from the Martin's Down bank barrow which clearly channel movement towards it from the west, in this case from the upper reaches of the South Winterborne valley with its series of important Bronze Age barrow cemeteries, stone circles and standing stones (Bradley 1983; Bailey 1984; Woodward 1991: 131; Thomas 1996: 190). The idea put forward by the RCHME that the course of the Ridgeway itself conceptually constituted a kind of open and undefined cursus monument, or a gigantic 'natural' bank barrow, its slopes being the 'ditches', is a pertinent one to explore further in terms of the ritual processions between the monuments that might be expected to have taken place. The linearity of this putative movement of people along the ridge top, and the distances involved, clearly contrasts dramatically with the localized and intimate patterns of movement and artefact deposition taking place within the late Neolithic and early Bronze Age circular monuments and enclosures to the north of the River Winterborne (see Thomas 1996: ch. 7). While ritual activities at these locales took place within the prescribed limits of the monuments set *within* the landscape, those taking place along the course of the Ridgeway may have had more the qualities of processions and pilgrimages of an 'integrative' character, drawing together wider and more generalized meanings about relationships *between* topography and places.

The sea to the south and the rolling chalk downland to the north are visible from virtually all the barrows located along the ridge top, with but a few exceptions. They were obviously located with reference to the sea and this visual perspective was of essential significance to their meaning. Approaching these ridge-top barrows from the north they invariably mark an important point in one's visual perspective on the world. Reaching the barrow line the sea becomes visible for the first time. By contrast, from the barrow sites located on the lower northern spurs of the ridge top, 50 m or considerably less from it, the sea is invisible. From these barrows there is an utterly different view of the world, a more sheltered, less open and dramatic inland view, studded with other barrows and monuments.

The barrow groups along the course of the Ridgeway are invariably located with reference to transition points in the landscape. Two types of transition can be distinguished. One is a transition interiorized in terms of walking along the Ridgeway itself: points at which the land begins to rise or fall away in front or behind along the course of the chalk ridge. The other transition is in terms of the relationship between the Ridgeway and the surrounding landscape: coombes sweeping in and breaking up the chalk: an exteriorized transition. The majority of the Bronze Age barrow cemeteries have coombes as a central 'focus' or the coombes constitute and mark spatial breaks or divisions between different barrow groups (see Figures 6.7, 6.8, 6.9, 6.12).

It is obvious that the barrows were meant to be *seen*. But there are various modes of seeing which may be distinguished: first, from barrow to barrow or barrow group to barrow group along the course of the Ridgeway. The linear groups of barrows are in most cases staggered so that you can see long lines of mounds as you walk along, and this is why they do not form neat and exact linear lines. Second, there is the viewing of these barrows from off the Ridgeway, primarily from the south or the north. So we can distinguish between 'internalized' visibility along the Ridgeway and 'externalized' visibility from off it. The third case is, of course, the barrows being sited so as to be visible both 'internally' and 'externally'.

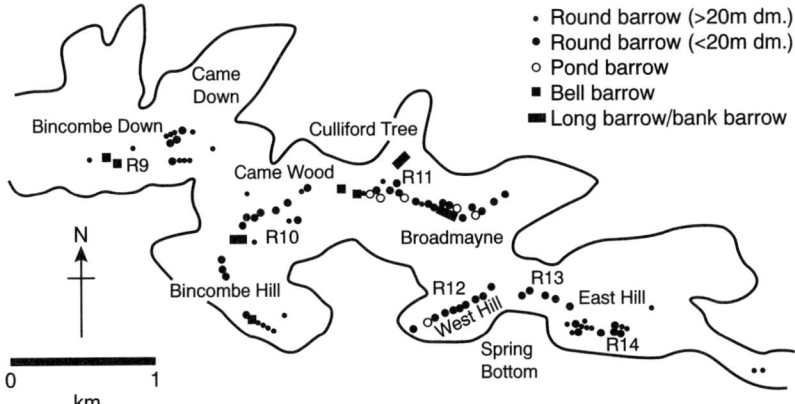

Figure 6.7 Barrow groups along the south Dorset Ridgeway from Broadmayne to Bincombe Down. Barrow distribution after RCHME (1970). The 130 m contour is marked.

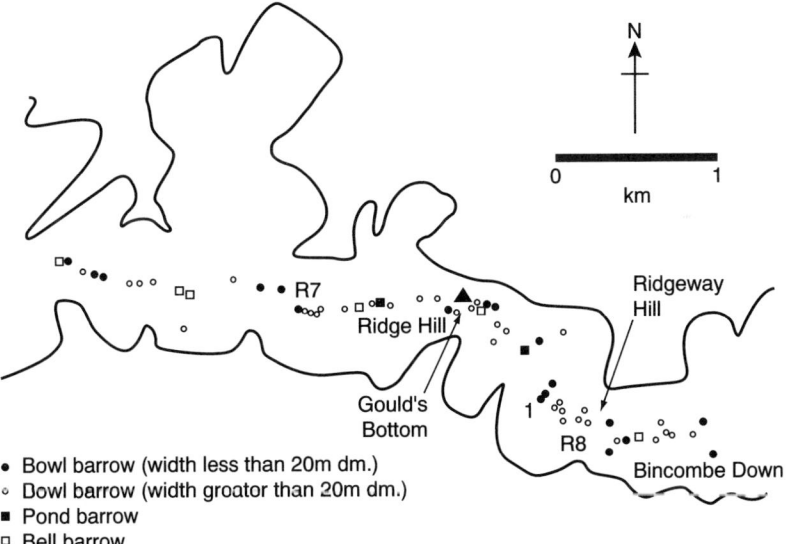

Figure 6.8 Barrow groups along the south Dorset Ridgeway from Bincombe Down to Bronkham Hill. The 130 m contour is marked. Arrows indicate bottoms of dry valleys cutting into the Ridgeway. Barrow distribution after RCHME (1970). Numbered barrow refers to text.

From Broadmayne to Bincombe Down (Figure 6.7)

The barrow groups at the eastern end of the Ridgeway form two great arcs. One stretches from just east of the Broadmayne bank barrow to Bincombe Hill in the south-west. These 48 barrows make up an almost continuous staggered group 1.1 km long, defining the very highest part of the ridge encircling a broad valley cutting into the chalk from the south. All but one of the 'fancy' barrows cluster in the vicinity of the Broadmayne bank barrow. The second group of 30 barrows runs for 600 m along the southern escarpment of the ridge, clustering around the steep declivity of Spring Bottom, the source of the River Jordan running south to the sea. All but one (a pond barrow) are bowl barrows, nine with extant surrounding ditches. The fall of the land here and at Bincombe Hill is quite dramatic. The barrows in both groups are placed in what might be termed points of transition on the lips of sloping land, usually just above points at which it begins to plunge away more or less steeply. Their spatial arrangements more or less exactly replicate the lie of the land. Closely located barrows are normally staggered rather than occurring in precisely orientated linear rows, so that if one stands at one barrow site up to four or more others are visible down the line.

From the majority of these barrows there are extensive views south to the sea and the Isle of Portland and to the north across the rolling chalk downland. Views west along the Ridgeway itself are restricted by the rise of Bincombe Down. The late Neolithic and Bronze Age enclosures to the north (Maiden Castle, Maumbury Rings and Mount Pleasant) are not visible.

The eastern approach to the top of the Ridgeway, along the present road from Broadmayne, involves climbing a gentle and gradual slope (about 100 m vertically to the ridge top in just under 3 km). The first monuments encountered are a series of round barrows strung along either side of the road forming a corridor. The road gently climbs to its highest point at the beginning of the Ridgeway proper at the eastern terminal end of the bank barrow. After passing two round barrows on the right-hand side and reaching one on the left, part of the terminal end of the bank barrow is first visible from about 150 m away. It appears as if it might be part of the profile of another round barrow. It is only once one has passed by another barrow pair (pond to the left and round to the right) that the entire length of the bank barrow and its associated round barrows can be seen stretching away into the distance.

From the barrow sites there are dramatic views of the Isle of Portland and the Chesil Beach stretching out and joining it to the mainland. This eastern end of the Ridgeway is the only area from which the link of the Chesil Beach to the mainland is visible. Elsewhere it is obscured by the low coastal hills around Weymouth. From the extreme eastern end of the barrow line at Broadmayne, the very northern tip of Portland is first visible when standing on top of the barrows but not beside them. It is fascinating to note that from the western end of the bank barrow the Bronze Age barrows parallel and continue its course, extending the visual perspective of Portland and the Chesil Beach. Before reaching the bank barrow, the orientation of the line of Bronze Age barrows is different, simply following the sloping route up to the ridge top from the south marked by the bank barrow. Walking below the bank barrow along its northern edge the view of Portland and the Chesil Beach is entirely obscured. From the southern side of the barrow only the tip of Portland is visible except at the western end. It is only from the top of the barrow that the line of the Chesil Beach is continuously visible from the western to the eastern end. Stepping off the mound at the eastern end it suddenly vanishes. Walking from east to west along the barrow top the view of Portland becomes more and more distinctive, the site of the most westerly Bronze Age barrow immediately to the north of the bank barrow marking the point at which it first becomes readily apparent that Portland is an island surrounded by sea, the Chesil Beach its only link with the mainland.

From the western end of the bank barrow the land dips away very gently to the west for about 350 m to a meeting of tracks (now a modern crossroads): the Ridgeway itself and one running up to the Ridgeway from the south and another to the north. This meeting point of trackways may explain the close location of the two long barrows here. By this meeting of tracks there are two pond barrows. From here the land gently rises once more until the last barrow in the western part of Came wood is reached, marking the point at which the great arc of round barrows runs away to the south-west following the very highest ground. Following the line of barrows west from the Broadmayne bank barrow, the line of the Chesil Beach is first obscured by Bincombe Hill at the point at which the barrows begin to curve round to the south. Only the very top of the Isle of Portland is visible from the Bincombe long barrow, but on reaching the other barrow groups to the south the view of Portland and the Chesil Beach dramatically reappears.

Beyond this barrow moving west the land dips away gently once more before rising and dipping to the end of Came wood. At this point a deep coombe cuts into the Ridgeway from the south. Continuing to walk west the land rises once more to Came Down (a northern spur of the Ridgeway) and Bincombe Down along the Ridgeway itself. The rise of Bincombe

Down blocks views further west. On the eastern slopes a linear cemetery of four barrows is situated. The highest land is occupied by a cluster of seven barrows on the southern part of Came Down. Approaching these up-slope from the east, Maiden Castle is first visible to the north-east from these barrow sites. On the upper eastern slopes of Bincombe Down there are two impressive bell barrows which dominate the view when approached from the east. There are stupendous views from these massive barrows of the whole of the eastern coast of Portland, as opposed to its towering northern cliffs, the only part of the island visible previously along the Ridgeway. These two barrows are not intervisible with the group on the western slopes of Bincombe Down. It is only after reaching the top of the Down that Black Down can be seen in the distance for the first time since leaving the Broadmayne bank barrow.

From Bincombe Down to Bronkham Hill (Figure 6.8)

From the top of Bincombe Down a long staggered row of barrows is visible stretching away down-slope and up again to the top of Ridgeway Hill to the west, the top of which is broken by the profile of a single prominent barrow. Walking down the steep slope, Black Down gradually disappears over the horizon and is only visible once more just before reaching the barrow on the top of Ridgeway Hill. It is only when this barrow is reached that those on the eastern part of group R7 are visible. From the barrow on the top of Ridgeway Hill the land gradually slopes down to the symbolic centre of the R7 group marked by an enormous barrow, unique on the Ridgeway in terms of form (intermediate between a disc and a bell barrow) and size (largest in overall diameter). From the barrow sites on the western slopes of Bincombe Down, the southern tip of Portland, Portland Bill, is clearly visible. Portland and the Chesil Beach gradually slip out of sight as one walks down the slope of Bincombe Down in a westerly direction, both being entirely obscured from view when reaching the bottom of the slope and the modern (and Roman) road from Dorchester to Weymouth. From the lowest barrow on the western side of Bincombe Down Portland is only visible from the top of the barrow mound, being obscured as one stands beside it. Walking up the western slopes of Ridgeway Hill Portland first becomes visible at the lowest barrow, and soon after the line of Chesil Beach linking it to the mainland. They both remain visible until passing the barrow on the crest of the hill, when they disappear out of sight. From this point onwards the stretch of Chesil Beach linking Portland to the mainland remains invisible along the rest of the Ridgeway. For the next

700 m Portland is only visible from the tops of the larger barrows. It is invisible from the top of the massive disc/bell barrow just to the north of the declivity of Gould's Bottom and the sea is not even visible from the summit of the barrow mound. By contrast, Portland and the sea are clearly visible from the barrow sites no more than 30 m to its south. Portland and the sea remain in sight from all the barrows along the next 5 km stretch of the Ridgeway to the summit of Black Down.

Unusually, the enormous bell-disc barrow is situated not on a high point, the norm for the largest and most impressive barrows, but in a dip on the Ridgeway with the land rising steeply to the west of it, more gently to the east. It is located on a north–south slope with the land rising above it to the south. This means that this barrow is not visible from off the Ridgeway to the south, being hidden by rising land above it. The top of the mound is first visible from the barrow on the summit of Ridgeway Hill 750 m away to the east, but from only 250 m away to the west. From both these vantage points one looks *down* on the barrow. Only the central mound is visible from the east until an observer reaches the two barrows immediately adjacent to it on the eastern side and passes beyond them. The entire barrow with central mound, wide berm, ditch and external bank is visible from the west, but only from a short distance away. Approaching from the south it is only visible when the crest of the Ridgeway has been reached about 60 m away. It seems to have been placed in a deliberately hidden location at the *lowest* point on the whole of the Ridgeway between the Broadmayne and Martin's Down bank barrows. It is only visible from a long distance away from the north, where it appears as prominent and skyline sited from the Maiden Castle bank barrow 1.9 km away. It must have been deliberately sited to have been seen from this direction and location. This huge round barrow was thus constructed in this location so as to explicitly reference the bank barrow. The bell/disc barrow is sited at the head of two dry valleys. One long narrow valley cuts into the Ridgeway from the north; another, much deeper valley, Gould's Bottom, from the south. Standing on the Maiden Castle bank barrow an observer's eye is drawn up the coombe to the bell/disc barrow at its head. From the barrow site itself views along the Ridgeway are very restricted. To the west the rising slope blocks the view after a few hundred metres, with the large barrows on the top of Ridge Hill being invisible. To the east, views are restricted by the rise of Ridgeway Hill. Bincombe Down is only visible from the top of the mound. Rising ground blocks any view off the Ridgeway to the south. It is only when passing over the ditch and bank on the southern side of the mound that there is a merest glimpse of the sea and

Plate 6.4 Part of the barrow line looking east from below Bronkham Hill towards Ridge Hill.

the landscape beyond, but this only becomes properly visible from the top of the Ridgeway south of the barrow.

Leaving this barrow one walks west up a steep slope to the top of Ridge Hill surmounted by an impressive string of barrows. These are skyline sited and highly visible from both the north and the south off the Ridgeway (Plate 6.4). Black Down comes into view just before reaching the top of the slope. From these barrows there are panoramic views across the landscape. Looking west an unbroken chain stretches away towards Bronkham Hill and Black Down. The land dips away gently at first from the summit – marked by the barrows to the north and south – and then more steeply. From the summit of Ridge Hill the western course of the Ridgeway itself dips away gently for about 2 km before rising up steeply to Bronkham Hill. Bronkham Hill and Black Down, the latter blocking all views of the rest of the Ridgeway, are the most distinctive westerly skyline features apart from the barrows themselves.

Glimpses of the Fleet and the Fleet stretch of the Chesil Beach are visible from the barrow sites between Ridge Hill and Bronkham Hill, but it is only from the first of the larger barrows lining the ridge of Bronkham Hill that the Fleet and the Chesil Beach become major visible and impressive features of the coastal landscape.

Bronkham Hill and Black Down (Figure 6.9)

At the western end of Bronkham Hill a shallow coombe cuts into the Ridgeway from the south and another, Ridge Bottom, from the north.

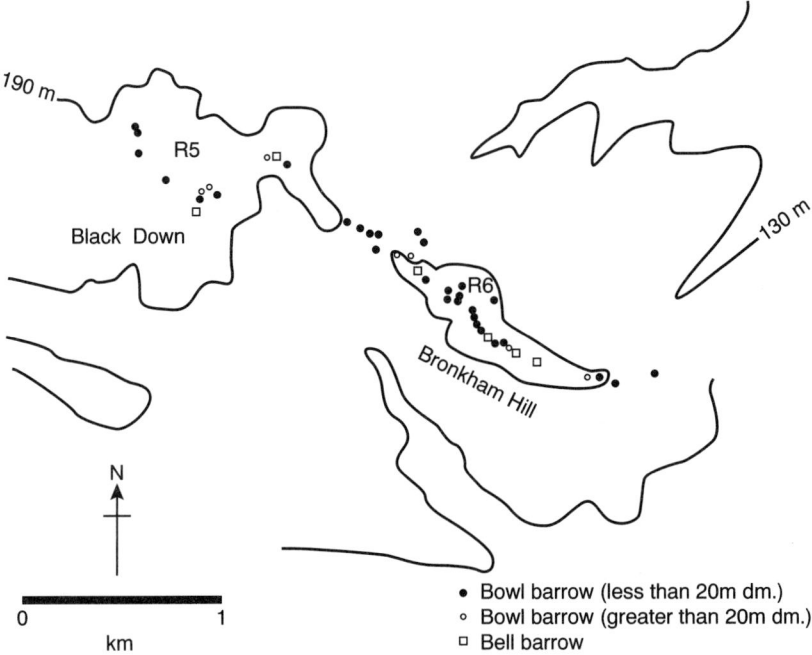

Figure 6.9 The barrow groups along the south Dorset Ridgeway from Bronkham Hill to the Black Down summit. The 130 m and 190 m contours are marked. Barrow distribution after RCHME (1970).

This marks a low point on the Ridgeway before the land rises steeply to the summit of the hill. Bronkham Hill is situated at the midpoint of the Ridgeway. It marks another important transition point, a change in the overall directional orientation of the ridge top from being almost exactly west–east to north–west to south–east. From the dip where the coombes meet four prominent barrows are visible studding the skyline of the hill.

The character of the land on the top of both Bronkham Hill and Black Down differs markedly from the chalk areas surrounding them. Here there is a thick capping of Bagshot gravels with heath development. The ground is rich in flint pebbles which were used to construct the monuments – essentially flint cairns of various colours. The tactile qualities of heather and bracken, flint and black peaty soil give these hills an utterly distinctive feel compared with other parts of the Ridgeway. The only other comparable area is Bincombe Down, but there the pebble gravels capping the chalk are thinner, less extensive and well developed. These two hills are also the highest points along the Ridgeway, the roofs of the world where one is in the closest contact with the sky. Black Down is slightly higher than Bronkham Hill, but while the top of Black Down is broad and relatively amorphous in shape, Bronkham Hill forms a long and narrow spinal ridge, rising up both from the eastern and western ends, with the land dropping away sharply to the north-east and the south-west. An unbroken 1.8 km line of thirty barrows is studded along the restricted spine of the ridge up along the eastern and western slopes of the hill. Of these, four are bell barrows, the largest and highest concentration of barrows of this form anywhere along the Ridgeway. The highest point on the hill is occupied by the largest bell barrow. One of the other bell barrows is situated on the north-western slope of the hill, the other two on the south-eastern slopes. Apart from the bell barrow on the north-western slope all the other most impressive and prominent barrows are situated on the south-eastern slopes and are meant to be seen from the Ridgeway itself as well as from off it to the north and the south. West of the large bell barrow on the hill summit there is a small, flat plateau area. Here the arrangement of the barrows becomes more clustered. The mounds of these barrows, in contrast to those situated on the narrowest parts of the ridge, are all small and relatively inconspicuous. Beyond barrows 12 and 13 (see Figure 6.10) the land begins to dip down and becomes very undulating. The remaining eleven barrows in the group are situated on sloping land, mostly on spurs or small knolls with the land dropping away steeply to the north and east of them. This repeats the pattern found in barrow location on the south-eastern part of Bronkham Hill, where again the land, in the majority of cases, drops away steeply to the north of the barrows. Hugging the line of the ridge the barrows were deliberately positioned so as to be most prominent when seen from the north, south and east. The siting of some of the barrows on small knolls considerably increases their profiles when viewed from afar. Moving along the line of barrows from east to west or west to east, barrow intervisibility in the cemetery is restricted. From bell barrow 10 it is possible to see the other barrow sites to the west, but only a couple of other barrows to the east. It is only from the bell barrow at the highest point that the majority of barrows both to the west and east are visible. Inter-barrow visibility is extremely restricted on the south-east slopes of the hill, with the majority of barrows out of sight to the west. The largest bell barrow on top of the hill marks the point at which (1) the majority of barrows are visible and (2) the 'hidden' plateau area is not visible from the eastern slopes of the hill. Walking up the slope of the hill following the line of the barrows Black Down only comes into view from the tops of the barrow mounds until the summit and the bell barrow (no. 20) is reached. Thereafter the ground slopes away to the north-west and

Black Down is continuously visible to the west. The finest and most extensive views of the Chesil Beach and the Fleet lagoon are obtainable from the vantage point of the largest and highest bell barrow on the summit of Bronkham Hill, where two continuous stretches of the lagoon and the beach are visible: parts of the east and west fleet. Descending Bronkham Hill views of the lagoon and the beach become less striking and impressive until one reaches the barrows on the summit of Black Down.

Undoubtedly the most remarkable feature of Bronkham Hill is that the entire ridge is studded with over 200 dolines or sink holes, some of which are very large, deep and impressive. Seen from a distance the ridge resembles a lunar landscape (Plate 6.5). On the ground these dolines are only visible from a short distance away, surprising an observer when one is on top of the hill and having to walk around and between them. They are all almost perfectly circular in shape, ranging in diameter from around 4 m to 15 m or more (the average diameter is 8 m) and may be up to 4 m deep (House 1991: 149–53). Apart from a small group of dolines in an area on the top of Black Down where Bronze Age barrows also cluster (around the Hardy monument), they occur nowhere else along the Ridgeway.

These circular hollows are depressions formed in the chalk by subsurface solution in areas where there is a cover of gravel and sand deposits (Bird 1995: 58). These surface deposits collapse into the solution holes invisibly formed beneath them to create a dramatically pock-marked topography. The sink holes on Bronkham Hill are particularly striking not only because of their size and depth but also their close association and juxtaposition with the burial mounds, something that surprisingly has been completely ignored in the archaeological literature on the Dorset Ridgeway. Standing near to some of the largest barrows it appears as if the barrows themselves have been thrown up out of the largest of the dolines. The dolines themselves may indeed have been enlarged or at the least have provided a ready source of building material for barrow construction. One is a transformation or inversion of the other. The circular shape of both serves to emphasize this connection. There exists a strong relationship between barrow and doline distributions. In the densest concentrations of some of the largest and deepest dolines the largest and most impressive of the barrows are also situated (Figures 6.10 and 6.11). Three of the four bell barrows have dolines in their surrounding ditches. Five of these dolines almost encircle the ditch of the largest and highest bell barrow (no. 20). Three occur in the eastern side of the ditch of barrow 10 and two in the northern part of the ditch of barrow 26. The remaining bell barrow (no. 25) has no dolines in its ditch but is surrounded by large dolines to the north and south. The

Plate 6.5 The summit area of Bronkham Hill showing barrows and dolines. Crown copyright: RCHME.

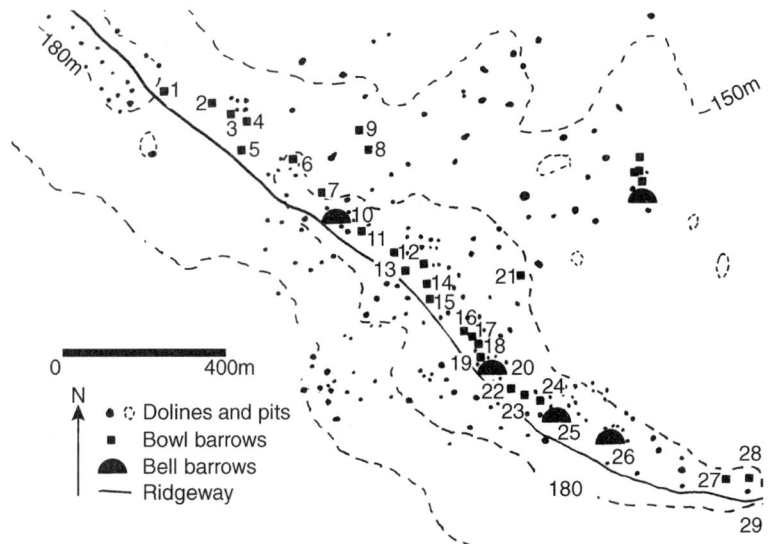

Figure 6.10 Bronkham Hill: the distribution of dolines and barrows (numbered). Doline distribution after House (1991).

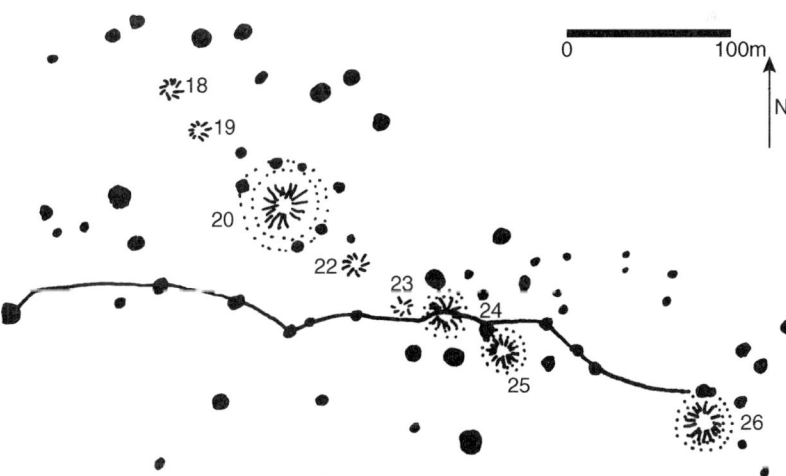

Figure 6.11 The distribution of dolines and barrows (numbered) on the summit of Bronkham Hill. Note the group of dolines linked together by a 'Romano British' cross-dyke running over the top of barrow 24. Doline distribution after House (1991).

dolines in the barrow ditches are usually considerably smaller in diameter than those encircling and surrounding them. A remarkable series of deep doline holes completely encircles a large ditched bowl barrow (no. 24) situated between two of the bell barrows on top of the hill and bounding it off from them. A much smaller bowl barrow is precisely situated at a point where there are no dolines in the circuit surrounding the barrow, thus completing the ring (see Figure 6.11).

Some of these dolines hold water in wet weather. House has noted that a few on the northern side of the hill have developed spring hollows (House 1991: 149). There is thus a clear association with sources of fresh water, springs and these doline holes. The precise date of the formation of the dolines remains unclear, but it seems to have taken place over a very long time period well before the construction of the Bronze Age barrows and up to the present day. Their appearance on the ground surface can be quite sudden and dramatic. Wilson et al. state that

> during the [geological] survey of this area [1931–46] two of these solution pits showed evidence of the process of their formation. On the top of Bronkham Hill, beside the largest tumulus, a hole about a foot in diameter appeared on the surface. Beneath it was a large cave about 20 ft in diameter and 20 ft deep. In a field 630 yd W.S.W of the Hardy Monument a solution pit was formed within five years. (Wilson et al. 1958: 179)

House attempts to date most of the dolines on Bronkham Hill as being later than the barrow construction: 'it seems unlikely that such splendid tumuli would have been erected on a site considerably pockmarked by deep solution hollows...the probability is that the surface was relatively smooth at the times of the burials' (House 1991: 153). I want to argue precisely the reverse. It was *because* of the presence of the dolines that the barrows were constructed here. It seems highly unlikely that dolines should develop by chance exactly in the ditches of three out of the four of the finest and largest monuments, the bell barrows, on the ridge and that some of the most impressive dolines should be situated so close to the barrows as to surround and encircle them. Unequivocal evidence of an intimate relationship between dolines and monument construction is shown by a cross dyke of probable Iron Age date which runs over the top of one of the Bronze Age barrows and links a series of doline holes which clearly pre-date it and were used as part of the structure of the dyke (Figure 6.11). It is pertinent to note that no new doline holes cut the dyke. It is not hard to imagine that during the Bronze Age these circular sink holes were conceptualized as sites of ancestral activity: the places where the ancestors entered and exited into the land to a sea of the underworld existing below. Their close association with the barrow ditches and sites is thus readily explicable. The dolines formed an essential part of the mystery and power of the place.

As already noted, on both Bronkham Hill and Black Down the overlying deposits are of Tertiary age, the Bagshot beds. The mounds of the Bronze Age barrows, visible in disturbed patches, are constructed out of these gravels which include 'flint cobbles, pebbles of flint and quartz, jasper from Cornwall, slate, chert and grit from the Upper Greensand and silicified Purbeck limestone [and] a matrix of yellow and white quartz sand' (ibid.: 40). These burial mounds thus contrast with all others along the Ridgeway in terms of the gravelly and pebbly nature of their construction and the numerous colours and textures of the material. The numerous smoothed pebbles occurring in these Bagshot beds are frequently exposed in the sides of the doline holes and bear a remarkable resemblance in colour, texture, shape and size to those forming the Chesil Beach 6 km away to the south. Bronkham Hill and Black Down are both within sight and sound of the sea, the Isle of Portland and stretches of the Fleet lagoon and the line of the Chesil Beach itself. These gravel and pebble sediments, in geological time, were carried and deposited here by a river draining from Dartmoor and the Haldon hills eastward across Lyme Bay; their waterborne origin is obvious. To the prehistoric people the pebbles on the top of Bronkham Hill and Black Down must have represented the tangible ancestral remains of a *beach in the sky*.

At the end of the Bronkham Hill barrow cemetery the land gradually dips down and then winds up to the top of Black Down. Two small barrow groups on the way are constructed on small knolls, thus emphasizing their size. Just before the Black Down summit is reached the land rises very steeply. On Blackdown there is a group of eight barrows, the largest on the summit. From this vantage point there are sweeping vistas along the Ridgeway in both directions. The Martin's Down bank barrow at the north-west terminal point is also just visible on the horizon. To the south, Portland is visible and stretches of the Fleet lagoon enclosed by the sweep of the Chesil Beach, the same view as from the top of Bronkham Hill. More immediately the doline-pitted and barrow-studded spiny ridge of Bronkham Hill is visible below, appearing as if in an oblique aerial photograph. For the first time one can see the westward stretch of the coast of Lyme Bay and the distinctive profile of Golden Cap.

The top of Black Down around the Hardy Monument, like Bronkham Hill, is studded with dolines. It is here, as on Bronkham Hill, that the main cluster of barrows occurs, again in close association with the doline distribution. However, in comparison with those on Bronkham Hill, these dolines are less numerous, generally shallower and far more irregular in shape. Given the usually close association between height and spiritual power in the Bronze Age it is somewhat surprising how few barrows occur on the Black Down summit. The surviving summit barrows are not prominent today and it is unlikely that they ever were. They are modest constructions. Only one (now destroyed) is a fancy barrow and this is situated south, down-slope from the highest point. These barrows are in place, mark the place, but were not intended to be visually prominent from any distance away. It is therefore unlikely that Black Down was the most important sacred hill along the Ridgeway, despite both its towering height and the magnificent views in all directions. It can be understood better as a large 'viewing platform' in which populations were able to look down, as today, and fully appreciate the mystery of Bronkham Hill with its pronounced dolines, barrows constructed out of pebbles and its narrow *ridged* resemblance to the Chesil Beach.

From Black Down to Martin's Down (Figure 6.12)

From Black Down to Martin's Down the character of the Bronze Age barrow distribution differs markedly from that occurring along the previous stretches of the Ridgeway. The barrows are either isolated or cluster in clearly defined groups rather than form an almost continuous line along the ridge top. The north-west arm of the Ridgeway is remarkable for the regularity in barrow placement: single barrows or barrow clusters occur at distances of between about 400 and 600 m. There is a gradual increase in numbers of barrows as one moves away from Black Down, from pairs of barrows or single barrows to large barrow groups, the last two groups both focused around long barrows, the final point being the remarkable Martins's Down complex consisting of a massive bank barrow with possibly an associated cursus leading up to it. There is thus an increase in monumentality as one moves north-west. Fancy barrows only occur in the last two groups.

Three small flint-pebble cairns were built a little way down-slope from the top of Black Down to the west. Only one, the largest, is visible from the summit. Two smaller cairns are sited on the margins of the highest land. To the west and north of them the land plunges away. From here the profile of the long barrow at Cowleaze, running along the upper slope of the Ridgeway in the distance, acts as a prominent visual marker. The broader south-east end is orientated directly up to the Black Down summit

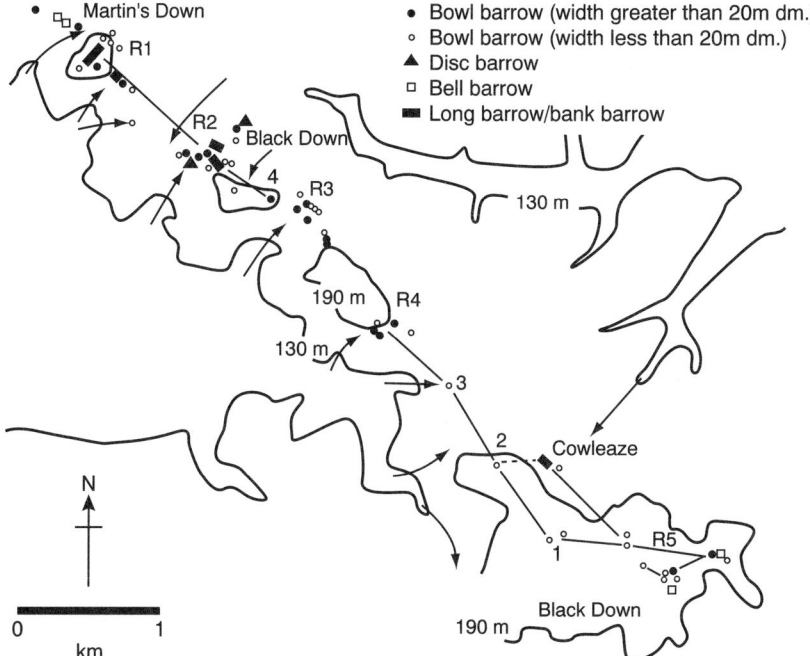

Figure 6.12 Barrow groups along the south Dorset Ridgeway from Black Down to Martin's Down. The relationship between barrow groups and dry valleys cutting into the Ridgeway from the south and north is shown by arrows. Intervisibility between barrows or barrow groups is shown by connecting lines. R1–R5: barrow groups. Numbered barrows refer to text. Barrow distribution after RCHME (1970).

in one direction and precisely along the remainder of the Ridgeway at the narrower north-west end, establishing a general direction in which to walk. Leaving the Black Down summit, the Fleet and the Chesil Beach disappear out of sight when one walks east past the last of the summit barrows. Henceforth, views of the sea from the next stretch of the Ridgeway from Black Down to Martin's Down are those of Lyme Bay. This part of the sea and the coast is visible from the majority of the barrow sites, constituting a completely different perspective on the world.

The western slopes of Black Down are gentle. Moving downwards and westwards one encounters a pair of barrows situated beyond the margins of the Bagshot pebble gravels. They are located at the top of a western arm of a dry coombe, part of the Valley of Stones, with prominent exposed sarsen boulders in its depths. These barrows are sited so as to be most prominent from below to the west and south. Viewed from these directions they

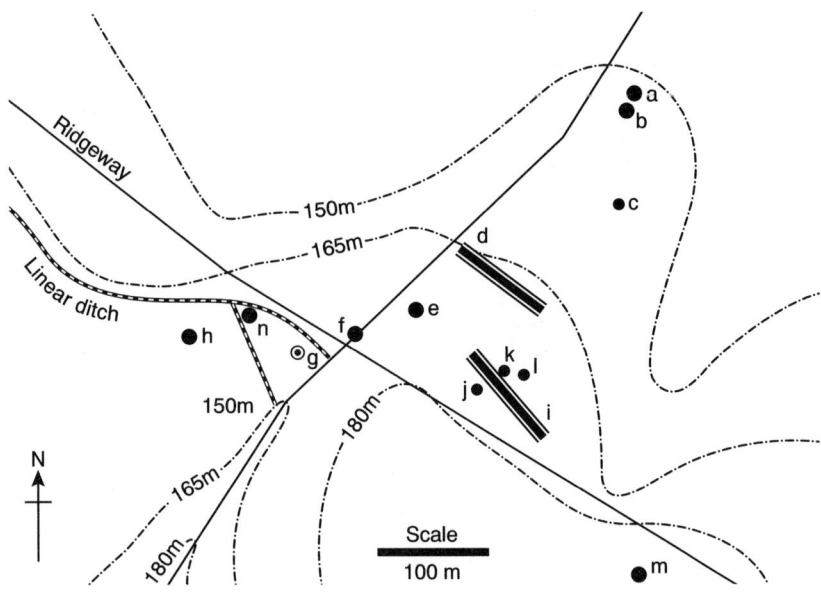

Figure 6.13 Barrow group R2.
Source: after Bailey (1980)

appear to mark the top of the hill and the Black Down summit is invisible beyond. Directly north-west another prominent barrow is visible, at a distance of just over 600 m (Figure 6.13, no. 2). The land slopes down gently for 250 m and then is flat until this barrow is reached. It is situated on a break of the slope. To its north and west the land plunges away quite steeply. The previous barrow is skyline sited from here. The next barrow, also located at a distance of 600 m, would have been prominent from here (Figure 6.14, no. 3). It is now much ploughed down, obscured by a wood and a hedge. The way to it replicates the previous move between barrows 1 and 2 (see Figure 6.12). At first there is a gentle slope and then a flat stretch of ground in the middle of which the barrow is placed. It is located just to the west of an arm of the Bride valley, forming a steep wooded coombe, at the point at which the dip finally disappears into the ridge. It clearly marks a point of topographical *transition*. From it the Cowleaze long barrow is clearly visible. Barrow group R4 (the centre of which is again situated about 600 m away) would originally have been prominent from this barrow. The walk to them is flat for the first 400 m. The ground then slopes up gently to the north-west where the barrows are sited. They are located so as to be prominent when seen from the south-east. Beyond them the view of the Ridgeway is blocked by rising land. This rise is conspicuously absent of barrows and it is only when reaching the top at 190 m that the next barrow group can be seen below. Martin's Down can also be seen from this point. The only prominent visible barrow in group R3 is the one farthest to the north-west at its terminal point (Figure 6.12, no. 4).

Barrow group R3 consists of eleven barrows in two staggered rows aligned north-west to south-east. The most prominently sited is the most north-westerly barrow in the group (just visible from the summit of Black Down). It and the three most southerly barrows in the group are sited at both ends of a shallow dip in the terrain, in the middle of which the others are sited. So these terminal barrows in the group are sited on transition points along the Ridgeway where the land rises and falls (Figure 6.13). Just to the south of the centre of the dip and the barrow group is an impressive arc-shaped coombe cutting into the chalk from the south. The higher ground at the western end of the dip effectively blocks any view along the remainder of the Ridgeway to Martin's Down and it is only when one reaches the western terminal barrow in the group that Martin's Down with its bank barrow can be seen in the distance. This is the first point along the whole of the Ridgeway when the massive bank barrow and its associated long and round barrows can be seen clearly and in their entirety (a hazy outline of the bank barrow seen with strained eyes on the summit of Black Down excepted). So the westernmost barrow in group R3 marks a very important point in an observer's visual field. Beyond it the bank barrow is an increasingly prominent feature on the horizon, never slipping out of view but blocking any view of the land beyond it. Barrow 4 is the only one in group R3 visible from groups R2 and R1, looking east. It commands a two-directional visual field along the Ridgeway and is also a prominent skyline feature seen from off the course of the Ridgeway from both the north and the south.

Beyond it the land slopes down gently to group R2, the beginning of which, marked by the end of a long barrow, is 400 m distant. The terminal end of this barrow is the only monument in group R2, apart from three outliers to the north, visible from this point.

Group R2, a diffuse clustered group, consists of two long barrows of great length, ten bowl barrows (four with surrounding ditches) and two disc barrows. It is only prominent as a group from Martin's Down in the north-west, being almost invisible until it is reached when approached from the south-east. The northern long barrow is aligned directly along the top of a slope (165 m contour) dipping down steeply to the north and this barrow and the rest of the barrow group appear prominent when seen from off the Ridgeway from the north, but are invisible from the south. Black Down is not visible from any of the monuments in this group and the bank barrow on Martin's Down blocks any view beyond it further west, an impenetrable barrier. While the round barrows cluster around the long barrows, clearly the focal point for the group, none of the round barrows are placed so as to be directly in line with the orientation of the axis of the long barrows. Only one round barrow, centrally located, is intervisible with almost all the others. This is the most prominently sited barrow, the only one in the group that is visible when walking all the way towards it from Martin's Down.

The group is located at a number of significant transition points, both internally with reference to the course of the Ridgeway, and externally:

1   The south-eastern end of the group, marked by barrow *m* on a high point, is due south of a shallow coombe cutting into the Ridgeway from the north (see Figures 6.12 and 6. 13).
2   Barrow *g* is situated just at the head of a deep coombe cutting into the Ridgeway from the south.
3   Barrows *f*, *e* and the end of long barrow *d* mark a break of slope where the land begins to dip away steeply to the north-west along the course of the Ridgeway itself.

From group R2 the round barrow by the Martin's Down bank barrow and in staggered alignment with the long barrow and two other barrows to its south, although not particularly large, is extremely prominent. From group R2 the Martin's Down bank barrow marks the termination of the world of the Ridgeway. Nothing is visible beyond it. Walking at first down-slope and then up-slope it completely dominates the horizon. It becomes the horizon of horizons.

The distance between the long barrows in group R2 and the Martin's Down bank barrow is about 1 km. The land dips down into a shallow, wide coombe cutting into the Ridgeway from the north for 300 m and then steadily rises up to the bank barrow. Another steep, narrow coombe cuts in from the south and at the head of this the first barrow in group R1 is sited. The others are scattered on sloping land rising up to the bank barrow. Two barrows are directly aligned in relation to its long axis, one at the southern end and the other at the northern end. Group R1 is clearly meant to be seen from group R2 along the Ridgeway. The bank barrow is hardly visible from the cluster of three barrows (two of which are very prominent bell barrows) below and beyond it to the north-west.

This terminal group R1 consists of eight bowl barrows — three with ditches — the massive bank barrow itself and a small long barrow with its long axis orientated up to the former. Walking up the slope the bank barrow dominates the horizon and it is not until passing around it or walking over it that the hills beyond can be seen. The land dips away sharply to the north-west of the bank barrow to a dip marking the top of a coombe slicing into the Ridgeway from the south. In the middle of the dip two massive bell barrows and a smaller bowl barrow cluster. The bank barrow is sited on the highest part of the Ridgeway (195 m) to the north-west of Black Down. The massive cross-bank is reminiscent of the terminal bank at Thickthorne Down of the Dorset cursus (see Tilley 1994). The bank barrow makes a dramatic impact on the landscape (Plate 6.3). Two-thirds of the way along it there is a curious break in the profile of the mound. Walking along the length of the barrow on the eastern side it is only through this gap that the hills beyond can be seen. No monuments are visible through it. As Bradley has noted the ditches on both sides are continuous and unbroken, so it is unlikely that the gap marks a trackway cut through the mound. It might be an antiquarian excavation, but another possibility suggested by Bradley (1983) is that the barrow was at some point extended and originally was a shorter, less imposing structure, and one that would not completely block an observer's visual field from the east. It was something added to create this effect, to terminate the Ridgeway, restricting flexibility of movement, visual knowledges and access to that lying beyond.

The Ridgeway as an Ancestral Beach

The transformation of the entire course of the Ridgeway into an almost continuous barrow cemetery in the Bronze Age can be understood as part of a process in which a set of pre-understandings, cosmological meanings and associations extending back to the Mesolithic were both extended and transformed. During the Neolithic the most sacred areas of the Ridgeway, the high points of Bronkham Hill and Black Down, were avoided. During the Bronze Age barrows were constructed in these places among the sink holes. This clearly must have involved an active appropriation of the ancestral powers associated with and invoked by these areas of the ridge. If the old Neolithic bank barrows represented beaches in the sky, cultural representations of the Chesil Beach manipulated in ritual practice, then in the Bronze Age this idea seems to have been extended to encompass the whole of the Ridgeway, which itself became reconceptualized, in ancestral mythology, as an enormous ancient raised beach on which the barrows were now constructed, studding the beach crest.

There are a number of specific analogies which link the Ridgeway and the Chesil Beach, features that would have demanded a cosmological explanation and understanding:

1   Both are ridges which run roughly parallel to each other in a westerly to easterly direction and terminate due north of each other at either end.
2   The profiles, or cross-sections, of both ridges are very similar: steep on the south side with much gentler slopes on the northern faces.
3   The Chesil Beach is composed of smooth and water-worn chert and flint pebbles. Smooth and water-worn chert and flint pebbles are similarly exposed on the highest points of the Ridgeway where the Bagshot beds cover the chalk: on Bincombe Down, Bronkham Hill and Black Down. The construction of the barrows in these areas would have systematically unearthed and exposed these pebbles which were used to construct the burial mounds.
4   Along the northern and landward side of the Chesil Beach circular canns or seepage hollows regularly and catastrophically form during storms. Similarly, almost perfectly circular dolines or sink holes catastrophically appear in areas of the chalk covered with thick Bagshot bed (pebble) material: on Bronkham Hill and Black Down which may temporarily fill with water. On these areas of the Ridgeway the barrows are surrounded by these circular sink holes.
5   The Chesil Beach is marked on either side by water, the Fleet lagoon and the sea, and seawater seeps through and issues out of the shingle bank. Similarly, the chalk of the Ridgeway is defined by the presence of water at its base and acts as a repository for it. The water flows out of the base of the chalk ridge from a series of springs seasonally giving birth (hence, the common village name Winterborne) to small streams to the south of the ridge and the River South Winterborne to the north. Like the Chesil Beach it forms a barrier and like the beach it is steeper on the southern than the northern (inland) side. Spring waters from the Ridgeway flow south to fill the Chesil lagoon and almost the entire length of Ridgeway itself is bordered to

the north by the River South Winterborne, which although small is the most important water course in the area, with its source only a few km from the Martin's Down bank barrow. The relationship of the River South Winterborne to the Ridgeway is thus in many ways analogous to that between the Chesil Beach and its lagoon. Both form protective dry barriers impounding water to the north which flows east. The Ridgeway acts, then, to the River South Winterborne as the Chesil Beach does to its lagoon. But it feeds and gives birth to both.

Now, all these geological similarities would have been well known to the Bronze Age populations (whose intimate knowledge of the landscape in which they lived we can scarcely hope to appreciate). They would have required an explanation. Why the pebbles up on the ridge, clearly worn by water and so similar to those occurring on the Chesil Beach? Why the sink holes and the seepage hollows? Why the steep profile of both the Ridgeway and the Chesil Beach to the south? etc. The suggestion here is that their mythological explanation must have involved, in some particular narrative form, the notion that the Ridgeway itself was a raised ancient and ancestral beach. For the Bronze Age populations it would have represented a 'prehistoric' version of the Chesil Beach – a beach along which the waves had once washed but had been thrown inland and landlocked in mythological time. And no more fitting or appropriate location could be imagined for the burial of the ancestral dead, for their corpses were being inserted into an ancient marine bank which had been sanctified and raised up from the sea to rest in the sky closest to the moon, the sun and the stars. In myths and stories the Ridgeway, like the Chesil Beach, must have been viewed as an ancestral creation. Tangible proof of this would have been provided by the metaphorical analogies listed above. But it must have been conceived as an older creation, no longer by the sea, but a raised beach in the sky, perhaps connected through the sink holes with the beach by the sea.

From the Neolithic to the Bronze Age, then, a fundamentally different consciousness of the landscape develops and is related to monument construction and ritual performance elaborating on pre-existing cosmological principles concerning the place of humanity within the cosmos. In the Neolithic the bank barrows marked out the Ridgeway as being of mythic and symbolic importance and these barrows were visual mimetic reminders of the Chesil Beach, an explanation and understanding of which were fundamental to local cosmologies. Gradually, during the course of the Neolithic, virtually the whole of the top of the Ridgeway and its northern spurs were cleared of both primary and secondary forest. The Neolithic long barrows and the two bank barrows cluster at the western and eastern ends of the Ridgeway. There appears to have been little or no Neolithic activity on the central and highest parts of the course of the Ridgeway. A small isolated long barrow at Cowleaze (Figures 6.4 and 6.12), the only one to be positioned in a central area of the Ridgeway, is set on a northern lower spur of the chalk well below Black Down. It references the hill through the orientational axis of the mound pointing towards it across the landscape, but it was not until the Bronze Age that the summit area became a major focus for funerary activity. The process of clearing the course of the top of the Ridgeway was probably only completed by the beginning of the early Bronze Age (Woodward 1991: 140). This stripping of the forest cover would have had the effect of revealing the overall morphology of the Ridgeway much more clearly. It would have exposed the pebbles of the Bagshot beds, revealed and emphasized the sink holes and, indeed, because of faster ground-water percolation would have further stimulated their development. It is very likely that these sink holes, situated on the very highest points of the Ridgeway, were conceived, as in contemporary Australian Aboriginal cosmologies (see Tilley 1994), as places where the ancestors entered and left the earth. The sink holes would have acted as points of intersection or doorways between the material and the spiritual worlds. Hence, it is not surprising that one of the most dramatic and important Bronze Age cemeteries along the entire Ridgeway occurs on Bronkham Hill, which is also its approximate geographical centre.

This process of revealing the bones of the land stimulated the redefinition of the old Neolithic mythic cosmologies in order to aid an understanding of what had now been revealed. These new mythological structures in turn became linked with the new mode of burial practice in round barrows and the establishment and maintenance of ancestral ties and genealogies through the development of the entire Ridgeway as a dedicated area for funerary practice. The uniqueness of the bank barrows of south Dorset and the equally unique linear accummulation of Bronze Age barrows along the course of the Ridgeway, between them have a common origin as explanatory landscape metaphors, activated in ritual performances, for the Chesil Beach that runs below them, one of the most striking features of the British coastline, and still regarded by many today as one of the wonders of the natural world.

7

Performing Culture in the Global Village

'The strangest thing in a strange land is the stranger who visits it.'
(Opening line in O'Rourke's film *Cannibal Tours*)

The Wala Island Tourist Resort is situated on a small coral island, one of a series known collectively as the Small Islands, just off the coast of northeast Malekula, one of the large islands in the northern part of the archipelago making up Vanuatu (former New Hebrides) (see Figure 4.1). An essential element of the experience for a visitor interested in anything more than sun, sea or sand is a visit to the Small Nambas on the Malekulan mainland, who have been busily reviving their customs during the past few years. Our guide, part-time local family planning adviser, close relative to the resort manager and occasional escort to visitors, took the party of six across the narrow strait of water to the village of Sanaliu on the Malekulan mainland. Wearing a floral skirt and Chanel Paris T-shirt she told us we would be fed: 'they'll provide the rice, you provide the meat!', a reference to the traditional practice of cannibalism, much stressed in the chapter on Malekula in the Lonely Planet guide to Vanuatu (the visitor's bible: everyone seemed to possess one). We followed a path through gardens in the bush, stopping at a huge banyan tree next to which were some small stone tables, the only visible remains of the site of an ancient *nimbaur* (men's house).

Nearby was a blue and white painted signboard. The overall organization of the design resembled that on a beer bottle. Highlighted areas in the top-left and right-hand corners read: 'Malekula 25 August '93' and 'Amel [dancing ground] Bouas'. Beneath in an oval band: 'Welcome to Small Nambes in Malekula Region.' Inside: 'Walla Kalja Club Organization of Foil Art. To promote understanding between people. Custom Dancing'.

Shortly, drumming broke the silence and we were led into the dancing ground. Chief Stephan greeted us dressed in a penis sheath supported by a bark belt, decorated arm band, and a curved pig's tusk hanging around his neck. A group of men, similarly dressed, were playing on upright and horizontal slit drums in the shade of an open high-roofed thatched house surmounted with a hawk sculpture with outstretched wings. Lining one side of the rectangular dancing ground on both sides of the central structure were ten houses, each with palm-leaf thatched roofs bound with lianas covering a coral monolith at the rear with small stone tables and a carved wooden anthropomorphic sculpture in front (Plate 7.1). Each sculpture, individually carved and utterly distinctive, had a large face and an extended upper torso. In two cases arms were represented; none had legs. Some of the faces of the effigies were painted in two halves, blue and red, divided down the bridge of the nose.

In one ancestor house an unpainted black tree-fern carving substituted for one of the wooden sculptures (Plate 7.2).

The two houses next to the central structure with the slit drums also had hawk sculptures affixed to the end of the roof ridge poles. Each of these houses was surrounded by a square of coral stones, and behind them there was a wall surmounted by a bamboo fence. Our guide explained that these were the ten ancestor houses erected along the men's side of the dancing ground in connection with the great *maki* ceremony that inaugurated it on 23 August 1993, the first such ceremony in living memory. Much smaller coral stones and stone tables, without any wooden sculptures or ancestor houses, lined the women's side of the dancing ground where we stood. Behind was a house with plaited bamboo walls and palm thatch. An awning provided welcome shade; a wooden table and benches stood outside.

Posted on the wall of the house was a small piece of paper with writing: a rota of duties connected with the maintenance of the dancing ground.

The women, more of our 'Small Nambas' hosts, clustered on their side of the dancing ground, dressed in pandanus mat skirts, bare breasted, with decorative arm bands, feathers in their hair and multiple strings of white beads hanging down to their stomachs. They gave us a cooling coconut

Plate 7.1   The central part of the 'Small Nambas' dancing ground: male side.

Plate 7.2   Ancestor house with tree-fern carving.

Plate 7.3   The 'Small Nambas' male dance troupe.

welcome drink. Small bamboo straws were provided to drink through a hole bored in the top of a coconut, complete with outer husk.

The six white, sweating British and Canadian guests were laden with all the latest reproductive technology: video and automatic cameras, tape recorder, and more primitively, notebook and pencil. The event was going to be framed and recorded in the greatest possible detail, from sight to sound to movement and back again. There was no mechanical means of recording touch and taste and smell. Our guide said we could photograph and look at whatever we want, ask questions, obtain information about traditional customs.

The drum beat changed. A male dance troupe with elaborate head decorations, *nambas*, ankle rattles and dance staffs rushed out into the centre of the dancing ground (Plate 7.3). A succession of three lengthy dances were performed: men at the centre; women on the periphery. The visitors watched from the sidelines, cameras flashed and clicked, the video and tape silently recorded. Sometimes they watched the dancers intently, sometimes other things: the buildings, and each other. Next, there was a visit to the male side of the dancing ground: past the ancestor houses, through the central structure, beyond the slit drums, to see another house. At one end there were two small wooden sculptures and a coral table on

Plate 7.4 The coral platform with displays of pigs' jaws.

which a large conch shell was placed (Plate 7.4). The ridge pole of the house, open at both ends, was supported by a tree-fern carving. Inside the house there was a coral platform with two parallel rows of pig's jaws, the two in front with spectacular curved tusks. Chief Stephan looked directly into the cameras. He explained in *bislama* (pidgin English) that this is the proof that a big *maki* (grade taking ceremony) took place involving the sacrifice of pig wealth (tusked boars). The fact that there is only one line of stones along the dancing ground demonstrates that there has only been one such ceremony. We were then taken to the men's house: another traditional structure of bamboo and palm thatch, an old canoe hull covering the ridge pole on the outside. At the entrance was a carved roof support: a complex face design painted red and white, 'the colours of initiation'. Only initiated men may enter the house (guests excepted: honorary initiates and honorary men). Inside, hanging from the wall and roof, various pieces of traditional culture were displayed: brightly painted paddles with attached feathers ('used in the paddle dances'), carved clubs ('ritual pig killing club'), headdresses and other items of dance costume. After we left the *nimbaur* three men displayed fire-making techniques. After a number of abortive attempts smoke began to rise from the

Plate 7.5 Serving *laplap*.

hollowed log and was fanned into flames. We were taken to see the women sitting in the shade weaving different types of baskets from coconut fronds and pandanus. The partner of one of the tourists was complemented for having fed him up so well (it turned out that he did the cooking). Two women with painted faces displayed techniques of yam planting, after which it was time for lunch. *Lap lap* (made from grated yams cooked with chicken and served with rich coconut milk) wrapped in banana leaves was taken from a smouldering stone-lined fire pit and brought to the table on the women's side of the dancing ground (Plate 7.5). We washed our hands in water contained in a banana leaf and were shown how to cut up the pudding with bamboo knives and dip it into the milk before eating. The second course was a choice of papaw or grapefruit.

A pink and white check cotton tea towel lay on the table.

During the meal the Small Nambas observed the ungraceful eating habits of the tourists at a distance. The male dance troupe then performed three more dances, each telling its own story. The show was over, or almost, for we were given a brief display of leaf magic as an after-thought. Chief Stephan showed us a photocopy of an old photograph taken from the archives of the Port Vila Cultural Centre, showing his grandfather from whom he learnt about traditional culture, and some notes copied out from Layard's anthropological account of the island of Vao, north-east Malekula,

Stone Men Of Malekula (1942): dual proofs of the authenticity of what we have seen. Some traditional artefacts, mainly wooden carvings, were available for sale. Purchases were duly made. Chief Stephan collected our 2,500 vatu each (£14). The show lasted over four hours. The dancers lined up, the tourist 'big man' made a thank-you speech describing the show as the best he had seen. Delighted, Chief Stephan presented him with a large wooden carving. We all shook hands with our hosts before leaving.

The six tourists were anthropologists and their affines.

Cultures in Performance

Everywhere, throughout the world, local peoples in response to the opportunities afforded by the global tourist industry are putting their culture on display. The Small Nambas, in common with other indigenous populations of the 'periphery', are earning a living through selling traditional artefacts, villages, music, dance, shrines and ritual acts: material metaphors of place and social identity.

This performance of 'ethnic lives' for a transitory and travelled audience is the equivalent in the developing 'third' and 'fourth' worlds of the heritage boom in the developed one. The staging of medieval jousts in a medieval castle or civil war battles in Britain or the United States has its counterpart in the Small Nambas show, in 'cannibal tours' up the Sepik river of Papua New Guinea or a visit to a Bali Aga village on the shores of Lake Batur. In all these cases it is the 'past' and 'tradition' that is being metaphorically put on display for consumption.

This has become the only potential locus of a search for cultural authenticity in the hyperreality of a global culture increasingly characterized by massive transnational flows of people, information, money and things. In a postmodern 'economy of signs and spaces' (Lasch and Urry 1994) and an age of 'travelling cultures' (Clifford 1992) localized places and global processes intersect in an increasingly creolized and hybridized world of peoples and experiences. The isolated village culture, the hallmark of a traditional anthropology in search of native simplicities, has become, like everywhere else in the world, a kind of borderland. A highly ambiguous 'contact zone' (Clifford 1997) of competing, changing and emerging identities is created wherever ethnicity and tradition are placed on display and become the focus of attention.

Global culture has been frequently imagined to be the spread of otherwise localized artefacts, products and technologies. But it is much more than this: an imploding world of diasporic 'ethnoscapes', 'finanscapes', 'mediascapes', 'technoscapes' and 'ideoscapes' (Appadurai 1990). Another item might be added to this list: 'travelscapes'. The world is significantly fashioned by tourism, which is now the planet's single biggest industry, generating the largest mass movement of peoples outside wartime. In an age of tourism the sojourn of the anthropologist is no longer isolated, if it ever was. To escape Western modernity in the ethnographic present is now solely the consolation and domain of an archaeology. The global travelscapes of tourism are entirely dependent for their success on the production or finding of authentic cultural difference. The world becomes an array of localities which might be experienced. There must be different things to look at, eat, touch, buy and see. As such the study of tourism forms part of a revitalized interest in the anthropology of consumption (Miller 1987; 1994a; 1995). What is being consumed in touristscapes, however, goes far beyond commodities extending to a metaphorical economy of signs, images and places which can only be carried away in snapshots and memories, but nevertheless may constitute a significant, if largely intangible, element of personal cultural capital and a means of self-distinction and self-definition. It is a peculiar form of consumption in so far as it usually entails producers and consumers actually confronting each other in person.

The negative consequences of tourism resulting in the production of the past and 'primitive culture' as commodities have been foregrounded over and over again in the critical sociological literature on the subject (see discussions in Crick 1989; MacCannell 1976; 1992; Urry 1990). The tourist has been almost universally reviled and condemned as an (unwitting) agent of cultural destruction. Many tourists themselves are increasingly embarrassed by the pursuit: far better to be a 'traveller'. Or finding 'out there', in distant places, a simulacrum of what may be already consumed 'back home', the 'post-tourist' (Feifer 1985) revels in decoding the games of traditional culture and staged ethnicity which 'primitives' have learned to play.

If the effects of global tourism on peripheral peoples have turned out to be cultural differentiation, 'revivals' and inventions of ethnicity, rather than cultural homogenization, as initially predicted, the analysis of the results has nevertheless been pretty much the same: an inauthentic postmodern pastiche is being produced in which populations pretend to be pre-modern in order to continue to purchase their modernist identity spaces in a world of mass movement, mass production and mass consumption. Peripheral peoples market themselves simply because they have little else to sell and this is what the tourists have, after all, come to see. Combining a calculating market rationality while donning banana-leaf skirts and feathers they can cynically be regarded as being as much 'exploiters' as the 'exploited' from this perspective. The gullible tourists are only transitory 'guests', easily manipulated by the wealth of experience acquired by their welcoming 'hosts'.

There is something, however, that seems to be deeply disingenuous about much of the critical literature on tourism (as opposed to that nakedly concerned with its promotion, marketing, planning, etc.), in that we can be sure that the self-same critics are, have been and will be tourists, travellers or post-tourist cynics. The interactions between tourists and indigenous groups are seldom simply reducible to various forms of self-interested mutual exploitation, manipulation, marketing strategies and trivialized, objectified and commodified experiences. They may involve all of these elements of course, but the literature has generally been insensitive to relationships which are both more complex and more muted. An anthropology of tourism is still in its infancy and there has been little sustained analysis. Books by Graburn (1976), Smith (1989), Gewertz and Errington (1991), Selwyn (1996) or O'Rourke's (1987) film *Cannibal Tours* are exceptions which prove the rule. Part of the reason may be an uncomfortable kindred between anthropologists (sophisticated or dedicated long-stay tourists) and non-professionals similarly interested in the cultures of Others (Crick 1985).

I want to attempt to discuss here what it means to perform traditional culture for tourists in a third world context. In the account which follows I attempt to highlight and emphasize the contradictions involved in both the performance of the Small Nambas show itself and its reception by tourists and local people, emphasizing that it is the site of many paradoxes and different interpretations that have no easy resolution.

The format of the Small Nambas show is basically the same for each group of tourists, although the dances vary. The Small Nambas started out as a local dance troupe, one of many within Vanuatu, and a development stimulated by politicians who have vigorously promoted *kastom* (custom) as a means of constituting national consciousness since the country became independent in 1980. The former deputy prime minister Sethy Regenvanu, born on the Small Island of Uripiv, with his constituency in north-east Malekula, arranged for the group to represent Vanuatu in an 'exposition of kastom and kalja' in New Caledonia in 1993. Chief Stephan put the dance troupe together and acted as leader and spokesperson. Having been paid a fair amount of money for the New Caledonian performances the commercial potential of 'performing culture' became evident. The eventual outcome was Chief Stephan going into partnership with the manager of the Wala Island Resort to create the Small Nambas tourist attraction. The present location of the dancing ground on the Malekulan mainland opposite Wala island is basically a matter of expediency and compromise following a long series of financial and land disputes, and splits between various local factions. It is cut from the bush on land Stephan owns, and is only visited by tourists staying at the Wala resort.

The Wala resort opened in July 1993 with virtually only word-of-mouth publicity in a few tourist centres in the capital of Vanuatu, Port Vila on Efate island. It is a small resort consisting of six bungalows built with traditional materials, and a dining hall in the style of a *nimbaur* or men's house. The resort manager and owner, Peter Fidelio, financed the entire project himself from savings built up during fourteen years working away from Wala in the Hotel Rossi, Port Vila and on merchant ships plying Asia and the Pacific. Peter and his immediate family do all the catering and cleaning. Facilities are basic: an el san toilet is complemented by an upturned oil drum serving as a water source for a shower. The resort is run as a collective between Peter and the five clans (*namil*) on Wala, between whom the profits are shared. The government of Vanuatu provided no financial support and demonstrated little interest in the project before it started. A small amount of finance capital was provided by the New Zealand High Commission, which gave money for a generator to provide electricity for the dining area, and subsequently financed the recent installation of two flush toilets and showers (August 1995). A solar-powered telephone was also installed at the same time when the 11th annual meeting of the Melanesian heads of state (the Melanesian Spearhead Group) was held on Malekula island involving a Sunday afternoon visit to the Wala resort for lunch and a seminar. This visit was also promoted by Sethy Regenvanu and resulted in the upgrading of the airstrip at Norsup on the Malekulan mainland from a grass to tarmac surface, and improvements to the pot-holed roads both north towards Wala and south to the administrative centre of Lakatoro on the Malekulan mainland.

Prior to the establishment of the Wala resort the islanders had no experience of tourists and were dubious about their impact and the benefits which might be forthcoming. The location of the Wala resort, like the Small Nambas dancing ground, is a compromise. Other possible locations were blocked by land disputes. The resort is situated in the village of Serser by the coast on the south-east tip of Wala island, where virtually the entire population lives today and where there is no room for further expansion. The manager has plans to establish another and much larger resort on land he owns along the coast on the Malekulan mainland opposite Wala. He hopes to develop package tours from Port Vila in the future which will involve tourists flying out to Malekula for short visits of one or two nights. The present resort on Wala island might cater more to a 'luxury' end of the market, a 'real pacific island experience', while the proposed resort on the mainland would cater to the cheaper 'mass tourism' market.

So far, visitor numbers to Wala have been low. In 1993 only seven visitors stayed at the resort; in 1994 there were seventy-nine and in 1995 (January–August) fifty-four. Two nights is the average stay. Most tourists arrive from Port Vila. Others exploring the coastline of Vanuatu arrive on private or hired yachts. Most, but not all, visit the Small Nambas during their stay on Wala. A party of six tourists watching the show is large, the average being three or four.

The Wala resort is the first to have been established in Malekula, and at present the only one. Until the early 1990s the policy of the Vanuatu government was to restrict tourism to a few of the islands of the archipelago: Efate with the capital Port Vila – where the bulk of the approximately 30,000 annual tourists who visit Vanuatu remain (they are mainly from Australia and New Zealand) (Jayarama and Andeng 1993) – Tanna and Espiritu Santo. The state has recently adopted a more liberal, *laissez-faire* attitude and is now actively stimulating further tourist development throughout the archipelago. The inclusion of the Wala resort and the Small Nambas in the second edition of the Lonely Planet guide to Vanuatu (Harcombe and O'Byrne 1995) will, no doubt, considerably increase visitor numbers in the future.

The Small Nambas show has to be understood in the context of other activities connected with and stimulated by tourism on Wala. These include the demonstration of traditional sand drawings, together with a project to market these as T-shirt designs, to be produced on Wala as a cottage industry and sold there and in shops in Port Vila; guided tours around Wala island to visit the old dancing grounds (three of which have been cleared from the encroaching bush), the manufacture of wooden artefacts, (canoe prow heads, clubs, miniature slit drums, etc.), mats and baskets to be sold to tourists. *Kava* (a mild narcotic beverage) can also be drunk by tourists in the Seisei bar next to the resort dining hall. The visit of the MSG stimulated the building of six new canoes in traditional style to carry the heads of state, and subsequently tourists, over to the island (see Chapter 4). There are also plans to write down the history of Wala island

and perhaps set up a small museum and exhibition centre to display and increase knowledge of traditional culture for both tourists and local people alike. The brother of the resort manager, employed by the Vanuatu Culture and Historical Sites Survey (VCHSS), is actively involved in promoting this last scheme. The total package is conceived as a vibrant revival of local *kastom*, providing entertainment for tourists and increased local knowledge of traditional practices.

Justifications and reactions

It was stressed to me on many occasions by Peter Fidelio that tourism would act as a catalyst to preserve traditional *kastom*. It would act as a counterweight to colonial and missionary influence which had all but destroyed local traditions. Western influence, having had such pernicious corrosive effects in the past, would now, in the era of independence and decolonization, act through tourist development to regenerate a culture in danger of being lost. It would also stimulate the local economy, providing jobs and income and helping to counter migration to Port Vila and beyond Vanuatu by people in search of employment. While tourists might expect the luxuries of showers, electricity and flush toilets, the rest of the island population should retain their traditional ways and not be seduced by such amenities. Peter Fidelio's brother was keen for the people to learn their own history so that traditional knowledges and practices could be maintained. Chief Stephan stressed that it was important to perform culture if it was to be preserved. It was no good just writing it down. To keep culture alive it must be lived. While most of the Small Nambas group were willing to perform only because they were paid for it, Stephan expressed a wish to actually live and dress in the style portrayed in the show. The motives were somewhat contradictory. A growing cash economy made it expensive and difficult to live and money was needed. However, in the past people were much richer and happier and had all that they required. They had no need for money. And yet the show was being performed for cash and the money obtained was being banked. By performing the past one could purchase a better future.

Many tourists staying at the Wala island resort wrote comments in the visitor's book. Virtually all mentioned the Small Nambas show and most seem to have been genuinely impressed: they wrote that they felt that they had learnt a great deal about traditional customs. Only a few of the tourists I interviewed did not appreciate the show. Preferring to describe themselves as 'travellers', they felt it was all make-believe. They were much more interested in seeing how people really lived today: watching people walking down a road or buying things in a trade store. One couple, who had been shown around the ancient dancing grounds on Wala island and then attended the Small Nambas show the following day, said that they enjoyed the visit to the old stones far more: 'we knew the guide was just telling us stories about them and they weren't really true, but we weren't concerned about the real meanings of the stones. We were just happy to look and be told stories'. They were appalled by the show: 'we have not seen anything like that before. A Disneyland in Vanuatu. We did not come for that'. What is interesting about these comments is that while these tourists were quite happy to listen to a story made up for them about the past, they reacted very strongly to the Small Nambas making up a story about their own lives in the present: 'custom living'.

Wala islanders themselves had similarly different sets of reactions to the Small Nambas show. Naturally, those working for or connected with the Wala resort regarded it as an entirely positive thing providing jobs, income and strengthening *kastom*. Other people, not so closely connected, criticized the show for being 'fake'. First of all it was felt that since Stephan was already connected with one ancient clan dancing ground on Wala it was entirely inappropriate for him to go and set up a new one on the mainland and pretend to be a chief. He was described to me as a 'rolling stone' and stones should not roll. Stones (those in the ancient dancing grounds) fix and root your identity in the land and this cannot be changed. 'A true *Maki* (pig sacrifice) ceremony should last for thirty days, Stephan's only took place over two days and proper tusked boars were not sacrificed.' The women's skirts were 'correct', the men's *nambas* were 'made up'. But the most bitter criticism was that the Small Nambas were only doing it for the money.

An 'authentic' culture?

Information providing the basis for the Small Nambas show came from a variety of sources. The traditional dances and music were taught to Stephan by his father and grandfather. Chief Stephan says he knows twenty-three different dances, all of which are 'authentic' and he claims not to have invented any new ones. Many of the general ideas behind the construction of the dancing ground came from the same sources. *Stone Men of Malekula* (Layard 1942), the work of the anthropologist Layard, who lived on the neighbouring Small Island of Atchin between 1913 and 1914, was consulted for 'details', principally the photographs and illustrations in the book. Information on traditional culture was also provided by Kirk Huffman, former director of the Port Vila cultural centre.

The Small Nambas show clearly works for most tourists. It is precisely the kind of traditional culture that most have come to see in this still rather remote area of Vanuatu. It satisfies the kinds of expectations anticipated and generated by brochures and guidebooks: unaltered and ancient customs. The show itself is clearly a bricolage of different knowledges: memories of Wala islanders, the work of Layard, information from the Port Vila cultural centre and its former director. Layard's book was not about Wala island, nor about Atchin island where he lived for most of the time, but the most northerly of the Small Islands, Vao (see Figure 4.1). Towards the end of a book running to 816 pages he states: 'we have gained some idea of the complex series of rites that go to build up the Maki on Vao . . . I have myself records of the corresponding institution on Atchin, enough to occupy at least one volume without repetition of any of the material here published on Vao. The same applies to the neighbouring island of Wala' (Layard 1942: 687–9). Throughout Malekula, as elsewhere in Melanesia, there is enormous linguistic and cultural diversity. The details derived from Layard's work for the Small Nambas reconstruction are those pertaining to Vao rather than Wala island culture, and are re-presented as their own. The events and reconstructions in the Small Nambas show provide, at the very least, a generic representation of a variety of Small Islands cultures rather than a 'pure' sense of indigenous Wala culture. The carving style of the slit-drum orchestra does indeed resemble depictions in Layard's book, as does the carved pole supporting the roof of the reconstructed men's house (Layard 1942: Plate XII). The anthropomorphic wooden ancestor images appear to be adaptations combining traditional and modern elements (in particular, the addition of more 'realistic' human faces), with no formal counterparts in Layard's book. Tree-fern ancestor images, present in one of the ancestor houses in the Small Nambas dancing ground and by the platform displaying the pigs' tusks, were not traditionally used in any of the Small Islands of north-east Malekula. Only a couple of the sacrificed pigs' jaws on display have curved tusks of the requisite size and shape for a traditional *Maki* ceremony. The ancient dancing grounds on Wala are all shaped in the form of canoes and bear little resemblance in form to the rigid rectangular morphology of the Small Nambas dancing ground. The penis wrappers from north-east Malekula depicted by Layard and Speiser (1990 [1923]) bear little resemblance to the modern counterparts worn by the Small Nambas. A banyan tree, an essential element of any traditional dancing ground, is absent. The name 'Small Nambas' (literal meaning: small penis sheaths) is a European classificatory device, used by missionaries and traders and adopted by Layard (1942) and Deacon (1934), not an indigenous term, and bears no correspondence to any real single ethnic group in Malekula, past or present. The term as used today owes much to its vigorous promotion in tourist guide books. The name, with all its implied ethnicity, as applied to Chief Stephan's dance troupe and show, fits well with the expectations raised by such tourist discourses (our guide had, on occasion, dressed and danced as a 'Small Namba'). The Small Nambas are devout Catholics worshiping at the nearby Wala/Rano mission. Many have close relatives on Wala. Stephan and Peter Fidelio both belong to Ama *namil*, one of five exogamous patrilineal clans on Wala, each connected with an ancient dancing ground in the centre of the island. The Small Nambas effortlessly slip out of their nambas and mat skirts and into their modern Western cotton clothing and back again.

It would be only too easy, in the above manner, to continue to deconstruct details of the Small Nambas show and demonstrate its 'inauthenticity', a point of evident concern for some Wala islanders too. But this raises the wider question of whether any reconstruction could hope to be authentic and whether this term 'authenticity' is either useful or relevant in understanding what the show means or its relationship to cultural tradition. At stake here is an issue of what the terms 'ethnicity' and 'culture' might actually refer to in north-east Malekula anyway.

Commodification and the past

One way of describing the Small Nambas show is that it is an empty vessel of tradition, form without sentiment. The performance of culture within the reconstructed dance arena is essentially divorced from mythological structures, ritual and cosmological beliefs. The culture on display is reduced to a series of material structures, ancestor houses etc., dance routines and drum beats: a parody of their original meaning and moroever a parody in which the performers sell their own bodies as part of the event. Visually striking, it lacks credibility simply because it is a show, theatre. Certain traditional elements of culture may be conveyed but they are not felt. Tradition does not outlast its performance. It is a kind of cultural gift-wrapping paper concealing a void. The show is a mixture of what might be termed living elements of contemporary Wala culture (dance and music, yam planting and *laplap*) and dead revived elements (ancestor houses and images, fire-making, erasure of modern elements, costumes, reference to *Maki* ceremonies and pig sacrifice) which only have any meaning within the context of the show that deliberately sets out to resurrect a sense of cultural alterity. Like some Wala islanders it is easy to conclude that an invented tradition is simply being marketed and sold to a gullible tourist public who can capture the spectacle on film for the folks back home and confirm the Lonely Planet message that Malekulans have indeed successfully preserved their customs and we were able to see them: the bare-breasted women and men dressed only in penis wrappers. Western influence, having successfully destroyed traditional culture, is now, through tourism, picking over its bones in a show which heartlessly reduces it to an exoticized spectacle for entertainment. The relationship between the dominant and the dominated is simply being reproduced in the post-colonial context in a new virulent form, a prostitution of culture. The exploitation involved substitutes the physical violence and land alienation of colonialism for a more subtle and insidious symbolic violence in which people sell themselves as part of a pan-Pacific human zoo, and thereby their souls. The tourist is a metaphoric cannibal, in an ironic twist in the Small Nambas case, being taken on a cannibal tour of ex-cannibals. With MacCannell it is only too easy to agree that

> the image of the savage that emerges from these primitive performances completes the postmodern fantasy of 'authentic alterity' which is ideologically necessary in the promotion and development of global monoculture. The 'primitivistic' performance is *our* funerary marking of the passage of savagery. In the presence of these displays, there is only one thing we can know with certainty: we have witnessed the demise of the original form of humanity. (MacCannell 1992: 19)

Objectifying culture and inventing tradition

All Wala islanders I spoke to were as deeply concerned with preserving their past and being knowledgeable about it as they were with securing their future. Tourism is undoubtedly an easier, potentially more secure and lucrative way of obtaining cash than selling copra (the other main local source of cash income) – subject to wild price fluctuations on the global market – has ever been. Chief Stephan wanted to put on a good show for the tourists and this was clearly a matter of personal pride and prestige in the presentation of traditional culture going considerably beyond simple financial gain. There would seem to be a fundamental difference between putting on a show, confined in space and time, and for the Wala community itself to become a 'museum' or a frozen time-lapse image of itself in which its participants become full-time *representations* of a vanished way of life. The past is part of the inalienable wealth of the people of Wala:

something that they can sell and give away while still keeping it. It is their history, their interpretation, their empowerment. This past requires an active and creative production on their part. The Small Nambas needed to research their show and in so doing informed themselves of part of what the European colonizers and missionaries and anthropologists have destroyed or taken away. Their invention of tradition is simultaneously and necessarily an interpretation of that tradition: a present-past.

A considerable amount of anthropological attention has been devoted to the theme of the 'invention of tradition' (Hobsbawm and Ranger 1983), both in Vanuatu and the Pacific more generally (e.g. Keesing and Tonkinson 1982; Keesing 1992; 1994; Linnekin and Poyer 1990; Carrier 1992; Jolly and Thomas 1992). At issue here has been the symbolic construction of community through the past. The Small Nambas show is clearly an invented tradition in so far as it is a deliberate and conscious creation. However, to leave the analysis at that would be to miss a great deal. The entire discourse on the invention of tradition is clearly predicated on a notion that while some cultural practices are invented or objectified, others are not. Anthropologists, in one form or another, have been particularly concerned to unravel 'authentic' from 'inauthentic' customs, the latter being those indigenous productions of ethnicity and difference arising either from colonial encounters, or the post-colonial experience of nation-state building involving the promotion of *kastom* by a Westernized administrative élite. These are conceptually distinguished from *ur*-originary forms not so produced, in which some kind of direct continuity might be claimed from an untainted pre-colonial, pre-contact and pre-modern past. While a notion of 'authenticity' has great salience or relevance for some anthropologists, the same cannot be claimed from the 'native's point of view'. A very recent concern with knowing the 'true facts' (in a very empiricist sense) about an unsullied pure cultural past on the part of Wala and other Pacific islanders is a product of the same modernist Western sense of historical discourse which anthropologists concerned about these matters inhabit – and are beginning increasingly to critique.

A recurrent feature of the early anthropological works of Deacon (1934) and Layard (1942) on Malekula is reference to the fact that individual and group rights to cultural productions from magical spells to dances, to carving styles of artefacts such as slit drums to details of ritual performances, to styles of roofing on ancestor houses, were continually being bought and sold between different individuals and ethnic groups. This caused both Layard and Deacon insuperable problems in being able to either isolate or define an 'essence of ethnicity' conceived in terms of a stable body of beliefs, practices, routines, traditions, rituals or style horizons of material culture. Subsequent research in Malekula (Larcom 1982; 1990) has faced exactly the same difficulty. If we are looking for a cultural essence of ethnicity in Malekula, or in Melanesia more generally (see Harrison 1993), it is to be found in continual creativity, diffusion and change in which it is often the *combination* of different elements drawn from outside the ethnic group and combined and reinvented inside it in new forms, that creates cultural distinctiveness, not their simple presence or absence. Viewed from this perspective virtually all expressions of culture or ethnic identity are equally 'inauthentic' or borrowed. Furthermore, this very ethnicity was characteristically something which was being continually constructed or 'invented' through *commodity-like* forms of exchange, which Gell (1992b) has convincingly argued preceded colonial contact in Melanesia rather than being a substitute for gift exchange.

From such a perspective it would seem entirely inappropriate to develop a deeply moralist critique of the Small Nambas show as being a spurious invention of culture, or to criticize Wala islanders for selling their past. In fact it can well be claimed that in inventing their traditions and selling their culture these people are, in fact, expressing, through their actions, two of the most fundamental and original structuring principles of the constitution of their culture. By constructing a bricolage of different elements from different sources they are true followers of 'ancestral ways'. Selling this invented culture to tourists rather than to neighbouring Atchin islanders, as in the past, is merely an adaptation to the exigencies produced by global modernity under conditions which are not of their own choice.

Constructing self-images

Setting the Small Nambas show in such a prior context further underlines the futility of asking whether or not it is an authentic or truthful representation of culture. It also highlights the power relations involved in any attempt to do so, most especially by an external commentator. Instead, there is a need to stress that ethnicity and culture are not ontological givens and discrete holistic cores but always already historically constituted. This requires a more nuanced understanding of the show as something bound up with sharing and controlling, recollecting and forgetting. It would seem to be more fruitful to ask: what kind of image are these people self-consciously constructing of themselves and whom do they wish to be? A good performance of the show is not simply to please tourists, and for them to evaluate. It is a dialogic encounter which is as much about self-worth and self-evaluation, and as the tourists gaze and take their photographs they are also being observed. By performing culture for tourists the Small Nambas are presenting an image of themselves which they want others to see and *feel*: dramatic dress, intricate wooden carvings, megalithic architecture, complex acoustics emanating from the mouths of the slit drums, elaborate dance movements. This is an image which is self-consciously not of Western modernity, but of a vibrant culture independent of it. What is being explicitly rejected here is that a desirable future will owe nothing to the past. But it is a past of a particular sort: a self-censored image excluding elements such as cannibalism (reduced to a joke by our guide) and warfare which they themselves find unacceptable as part of their contemporary modernity (representation of these elements, of course, would constitute a more memorable tourist spectacle). The wearing of 'custom dress' by men in Vanuatu has a very powerful significance far beyond simply being a display of the 'past' or a 'primitive' culture. It is part of a local political culture of *truth*: you simply can't trust a man in a suit: 'If you see someone who goes naked this man is one of yours, naked people of Santo! Someone who goes naked you can vote for' (political speech by Jimmy Stephens, insurrectionist leader in Espiritu Santo, cited in Philibert 1987). Here traditional ideas of political legitimacy are expressed through metaphors of nakedness and traditional knowledge in which the second skins of clothing and Western knowledges are distrusted. The Small Nambas show and associated tourist developments on Wala island are ways of negotiating an external relationship with outsiders through a project which is rebuilding a sense of *locality*. This does not at present represent, in any sense, a form of oppositional discourse or resistance to the Vanuatu state or Western practices in the manner of the Kwaio traditionalists of the Solomons (Keesing 1994) or the *kastom* villagers of south-east Pentecost in Vanuatu (Jolly 1994). At the moment it is 'safe', depoliticized and contained within the 'unity through difference' rhetoric of the modern state and its own production of generic metaphors of *kastom* unity through the symbolism of flags, anthems, plants, pigs' tusks, etc. (Philibert 1986; Jolly 1992). The power relations enabling the production of Small Nambas 'ethnicity' are translocal in origin and impetus, with both the state and tourism providing normative hinges. But once this production has taken place the seeds for a future oppositional discourse have been planted.

The present show is already the subject of a different kind of internal contestation to a certain extent. It is self-evidently both male orientated and male dominated. The male dancers take centre stage. Their activities and dances are foregrounded. The women and their activities remain on the sidelines. The women, I was informed, were embarrassed about performing in 'custom dress' and deliberately decorated themselves in multiple strings of beads to conceal their breasts. With an increasing social awareness and concern with traditional gender roles and inequalities within Vanuatu (Bolton 1993) the show itself may change increasingly to emphasize traditional women's activities. The future is likely to provide a reinterpretation and re-presentation of the past in which an increasing place for women will be found.

What time is this place?

The meticulous and scrupulous attention to detail in the Small Nambas show is quite striking. Virtually all signs of modernity have been erased. Only tiny details (the sign-board – soon forgotten – the hand-written note on the hut wall, the check cotton tea towel on the table) 'give the game away' that the Small Nambas may not actually live like this, that it is a reconstructed past that is on display for tourist consumption in the present. This same meticulous attention to historical detail is, of course, a basic element in most attempts to recreate folk life-ways in the West. The major difference would appear to be that while everyone knows and participates in the fantasy that a medieval joust in the past is in the present, for just the length of the show, the Small Nambas event is designed to provide the overriding impression that the past is a lived present-day reality, that the Small Nambas really do live like this, that the show is something more than a re-enactment. In a highly equivocal way the Small Nambas are both 'here' and 'there', of the present and of the past. This impression is only possible to convey because of the location of the show in a remote Pacific island which has supposedly escaped the full ravages of modernity. This highlights the ambiguities, the entertainment of the metaphoric possibility that 'then' might be 'here', that the past might be present, a sense of conflicting temporalities pervading the entire structure of the show. More precisely, what we have here is a *third* space and time of representation in the third world, neither exactly here *nor* there, neither of the present *nor* of the past, neither inside culture *nor* outside it: an interposed 'liminal' structure of communication. This third space is both supported and made possible by the presence of an exterior discourse for the show's audience in which distance in space and time become coeval. We can read in the Lonely Planet guide to Vanuatu that 'while townspeople's lives in Vanuatu have altered considerably in recent times, village life is much as it has always been' (Harcombe and O'Byrne 1995: 37); 'generally speaking, Malekulans have preserved their traditions more successfully than other ni-Vanuatu . . . these small islands are among the world's last megalithic cultures' (ibid.: 184); and more specifically:

> the deep, primeval throbbing of a tamtam [slit drum] shattered the quiet as I walked along the jungle path to Amelboas natsaro. I was with Peter Fidelio, manager of the Wala Island Resort, and we were on our way to see something of the ancient traditions of the Small Nambas people. The drumming had a menacing quality, perhaps because of the gloomy conditions. . . . Suddenly we broke out of the trees at the edge of a large, fenced clearing lined with thatched shelters and carved nimangki figures. Chief Stephan Lelektei, 'bigman' of this particular natsaro, stepped forward with a smile of welcome. He was a young man resplendent in blue and yellow body paint, and wearing only a penis sheath, a headdress and a pig's tusk. The latter hung around his neck as a symbol of his chiefly status. (Ibid.: 193)

Conclusion

By virtue of the practice of objectifying culture in the show people are beginning to learn that they have to *negotiate and transform* it. The show is not, and can never be, a representation of Bourdieu's (1977) 'habitus', a realm of reproducible practices and dispositions. Instead, it provides an arena for the exercise of conscious choice, contextualizing practices, modes of representation, the articulation of metaphors, rationalization and justification. In short it promotes increasing self-reflexivity. Wala islanders are very far removed from Hobart's 'terminally tranquillized natives enacting tableaux of their former selves' (Hobart 1995: 54). The culture displayed by the Small Nambas is thoroughly mediated by performing it to tourists, and this is indeed its origin, but it is in no simple sense determined by the expectations of such an audience. It contains the warp and weft of signs of an imagined community which, once woven, has the potential of being spun again in a different way, and by so doing, providing community empowerment. Through constructing this past they are better able to talk about themselves to themselves and secure a place in the global future. The contradictory capacity of the Small Nambas show is the production of a performance which can simultaneously, through metaphor, evoke a vanished past and constitute an imagined future.

8

Conclusions

On the basis of the discussions in Chapters 3–7 and in relation to the general issues raised in Chapters 1 and 2, in this conclusion I attempt to isolate some of the main tenets of a general theory of material culture as metaphorical form, and emphasize important differences between linguistic and material metaphors, while insisting on their complementary and fundamental role in the invention and mediation of culture.

When the Bororo told Karl von den Steinen 'We are parrots', or the Nuer, Evans-Prichard, that 'twins are birds', or the Telofol, MacKenzie, 'the *bilum* is our mother', they were all making fundamental statements about themselves, and their relationship to the world, which cannot be ignored. The villagers of Baan Phraan Maun would not, of course, explicitly recognize or discuss all the structural homologies and metaphorical correspondences that Tambiah draws out, nor the Yekuana the meanings Guss finds in their basketry. Nor did the men fabricating the canoes on Wala island acknowledge all the different metaphors I claim to be at work in Chapter 4. This does not mean that the connections do not exist or cannot be made. All that it implies, minimally, is that they are not discursively constructed, except by the anthropologist. Some, or many, may reside at a practical level of consciousness, part of what

Bourdieu (1977) refers to as the 'habitus' as dispositional tendencies and generative principles for social practice. But the process of analysis is not and can never be one in which the anthropologist's meanings must try and mirror their explicit or implicit constructs. An archaeologist cannot read past minds. The process of interpretation is a discursive act that produces something new. It is necessarily a metaphorical extension and networking of metaphor, a tropic interplay or dialectical weave in which what has never been said is produced on the basis of discursive attempts at self-understanding. From initial metaphorical statements the anthropologist draws out lateral and vertical connections to invent or reconstruct culture between different domains of the life-world. The latter are no more, or less, real than the initial unmediated recorded 'facts' of the matter. Both are equally 'made up' interpretative statements. Both may be held to have their ontological grounding in the fact that all human beings think metaphorically with an embodied mind. This is perhaps one of the few cultural universals that exist beyond basic biological necessities. This is simply to assert that human logic is fundamentally an analogical logic grounded in bodily perception and action. The specific *content* of this logic, the types of connections drawn between familiar and unfamiliar domains, is culturally produced in determinate social and historical circumstances. People draw metaphorical connections, but not just as they please. The types of connections made are clearly constrained by environment and cultural tradition. Pigs' tusks would be as meaningless to the Dinka as ox horns to the populations of Malekula. High-flying birds would not do as a metaphorical source domain for the Nuer concept of twins. The Batammaliba house would have little cultural salience among the Sabarl, Yaka healing rituals would not work among the Baktaman. Bank barrows might have little significance outside Dorset. The manner in which the Small Nambas are creating a sense of place and identity is unlikely to be just as effective elsewhere.

The Bororo could, theoretically, have chosen to describe important features of their world in a more literal way. What is significant is that they did not, for the metaphorical phrase they chose captured and expressively conveyed a fundamental aspect of their Being in the world in a manner which would have otherwise been impossible. And the vividness of their self-description worked quite dramatically. It has now become a little discursive treasure of anthropology, endlessly recycled in texts, something that has not been forgotten for over a century.

A story is told by Simone de Beauvoir in her autobiography about a meeting between Aron and Sartre in Paris:

> We spent an evening together at the Bec de Gaz in the Rue Montparnasse. We ordered the speciality of the house, apricot cocktails; Aron said, pointing to his glass: 'You see, my dear fellow, if you are a phenomenologist, you can talk about this cocktail and make philosophy out of it!' Sartre turned pale with emotion at this. Here was just the thing he had been longing to achieve for years – to describe objects just as he saw and touched them, and extract philosophy from the process. (De Beauvoir 1965: 135)

The linguistic description of objects is, of course, crucial to their understanding and the metaphorical connections (philosophy) that can be drawn out of them. Alternative, always culturally constrained modes of description provide the basis for exploiting the different metaphorical possibilities in the production and representation of culture. But there is something more. The Daribi explained this to Wagner: 'eat our pandanus fruit, smoke our tobacco, and you will know our language' (Wagner 1975: 114). What the Daribi philosophers were referring to was not a language of words, description and the naming of things, but a different way of telling, one involving things and actional context: solid as opposed to verbal metaphor.

Pandanus fruit and tobacco smoke are material metaphors as essential to encoding and making sense of the world in Daribi culture as words. The Bororo cannot realize their cultural essence without red macaw feathers, men participating in *kula* exchanges cannot acquire fame without shells, in Malekula men require pigs to receive their souls. Without a corpse of axes Sabarl islanders cannot remember to forget the deceased. The Small Nambas require their reconstructed dancing ground. The general point is that persons require things to make and transform themselves. This objectification of culture is as essential to its understanding as its phenomenological verbal description. Just as persons make things, things make persons. The dualistic fashion in which we have a tendency to think of persons as active subjects and things as passive objects hinders an understanding of the manner in which material metaphors work in relation to persons and their self-knowledge and understanding of the world.

Solid, or image, and verbal metaphors have complementary roles in the constitution of cultural form. Words inform an understanding of things and things permit an understanding of words. It is not a question, therefore, of stressing or arguing for the primacy of one as opposed to the other, or trying to make the claim that in small-scale societies solid metaphor dominates whereas in Western culture words have more significance than things. What is the case is that the analysis of words has taken precedence over things in the Western philosophical tradition, an arbitrary fold in thought that could be otherwise.

Underlying both verbal and solid metaphor is polysemy. The polysemy of words and the polysemous condensation of meanings in things both permit metaphorical elaboration. The anthropological and archaeological analyses of material culture discussed in this book display a persistent tendency in which the polysemy of words in the naming of a thing becomes an avenue for understanding its metaphorical properties (e.g. the discussion of megaliths in Chapter 3 or canoes in Chapter 4). But this need not always be the case in understanding the metaphoric 'code' of the object. Linguistic metaphors unfold in time and sequence (it requires time to read or utter a sentence which one follows), solid metaphors are spatial. There is no obvious starting point from which to read them. There is no necessity to start reading a *malangan* carving or the depictions carved on the rocks at Högsbyn (discussed in Chapter 5) from the top and then work down to the bottom or from one side to another. We see the images all at once. Linguistic or solid metaphors may become the subject of discursive discussion in order to understand or explain them, but the former, as already constituted in words, lend or give up themselves to this process of discussion more readily. Solid metaphors are not substitutes for linguistic metaphors or translations of them into material form. They act most subtly and powerfully precisely when they are not linguistically translated, at a non-discursive level of consciousness and as part of the routinization of action. In this manner they are thus a primary element of the unconscious in culture. Their material presence permits the unsaid to be said. Words are poor substitutes for the mental images and associations a rock carving or a plume of tobacco smoke may express. Similarity and difference can often be much more subtly conveyed through the colours, textures, shapes and smells of things than through words (Miller 1994b). We may very well say that words domesticate and partially destroy the metaphorical powers of things. The paradox here is that to analyse *either* a solid metaphor or a linguistic metaphor may be to detract from their cultural efficacy, for both share the power of suggestiveness. This is especially the case in solid metaphors since they typically condense meanings in a manner which would require an entire string of different linguistic metaphors to accomplish a similar effect. Their economy of form resides in their metaphorical condensation.

The basis of the manner in which solid metaphors work to link different cultural domains and construct meaning relates first of all to their internal qualities, their shape, structure, colour, texture and form. As discussed in detail in Chapter 6, aspects of any of these multifarious qualities of things may be the analogical basis for recalling an attribute of another object, as same or similar or regarding it as fundamentally different and other. People will typically understand the design of one monument or artefact in terms of another. The more unfamiliar an object the more it is likely to be metaphorically compared to what is previously known, a mapping of experience from one domain to another, the culturally determined 'code' restrictions, guiding the reading of meaning.

Second, material metaphors need to be understood temporally in their actional and biographical contexts: how the artefact is produced, and from what sources and raw materials, the manner in which these materials may be combined in a technological process, its subsequent exchange and consumption contexts, how it may be destroyed, what is done to the thing, how it is used and in what sequence it occurs in relation to other artefacts in a series of events. Chapters 4–7 reiterate this point.

Because material metaphors are solid and spatial, rather than spoken and transitory, the process of 'reading' them is immediate. There is no need to explicitly name, delimit or identify them. Material metaphors have a quality of density in that every aspect of an artefact contributes continuously to its meanings and is interdependently significant. By contrast written language is not dense and is discontinuous in nature. Solid metaphor operates, for the most part, at the routinized level of practical consciousness of social actors. The effect of solid metaphors on social actors may often be effortless in as much as they surround persons and frame activities without the requirement of an active intentional process of listening and reading which speech and written texts require. Their solid materiality constantly presents them without foregrounding them in experience: a speech like the sound of a stream, always there and taken for granted except when it stops. Because material metaphors are as often as not responded to inattentively as a series of taken-for-granteds, they require repetition and over-coding: one moves around, enters and uses a house without constantly scrutinizing its architectural detail. Material forms may most frequently attract our attention when we realize that there is something wrong with them – an absent feature or a new attribute. It is usually only in special circumstances, in the performative contexts of ceremonial practice and ritual, when material metaphors may be explicitly foregrounded and become the subject of verbal discourse. It is in these circumstances when innovations and novel metaphorical forms may be most likely to be produced. Ritual acts and utterances in which material forms produce and acquire contextual meanings are never simply repetitions of the same; they may require that the pre-existing meanings of things be reassembled, the structuring of structure, revitalizing domains of experience and participation (Kapferer 1986). Prior syntheses of the metaphorical meanings of things may get taken apart or further expanded when an artefact or aspect of it becomes referenced in relation to others. In linguistic discussions of metaphor a spatial analogy is normally used: metaphor is a process in which meaning is carried over or transferred. When we use one word for another we move an entity from one place to another. Solid metaphors, of course, can actually perform this work of meaning creation directly through being moved, replacing each other in particular situational contexts, real rather than linguistic spaces.

There may be varying degrees of coherence or structural homologies between material metaphors operating in different domains: body metaphors, house metaphors, landscape metaphors, artefact metaphors, animal metaphors, etc. but they may equally well be contradictory and convey different and conflicting meanings. Solid metaphors do not therefore dovetail together neatly to form some kind of totalizing cultural code. They work together to create cultural sense by a process that can be termed *parataxis* or the juxtaposition of things, for example the different architectural features of a house or qualities of an artefact. There is no *necessary* connection between house metaphors and those conveyed by the clothing of its occupants. In some cases systematicity may exist, as in Tambiah's analysis of connections between house spaces, animal and kin categories; in others the metaphorical connections will be partial or contradictory, as in Barth's analysis (see Chapter 1) of Baktaman ritual forms and the discussion of canoes in Chapter 4.

Unlike linguistic metaphors solid metaphors usually signify in a non-arbitrary way. The use of the colour red to symbolize blood or the colour white milk or semen is a non-arbitrary linkage. Similarly, as exemplified in Chapter 5, a foot (body part) may be used metonymically to signify the whole (the body), in a non-arbitrary manner. The ubiquitous anthropomorphism of metaphorical material forms all work in a non-arbitrary way. Consequently, it can be argued that material metaphors, although inherently polysemous, are always likely to be motivated, or take on meaning, in a manner different from language because, in any given culture, they are relatively constrained. The three questions 'what does this artefact mean?' 'what does this artefact do?' and 'why was this artefact chosen rather than another?' are intimately connected. This is because material forms, unlike words, are not just communicating meaning but actively *doing* something in the world as mediators of activity in the world of whatever kind: 'technological', 'economic', 'ritual', etc. in specific material contexts which are historically determined (Tilley 1996: 341). The process of analysis is one of finding the metaphorical and metonymic connections that link things together to create varying degrees of the condensation of meaning. The metaphorical 'depth' of any particular material form cannot be predicted in advance. Sometimes metaphorical condensation will be greatest in artefacts such as Yekuana basketery (see Chapter 1) or Wala canoes (Chapter 4) utilized in virtually every aspect of daily life. In other cases those artefacts with broad meaning ranges may only be seen and used infrequently in specific ceremonial or ritual contexts. Any one artefact may synthesize a number of different meanings and provoke a response in the person who perceives or receives the thing.

Solid metaphors work through image presentations which must always take on a specific form. They have the capacity to evoke the past (tradition) and become the subject, because of their very materiality and longevity, of being reinterpreted. Artefacts may thus 'grow' layers of metaphorical meaning like the rings of an onion and like the onion, as we strip layer from layer, we do not reach an inner core or kernel of metaphorical meaning. Rather, what we have is a wider outward growth and a series of transformations.

The Sabarl axe, Wala canoes, rock carvings, or the monuments and places discussed in the various chapters of this book, as tropic symbols, clearly work on a number of different meaning levels which are contradictory and cannot necessarily be privileged as more or less important or significant. The power of the imagery is in its condensation of reference. For example, when translated into linguistic terminology, the Sabarl axe or the Wala canoe are clearly mixed metaphors, something that traditional literary critics continually warn the author against. Mixed metaphors are a product of bad writing producing cognitive confusion, and are ultimately meaningless. Wagner has usefully distinguished between what he refers to as 'point metaphors' and 'frame metaphors' in the study of material symbols (Wagner 1986: 31). Perceptual images are point metaphors. Symbol as image involves 'the elicitation of multiple, condensed analogy, [bridging] between names as points of reference, bringing them into a relational field' (ibid.). These point metaphors are brought into a relational field through the referential coding of frame metaphors. A point of reference can only have significance in so far as it mediates among points of reference. The process of expanding point metaphors into frame metaphors is what Wagner refers to as 'obviation'. An artefact as image or point metaphor condenses meaning content into itself because all points of reference are collapsed into a single form. Meanings and metaphors are not strung out along the artefact as in a sentence with words. Point metaphor refers to the apprehension of the artefact as something that is only itself, an *image*. Referential coding or frame metaphor, by contrast, interpretatively, opens out a symbol to create meaning out of its constituent parts, codes or points of reference, and thus involving relationship to other symbols 'outside' and beyond the artefact. It expands, or obviates, an image by contextualizing it in relation to others which then become part of its meaning which is, therefore, culturally emergent rather than fixed within the artefact itself, which can no longer be conceived or understood in terms of being a bounded, fixed, 'static' and unique entity.

The Sabarl axe, Wala canoe or Dorset bank barrow as point metaphors can be simply understood as an image or symbol that 'stands for itself'. They can also be further coded and made meaningful through their relationship to other symbols whose own meaning have to be taken for granted at that point. In relation to the Sabarl axe Strathern comments:

> The bird-elbow intrinsic to the Sabarl axe has a shape that may also be explained as a map for kin relations; when these become points of reference for the axe, they take on assumed qualities of their own (are images of support, point metaphors). But the kin relations may then be opened to explanation, as happens in the give and take of the mortuary exchanges of which the axes are a part, in which case they cease to be taken for granted. The process of explanation by referencing or decoding deprives the image of its power to elicit taken-for-granted meanings. Conversely [as point metaphor], by itself, the Sabarl axe is not a simple illustration of meanings describable in other terms: rather, it presents to perception a particular *form* that is its own. What the Sabarl Islander grasps in handling the axe that can be verbally explained as 'the same as' kin relationships activated in exchange is not those kin relations in fact. (Strathern 1990: 35)

The important point here is that the metaphorical significance of the axe is not simply reducible to various verbal coding operations that explain its form. It is a complex unity of referential symbolic elements in itself working beyond and outside language. Its metaphorical power is derived from the way it works wider cultural referents within itself and acts so as to synthesize different meanings which have to be pulled apart in verbal exegesis, and in relation to other classes of artefacts. Such images need to be witnessed and experienced to have their effect on the mind. They cannot be represented *as they are* in words.

Material culture as image metaphor requires phenomenal experience for its understanding. Words provide no substitute for the power of the thing, for it acts synesthetically and simultaneously along a whole series of dimensions such as sight and sound and touch and smell. In producing and experiencing artefacts people are producing and experiencing themselves in the deepest sense. Artefacts permit people to know how they really are by virtue of the fact that artefacts always assume specific forms or images in the minds of the viewer in a manner impossible to convey with words. Material images, like words, may be substituted for each other in a succession of analogies. Your mental image of the moon or of a fox from the word may be very different from mine, relatively unconstrained. By contrast, we experience a *material* representation of the moon from a starting point that is the same image, empirically constrained, taking a particular form, although we may still 'see' very different moons or foxes in it.

Solid metaphor works in the same way as other metaphoric processes by mapping the structure of one domain onto that of another. Metonymic aspects of such mapping include such part–whole relationships as between attributes of houses such as floors, roofs, etc. and the whole structure, between body parts and substances and wholes, between attributes of graves (grave goods etc.) and the whole. Metaphoric aspects of mapping include such things as colour, shape, curvature, discontinuous/discrete. The metaphorical connections thus created are conceptual in nature: images in the mind forged from images in the world. It is the mind that relates and brings together the various perceptual physical images of the thing, picturing them in a particular manner. It is the existence of perceived common structure within material culture that allows and permits the mapping to take place. The artefacts work as prompts to perform processes of conceptual mapping between them. Perhaps the most common case of this is the perception of shared parts or elements such as bodies and pots and houses having openings or orifices or being containers, thus permitting them to be linked, or shared aspects of physical structure (e.g. houses and axe blades having a trapezoidal form), sharing the same shape or form. Technological processes such as weaving or potting or smelting may provide dynamic images of movement and change which may be compared with the movements of kin or animals or the seasons. Basic ideas such as a distinction between something being covered/uncovered can be used to liken clothing with house decoration or spatial distance to create analogies between forms of animal and human life. Colours may be mapped by virtue of them being shared and so on. Such metaphoric and metonymic mappings work because of the almost limitless proliferation of detail in the world of things in which a source image is mapped onto a target domain that is also an image. Metaphorically personifying a house (regarding it as a body) or an axe involves a relatively straightforward and everyday process of mapping attributes of the cultural image of one in terms of another. Once shared qualities have been recognized then the metaphorical meanings may be readily extended; so, for example, a whole host of cosmological ideas may become materially translated by the forms of houses or landscapes and can be further metaphorically mapped in terms of abstract target domains which are themselves not material images, e.g. ideas about time, life, death, descent and reciprocity. Sharing a meal with others can provide a metaphoric map for a concept of trust. Lakoff and Turner (1989: 99) usefully distinguish between image metaphors and image-schema metaphors. The former map rich mental images onto other rich mental images, in the case of material culture the rich physical attributes of the world of things in relation to each other. The latter are very general material structures such as bounded regions, paths, centres as opposed to peripheries, from which ideas about going out of, in to, along, from, between, etc. are derived. Such material image-schema mappings permit forms of spatial reasoning of the type: if house X is in a bounded space A and A is in bounded space B then house X is in B. They also provide the basic structure for rich mental images. To take an example from Devisch's discussion of Yaka infertility healing rites:

> The relationship between the patient's body and the shade hut, into which she is led backwards for seclusion, is one of encompassment. . . . Movements in and out of the shade hut, putting medicines in the mortar, pot or house, and extracting preparations from these containers and giving them to the woman to drink or splashing them over her body are metaphors both for purging the patient's body of intrusive elements and for making her into an agent capable of inclusion and life transmission. The shade moreover articulates ties with uterine descent. The patient hereby experiences 'embodiedness' and embodiment, feeling contained and herself able to contain. (Devisch 1993: 248)

This passage clearly indicates the fundamental role that the visual imagination plays in the formation of metaphor. Although verbal metaphors need not rely on or express visual imagery, the most powerful of them usually do, referring directly or indirectly to objects and experiences in the world, and these metaphors with visual aspects may be most closely related to non-verbal metaphors (MacCormac 1985: 228).

Solid metaphor cannot be reduced to a series of linguistic metaphors. Rather, we can suggest that the latter belongs in a domain of semantic processes, whereas the former relates more to a series of perceptual processes. As spatial images solid metaphors can be translated into linguistic statements, but much of their power becomes lost in the process. Solid metaphors contain what might be termed a literal memory component residing in the shape, form, colour, etc. that becomes sedimented as a non-verbal mental image of the thing in the mind (see the discussion of the *malangan* carvings in Chapter 2 and rock carvings in Chapter 5). As image in the mind solid metaphor then exists as a coding system of perceptual images for the storage and retrieval of information intimately linked to experiences with artefacts and events in which those artefacts are used. This perceptual trace of solid metaphor in the mind will, if the object becomes the subject of verbal discourse, elicit a verbal translation by means of which sensory, experiential and image-based analogic reasoning processes acquire semantic expression as linguistic metaphor, or it may alternatively elicit images of other objects at a non-verbal level (Paivio 1971: 8). A series of transformations may also occur involving images or words or both, serving a mediational role in perception and memory. Both solid and linguistic metaphors are alternative expressions or outcomes of analogical cognitive processes that result in a natural inclination in the mind to think metaphorically. Both have their basis in the ability to recognize similarities among the material attributes of things or among the semantic features of metaphorical referents. The production, exchange and consumption of things and linguistic experience of the naming and associations of those things provide the continuous possibility for the creation of new metaphorical links and understandings of the world. This work of the metaphorical mind in which one thing is conceived in terms of another is most likely to be activated in ritual and learning contexts where what is taken for granted needs to be explicated or re-presented. Novel metaphors produced in these performative contexts bring about changes in the manner in which people perceive the world, which in turn affects the way they act in that world.

To return to a linguistic analogy, we can posit that the literal meaning of the artefact resides in whatever utilitarian need it serves, its function as chair to sit on, house to live in, axe to chop down trees, animal as source of meat and protein, etc. The literal resides at a level of denotative meaning by means of which we identify and name a thing in terms of its standard or typical use. The metaphorical meaning of the thing by contrast operates at the level of connotation according to particular cultural conventions: white as signifier for milk or semen, house as body, cattle as kin relations, etc. While mixed metaphors are rarely effective in linguistic utterances they reside at the essence of material forms, which thereby have a metaphorical openness that works and conveys meaning through polysemous ambiguity. Material culture is an 'art of ambiguity' (Tilley 1991) that works through that which is despised in language: mixed metaphor. There may be dominant metaphorical meanings of a thing, it may usually be understood in a particular culture in a limited number of ways. There are also always secondary meanings which resist and play off the dominant cultural senses of a thing. But through time and through the unfolding of artefact biographies these may become the dominant meanings and those meanings that were dominant assume secondary significance.

Material metaphors do not just reflect social realities, they play an essential role in the description, definition and redescription of those realities. But how do they relate to a metaphorical mind? Dreyfus, following Merleau-Ponty (Dreyfus 1979: 248ff.) has made the point that the reason computers cannot be said to think, except metaphorically, is not because they do not have a mind but because they do not have a body. They therefore cannot enter into the complex realms of human action and meaning. Now the physical, tangible, *material* dimensions of material forms are essential in the creation of metaphoric meaning and significance. While the metaphors may operate on a connotative plane, as in language, there is a second level of meaning, through which metaphors operate, which – borrowing a term from Barthes (1982) – I want to refer to as the *punctual* significance of the artefact. In relation to the photographic image Barthes distinguished between the 'studium' and the 'punctum'. The former refers to its denotative qualities and the cultural connotations by which the meanings of the image may be decoded. The latter is psychologically analogical to a prick, pin-point or sting with its origins in photographic details or qualities, breaking or punctuating the field of the studium (ibid.: 26–7). There may be one or many punctums in an image which are subjectively recognized by an observer (most of Barthes's book concerns the punctual qualities, for him, of an image of his dead mother as a little girl, a photograph which he does not reproduce in the book for the disinterested studium of another spectator). While remaining a detail (e.g. a hand, a boy's bad teeth) for the observer it may, in a flash, fill the whole picture with an emotional power of analogical reference and association. The punctum of the artefact is the level at which it meets the embodied mind of the observer at an entirely pre-linguistic and personal level not subject to verbal discourse or linguistic mediation. The punctum of the artefact, its 'prick' or 'sting', is the mental image analogies and associations that it conjours up in relation to others in which seeing a thing, or an aspect of a thing such as its colour or shape, stings the memory into recalling other artefacts experienced and used in prior actional contexts. To give two examples from the present text: for me, as interpreter, the punctum of the Maiden Castle bank barrow discussed in Chapter 6 is its change in orientation, that of the Wala canoe discussed in Chapter 4, the female banyan root wrapped around the hull.

The manner in which artefacts are manipulated and used in ritual and performative contexts, expressly designed to have a dramatic and vivid effect on the social actor, may operate particularly powerfully at this punctual level to stimulate fresh metaphorical connections, new ways of thinking about and describing reality. This punctual level of analogical association may be fleeting and momentary, or it may become sedimented in the mind, such that it can enter into verbal and solid metaphor at a directly connotative referential level. The 'punctum' of the artefact performs its work because of the inalienable qualities of things, that they are subjects rather than objects, personified things through which people create themselves. It is the unique power of the thing that operates physically, emotionally, preverbally, evocatively. This is why words can never substitute for things, why if people could say it, they would not make it. This is to stress the deeply personalized relationship people develop with things made and things consumed, which works in a manner different from linguistic experience because it is a physical, synaesthetic, material experience threatening to overwhelm the senses and inbuilt into the thing (usually) is the passage of time in its making, exchange, uses, movements and modes of consumption, properties not shared with the fleeting and momentary spoken word.

The problem with the work of Lévi-Strauss is not that he posited a universal mode of the operation of the human mind, but the manner in which he characterized that mind as a kind of potato chipper taking the raw materials of experience and processing the form of the finished product in just the same way. The abiding significance of the work of Lévi-Strauss, for the study of material culture, is not the trappings of a structuralist mode of analysis isolating binary oppositions, but that he is a master of metaphor. By employing metaphor and metonymy to the full he is able to create interpretative sense from often the most refractory of materials. To characterize the human mind as a mind that makes sense of the world through the creation of metaphorical analogies avoids the reductionist determinism, ahistoricism and anti-individualism underlying Lévi-Strauss's appropriation of structural linguistics to study culture. It is to stress instead the active generative qualities of the human mind which result in fundamentally different cultural systems of meaning that are genuinely transformative in time and space, historically situated and determined within the praxis of individual social action. The social world is not reduced to a series of chess games in which the structural rules always remain the same, while the different moves of the pieces in each game are reduced to an insignificant level of parole. It might be claimed that there is in fact only one invariant cultural rule of any real significance: the rule of metaphor.

References

Andersson, T. (1992) 'En kult-procession på hällristningarna i Högsbyn', *Adoranten* 36–8.
Andersson, T. (1994) *Skurna figurer på Hällristningar i Högsbyn*, Bengtsfors.
Andersson, T. (1995) 'En märklig hällristningshäll i Högsbyn, Tisselskog', *Hembygden* 63–6.
Appadurai, A. (1986) 'Introduction: commodities and the politics of value' in A. Appadurai (ed.) *The Social Life of Things: Commodities in Cultural Perspective*, Cambridge: Cambridge University Press.
Appadurai, A. (1990) 'Disjuncture and difference in the global cultural economy', *Public Culture* 2: 1–24.
Aristotle (1924) 'Poetics' in W. Ross (ed.) *The Works of Aristotle*, Oxford: Oxford University Press.
Bailey, C. (1980) 'The excavation of three round barrows in the parish of Kingston Russell', *Proceedings of the Dorset Natural History and Archaeology Society* 102: 19–32.
Bailey, C. (1984) 'Fieldwork in the upper valley of the South Winterborne', *Proceedings of the Dorset Natural History and Archaeology Society* 106: 134–7.
Balaam, N., Corney, M., Dunn, C. and Porter, H. (1991) 'The surveys' in Sharples (1991b) *Maiden Castle*, London: Historic Buildings and Monuments Commission for England.
Bapty, I. and Yates, T. (eds) (1990) *Archaeology after Structuralism*, London: Routledge.

Barrett, J. (1994) *Fragments from Antiquity*, Oxford: Blackwell Publishers.
Barth, F. (1975) *Ritual and Knowledge among the Baktaman*, New Haven, Conn.: Yale University Press.
Barth, F. (1987) *Cosmologies in the Making*, Cambridge: Cambridge University Press.
Barthes, R. (1982) *Camera Lucida*, London: Jonathan Cape.
Basso, K. (1984) '"Stalking with stories": names, places and moral narratives among the Western Apache' in E. Bruner (ed.) *Text, Play and Story*, Prospect Heights, Ill.: Waveland Press.
Basso, K. (1996) 'Wisdom sits in places: notes on a Western Apache landscape' in K. Basso and S. Feld (eds).
Basso, K. and Feld, S. (eds) (1996) *Senses of Place*, Albuquerque: University of New Mexico Press.
Battaglia, D. (1983) 'Projecting personhood in Melanesia: the dialectics of artefact symbolism on Sabarl island', *Man* 18: 289–304.
Battaglia, D. (1990) *On the Bones of the Serpent: Person, Memory, and Mortality in Sabarl Island Society*, Chicago: University of Chicago Press.
Beck, B. (1978) 'The metaphor as a mediator between semantic and analogic modes of thought', *Current Anthropology* 19/1: 83–97.
Becker, A. (1995) *Body, Self and Society: The View from Fiji*, Philadelphia: University of Pennsylvania Press.
Bertilsson, U. (1986) *The Rock Carvings of Northern Bohuslän*, Stockholm: Akademitryck.
Bertilsson, U. (1989) 'Space economy and society in the rock carvings of northern Bohuslän' in T. Larsson and H. Lundmark (eds) *Approaches to Swedish Prehistory*, Oxford: British Archaeological Reports. International Series: 500.
Best, M. (1965) 'Excavation of three barrows on the Ridgeway, Bincombe', *Proceedings of the Dorset Natural History and Archaeology Society* 86: 102–3.
Bird, E. (1995) *Geology and Scenery of Dorset*, Bradford on Avon: Ex Libris Press.
Bird-David, N. (1990) 'The giving environment: another perspective on the economic system of gatherer-hunters', *Current Anthropology* 31: 189–96.
Bird-David, N. (1992) 'Beyond "The original affluent society": a culturalist reformulation', *Current Anthropology* 33: 25–47.
Black, M. (1962) *Models and Metaphors*, Ithaca: Cornell University Press.
Black, M. (1993) 'More about metaphor' in A. Ortony (ed.) *Metaphor and Thought* 2nd edn, Cambridge: Cambridge University Press.
Bolton, L. (1993) *Dancing in Mats: Extending Kastom to Women in Vanuatu* Ph.D. thesis, University of Manchester.
Bonnemaison, J. (1994) *The Tree and the Canoe: History and Ethnogeography of Tanna*, Honolulu: University of Hawaii Press.
Borges, J. (1977) 'The book of sand' in J. Borges *The Book of Sand*, New York: Dutton.

Bourdieu, P. (1977) *Outline of a Theory of Practice*, Cambridge: Cambridge University Press.
Bourdieu, P. (1984) *Distinction: A Social Critique of the Judgement of Taste*, London: Routledge.
Bourdieu, P. (1990) *The Logic of Practice*, Cambridge: Polity Press.
Bradley, R. (1983) 'The bank barrows and related monuments of Dorset in the light of recent fieldwork', *Proceedings of the Dorset Natural History and Archaeology Society* 105: 15–20.
Bregulla, H. (1992) *Birds of Vanuatu*, London: Anthony Nelson.
Brennan, M. (1983) *The Stars and the Stones: Ancient Art and Astronomy in Ireland*, London: Thames and Hudson.
Brown, R. (1977) *A Poetic for Sociology*, Cambridge: Cambridge University Press.
Bulmer, R. (1967) 'Why the cassowary is not a bird', *Man* 2 (1): 5–25.
Butler, J. (1990) *Gender Trouble: Feminism and the Subversion of Identity*, London: Routledge.
Campbell, S. (1983) 'Attaining rank: a classification of Kula shell valuables' in J. Leach and E. Leach (eds) *The Kula: New Perspectives on Massim Exchange*, Cambridge: Cambridge University Press.
Care, V. (1979) 'The production and distribution of Mesolithic axes in southern England', *Proceedings of the Prehistoric Society* 45: 93–102.
Carmichael, D., Hubert, J., Reeves, B. and Schanche, A. (eds) (1994) *Sacred Sites, Sacred Places*, London: Routledge.
Carr, A. and Blackley, M. (1974) 'Ideas on the origin and development of Chesil Beach, Dorset', *Proceedings of the Dorset Natural History and Archaeology Society* 95: 9–17.
Carr, A. and Gleason, R. (1971) 'Chesil Beach and cartographic evidence of Sir John Coode', *Proceedings of the Dorset Natural History and Archaeological Society* 93: 125–31.
Carrier, J. (ed.) (1992) *History and Tradition in Melanesian Anthropology*, Berkeley: University of California Press.
Carsten, J. and Hugh-Jones, S. (eds) (1995) *About the House: Lévi-Strauss and Beyond*, Cambridge: Cambridge University Press.
Casey, E. (1996) 'How to get from space to place in a fairly short stretch of time: phenomenological prolegomena' in K. Basso and S. Feld (eds).
Chapman, R. (1981) 'The emergence of formal disposal areas and the "problem" of megalithic tombs in prehistoric Europe' in R. Chapman, I. Kinnes and K. Randsborg (eds) *The Archaeology of Death*, Cambridge: Cambridge University Press.
Childe, V. G. (1925) *The Dawn of European Civilization* 1st edn, London: Kegan Paul.
Childe, V. G. (1957) *The Dawn of European Civilization* 6th edn, London: Routledge and Kegan Paul.

Clausen, R. (1960) 'Slit drums and ritual in Malekula, New Hebrides' in *Three Regions of Melanesian Art*, New York: Museum of Primitive Art, University Publishers.

Clifford, J. (1992) 'Traveling cultures' in L. Grossberg, C. Nelson and P. Triechler (eds) *Cultural Studies*, London: Routledge.

Clifford, J. (1997) 'Museums as contact zones' in *Routes: Essays in Travel and Interculture*, Cambridge, Mass.: Harvard University Press.

Codrington, R. (1881) 'Religious beliefs in Melanesia', *Journal of the Anthropological Institute*, XXVI: 261–316.

Coleridge, S. (1971) 'Biographia literari' in *Coleridge: Select Poetry and Prose* (ed. S. Potter), London: Nonesuch Press.

Collett, D. (1993) 'Metaphors and representations associated with precolonial iron-smelting in eastern and southern Africa' in T. Shaw, P. Sinclair, B. Andah and A. Okopoleo (eds) *The Archaeology of Africa*, London: Routledge.

Corradi Fiumara, G. (1995) *The Metaphoric Process*, London: Routledge.

Crawford, O. (1938) 'Bank barrows', *Antiquity* XII: 228–32.

Crick, M. (1985) '"Tracing" the anthropological self: quizzical reflections on fieldwork, tourism and the ludic', *Sociological Analysis* 17: 71–92.

Crick, M. (1989) 'Representations of international tourism in the social sciences', *Annual Review of Anthropology* 18: 307–44.

Crocker, J. (1977) 'The social functions of rhetorical forms' in J. D. Sapir and J. C. Crocker (eds) *The Social Use of Metaphor*, Philadelphia: University of Pennsylvania Press.

Crocker, J. (1985) 'My brother the parrot' in G. Unton (ed.) *Animal Myths and Metaphors in South America*, Salt Lake City: University of Utah Press.

Culler, J. (1981) 'The turns of metaphor' in *The Pursuit of Signs*, London: Routledge.

Daniel, G. (1958) *The Megalith Builders of Western Europe*, London: Hutchinson.

Davies, S., Stacey, L. and Woodward, P. (1985) 'Excavations at Alington Avenue, Fordington, Dorchester 1984/5: interim report', *Proceedings of the Dorset Natural History and Archaeology Society* 107: 101–10.

Deacon, A. (1934) *Malekula: A Vanishing People in the New Hebrides*, London: George Routledge and Sons.

De Beauvoir, S. (1965) *The Prime of Life*, London: Penguin.

Derrida, J. (1982) 'White mythology: metaphor in the text of philosophy' in *Margins of Philosophy*, Brighton: Harvester Press.

Descartes, R. (1965) *Discourse on Method, Optics, Geometry and Meteorology*, Indianapolis: Indianapolis University Press.

Devisch, R. (1993) *Weaving the Threads of Life: The Khita Gyn-Eco-Logical Healing Cult among the Yaka*, Chicago: University of Chicago Press.

Douglas, M. (1954) 'The Lele of the Kasai' in D. Forde (ed.) *African Worlds*, Oxford: Oxford University Press.

Douglas, M. (1957) 'Animals in Lele religious symbolism', *Africa* XXVII (1): 46–58.
Douglas, M. (1963) *The Lele of the Kasai*, Oxford: Oxford University Press.
Douglas, M. (1966) *Purity and Danger*, London: Routledge and Kegan Paul.
Douglas, M. (1970) *Natural Symbols*, Harmondsworth: Penguin.
Douglas, M. (1996) 'Anomalous animals and animal metaphors' in *Thought Styles*, London: Sage.
Dreyfus, H. (1979) *What Computers Can't Do*, New York: Harper and Row.
Evans-Pritchard, E. (1940) *The Nuer*, Oxford: Oxford University Press.
Evans-Pritchard, E. (1956) *Nuer Religion*, Oxford: Oxford University Press.
Fainsilber, L. and Ortony, A. (1987) 'Metaphoric uses of language in the expression of emotion', *Metaphor and Symbolic Activity* 2: 239–50.
Feifer, M. (1985) *Going Places*, London: Macmillan.
Feld, S. (1996) 'Waterfalls of song: an acoustemology of place resounding in Bosavi, Papua New Guinea' in K. Basso and S. Feld (eds).
Fergusson, J. (1872) *Rude Stone Monuments in All Countries: Their Age and Uses*, London: John Murray.
Fernandez, J. (1986) *Persuasions and Performances*, Bloomington: Indiana University Press.
Fernandez, J. (ed.) (1991) *Beyond Metaphor: The Theory of Tropes in Anthropology*, Stanford: Stanford University Press.
Fleming, A. (1971) 'Territorial patterns in Bronze Age Wessex', *Proceedings of the Prehistoric Society* 37: 138–66.
Forde, C. D. (1930) 'Early cultures of Atlantic Europe', *American Anthropologist* 32 (1): 19–100.
Forge, A. (1979) 'The problem of meaning in art' in S. Mead (ed.) *Exploring the Visual Art of Oceania*, Honolulu: University of Hawaii Press.
Foucault, M. (1977) *Discipline and Punish*, New York: Vintage.
Frake, C. (1996) 'Pleasant places, past times, and sheltered identity in rural East Anglia' in K. Basso and S. Feld (eds).
Funabiki, T. (1981) 'On pigs of the Mbotgote in Malekula' in M. Allen (ed.) *Vanuatu: Politics, Economics and Ritual in Island Melanesia*, London: Academic Press.
Gadamer, H.-G. (1975) *Truth and Method*, London: Sheed and Ward.
Game, A. and Metcalfe, A. (1996) *Passionate Sociology*, London: Sage.
Garwood, P. (1991) 'Ritual tradition and the reconstitution of society' in P. Garwood, D. Jennings, R. Skeates and J. Toms (eds) *Sacred and Profane*, Oxford: Oxford University Committee for Archaeology Monograph 32.
Gell, A. (1992a) 'The technology of enchantment and the enchantment of technology' in J. Coote and A. Sheldon (eds) *Anthropology, Art and Aesthetics*, Oxford: Oxford University Press.
Gell, A. (1992b) 'Inter-tribal commodity barter and reproductive gift-exchange in

old Melanesia' in C. Humphrey and S. Hugh Jones (eds) *Barter, Exchange and Value*, Cambridge: Cambridge University Press.

Gell, A. (1995) 'The language of the forest: landscape and phonological iconism in Umeda' in E. Hirsch and M. O'Hanlon (eds) *The Anthropology of Landscape*, Oxford: Oxford University Press.

Gewertz, D. and Errington, F. (1991) *Twisted Histories, Altered Contexts*, Cambridge: Cambridge University Press.

Gibbs, R. (1994) *The Poetics of Mind*, Cambridge: Cambridge University Press.

Gill, J. (1991) *Merleau-Ponty and Metaphor*, London: The Humanities Press.

Graburn, N. (ed.) (1976) *Ethnic and Tourist Arts*, Berkeley: University of California Press.

Griaule, M. (1965) *Conversations with Ogotemmeli*, Oxford: Oxford University Press.

Grinsell, L. (1959) *Dorset Barrows*, Dorchester: Dorset Natural History and Archaeology Society.

Grinsell, L. (1982) *Dorset Barrows Supplement*, Dorchester: Dorset Natural History and Archaeology Society.

Guss, D. (1989) *To Weave and Sing: Art, Symbol and Narrative in the South American Rain Forest*, Berkeley: University of California Press.

Haddon, A. (1937) *Canoes of Oceania* Vol. 2. Honolulu: Bernice P. Bishop Museum Special Publication 28.

Harcombe, D. and O'Byrne, D. (1995) *Vanuatu*, London: Lonely Planet Publications.

Harrison, P. (1983) *Seabirds: An Identification Guide*, London: Croom Helm.

Harrison, S. (1993) 'The commerce of cultures in Melanesia', *Man* 28: 139–58.

Hawkes, C. (1940) *The Prehistoric Foundations of Europe to the Mycenean Age*, London: Methuen.

Hawkes, T. (1989) *Metaphor*, London: Routledge.

Hertz, R. (1960) *Death and the Right Hand*, New York: Free Press.

Hobart, M. (1995) 'As I lay laughing: Encountering global knowledge in Bali' in R. Fardon (ed.) *Counterworks*, London: Routledge.

Hobsbawm, E. and Ranger, T. (eds) (1983) *The Invention of Tradition*, Cambridge: Cambridge University Press.

Hodder, I. (1984) 'Burials, houses, women and men in the European neolithic' in D. Miller and C. Tilley (eds) *Ideology, Power and Prehistory*, Cambridge: Cambridge University Press.

Hodder, I. (1990) *The Domestication of Europe*, Oxford: Blackwell Publishers.

Hodder, I. (1992) *Theory and Practice in Archaeology*, London: Routledge.

House, M. (1991) 'Dorset dolines: Part 2, Bronkham Hill', *Proceeedings of the Dorset Natural History and Archaeology Society* 113: 149–53.

Ingold, T. (1996) 'Hunting and gathering as ways of perceiving the environment' in R. Ellen and K. Fukui (eds) *Redefining Nature*, Oxford: Berg.

Jakobson, R. (1956) 'Two aspects of language and two types of aphasic disturbances' in R. Jakobson and M. Halle, *Fundamentals of Language*, The Hague: Mouton.

Jarman, M., Bailey, G. and Jarman, H. (eds) (1982) *Early European Agriculture*, Cambridge: Cambridge University Press.

Jay, M. (1993) *Downcast Eyes: The Denigration of Vision in Twentieth Century French Thought*, Berkeley: University of California Press.

Jayarama, T. and Andeng, J. (1993) 'Tourism sector in Vanuatu', Working Papers, Research School of Pacific Studies, Canberra: Australian National University.

Johansen, O. (1979) 'New results in the investigation of the Bronze Age rock carvings', *Norwegian Archaeological Review* 12 (2): 108–14.

Johnson, M. (1987) *The Body in the Mind*, Chicago: Chicago University Press.

Jolly, M. (1982) 'Birds and banyans of south Pentecost: Kastom in anti-colonial struggle', *Mankind* 13: 338–56.

Jolly, M. (1984) 'The anatomy of pig love: substance, spirit and gender in South Pentecost, Vanuatu', *Canberra Anthropology* 7: 78–108.

Jolly, M. (1991a) 'Soaring hawks and grounded persons: the politics of rank and gender in north Vanuatu' in M. Godelier and M. Strathern (eds) *Big Men and Great Men*, Cambridge: Cambridge University Press.

Jolly, M. (1991b) 'Gifts, commodities and corporeality: food and gender in South Pentecost, Vanuatu', *Canberra Anthropology* 14: 45–66.

Jolly, M. (1992) 'Custom and the way of the land: past and present in Vanuatu and Fiji' in Jolly and Thomas (eds) *The Politics of Tradition in the Pacific*, special issue of *Oceania* 62 (4).

Jolly, M. (1994) *Women of the Place: Kastom, Colonialism and Gender in Vanuatu*, Camberwell: Harwood Academic Publishers.

Jolly, M. and Thomas, N. (eds) (1992) *The Politics of Tradition in the Pacific*, special issue of *Oceania* 62 (4).

Joussaume, R. (1988) *Dolmens for the Dead*, London: Batsford.

Kahn, M. (1996) 'Your place and mine: sharing emotional landscapes in Wamira, Papua New Guinea' in K. Basso and S. Feld (eds).

Kapferer, B. (1986) 'Performance and the structuring of meaning and experience' in V. Turner and E. Bruner (eds) *The Anthropology of Experience*, Urbana: University of Illinois Press.

Kaul, F. (1995) 'Ships on bronzes' in O. Crumlin-Pedersen and B. Much Thye (eds) *The Ship as Symbol in Prehistoric and Medieval Scandinavia*, Copenhagen: Danish National Museum.

Keesing, R. (1987) 'Anthropology as an interpretative quest', *Current Anthropology* 28: 161–76.

Keesing, R. (1992) *Custom and Confrontation: The Kwaio Struggle for Cultural Autonomy*, Chicago: University of Chicago Press.

Keesing, R. (1994) 'Colonial and counter-colonial discourse in Melanesia', *Critique of Anthropology* 14: 41–58.
Keesing, R. and Tonkinson, R. (eds) (1982) *Reinventing Traditional Culture: The Politics of Kastom in Island Melanesia*, special issue of *Mankind* 13 (4).
Keller, J. (1988) 'Woven world: neotraditional symbols of unity in Vanuatu', *Mankind* 18: 1–13.
Kent, S. (ed.) (1990) *Domestic Architecture and the Use of Space*, Cambridge: Cambridge University Press.
Kittay, E. (1987) *Metaphor: Its Cognitive Force and Linguistic Structure*, Oxford: Clarendon Press.
Knauft, B. (1989) 'Bodily images in Melanesia: cultural substances and natural metaphors' in M. Feher, R. Nadaff and N. Tazi (eds) *Fragments for a History of the Body, Part Three*, New York: Zone Books.
Kopytoff, I. (1986) 'The cultural biography of things: commoditization as process' in A. Appadurai (ed.) *The Social Life of Things*, Cambridge: Cambridge University Press.
Küchler, S. (1987) 'Malangan: art and memory in a Melanesian society', *Man* 22: 238–55.
Küchler, S. (1988) 'Malangan: objects, sacrifice and the production of memory', *American Ethnologist* 15 (4): 625–37.
Küchler, S. (1992) 'Making skins: malangan and the idiom of kinship in northern New Ireland' in J. Coote and A. Sheldon (eds) *Anthropology, Art and Aesthetics*, Oxford: Oxford University Press.
Kuhn, T. (1993) 'Metaphor in science' in A. Ortony (ed.) *Metaphor and Thought* 2nd edn, Cambridge: Cambridge University Press.
Lakoff, G. (1987) *Women, Fire, and Dangerous Things: What Categories Reveal About the Mind*, Chicago: University of Chicago Press.
Lakoff, G. and Johnson, M. (1980) *Metaphors We Live By*, Chicago: University of Chicago Press.
Lakoff, G. and Turner, M. (1989) *More than Cool Reason: A Field Guide to Poetic Metaphor*, Chicago: University of Chicago Press.
Larcom, J. (1982) 'The invention of convention' in R. Keesing and R. Tonkinson (eds) *Reinventing Traditional Culture*, special edition of *Mankind* 13 (4).
Larcom, J. (1990) 'Custom by decree: legitimation crisis in Vanuatu' in J. Linnekin and L. Poyer (eds) *Cultural Identity and Ethnicity in the Pacific*, Honolulu: University of Hawaii Press.
Lasch, S. and Urry, J. (1994) *Economies of Signs and Space*, London: Sage.
Lawson, A. (1990) 'The prehistoric hinterland of Maiden Castle', *Antiquaries Journal* LXX: 271–87.
Layard, J. (1942) *Stone Men of Malekula*, London: Chatto and Windus.
Layard, J. (1955) 'The role of the sacrifice of tusked boars in Malekulan religion and social organization', *Ethnologica* 2: 286–98.
Layard, J. (1972) *The Virgin Archetype*, Zurich: Spring Publications.

Layard, J. (n.d.) 'Canoes', unpublished manuscript, John W. Layard Papers, MSS 84. Mandeville Special Collections Library, University of California, San Diego.

Leach, E. (1964) 'Anthropological aspects of language: animal categories and verbal abuse' in E. Lenneberg (ed.) *New Directions in the Study of Language*, Cambridge, Mass.: MIT Press.

Leach, J. and Leach, E. (eds) (1983) *The Kula: New Perspectives on Massim Exchange*, Cambridge: Cambridge University Press.

Lemonnier, P. (ed.) (1993) *Technological Choices: Transformations in Material Cultures since the Neolithic*, London: Routledge.

Lévi-Strauss, C. (1962) *Totemism*, London: Merlin Press.

Lévi-Strauss, C. (1966) *The Savage Mind*, London: Weidenfeld and Nicolson.

Lévi-Strauss, C. (1969) *The Raw and the Cooked*, London: Jonathan Cape.

Lienhardt, G. (1961) *Divinity and Experience*, Oxford: Clarendon Press.

Linnekin, J. and Poyer, L. (eds) (1990) *Cultural Identity and Ethnicity in the Pacific*, Honolulu: University of Hawaii Press.

MacCannell, D. (1976) *The Tourist: A New Theory of the Leisure Class*, New York: Schocken.

MacCannell, D. (1992) *Empty Meeting Grounds: The Tourist Papers*, London: Routledge.

MacCormac, E. (1985) *A Cognitive Theory of Metaphor*, Cambridge, Mass.: MIT Press.

MacKenzie, M. (1991) *Androgynous Objects: String Bags and Gender in Central New Guinea*, Melbourne: Harwood Academic Press.

Marstrander, S. (1963) *Østfolds Jordbruksristninger*, Oslo: Instituttet for Sammenlignende Kulturforskning.

Mauss, M. (1973) 'Techniques of the body', *Economy and Society* 2: 70–88.

Merleau-Ponty, M. (1962) *The Phenomenology of Perception*, London: Routledge.

Miller, D. (1987) *Material Culture and Mass Consumption*, Oxford: Blackwell Publishers.

Miller, D. (1994a) *Modernity: An Ethnographic Approach*, Oxford: Berg.

Miller, D. (1994b) 'Artefacts and the meanings of things' in T. Ingold (ed.) *Companion Encyclopedia of Anthropology*, London: Routledge.

Miller, D. (ed.) (1995) *Acknowledging Consumption*, London: Routledge.

Miller, D. and Tilley, C. (1996) 'Editorial', *Journal of Material Culture* 1 (1): 5–14.

Montelius, O. (1905) 'Orienten och Europa', *Antiqvarisk Tidskrift för Sverige* 13: 1–252.

Munn, N. (1977) 'The spatiotemporal transformation of Gawa canoes', *Journal de la Société des Océanistes* 33: 39–53.

Munn, N. (1983) 'Gawan kula: spatiotemporal control and the symbolism of influence' in J. Leach and E. Leach (eds) *The Kula*, Cambridge: Cambridge University Press.

Munn, N. (1986) *The Fame of Gawa*, Cambridge: Cambridge University Press.

Needham, R. (ed.) (1973) *Right and Left: Essays on Dual Symbolic Classification*, Chicago: University of Chicago Press.

Nilsson, S. (1868) [1838–43] *The Primitive Inhabitants of Scandinavia*, London: Longmans, Green and Co.

O'Rourke, D. (1987) *Cannibal Tours* (film), Canberra: O'Rourke and Associates.

Ortner, S. (1973) 'On key symbols', *American Anthropologist* 75 (6): 1338–46.

Ortony, A. (1975) 'Why metaphors are necessary and not just nice', *Educational Theory* 25: 45–53.

Ortony, A. (1976) 'On the nature and value of metaphor: a reply to my critics', *Educational Theory* 26: 395–8.

Ortony, A. (ed.) (1993) *Metaphor and Thought* 2nd edn, Cambridge: Cambridge University Press.

Paivio, A. (1971) *Images and Verbal Processes*, New York: Holt, Rinehart Winston.

Palmer, S. (1963) 'Prehistoric stone industries of the Fleet area, Weymouth', *Proceedings of the Dorset Natural History and Archaeology Society* 85: 107–15.

Palmer, S. (1967) 'Second interim report on the excavation of a Mesolithic site at Portland Bill', *Proceedings of the Dorset Natural History and Archaeology Society* 89: 119.

Palmer, S. (1968) 'A Mesolithic site at Portland Bill 1966', *Proceedings of the Dorset Natural History and Archaeology Society* 90: 183–206.

Palmer, S. (1970) 'The stone age industries of the Isle of Portland, Dorset, and the utilization of Portland chert as artifact material in southern England', *Proceedings of the Prehistoric Society* 36: 82–115.

Palmer, S. (1975) 'Interim note on excavations at the Culver Well Mesolithic site, Portland, 1975', *Proceedings of the Dorset Natural History and Archaeology Society* 97: 45–6.

Palmer, S. (1977) *Mesolithic Cultures of Britain*, Poole: Dolphin Press.

Parker-Pearson, M. and Richards, C. (eds) (1994) *Architecture and Order*, London: Routledge.

Parmentier, R. (1987) *The Sacred Remains: Myth, History and Polity in Belau*, Chicago: Chicago University Press.

Peers, R. and Clarke, D. (1967) 'A Bronze Age beaker burial and Roman site at Broadmayne', *Proceedings of the Dorset Natural History and Archaeological Society* 88: 103–5.

Peet, T. (1912) *Rough Stone Monuments and Their Builders*, London: Harper and Brothers.

Pfaffenberger, B. (1992) 'Social anthropology of technology', *Annual Review of Anthropology* 21: 491–516.

Philibert, J.-M. (1986) 'The politics of tradition: towards a generic culture in Vanuatu', *Mankind* 16: 1–12.

Philibert, J.-M. (1987) 'Consuming culture: a study of simple commodity consumption' in H. Rutz and B. Orlove (eds) *The Social Economy of Consumption*, Lanham: University Press of America.

Piggott, S. (1938) 'The early Bronze Age in Wessex', *Proceedings of the Prehistoric Society* 4: 52–106.

Porteous, J. (1990) *Landscapes of the Mind: Worlds of Sense and Metaphor*, Toronto: University of Toronto Press.

Preston Blier, S. (1987) *The Anatomy of Architecture: Ontology and Metaphor in Batammaliba Architectural Expression*, Chicago: University of Chicago Press.

Quinn, N. (1991) 'The cultural basis of metaphor' in J. Fernandez (ed.) *Beyond Metaphor*, Stanford: Stanford University Press.

Rankine, W. (1951) 'Artifacts of Portland chert in southern England', *Proceedings of the Prehistoric Society* 17: 93–4.

Rankine, W. (1962) 'The Mesolithic age in Dorset and adjacent areas', *Proceedings of the Dorset Natural History and Archaeology Society* 83: 91–9.

RCHME (Royal Commission on Historical Monuments, England) (1970) *An Inventory of Historical Monuments in the County of Dorset*, Vol. 2 South East, London: Royal Commission on Historical Monuments.

Renfrew, C. (1973) *Before Civilization*, London: Jonathan Cape.

Renfrew, C. (1976) 'Megaliths, territories and populations' in S. DeLaet (ed.) *Acculturation and Continuity in Atlantic Europe*, Brugge: De Tempel.

Richards, I. (1936) *The Philosophy of Rhetoric*, Oxford: Oxford University Press.

Ricoeur, P. (1978) *The Rule of Metaphor*, London: Routledge.

Rowlands, M. and Warnier, J.-P. (1993) 'The magical production of iron in the Cameroon Grassfields' in T. Shaw et al. (eds) *The Archaeology of Africa*, London: Routledge.

Sahlins, M. (1976) *Culture and Practical Reason*, Chicago: Chicago University Press.

Salmond, A. (1982) 'Theoretical landscapes: on cross-cultural conceptions of knowledge' in D. Parkin (ed.) *Semantic Anthropology*, London: Academic Press.

Schieffelin, E. (1976) *The Sorrow of the Lonely and the Burning of the Dancers*, New York: St Martin's Press.

Selwyn, T. (ed.) (1996) *The Tourist Image: Myths and Myth Making in Tourism*, London: Wiley.

Sharples, N. (1991a) *English Heritage Book of Maiden Castle*, London: Batsford.

Sharples, N. (1991b) *Maiden Castle*, London: Historic Buildings and Monuments Commission for England.

Sherratt, A. (1990) 'The genesis of megaliths', *World Archaeology* 22: 147–67.

Shibles, W. (1971) *Metaphor: An Annotated Bibliography and History*, Whitewater: Language Press.

Smith, V. (ed.) (1989) *Hosts and Guests: The Anthropology of Tourism*, Philadelphia: University of Pennsylvania Press.

Somerville, B. (1894) 'Ethnological notes on the New Hebrides', *Journal of the Anthropological Institute* XXIII: 363–93.

Speiser, F. (1990) *Ethnology of Vanuatu: An Early Twentieth Century Study*, Bathurst: Crawford House Press.

Strathern, M. (1988) *The Gender of the Gift*, Berkeley: University of Chicago Press.

Strathern, M. (1990) 'Artefacts of history events and the interpretation of images' in J. Siikala (ed.) *Culture and History in the Pacific*, Helsinki: Finnish Anthropological Society Transactions No. 27.

Svensson, K. (1982) *Hällristningar i Älvsborgs Län*, Uddevalla: Älvsborgs Länsmuseum.

Svensson, K. (1985) 'En kultplats i Dalsland', *Populär Arkeologi* 3: 29.

Tambiah, S. (1969/1973) 'Animals are good to think and good to prohibit', *Ethnology* 8 (4): 424–59. Reprinted in M. Douglas (ed.) (1973) *Rules and Meanings*, Harmondsworth: Penguin.

Thomas, J. (1984) 'A tale of two polities: kinship, authority and exchange in the neolithic of south Dorset and Wiltshire', in R. Bradley and J. Gardiner (eds) *Neolithic Studies: A Review of Some Current Research*, Oxford: British Archaeological Reports 133.

Thomas, J. (1991) *Rethinking the Neolithic*, Cambridge: Cambridge University Press.

Thomas, J. (1996) *Time, Culture and Identity*, London: Routledge.

Thomas, N. (1991) *Entangled Objects: Exchange, Material Culture and Colonialism in the Pacific*, London: Harvard University Press.

Thomas, N. (1995) *Oceanic Art*, London: Thames and Hudson.

Tilley, C. (1990) 'Claude Lévi-Strauss: structuralism and beyond' in C. Tilley (ed.) *Reading Material Culture*, Oxford: Blackwell Publishers.

Tilley, C. (1991) *Material Culture and Text: The Art of Anbiguity*, London: Routledge.

Tilley, C. (1994a) *A Phenomenology of Landscape: Places, Paths and Monuments*, Oxford: Berg.

Tilley, C. (1994b) 'Design structure and narrative in southern Scandinavian rock art', *Bulletin of the Institute of Archaeology* 34: 61–87.

Tilley, C. (1996) *An Ethnography of the Neolithic*, Cambridge: Cambridge University Press.

Treves, F. (1906) *Highways and Byways in Dorset*, London: Macmillan.

Turner, T. (1991) ' "We are parrots," "twins are birds"; play of tropes as operational structure' in J. Fernandez (ed.) *Beyond Metaphor*, Stanford: Stanford University Press.

Turner, V. (1967) *The Forest of Symbols*, Ithaca: Cornell University Press.

Turner, V. (1969) *The Ritual Process*, Chicago: Aldine.

Turner, V. (1974) *Dramas, Fields and Metaphors*, Ithaca: Cornell University Press.

Urry, J. (1990) *The Tourist Gaze*, London: Sage.

Wagner, R. (1975) *The Invention of Culture*, Englewood Cliffs, NJ: Prentice-Hall.

Wagner, R. (1986) *Symbols That Stand for Themselves*, Chicago: Chicago University Press.

Waterson, R. (1991) *The Living House: An Anthropology of Architecture in South-East Asia*, Oxford: Oxford University Press.

Weiner, A. (1992) *Inalienable Possessions*, Berkeley: University of California Press.
Weiner, A. and Schneider, J. (eds) (1989) *Cloth and Human Experience*, Washington: Smithsonian Institution Press.
Weiner, J. (1991) *The Empty Place: Poetry, Space and Being among the Foi of Papua New Guinea*, Bloomington: Indiana University Press.
Wheatley, J. (1992) *A Guide to the Common Trees of Vanuatu*, Port Vila: Department of Forestry.
Wheeler, R. E. M. (1943) *Maiden Castle, Dorset*, London: Society of Antiquaries.
Whittaker, J. (1978) 'The Fleet, Dorset: a seasonal study of the watermass and its vegetation', *Proceedings of the Dorset Natural History and Archaeological Society* 100: 73–99.
Wilkinson, G. (1978) 'Carving a social message: the malanggans of Tabar (Papua New Guinea)' in M. Greenhalgh and V. Megaw (eds) *Art in Society*, London: Duckworth.
Willis, R. (1974) *Man and Beast*, St Albans: Paladin.
Willis, R. (ed.) (1990) *Signifying Animals*, London: Unwin-Hyman.
Wilson, V., Welch, F., Robbie, J. and Green, G. (1958) *Geology of the Country around Bridport and Yeovil*, London: Memoirs of the Geological Survey of Great Britain, Her Majesty's Stationery Office.
Woodward, P. (1991) *The South Dorset Ridgeway: Survey and Excavations 1977–84*, Bridport: Dorset Natural History and Archaeology Society Monograph Series No. 8.
Wymer, J. (ed.) (1977) *Gazetteer of Mesolithic Sites in England and Wales*, London: Council for British Archaeology Research Report 22.
Yates, T. (1990) 'Archaeology through the looking-glass' in I. Bapty and T. Yates (eds) *Archaeology after Structuralism*, London: Routledge.
Yates, T. (1993) 'Frameworks for an archaeology of the body' in C. Tilley (ed.) *Interpretative Archaeology*, Oxford: Berg.

Index

Abbotsbury 190, 191, 192, 195
Aborigine cosmologies 238
adultery 57
Afek (god) 66, 67
Africa: Batammaliba 41–9; Cameroon Grassfields 58–9; Dogon 37–8; iron making 57–9; Zaire 39, 40, 50
Allington long barrow 199, 201
America, North, Western Apaches 181–2
America, South, Yekuana basketry 68–72, 244, 266
ancestor houses 111–12, 240, 241
ancestors: images 252; powers 235–6; relics 30
Andeng, J. 249
Andersson, T. 135, 153, 160, 165
androgyny 117–18, 128
anger, expressions for 18–19
animal metaphors: birds 23–4, 26–7, 260; dogs 54–5; and humans 49–50; oxen 51–2, 55; pigs 52–4; *see also* rock carvings

anthropology: consumption 246; discourse of place/movement 180; metaphor 25–6, 36–7, 260–1; tourism 247
anthropomorphism 38, 44–6, 48
Apaches, Western 181–2
aphasia 21–2
Appadurai, A. 75, 246
archaeology: interpretations 91–2, 96–8; metaphors of past 79–80; place/movement 180; processual/post-processual 85, 86, 87, 90, 91, 94, 95; texts deconstructed 100–1
architecture: anthropomorphism 44–6, 48; metaphor 40–9; metonymy 43–4, 45
Aristotle 4–5, 9–10
arrows 30, 66
artefacts: analysed 265–6; and discourse 130; meaning 103–4, 270; metaphorical power 267–8; Portland Bill 193; punctual significance 271; punctum 272;

social system 103; for tourism 245, 249
Atchin island 120, 123, 251–2, 256
Australian Aborigine cosmologies 238
authenticity 251–2, 253, 254, 255, 258–9
axes 72–5; *hinona* 72, 73–4; metaphorical power 267; mortuary feast 75, 262; tranchet 193

babies 45, 63, 64; *see also* childbirth
Bagshot beds 188, 223, 229, 236
Bailey, C. 215, 232
Bailey, G. 84, 85, 87, 90, 91
Baktaman people: growth symbols 32–3; pandanus palm 29–30; ritual 28, 265; water 31
Balaam, N. 203
bank barrows 185, 198, 210, 267; Broadmayne 205, 206, 207, 208, 212, 213, 214, 215, 218; and Bronze Age barrows 212; Maiden Castle 202–5, 206–7, 221; Martin's Down 205, 206–7, 208, 215, 229, 230, 234–5; myth/ritual 205, 237–8, 261; Neolithic 185, 237–8
banyan tree: canoe 108, 129; dancing grounds 108, 125, 126–7, 129, 252; male/female 117–18, 126–7, 129; symbolism 113; Wala Island Resort 239
Barrett, J. 208, 211
barrows: Bronze Age 208, 210–11; distribution 208–10, 217, 230, 231; Dorset Ridgeway 198–208; grave goods 210–11; orientation 212, 214, 215; positioning 213–14; and sink holes 225, 226, 227, 228–30, 236, 238; skyline siting 214–15, 221, 222; visibility 213, 214, 216; *see also* bank barrows; bell barrows; bell-disk barrows; bowl barrows; disk barrows; long barrows; round barrows
Barth, F. 28, 31, 265
Barthes, Roland 271
basket-making, Yekuana 68–72, 244, 260, 266

Basso, K. 181, 182
Batammaliba 45, 47–8, 178–9
Batammaliba architecture 41–2; anthropomorphism 44–6, 48; cosmogony 43; gender divisions 47; metonymy 43–4, 45; nesting of buildings 43–4; orientation 43, 47; silhouetting 43; skeuomorphs 44; synecdoche 44
Battaglia, D. 72, 73, 74, 75, 102, 113
bauer tree 108
beach, ancestral 235–8
beaches in the sky 206, 210, 229, 236
Beauvoir, Simone de 261–2
Beck, B. 8, 10, 11
Becker, A. 38, 39
beliefs, metaphor 10–11
bell barrows 224, 225, 235
bell-disk barrow 221
Bertilsson, U. 134, 151
Best, M. 210
betilok shrub 108, 111
bilum (netbags) 62–3; aesthetics 65–6; androgyny 118; as baby carriers 63; childbirth 64, 66, 67–8; ethnic identity 64; gender differences 64–5, 66–7; Kaluli 64; life-cycle 64; looping techniques 63, 64, 65, 66; metonymy 66; social significance 63–4, 65–6; spirit beings 64; Telefol 65, 66
binary oppositions 28
Bincombe Down 188, 196, 201, 219
Bincombe Hill 186, 214, 215, 218, 219
Bincombe long barrow 198, 199, 212, 213, 214
biographies 76, 179
Bird, E. 225
Bird-David, N. 50
bird metaphors 23–5, 110, 111, 113, 260
Black, M. 12, 13–14
Black Down: Bagshot beds 188, 229; enclosure 196; height 186, 223–4; long barrows 199, 200, 231–2; streams 191; visibility 220, 222
Blackley, M. 192, 193

INDEX

bodily emissions 38
body 180; and canoes 113–17; emotion 18–19; Fijian view 38–9; hexis 38; Melanesian view 102; metaphors 18–19, 34–5, 37–40; metonymy 265; and place 177; social system 37, 39, 40; Wala islanders' view 129–30; Western view 38, 102; *see also* rock carvings
Bohuslän rock carvings 151
Bolton, L. 258
Bonnemaison, J. 112, 113
Borges, J. 36
Bororo people 26–7, 260, 261, 262
Bourdieu, Pierre 38, 39, 41, 147, 259, 261
bowl barrows 233, 235
Bradford Peverell long barrow 199
Bradley, R. 198, 203, 204, 215, 235
Brazil, parrot metaphor 26–7
Bregulla, H. 110
Brennan, M. 148, 149
Bridge Valley 232
Broadmayne 186, 201; bank barrow 205, 206, 207, 208, 212, 213, 214, 215, 218; long barrow 199
Bronkham Hill: Bagshot beds 188, 229; and Chesil Beach 230; coombe 222; height 186; solution pit 228; as transition point 223–4
Bronze Age: barrows 208, 210–11; burial mounds 185, 189; cairns 134; cemetery groups 211–12; Dorset Ridgeway 208–11, 238; *see also* Högsbyn rock carvings
Brown, R. 11
buffalo 55
Bulmer, R. 49
burial mounds 185, 189
burials 99, 210–11
Butan (god) 41
Butler, J. 102

cairns 134, 230
Came Down 219–20
Came Wood barrow 219
Cameroon Grassfields, iron making 58–9

Campbell, S. 179
Cannibal Tours film 239, 247
cannibalism 239, 257; metaphorical 254
canns 190, 236
canoe tree 107
canoes: banyan tree 108, 129; as big man 115–16, 117; and body 113–17; and club houses 112–13; consecration rites 123–4; dancing grounds 125–7; double bird prow-head 121; elaboration 104; figurehead 109–10, 116; good to think 130; identity 124, 126; metaphors 79, 80, 112, 260; mourning rituals 105; sails 121, 122–4; and slit drum 127–9; symbolism 106; taboo for women 122, 124; as womb 118; wrecked 105, 124
canoes, types: coastal 104–5, 119–20; Gawa 106–7, 112; sea-going 114–15, 119–20, 121–2; *see also* Wala canoes
Care, V. 194
Carr, A. 189, 192, 193
Carrier, J. 255
Carsten, J. 41
carvings: axes 72–3, 74; tree-fern 240, 241, 243, 252; *see also* rock carvings; sculptures
Casey, E. 178
cassowary 29, 30, 67
cattle 51–2, 55
causewayed enclosure 195, 196–7, 202–3
Chapman, Robert 84, 85, 87, 90, 91, 98
chert 185, 192, 193, 194, 236
Chesil Beach 189–92; and Bronkham Hill 230; cultural representations 236; and Dorset Ridgeway 191–2, 236–7; and Maiden Castle bank barrow 204–5, 206; pebbles 191, 192, 193, 229, 236; views of 195, 218, 219, 220–1, 222, 225
childbirth, and *bilum* 64, 66, 67–8

INDEX

Childe, V. Gordon 83, 84, 85, 87, 90, 91, 96, 98, 99–100
Clandon 199, 201
Clarke, D. 210
Clausen, R. 128–9
Clifford, J. 245
cloth 57
club houses 111–13, 125
Codrington, R. 122
cognition 34–5
cognitive psychology 16, 17–18
Coleridge, Samuel Taylor 7
Collett, D. 58
colour words, cattle 51–2
compactness thesis 7–8
concepts 16, 17, 18, 21, 180
consumption 246–7
context for metaphor 14, 261
Coombe Farm 199, 200
coombes 214, 216
Corradi Fiumara, G. 9
cosmologies 43, 238
Cotswold–Severn tombs 97, 101
Cowleaze long barrow 199, 200, 212, 230, 232, 238
Cranborne Chase 194
Crawford, O. 198
Crick, M. 246
Crocker, J. 26
croton leaves 116–17
Culler, J. 4, 19, 33, 35
Culliford Tree long barrow 199, 201, 212, 213, 214, 215
cultural productions 27, 40, 255–6
culture: authenticity 251–2, 253, 255; global 245–6; and linguistics 272–3; metaphor xiv, 11, 21–7, 36; and nature 22–3, 26, 50–1; objectified 254–6, 259, 262; performance 245, 246–51, 253; polysemy 36; preservation 255
Culver Well 192
cursus 210, 215, 230
custom dress 257, 258; *see also kastom*

dancing ground 125–7; banyan trees 108, 125, 126–7, 129, 252; canoes 125–6; men 123; stones for 105; tourism 240, 241, 248, 249
Daniel, Glyn 82, 83, 84, 85, 86, 87, 90, 91, 97, 98
Davies, S. 199
Deacon, A. 253, 255
deconstruction: archaeological texts 100–1; megalith 98–9
Derrida, Jacques 9, 20, 101
Descartes, René 21
Devisch, R. 39–40, 269
dew 32
Dinka, oxen 51–2, 261
disk barrows 233
Dogon, West Africa 37–8
dogs 54–5
dolines *see* sink holes
Dorchester timber henge 208
Dorset Ridgeway 186–9; as ancestral beach 235–8; ancestral powers 235–6; beaches in the sky 206, 210, 229, 236; from Bincombe Down to Bronkham Hill 220–2; from Black Down to Martin's Down 230–5; from Broadmayne to Bincombe Down 217–20; Bronkham Hill and Black Down 222–30; Bronze Age 208–11, 238; and Chesil Beach 191–2, 236–7; Early and Middle Neolithic 195–208; Later Neolithic 198–211; Mesolithic 192–4; as natural monument 215–16; as path of movement 215–16; stripping of forest 238; valleys and coombes 214; *see also* barrows
Douglas, Mary 29, 37, 49, 52
Dreyfus, H. 271

edibility distance 54, 55–7
elders, deceased 47–8; *see also* ancestors
emotion 18–19
Errington, F. 247
ethnicity 245, 257
etiquette: edibility distance 54, 55–7; social distance 54, 56; spatial

distance 54, 56
Evans-Pritchard, E. 23, 24–5, 51, 52, 260
exchange 76; *see also kula*

Fainsilber, L. 6
family, and house 46–8
feathers for decoration 66–7
Feifer, M. 246
Feld, S. 180
Fergusson, James 83, 84, 85, 86, 87, 90, 91, 96
Fernandez, J. 10, 27, 36
fertility 58–9
Fidelio, Peter 248, 250, 259
figure-head, bird 109–10, 116
Fiji, body and self 38–9
Fipa beliefs 52
fire-making 30, 243–4
Fleet lagoon 190, 191, 192, 222, 225, 229
Fleming, A. 208
flight metaphors 27
flint scatters 192, 193, 195–6
flying fish design 110–11, 120
Forde, Daryll 84, 85, 86, 87, 90, 91
Forge, A. 130
Foucault, Michel 39
Frake, C. 178
frame metaphors 266, 267
Frampton long barrow 199
frigate bird 110, 111, 113, 118, 120
Frome valley 186, 192, 197, 198
Funabiki, T. 53
funerary activities 57, 210

Gadamer, H.-G. 8
Game, A. 7, 12
Garwood, P. 211
Gawa canoes 106–7, 112
Gell, A. 59, 180, 256
gender: banyan trees 117–18, 126–7, 129; *bilum* 64–5; canoes 128–9; constructions 102; house design 47; identity 168; roles 44; slit drums 128, 129; Small Nambas show 257–8; Vanuatu 258

Gewertz, D. 247
Gibbs, M. 16, 17–18, 21
Gibbs, R. 6, 9, 12, 13, 35
Gill, J. 34
Gleason, R. 189
Gould's Bottom 221
Graburn, N. 247
grave goods 99, 210–11
Grey Mare and Her Colts 199, 200
Griaule, M. 37–8
Grinsell, L. 199, 208
growth symbols 32–3
Guss, D. 68, 70, 71, 72, 260

habitus 259, 261
Haddon, A. 104
hair 30, 32
Hambledon Hill 196
handedness, symbolism 38
Harcombe, D. 249, 259
Hardy Monument 228, 229
Harrison, P. 110
Harrison, S. 256
Hawkes, C. 83, 84, 85, 87, 90, 91, 98
Hawkes, T. 9
Hell Stone 198, 199, 200
Hertz, R. 38
hillfort 197
hinona metaphor 72, 73–4
history, spatial mapping 183
Hobart, M. 259
Hobsbawm, E. 255
Hodder, Ian 83, 84, 85, 86, 87, 90, 91, 92, 94, 95–6, 98, 100
Hog Hill 197
Högsbyn rock carvings 133–5; abstract designs 138, 146–9; ceremony 171; design classes 135–8; design combinations 138–41, 142; design form 143–50; identity 168, 171; landscape settings 158; meanings 172; merged designs 141–3; narrative structure 171, 173; Ormvindlingshällen 141, 144, 158–61, 162, 167; polythetic structure 153, 173; Ronarudden

peninsula 155, 167; as seasonal site 173; visibility 153, 172, 263; zonation 150–3, 155–67; *see also* rock carvings
Homer 57
hornbill 67
House, M. 225, 227, 228
house: as family 46–8; human/social body 40–1; and megaliths 92; metaphorically personified 268–9; and tomb 48, 92–4
Huffman, Kirk 252
Hugh-Jones, S. 41
humans 12, 49–50; *see also* rock carvings
hunter-gatherers 50

identity: and burial 210–11; canoes 124, 126; clan 183; gender 168; Högsbyn rock carvings 168, 171; personal 178; social 103, 113, 210–11
indigenous people, and tourists 247, 256–7
inexpressibility thesis 7
Ingold, T. 50–1
initiation rites 154–5, 167–9
interaction view 13–14
iron making 57–9

Jakobson, R. 21, 22, 28
Jarman, H. 84, 85, 87, 90, 91
Jarman, M. 84, 85, 87, 90, 91, 98
Jay, M. 21
Jayarama, T. 249
Johansen, O. 154
Johnson, G. 16, 17, 18, 19, 21
Johnson, M. 35, 180
Jolly, M. 53, 102, 113, 255, 257
Jordan River 218
Joussaume, Roger 83, 84, 85, 86, 87, 90, 91, 95

Kahn, M. 182–3
Kaluli, *bilum* 64
Kapferer, B. 265
kastom 106, 131, 247, 250, 255, 257
Kaul, F. 133

Kava (alcohol) 249
Kayapo people 26, 27
keda (paths) 179
Keesing, R. 130, 255, 257
Keller, J. 102
Kent, S. 41
Kittay, E. 12
Knauft, B. 38
Kopytoff, I. 76
Küchler, S. 60, 61, 62
Kuhn, T. 11
Kuiye (god) 41, 43, 44, 47
Kula exchange 53, 179, 262
Kwaio traditionalists 257

labour division 65, 123
Lakoff, G. 16, 17, 18–19, 21, 34, 35, 269
landscape: Högsbyn rock carvings 158; Maori view 180–1; metaphorical 177–8, 181–2, 185–6; moral 182; Neolithic monuments 200–1; oral narrative 181–2; Papua New Guinea 182–3; phenomenology 180; South Dorset 186–92; synaesthesia 180; Vanuatu 183–4; Western Apache views 181–2; Western view 180
language xiv, 15, 17–18, 19–21
Lasch, S. 245
Lawson, A. 208
Layard, J. 53, 54, 104, 114, 115, 116, 119–20, 121, 122, 123, 124, 126, 127, 128, 129–30, 244–5, 251, 252, 253, 254, 255
Leach, E. 49, 179
Leach, J. 179
leaf magic 244
Lele people 52
Lemonnier, P. 59
Lévi-Strauss, Claude 22–3, 24, 25, 28, 29, 49, 272
Lienhardt, G. 51, 52
liminality 154–5
linguistics 3–4, 22, 272–3
Linnekin, J. 255

logic, analogic/digital 28–31
Lonely Planet guide to Vanuatu 249, 254, 258
long barrows 199, 200–1;
  Allington 199, 201; Bincombe 198, 199, 212, 213, 214; Black Down 199, 200, 231–2; and Bronze Age barrows 212; Cowleaze 199, 200, 212, 230, 232, 238; Culliford Tree 199, 201, 212, 213, 214, 215; Martin's Down 199, 200, 233–4; Neolithic 198, 238
Longlands 199, 200
Longwalls 199, 201
lunar cycles 148
Lyme Bay 229, 231

MacCannell, D. 246, 254
MacCormac, E. 269
maceheads 193
MacKenzie, M. 62, 64, 65–8, 102, 118, 260
Maiden Castle 192, 195, 196, 197, 199, 201, 220
Maiden Castle bank barrow 202–5, 206–7, 221
Maki ceremonies 53, 122, 126, 243
malangan sculptures 59–62, 263, 270
Malaysia: Batek people 50; hunter-gatherers 50
Malekula: airstrip 248; anthropological studies 255–6; canoe types 118–19; club houses 111–13, 125; pigs' tusks 261; Small Islands 53, 104, 239; Vao island 111–12, 121, 122, 126, 244–5; *see also* Wala island
Maoris 180–1
marriage preparation 69–70
Marstrander, S. 150
Martin's Down: bank barrow 202, 205, 206–7, 208, 215, 229, 230, 234–5; flint/pebbles 188; long barrow 199, 200, 233–4; visibility 233
Massim communities 106–7, 179
material culture: ambiguity 270–1; metaphor xiv, 36
material metaphors 28, 32, 245, 262, 264, 271
Mauss, Marcel 37
meaning: ambiguity 270–1;
  artefact 103–4, 270; and form 28; metaphor 4–5, 12, 14–15, 17, 32, 263, 265; metonymy 5–6; rock carvings 266; Wala canoes 266
megalith 79–80, 82–3, 84–7; associated words 88–9, 91; concepts covered 96–8; deconstructed 98–9; as frozen metaphor 86; and houses 92; as monument 85–6, 99; narrative of 95–6; origins 98, 99; polysemy 80, 100; studies of 83, 84, 85, 87, 90, 91; as tomb 97, 99; traditional thinking on 94–5
Melanesia: artefact/discourse 130; body concept 102; body metaphors 38; pigs 52–4; rootedness/voyaging 113; stones 183
Melanesian Spearhead Group 106, 248, 249
melior tree 108
memory 8, 59–62
men's house 239, 243
Merleau-Ponty, M. 34, 271
Mesolithic, Dorset Ridgeway 192–4
metaphor 6–11, 13; anthropology 25–6; anthropomorphism 38; archaeology 79–80; architecture 40–9; belief systems 10–11; cognitive psychology 16, 17–18; compactness thesis 7–8; comparison 12; context 14, 261; and culture xiv, 11, 21–7, 36; hermeneutics of 81; inexpressibility thesis 7; interaction 6–7, 9, 13–14; isolated 20–1; and landscape 177–8, 185–6; and language xiv, 11–16; logic in culture 28–31; meaning 4–5, 12, 14–15, 17, 32, 263, 265; and memory 8, 59–62; ontology 7, 33–5, 51; in poetry 7, 13; polysemy 263; primitive mind 22, 23; rhetoric 3, 4, 9–10; ritual 10, 264–5; in social world 11, 33–4, 272–3; and subjectivity 4;

substitution function 11–12, 15–16; technology 57–9; tenor and vehicle 13, 15; tension theory 14, 16; and thought 16–19; vividness thesis 8
metaphor, examples: animals 23–4, 26–7, 49–54, 110, 111, 113, 262; artefacts 260, 267–8; beaches in the sky 206, 210, 229, 236; body 18–19, 34–5, 37–40; canoes 79, 80, 112, 260; flight 27; floating forest 107–9; *hinona* 72, 73–4; landscape 177–8, 181–2, 185–6; rock carvings 79, 80; thinking reed 12; twins 23–5, 260, 261
metaphor, types: dead 20, 21; frame/focus 13–14, 15, 266, 267; frozen 13, 19, 86; linguistic 263; living 20, 21; material 28, 32, 245, 262, 264, 271; mixed 270; novel 13, 15, 33–4, 270; point 266–7; solid xiv, 79, 80, 262, 263, 266, 268, 269–70; verbal 10–11, 269; visual 180
Metcalfe, A. 7, 12
metonymy 5–6; abstract concepts 16; aphasia 21–2; architecture 43–4, 45; *bilum*/woman 66; body 38, 265; men/boar relationship 53–4; and metaphor 11, 25–6
middens 192–3
Miller, D. xiv, 246, 263
missionary impact 250, 255
Montelius, Oscar 83, 84, 85, 86, 87, 90, 91, 92, 95, 98–9
monuments: Dorset Ridgeway 208, 215–16; and megaliths 85–6, 99; Neolithic 195, 200–1; as term 90, 91; and topography 183–4
mortuary ceremonies 60–1, 62, 75, 124, 262
mourning rituals 105
Munn, N. 102, 106–7, 112, 113, 179
myth 10, 22, 26, 29, 30–1, 205, 237–8

nakedness, cultural meaning 257
namba (penis sheath) 115, 116, 240, 251, 252, 259
nature and culture 22–3, 26, 50–1
Needham, R. 38
Neolithic: bank barrows 185, 237–8; Bronze Age cemetery groups 211–12; Dorset Ridgeway 195–211; long barrows 198, 238; monuments 195, 200–1
neuru tree 108, 111
New Caledonia exhibition 247–8
New Zealand High Commission 248
nilak plant 120
Nilsson, Sven 92, 93, 94
nimbaur (men's house) 239, 243
Norway, rock carvings 154
Nuer 23–5, 51–2, 260, 261

objectivism 33, 254–6, 259, 262
O'Byrne, D. 249, 259
ontology and metaphor 7, 33–5, 51
oral narratives 181–2
Ormvindlingshällen 141, 144, 158–61, 162
O'Rourke, D. 239, 247
Ortner, S. 31, 32
Ortony, A. 6, 8
Other 25, 37, 247
oxen 51–2, 55, 261

paddle dances 105, 117
Paivio, A. 270
Palmer, S. 192, 193, 194, 196
pandanus palm 29–30, 123, 244, 262
Papua New Guinea: axes 72–5; Baktaman ritual 28, 265; *bilum* 62–8, 118; Gawa canoes 106–7, 112; *Kula* exchange 53, 179, 262; landscapes 182–3; *malangan* sculptures 59–62, 263, 270; water 31
Parker-Pearson, M. 41
Parmentier, R. 179
parrots 26–7, 260
Pascal, Blaise 12
paths 48, 178–9, 215–16
pebble maceheads 193
pebbles, Chesil Beach 191, 192, 193,

229, 236
Peers, R. 210
Peet, T. Eric 83, 84, 85, 86, 87, 90, 91, 96
Penelope, in *Odyssey* 57
penis sheaths 30, 115, 116, 240, 251, 252, 259
Penn Hill 199, 201
perception: point metaphors 266–7; spatial 179–80; synaesthetic 180
performance: culture 245, 246–51, 253; ethnic lives 245; production 103; Small Nambas 250, 252
personification 268–9
persuasion 10
Pfaffenberger, B. 59
phenomenology 34, 180
Philibert, J.-M. 257
Pigeon House 199, 201
Piggott, S. 98, 210
pigs: Baktaman 32–3; fat 32; hermaphrodite 52; rites 53; sacrificed 123, 124, 125, 126, 127; tusks 53, 122, 126, 243, 252, 261
place, as concept 177–8, 180
poetry 7, 13, 17–18
point metaphors 266–7
poisons, Yekuana 70, 71
polysemy: culture 36; *malangan* 61; megalith 80, 100; metaphor 263; of words 14–15, 16
Porteous, J. 180
Portland, Isle of 189; history 192; as quarry site 194; views of 195, 218–19, 220–1, 229
Portland Bill 192–3, 196
Portland chert 185, 193, 194
postmodernism 245, 246–7, 254
pottery finds 195, 196, 210
power relations, tourists/indigenous peoples 256–7
Poyer, L. 255
Preston Blier, S. 41–2, 43, 44, 46, 48, 178–9
primitive mind 22, 23
procreation 57–8
production: cultural 27, 40, 255–6; performance 103; and producers 102–3; and reproduction 27; Small Nambas 257
prow-head 108–11, 120–1
public/private sphere 65
punctum/studium (Barthes) 271, 272

Quinn, N. 34

Ranger, T. 255
Rankine, W. 192, 194
RCHME 208, 209–10, 215, 217, 223, 231
Red Barn 201
redness 29, 30, 116, 121, 123, 262, 265
Regenvanu, Sethy 247, 248
Renfrew, Colin 84, 85, 87, 90, 91, 95, 97, 98, 100
reproduction 27, 57–8, 62
rhetoric and metaphor 3, 4, 9–10
Richards, C. 41
Richards, I. 13
Ricoeur, P. 7, 14–16, 17
Ridge Bottom 222
Ridge Hill 222
Ridgeway Hill 220, 221
rites 29, 40, 123–4, 154
ritual: analogic code 29, 30–1; Baktaman 28, 265; bank barrow 205; bodily emissions 38; cycles of year 147; healing 39, 40, 261, 269; metaphor 10, 264–5; and myth 26, 205; physiological phenomena 31–2; as praxis 39–40; rock carvings 154
rock carvings 133–5, 151; animals 140, 141, 143, 151–3, 164; boats 139, 140, 141, 144, 145, 149–50, 151–3, 158, 159–60, 164; body parts 139, 140, 141, 143, 144, 145, 149–50, 151–3, 157, 161, 163, 164, 170–1; Bohuslän 151; circle cross designs 139, 140, 141, 142, 147–8, 157; cupmarks 135, 138, 139, 140, 141, 142, 146–7; humans 139, 140, 141, 143, 149, 150, 151–3, 157, 163, 164–5, 167–71; and landscape 158;

meaning levels 266; metaphor 79, 80; Norway 154; ritual use 154; shoe soles 139, 140, 141, 143–4, 145, 149, 151–3, 163, 164, 170–1; spirals 140, 166; wavy lines 139, 140, 142, 148–9, 157, 159–61; *see also* Högsbyn rock carvings
Ronarudden peninsula 155, 167
roof ridge poles 240
root imagery 111–12, 113
round barrows 210, 211, 212, 214–15, 219, 234, 238
Rowlands, M. 58, 59

Sabarl: axes 73, 74, 266, 267; islanders 261, 262; mortuary feast 75
sacrifice: fowl 123, 124, 125; pig 123, 124, 125, 126, 127
Sahlins, M. 49
sails for canoe 121, 122–4
Salmond, A. 180
Sartre, Jean-Paul 261–2
Saussure, Ferdinand de 21, 28
savage mind (Lévi-Strauss) 22, 23
scallop shell 193
Schieffelin, E. 64
Schneider, J. 57
sculptures: dancing ground 240, 242; *malangan* sculptures 59–62, 263, 270
seepage hollows 190, 236
self-images, constructed 256–8
self-reflexivity 8–9, 259
Selwyn, T. 247
separation rites 155
sexuality, and hair 30
Sharples, N. 196, 197, 203–4
shell middens 192–3, 195
shells 179, 193, 197, 262; *see also Kula*
Sherratt, A. 92
Shibles, W. xiv
shore orache 197
similes 5, 12
sink holes 225, 226, 227, 228–30, 236, 238
skeuomorphs 44
skin 38, 61

skyline siting of barrows 214–15, 221, 222
slave labour capture 122
slit drums 127–9; hermaphrodite 128, 129; for tourists 240, 252, 259
Small Islands, Malekula 53, 104, 239; *see also* Wala island
Small Nambas 239–43, 247–8; attention to detail 258–9; dancing ground 262; *kastom* 247, 250–1, 252; male dominated 257–8; name 252–3; as observers 244; performance 250, 252; preserving culture 252, 255; as production 257; significance 261
Smith, V. 247
snakes 70, 71
social constructions: memory 60–1; place 177–8
social distance 54, 56
social identity 103, 113, 210–11
social reproduction 62
social sciences 10, 11, 33–4
social system: artefacts 103; and body system 37, 39, 40; metaphor 11, 31, 33–4, 272–3
solid metaphor xiv, 79, 80, 262, 263–6, 268, 269–70
Solomon Islands 257
solution pit 228
Somerville, B. 122–3
South Winterborne river 237
South Winterborne river valley 186, 196, 198, 208, 215, 216
space 18, 54, 178, 179–80, 263–5
Speiser, F. 104, 111, 115, 116, 119–20, 121, 252
spirit beings 64
Spring Bottom 218
springs 214, 228, 236–7
Steinen, Karl von den 260
Stephan, Chief 240, 243, 245, 247, 248, 250, 251–2, 254, 259
Stephens, Jimmy 257
stone circles 215
Stonehenge 208
Stones, Valley of 231

stones: dancing grounds 105; standing stones 215; stories of 183; Wala island 251; *see also* pebbles
story-telling 68, 181–2
Strathern, M. 102, 103, 267
structuralism 3, 11, 27, 28–9
studium/punctum (Barthes) 271
substitution, metaphor 11–12, 15–16
Sutton Poyntz 196
Svensson, K. 135, 143, 153, 156, 160, 166
Sweden, rock carvings 133; *see also* Högsbyn
symbols: animals 49, 54; basketry 70; canoes 106, 113–14; metaphorical meaning 32; summarizing/elaborating 32
synaesthesia 180
synecdoche 6, 25–6, 44

Tambiah, S. 49, 54, 55, 56, 260, 265
Tanna island 112
technology 57–9
Telefol people: Afek 66, 67; giving birth 66, 67; labour division 65; *see also bilum*
tension theory of metaphor 14, 16
Thailand, animal symbolism 54, 55
things concept 75–6, 262
Thomas, Julian 84, 85, 86, 87, 90, 91, 97, 100, 198, 204, 208, 209, 210, 211, 215, 216
Thomas, N. 102, 255
thought 16–19, 94–5
Tilley, Christopher xiv, 8, 22, 103, 138, 177, 180, 235, 238, 265, 270
timber henges 208
tombs 48, 86, 90, 91, 92–4, 97, 99
Tonkinson, R. 255
topography 181, 183–4, 210
totemism 22, 23
tourism: anthropology 247; artefacts 245, 249; facilities 250; global 246–7; impact 246–7; *kastom* 250; Vanuatu 249; Wala island 239–45, 248–9
tourists: and indigenous people 244–5,

247, 256–7; as metaphorical cannibals 254; observed 244; recording experiences 242; Small Nambas 250–1, 252
tradition 94–5, 255
tree-fern carvings 240, 241, 243, 252
Treves, F. 191
turmeric 122
Turner, M. 19, 269
Turner, Terence 23–5, 26
Turner, V. 31, 154
twin metaphors 23–5, 260, 261

Urry, J. 245, 246

Vanuatu 239; gender roles 258; landscape 183–4; Lonely Planet guide 249, 254, 258; New Caledonia exhibition 247–8; Pentecost 257; pigs 52–4; Tanna island 112; tourism 249; *see also* Atchin island; Malekula; Vao island; Wala island
Vanuatu Culture and Historical Sites Survey 250
Vao island 111–12, 121, 122, 126, 244–5
violence 58–9
visual concepts 21, 180
votive deposits 193, 197

Wagner, R. 27, 36, 262, 266
Wala canoes 260, 266; as big man 115–16, 117; and club house 112–13; consecration 123–4; construction 107, 108–9, 122–3; decorations 108–9, 113–14; ethnohistory 118–20; figure head 109–10, 116; floating forest metaphor 107–9; gender 117–18; importance 104–6, 121–2; meaning levels 266, 267; 'moustaches' 114–15, 116, 120, 130; prow-head 108–11, 120–1; relationships 131; taboo for women 122; tourism 130–2; uses 104–6
Wala island: body concepts 129–30; community as museum 254–5;

dancing grounds 125–7; fresh water 104–5; history 249–50; tourism 239–45, 248–9
Wala Island Resort 239, 248–9, 259
war canoes 122
warfare 257
Warnier, J.-P. 58, 59
Waterson, R. 41
weaving 40, 57
Weiner, A. 57, 129
Weiner, J. 179
West Hill 186, 214
Western thought: body 38, 102; landscape 180; things/words 75–6; tradition 94–5; visual concepts 21
whaleboats 122, 124
Wheatley, J. 108
Wheeler, R. E. M. 197, 198, 203
whiteness 270
Whittaker, J. 190
Willis, R. 49, 52
Wilson, V. 208
Woodward, P. 192, 196, 204, 208, 209, 210, 211, 215
words and things 75–6, 262
Wymer, J. 192

Yaka healing rituals 39, 40, 261, 269
Yates, T. 168
Yeats, William Butler 12
Yekuana 260; basketry 68–72, 244, 266; house design 71, 72; indigenous/outside objects 68–9; poisons 70, 71; snakes 70, 71

Zaire: Mbuti people 50; Yaka healing rituals 39, 40, 261, 269